Totems and Taboos

Totems and Taboos

Risk and Relevance in Research on Teachers and Teaching

Jeanne Adèle Kentel
Leeds Metropolitan University, United Kingdom

Andrew Short
Brock University, Canada

Assistant Editors
Jill Grose
Kevin Ker
Carol Maingot

Forward
Michael Kompf

Cover Design
Peter Vietgen

Cover Layout
Herman Yu

Illustrator
Helen Shaw

SENSE PUBLISHERS
ROTTERDAM / TAIPEI

A C.I.P. record for this book is available from the Library of Congress.

ISBN 978-90-8790-565-1 (paperback)
ISBN 978-90-8790-566-8 (hardback)
ISBN 978-90-8790-567-5 (e-book)

Published by: Sense Publishers,
P.O. Box 21858, 3001 AW
Rotterdam, The Netherlands
http://www.sensepublishers.com

Printed on acid-free paper

TABLE OF CONTENTS

FOREWORD

To paraphrase the late Dorothy Parker this is not a book to be taken lightly it should be flung with great force towards colleagues, students and anyone willing to take some steps beyond the usual stuff of edited academic text books having to do with learning, teachers or teaching.

The title was used as the conference theme for the 13th biennial meeting of the International Study Association on Teachers and Teaching (ISATT) which took place at Brock University, Canada in July 2007. ISATT last met at Brock in 1995 and produced a volume of similar ilk with the title "Changing Research and Practice". Fortunately the superior contents forgave the unfortunate acronym provided by the title. The title of this volume "Totems and Taboos: Risk and Relevance in Research on Teachers and Teaching" is a good one that conveys the hopes held for the meeting; to discover and discuss members' ideas that were close to or beyond the edge of conventional inquiry in education. The 'safe' papers that usually make up the proceedings of mainstream educational gatherings tend to represent well-trodden ground on which fresh footprints are barely noticeable. This is not, nor has it ever been, the way of ISATT. During the two and one-half or so decades that ISATT has existed, members have been encouraged to anticipate meetings as safe havens for risky discussions about research ideas that matter and are most likely to make a difference as the global village moves forward. In spite of geographic, cultural and linguistic diversity, common grounds have always been found in an authentic collegial, congenial and critical community of scholars and thinkers.

This volume contains the thoughts ideas and words of academic novices, veterans and those in-between. The selected papers give an indication of topics chosen with personal interest and curiosity as guides rather than disciplinary boundaries or national borders. The contributors represent countries and institutions from around the globe yet raise common concerns and queries against a backdrop of hopefulness for greater understanding and positive educational futures. The papers in this collection were selected as excellent examples of forward-looking research. The topics are issues that will be paid much attention in times ahead. Each paper is intended to spark conversation, debate and further research. This is what academics do when encouraged to query and write about what they find between the lines of reports, articles and media bits addressing needs and cares of learners, families and society.

To the contributors, the editors and their families go thanks for time, trust and care. To ISATT members go thanks for participation, feedback and further opportunities. To Sense Publishers go thanks from ISATT and kudos for choosing a name that fits with an admirable mission. Please check out isatt.org for a full list of publications and activities.

Michael Kompf
Chair, ISATT

ACKNOWLEDGEMENTS

The papers in this book were presented at the 2007 ISATT conference held at Brock University, St. Catharines, Ontario, Canada. The conference, and subsequently, this book would not have been possible without the participation and work of many contributors. The first thanks must go to the community of scholars who came together at Brock to present their work, exchange ideas, and share in conversations that renewed and created friendships.

We would like to extend our gratitude to the ISATT conference 2007 organizing committee (especially those who brought the cookies and coffee). The ISATT executive was instrumental in ensuring that the planning process ran smoothly. In particular, the advice of Pam Denicolo, and the assistance of Daniela Hotolean were much appreciated. We would also like to recognize Brock University, especially the Faculty of Education, the Centre for Teaching, Learning & Educational Technologies, and conference services for use of university services and facilities. In addition, we give credit to Table rock Restaurant for the conference dinner, and to the Four Points Sheraton Hotel for the housing of guests.

Our appreciation is extended to Michel Lokhorst for his guidance during the construction of this book. There was much editorial work to be completed and this would not have occurred without the participation of Jill Grose, Carol Maingot, and Kevin Ker. Particular thanks to Jill and Carol for going above and beyond the call as regards the preparation of the papers for the manuscript.

Special thanks is given to Peter Vietgen for his creative cover design, Helen Shaw for her skilful chapter illustrations, Michael Kompf for the foreword, and Herman Yu for his technical assistance.

We truly appreciate the patience of those who read, reviewed, and commented on papers submitted for this book. We remain grateful for the support of friends, family and colleagues and for their patience in this endeavour.

Jeanne Adèle Kentel & Andrew Short

PROLOGUE

The International Study Association on Teachers and Teaching (ISATT) held its biennial meeting at Brock University, St. Catharines, Ontario, Canada in July 2007. The daring feats performed at Niagara Falls such as tightrope walking and barreling down the drop acted as the impetus for the conference title, *Totems and Taboos: Risk and Relevance in Research on Teachers and Teaching.* The conference committee thereby called for papers that were edgy, risky, and examined relevant and precarious teaching and learning.

This book comprises an elite selection of the papers and ideas that were generated. We use the intricacies of funabulism to present the provocative works of 42 authors. Derived from the Latin terms *funis* meaning rope and *ambulare* denoting walk, funabulism requires a high level of expertise as well as fortitude in order to successfully performed. The tightrope walker must employ the mechanical principles of inner balance, centre of gravity, and rotational inertia in order to successfully follow the path along the rope. The funabulist must also possess bravado, imagination, and have a proclivity for the theatrical. These exemplary papers are examples of such characteristics and as such are included in this collection.

FOCUS

The opening section comprises papers generated from the keynote addresses given by Kieren Egan, Shannon Moore, and Keith Trigwell. The first paper entitled, *Emotion and Imagination in Teaching* compels one to consider understanding holistically. Chodakowski and Egan argue for a pedagogy that considers emotions and imaginations in bodily experience. They examine the body's toolkit and further question forms of schooling, which have traditionally overlooked the significance of the body in learning.

The second paper submitted by Shannon Moore challenges readers to consider and reconsider the integrity of children in a world whereby justice for all can flourish. In *Social Justice and Education in 'A World Fit for Children?'* Moore focuses upon the groundbreaking work of Tomaševski who observes that the right to education is central to achieving all other justices for children and youth.

The closing paper of Part I provides an overview of higher education research carried out by Keith Trigwell and his colleagues. *Quality Teaching: Some Insights from Higher Education Research* examines a conceptual change/student-focused (CCSF) approach to teaching and learning. They argue for pedagogical approaches, which provoke deep learning and *a way of thinking* where there is greater concentration on what the student is perceiving and doing than on teaching practices.

We focus upon the blindfold worn by Blondin; or rather, the absence of the dominant sense of sight to feature these papers. When blindfolded the funabulist must tap into the remaining senses in order to maintain dynamic balance and control while walking the tightrope. This genus of sensory isolation permits the other senses to thrive. The scholar engages in this sort of sentiment each time he or she steps aside to allow another (i.e. person or idea) to thrive. Academia continually requires a refocusing on the other. As we move towards the notion of generous scholarship we must indeed regard others in ways we have not considered before. Through this process dominant discourses are challenged and opened to the potential of transformative pedagogy. This further requires one to give full consideration to the pervading hegemonic language, which causes the other to be overlooked. When blindfolded, the funabulist must call upon the other, that is, the sensing body in order to experience the path through inner balance, touch, and the faith of the heart.

ANNE CHODAKOWSKI AND KIERAN EGAN

EMOTION AND IMAGINATION IN TEACHING

Considering emotions and imaginations in teaching inclines us to focus attention on aspects of ourselves, and learners, that we commonly neglect. Our emotions and imaginations seem to come with us from our earliest times, so we might usefully begin to consider their sources in our early bodily experience. In this paper, we argue that only by attending much more closely to the kind of body we have and how it, in part, constitutes and interacts with our minds will we be able to construct adequate notions of how to educate. We will focus particularly on the body's emotional responses and attachments, its musicality and humour, and also with bodily senses. We will explore how these features of our bodies learned most intensively during our earliest years—though also educable throughout our lives—remain crucial in all future intellectual education. We explore also how these are also features closely implicated in the development of our imaginations.

We explore some of the fundamental tools that are available to us as we grow up, with the kinds of bodies we have, in a modern society. We examine the meaning-making toolkit we have available in our bodies and how this toolkit remains important in our future intellectual education. We look also at the toolkit that is available to us when we learn an oral language, and explore how this toolkit is intimately tied to the first toolkit that comes with our bodies. We will also explore the ways we might educate children better by observing how our body's "toolkit" continues to be important during later schooling. We focus only on primary schooling, and consider how this perspective might change some long-held assumptions about how best to educate children in those years.

INTRODUCTION

Most educational theorizing, and practice, seems to go on as though humans were disembodied brains. While it is indeed the strange distinctiveness of our brains that is of great importance in education, it is also crucial to recognize that these brains are parts of our bodies, and that the distinctive human body remains central to all forms of education. In this paper, we argue that only by attending much more closely to the kind of body we have and how it, in part, constitutes and interacts with our minds will we be able to construct adequate notions of how to educate. We will focus particularly on the body's emotional responses and attachments, its musicality and humour, and also with bodily senses. We will explore how these features of our bodies learned most intensively during our earliest years—though also educable throughout our lives—remain crucial in all future intellectual education.

J. A. Kentel and A. Short (eds.), Totems and Taboos: Risk and Relevance in Research on Teachers and Teaching, 3–16.

We want to draw on Vygotsky's notion of how our intellectual growth occurs by our picking up an array of the cognitive tools that are available in our society and in the local human and natural environments with which we interact. "Cognitive tool" is perhaps not the best term to use for the set of bodily "tools" we bring to bear on early meaning-making, but it is the term most commonly used so we will ask our readers only that they understand it in the sense that has been developed in Vygotsky's usage and that of others since and allow for a degree of metaphoric looseness (see, e.g. Vygotsky, 1981, 1997; Wertsch, 1991, 1997).

In this paper we want to explore some of the most fundamental tools that are available to us as we grow up, with the kinds of bodies we have, in a modern society. So we want to look, first, at the kind of meaning-making toolkit we have available given our bodies and how this toolkit remains of crucial importance in our future intellectual education. We will look also at the toolkit that is available to us when we learn an oral language, and explore how this toolkit is intimately tied to the first toolkit that comes with our bodies. We will also explore the ways we might educate children better by observing how our body's "toolkit" continues to be important during later schooling. We will focus here only on primary schooling, and consider how this perspective might change some long-held assumptions about how best to educate children in those years.

The Body's Toolkit

We will introduce this "toolkit" quite briefly, just establishing the kind of categories we wish to deal with, and giving a paragraph or two elaboration of what we mean by each element of the "toolkit" that we will focus on. Thereafter we will explore how these tools persist as language develops and school begins.

Senses. The inescapable elements of our body's toolkit are our senses—our sight, hearing, touch, taste, and smell, which we value more or less in that order. (We could add others, like balance, proprioception, nociceptivity, attention, temporality, and some others that have been nominated here and there with greater or lesser general acceptance.) These senses are stimulated in our earliest years, and babies take a particular delight in games that combine a number of them: plops, clicks, and squeaks that create, then follow, patterns that involve sight, touch, and taste. Our senses are necessary for our initial understanding of the world and allow us to perceive and deal with a certain range and scale of the phenomena of our environments. Several theorists suggest that all of our later meaning-making actually emerges from this initial understanding by means of the body, a point upon which we shall elaborate later. Indeed, many of us do seem to have great difficulty later in life understanding things that are not an extension of these senses. For example, most of us can happily follow Einstein as he invites us along to ride on the back of a light-wave, but lose him sadly when it all dissolves into mathematical formulae and abstractions. Similarly, while we might scoff at the unlamented Taliban education minister of Afghanistan scoffing at the notion that the sun is more than 90 million miles from the earth, because, as he reasonably pointed out, "There is no tape measure long enough to reach it!" we also can feel some sympathy for a person who wants a way of measuring such distances based on familiar senses.

Emotions. A central feature of our bodies' meaning-making toolkit is its emotional nature. These emotions will persist and develop as the most basic orientors and organizers of our cognition throughout our lives; in other words, while emotions are essential to understanding by means of the body, they are clearly not specific to this type of understanding. The way in which we respond to the physical and social world around us depends, importantly, on our emotions: from an early age we experience profound emotional patterns such as expectation and frustration, or satisfaction, of the expectation.

Indeed the way we interpret events, including our later ability to critically analyse them, will always be shot through with emotions. Delight, distress, elation, horror, satisfaction, anger, compassion, or fear constitute elements of the underlying matrix that shape our responses, and thus even rationality itself. David Kresch coined the neat term "perfinkers" (in Bruner, 1986, p. 69) to highlight the fact that we perceive, feel, and think together. If we recognize the foundational development of our bodies' emotional core, we will be less likely to see cognition, and cognitive tools, as somehow separate from our emotional lives; however sophisticated our thinking becomes it will always be oriented and shaped by the emotions of the body within which it occurs. Damasio, criticizing so much of modern psychology for viewing the mind as some kind of epistemic engine of behaviour, provides a powerfully suggestive image of human beings as creatures whose consciousness is driven by emotions. He distinguishes six universal emotions, namely happiness, sadness, fear, anger, surprise, and disgust, which is the same set as in Ekman, 1992. (See also deSousa on the rationality of the emotions, 1987).

Pattern and Musicality. Stephen Mithen's *The Singing Neanderthals* has helped to show how profoundly we are musical animals. Our musicality seems a central feature of our body's toolkit, perhaps, as Mithen suggests, from early in our evolution as modern humans. We walk according to particular patterns that easily lead us to dance, and we sing, and sing together, in ways that are profoundly central to being human. Our bodies recognize, track, compose and respond to patterns in the physical world (including patterns of sound), that seem to have no particular utility to us, though no doubt our massive elaboration of those patterns is based on earlier forms of them that are tied to our survival. This peculiarity of our meaning-making seems to give humans in all cultures, and perhaps babies more than anyone, great aesthetic delight.

Rhythm and pattern are recognized in some form by all animals, but humans' sense of both is rich and quickly "bootstraps" into more complex forms that find expression through all our senses. We look for meaning in patterns from our earliest years, even when what we see, hear, or touch may be quite random. But we quickly recognize those recurring regularities that give us our most basic understanding of the world we find ourselves in, of its significant patterns of sound, sight, touch, taste, and smell. We begin to construct that uniquely human kind of meaning on the back of these patterned regularities our senses deliver to us. There is, of course, a huge amount of recent research showing the importance of pattern recognition in infants' learning, in language learning and visual recognition of their world (see, for example, Kirchhoff and Schimmel, 2005; and the multitude of studies from the Stanford University Centre for Infant Studies: http://www-psych.stanford.edu/~babylab/index.html).

Humour. Another prominent component of our bodies' toolkit is humour, although, as with the earlier components discussed, humour is, of course, hardly limited to bodily meaning-making. While educators have typically neglected humour, or treated it as some relatively casual frill, the presence of humour in our earliest interactions suggests that its stimulation and development might be profoundly important to us, and consequently should be considered as a constituent of any adequate program of education. It is useful to remember that humour, in many of its forms, is based on incongruity. The intentional interruption of any normal pattern of activity—even if that pattern has just been created for the game—can stimulate a humorous response, as can unintentional interruptions of normal patterns, of course, as the proverbial banana skin can testify. The interruption conditions the baby to incongruity. Ability to deal easily and pleasurably with incongruity contributes to flexibility of mind, which is an important component of an educated person. Humour is important for many things, not least the delight it can give to experience, but it has a distinctive educational importance in its contribution to flexible, imaginative, and creative thinking.

Our bodily sense of humour becomes evident in such early activities as the mutual sticking out of tongues, tickling, the hiding and revealing of peek-a-boo, and other forms of pretend that so delight babies and elicit laughter. All our behaviours seems accessible to a sense of humour, both to enrich the experience itself and to recognize it as parts of contexts that we can also transcend. That is, even in those peek-a-boo games, we engage in a form of behaviour while recognizing that the overt behaviour is only a part of what is going on. Of course, babies cannot express this, but their positive response and their grasping of the "rules" of such play indicates clear understanding. The fuller meaning, as Mithen suggests, may lie in the fostering of affection and communication; what is happening, again, is only a part of what is happening.

There is a range of research now available showing a number of dimensions of learning that are aided by humour (for a good summary of this material, and further support, see Garner, 2005; see also Garner, 2006).

Mimetic Intentionality. Merlin Donald (1991) argues that mimesis, intentional representations that are invented, is central to early forms of humans' learning behaviour. While numerous other species mimic (or even according to Donald's categorization, imitate) the physical movements and sounds of other individuals in their community, it is only humans that seem able to combine such gestures or sounds in novel ways, or indeed invent new gestures derived from known ones. For example, a young child might cover her face and bow her head to indicate grief;

such types of gestures, involving "a representational dimension to imitation" (p. 169), are not performed by apes and other animals, even though one does see such conventional responses to emotions in our ape family (see Call & Tomasello, 2007). We use our bodies while interpreting the gestures of others, of course, as well as in inventing novel gestures for communicative purposes. Such types of interactions, Donald argues, "interlock the infant's growing mind with those of its caretakers and ultimately the broader society" (p. 255). Attachment of infants to caregivers is one of the most studied topics in psychology, from Bowlby's landmark work (1969) to a recent discussion of the range of modern research (e.g. Cassidy & Shaver, 1999).

If you are sitting next to a one-year-old and a cat and you point at the door, the toddler will usually look at the door and the cat will look at your finger. The toddler will also point to things, something the cat, or a chimpanzee, will not do. We very early develop the power to read the intentions of others' in their actions and anticipate their reading ours in our actions. We represent the world in the mind, and relate to the external world so composed in the mind, in a way that is unique in the animal world.

In the following section, we will discuss something of how the body's toolkit influences the development of the toolkit that comes along with an oral language. While we could go on to explore how the body's toolkit influences the toolkits that come with literacy and theoretic thinking, because our immediate purpose is to see how important it is to recognize the bodily bases of our later cognition, in some fairly simple and explicit ways not much attended to in primary (or later) education, it will be enough at present to connect the previous set of tools with a related set we can identify as the toolkit of oral language.

The toolkit of oral language includes such things as story structuring and recognition, metaphors, abstract binary opposites, rhyme, meter, and pattern, jokes and humour, forming images from words, and the sense of mystery. We will describe each of these below, indicate why they are reasonably considered significant components of the toolkit of oral language, and show how they are in turn shaped by the body's toolkit.

All these categories are attempts to identify features of our developmental profiles that are not much explored either in psychology or education. The kind of category we are trying to bring into focus is one that is, we believe, better suited for educational purposes than those that are more familiar from psychological theories, whose extrapolation to education seems to us to have nearly always been unsuccessful. This is not an argument to pursue here, but is simply an attempt to account for the unusual features of our main "tools." The complexity of human development is such that these crude and general categories are inevitably imprecise so it would be a mistake to assume that each of the previous tools will morph in some direct way in the tools we will explore in this section. Indeed, these are fairly general categories, and not very well sorted into a coherent set; story, metaphor, and binary opposites, for example, may seem to be at different "levels" or, at least, are not, apparently, items of the same set. So we should not expect any simple and direct movement from, say, our senses to our use of metaphors even though we will be suggesting there are important connections. Even in the case of bodily humour and oral jokes, the connections are far from simple, and bodily humour slops over in ways that bits could be picked up by other oral language tools, such as rhyme, or stories. While one is wise to remember that there isn't anything simple or straightforward about the way these few categories try to capture some features of the enormous complexity of human development, we will try to clarify, as simply and straightforwardly as possible, these admittedly messy connections.

THE TOOLKIT OF LANGUAGE

At the very simplest level of language development we can see the strong constraints the body places on language. The unique physiology of our speech organs gives us remarkably more sound options than those exhibited by our primate cousins. We suck air into our lungs and gradually let it seep out and be shaped by the pharynx, the larynx, and tongue to make those commonly accepted sounds that form the basis of human language. We could say that, at least to some extent, the thoughts we have are shaped by the amount of air we can pull into and emit from our lungs in one go: generally, this constrains our expression into clauses and sentences. Stephen Pinker (1994) called the sentence a case of syntax overriding carbon dioxide, though we might more appropriately see the limits of the sentence as carbon dioxide's triumphant determination of syntax.

Lakoff and Johnson (1980) and Johnson (2007) argue that our language itself evolves from our bodily experience of phenomena and that bodily-based metaphors pervade our understanding of many of the world's most fundamental physical forces and operations. These body-based metaphors provide "a pervasive principle of human understanding that underlies our vast network of interrelated literal meanings" (Johnson, 1987, p. 65.) For example, such simple concepts as up and down may indeed be based in our bodily experiences of the world, so that positive emotions, (such as happiness) and increases in quantity (such as more) go up and negative emotions (such as sadness) and decreases in quantity (such as less) go down. We subconsciously continue complex orientation and meaning in language from the orientation to the world first established by our bodies in our use of such bodily-based metaphors as "in," "out," "force," "balance," and so on. These basic concepts, while grasped by individuals in slightly different ways as a result of our particular bodily experience and our emotional responses to that experience, are, of course, somewhat culturally bound, but generally publicly shared and understood by everyone.

Besides these direct ways in which the physical world and our own bodies shape the particular sounds we can make and the words we "choose," there are other ways in which our bodies shape the understanding we acquire with oral language. For example, we might say that the bodily constraints that shape the sentence also give us the story as the sentence writ large. The relationship between those rituals of expectation and satisfaction the baby experiences from the beginning, such as hunger and feeding, or hunger and not being fed sufficiently quickly and so frustration, then satisfaction, and the thousand variations we all know from the beginning of our experience, can be seen when language develops in the plots of stories. We set up expectations in stories, complicate them, then satisfy them, or fail to satisfy them in more complicated plots. So these bodily patterns of our emotional lives are evident in the shapes of our later stories.

It is not too difficult as well to see clear parallels between the structure of sentences and those of stories. The rules that bind sentences (grammar) create syntax; the rules that bind stories (verisimilitude, etc.) create plot. Or we could say that as morpheme is to syntax, so event is to plot. (For further examples of some of the more subtle ways in which sentences, shaped by bodily constraints, are analogous to the structure and composition of stories, which also bear the more distant marks of our bodies, see Egan, 1978).

Understanding based on the mediation of binary opposites, as is evident in meaning-making that comes with oral language, also seems to be a development of the kinds of mediation that we employ as part of bodily knowing. As babies, the events of our days are experienced in terms of our bodily senses of security and anxiety, pleasure and pain, expectation and satisfaction, happiness and sadness, and so on. We oscillate from pole to pole, rarely settling for long in the mediating condition between the two opposites. Such binary oppositions provide the basic structure for children's stories, such as *Cinderella, Hansel and Gretel* or *Jack the Giant Killer*. These fairy tales are all built on top of powerful, abstract, binary oppositions such as security and anxiety, pleasure and pain, expectation and satisfaction, happiness and sadness, and so on. Bettelheim analyses the "manner in which [children] can bring some order into [their] world by dividing everything into opposites" (1976, p. 74; see also Propp, 1985, Zipes, 1991). The body, then, provides a template on which our understanding of stories is fairly directly built.

Similarly, the rhymes, meter, and pattern of language are fairly straightforwardly built on the patterns and rhythms that our bodily awareness of the world establishes, and also on the patterns and rhythms of our bodily wants and needs. When we are pre-linguistic, we gain a sense of the world as involving regularities and patterns of seemingly infinite kinds. These absorb and are absorbed into our languaged perception of the world, so that new tools such as rhyme in language, pattern in numbers, and deliberate shapes and lines in art are built on and can give the same delight as the meaning-making patterning of our earliest bodily experience. The fundamental musicality of our physical make-up leads to our shaping sound into the shared patterns of language and then shaping language to give pleasure as well as to communicate meaning, and sometimes to do both together.

In much the same way as physical rhythm transforms into our languaged, rhythmed sense of the world, so too do our earliest bodily games and humour give birth to jokes; the physical fun of peek-a-boo becomes the fun of the concocted language of riddles, puns and other forms of jokes. Maybe you heard about the boy who fell into the sea and thrashed around shouting: "I can't swim! I can't swim!" A girl stood looking at him from the shore: "So what? I can't play the violin, but I don't go shouting about it." Or perhaps you know when cooks are mean? "When they beats eggs and whip cream." Jokes such as these, which typically delight young children, rely greatly on incongruity. The incongruity that is crucial to the humour of infancy (with a person disappearing and magically appearing again in a new location) now finds a role in the jokes that rely on deliberate misunderstanding, or perhaps misusing, of language (Klein, 2003). Both in the physical and oral form, familiarity with and use of such incongruity helps develop flexibility and creativity of mind, a capacity that can be furthered enormously by language. (The kind of joke that gives greatest delight changes as we grow older and more particularly as we pick up further toolkits of understanding—so don't try playing peek-a-boo with a 45 year old on the bus.)

Like humour, the array of images available to our minds, while somewhat limited in our early years, is suddenly enriched immensely by the acquisition of language. We seem unable to not form images as we hear events described in words, and a range of the effects of stories depends, to a great extent, upon listeners' ability to form images in their minds. We can, of course, treat vivid descriptions as though they are abstract terms, and resist creating images while listening, but it certainly requires effort. Normally images are brought into the mind seemingly effortlessly. The ability to call up precise and rich images is a unique feature of our minds and is clearly connected with the development of the imagination. It is also pervasive; most adults can still call up images from stories they heard as young children, and, indeed, their early memory is made up very largely of images (Cowan, 1998).

We could examine more ways in which our early bodily experience provides templates for our later languaged experience, but the above set should suffice for the purpose of the next section, in which we will consider some of the implications that such a way of thinking about our earliest tools of meaning-making can have on primary education.

IMPLICATIONS FOR PRIMARY EDUCATION

In Part One, we explored some features of our bodies' toolkit that seemed to us important to our future intellectual activity. In Part Two, we explored how those bodily tools morph gradually with language and "inhabit" important intellectual activities. Too often we see the languaged form and forget the somatic base from which it has grown, and forget the somatic features that remain within the languaged form. We have established a sub-set of tools with clear somatic bases in Part Two, such as the emotional structures that give us stories, binary opposites, jokes, and the ability to form images from words. In this third part of our essay we want to explore how the recognition of the fundamental meaning-making nature of these somatically shaped language tools can lead us to view early education in a somewhat new light. Our purpose is not to argue the commonly accepted principle that young children's senses should be actively involved in learning. This has been a prominent feature of progressivism for more than a century, and has been explicitly argued back to Pestalozzi and Rousseau. Rather, our aim is to point out that features of what we usually consider straightforward intellectual activities—stories, binary opposites, images, etc.—are intimately tied to their somatic sources in ways rarely acknowledged and recognized. Recognizing these somatic sources leads us to think about some aspects of primary education somewhat differently from what is currently normal. It is those differences we want to explore and emphasize here.

The story is one of the fundamental tools for engaging our emotions in establishing meaning, having grown from those patterns of emotion laid down in the beginning of our lives. By "story" we do not mean simply the "once upon a time" kind of story but also the kind we are interested in when a girl asks a friend, "What's the story on your new neighbours?" In this latter case, she is not asking the friend to make up a fiction; she is asking for the facts in a way that highlights their importance and emotional impact. This is the kind of "story" we read all the time in newspapers or hear on TV. We don't expect friends to make things up or the reporter to invent fictions, but rather to bring us the facts about neighbours and news items in a format that clarifies our understanding. It is this sense of the story that seems to us to have greater importance for primary education than is commonly recognized. Instead of beginning by pondering our objectives for a new unit, we might better ask first, "What's the story on this topic?" That is, we begin to organize lessons and units of study by first considering the emotional importance and how this can be brought out clearly to enhance students' understanding through the use of the cognitive tool that is most powerfully able to engage their imaginations in learning. As Ohler puts it: "I have come to appreciate that quite often when students say, 'This is too hard' or 'This doesn't make sense,' what they're really saying is 'Where's the story?" (2007, p. 118).

There are many texts that promote the importance of fictional stories as a part of children's education. Our point is quite different from this, however. We believe that students' imaginations will be routinely engaged in lessons if they are "story-shaped." Take, for example, the common topic of the butterfly. The story about the butterfly is one of dramatic extremes: from being constrained in its movements to great freedom and constant movement; from being a rather featureless, ugly creature to one of the most beautiful; from being a voracious eater to eating almost nothing; from being monochrome to variously dazzling colours. The butterfly has one of the most dramatic transformations in the animal world. Our lesson will, then, need to work out how to tell this story in all its dramatic extremes. Teachers considering how this might best be done can draw upon the bodily understanding from which the story structure emerges; and, of course, they will engage the students' senses in the process. What expectations can we set up and then later fulfil for the students in their experience of the "story" of butterflies? What activities can they engage in that help them to understand these physical extremes? How can we structure the unit to allow students rich opportunities to understand and represent this story both with their bodies and with oral language?

Generating images from words is another of the powerful cognitive tools that begins in somatic experience and develops in new ways with oral language. Its immense utility was discovered long ago in the creation of shared images and feelings about who "we"—our family, tribe, or nation—are, what we are doing here, and what we are supposed to do for the time we are here. In tandem with the story, this tool provides the conceptual glue that binds societies together and generates their sense of solidarity and identity. Americans learn a story about their country's founding and identity and they learn a set of images with appropriate emotional responses that support the story. Oddly enough, other countries do the same, in their peculiarly different ways—their stories and their potent images tend to leave us cold. (Whether these images are appropriate or otherwise is of huge educational importance, of course, but our point here is simply how meaning-making requires development of this tool in children, and too little attention is given to helping children shape images.)

Given the range of social and psychological functions this image-forming tool allows us to perform, it is clearly something we can use in educating and a tool we need, in turn, to educate. That is, when teaching mathematics, science, or history, we need to attend to the images that can make the concepts and knowledge engaging and vivid. We will also be sensible to consider the conditions, apart from frequent use, that will stimulate increasing flexibility and sophistication in use of this tool. You may scan educational textbooks till your brain crumbles and you will find hardly any mention of image generation from words, and no discussion of how teachers can stimulate and develop it. The practice and development of the ability to generate rich and satisfying images helps keep alive the acuity of our bodily senses: when we create powerful images, not only do we smell, taste, touch, hear and see with great specificity, we also feel significant emotional responses to the images we have generated.

Most commonly today we don't simply ignore this cognitive tool; indeed, we almost seem intent on suppressing it. Electronic media, such as TV, movies, video games and the internet, can be great enemies of this tool's development, as they constantly provide images for us and so undermine our capacity to generate our own unique images from words. Rather than foster our ability to create vivid, emotionally resonant images on our own, being bombarded with images may encourage the easy acceptance of stereotypical, often emotionally barren, images. Similarly, giving children storybooks full of illustrations may not be as beneficial as telling them oral stories and allowing them to generate their own rich images in response (which, of course, has been the condition of listeners to oral stories for countless generations into the dim beginnings of our history as cultural animals). Today many children never hear a story told. They tend to watch movies, or TV, or, at best, have a story read to them while they look at the pictures. Given that many children suffer impoverishment for this tool from the beginning, and its importance in the development of the imagination, we will want to foster it in our primary educational program. (We are not recommending an either/or choice here; some TV and some well-illustrated books can also be beneficial. Our purpose is to draw attention to what is most commonly neglected and of considerable importance in our development of our ability to generate mental images.)

When we begin planning a lesson or unit, then, it might be helpful for teachers to ask, "What emotionally charged images are central to this topic?" The image can communicate a level of meaning with force and clarity in a way that also engages the students' imaginations. If teaching about the properties of the air, for example, we can focus on how to represent to the students the fact that the "story" here is that the air they think of as empty when they enter a room is in fact full of the most amazing and varied things—radio waves, particles from the sun, dust (decayed human skin, and even decayed fly feces), pollen, and on and on. The emotionally charged image is not built just by showing students pictures of enlarged pollen, viruses or bacteria, but rather by achieving that vivid sense of the air as rich and crowded with more things than we can guess—in contrast to the things we do see and touch when we enter a room, which the students come to realize are really very dull and uniform. By using vivid description, telling stories, and asking children to play with their imaginations while considering the properties of the air—for example by imagining various entities as characters—students can create a repertoire of emotionally powerful images for the unit of study.

Let us consider a further couple of cognitive tools, which are connected, both to each other and to the story. These are children's recognition and orientation to new knowledge via binary opposites, and also their constant use of abstract ideas. We put these together because they seem to run counter to common current beliefs about young children's thinking and learning.

Think of the Grimm fairy stories, which have close equivalents in many cultures. Each story, just below its surface, has a simple structural element: emotionally charged binary opposites – like courage/cowardice, security/fear, love/hate, good/bad – give shape and provide access to the meaning of the events (Fisher, 1996). The story of *Hansel and Gretel* would be just one thing after another if it weren't carefully structured to attach our emotions of security and fear to the sequence of events. The story plays with those emotions and their interactions and conflicts. How fearful that the children should be hungry and lost in the forest; what a relief that they find an edible cottage and are invited in; how fearful that the wicked witch . . . In educational settings, we will want to abstract this feature of binary structures to use it in teaching algebra, history, or whatever.

A part of the folklore of educators at present, which has long bewildered us, is that young children are "concrete" thinkers. Now clearly this idea captures something about the way young children's thinking differs from adults; but it is generally taken to mean that young children therefore can't understand abstractions, among other intellectual deficiencies they are presumed to labour under. The trouble with such folk-lorish beliefs is that they tend to prevent those who hold them from seeing children except through those beliefs. But consider the foundations of those Grimm fairy stories – security/fear, courage/cowardice, good/bad: what more abstract ideas have you ever learned? Think also of the characters – they are not people in any rounded sense but representatives of beauty, simplicity, greed, terror, goodness, and so on. That is, it's not just the underlying structure of the story that rides on abstractions but the characters as well embody abstractions, and, of course, those abstractions are derived from earlier or present somatic experience.

Young children do not usually explicitly identify theoretic abstractions, but their own thinking is constantly suffused with abstractions. Indeed it seems to make better sense than to claim that young children are "concrete" thinkers to claim that they make sense of the "concrete" better when it is tied to underlying abstractions. It is the abstractions – love, hate, fear, security, anxiety, good, bad – that are more profoundly known and pervasively used in their thinking. Our educational program, then, will be sure to draw on, to stimulate, and to elaborate children's use of abstractions. These emotionally-charged abstractions are clearly another cognitive tool we will sensibly try to develop and use in curriculum selection and delivery.

The Grimm fairy-tales, children's games, and most of what engages young children's imaginations are built on abstract, emotionally-charged binary-opposites.

And if early schooling is to introduce children to the great stories and games of our culture—our history, science, mathematics, literature, and so on—we would surely be a little dense to ignore the structural feature we can see in all those other areas of their spontaneous engagement. Again, it might take a little ingenuity to see how to present mathematics and history in such terms, while ensuring they do not falsify what we want to teach. But only a little ingenuity is required and the rewards in terms of children's understanding can be enormous.

As time, experience, and education, continue, children learn to mediate between the opposites that provide their first grappling tools on knowledge. We each learn to build a conceptual world between the extremes—between the ideally good and bad, the totally secure and dangerous, the infinitely courageous and cowardly. Education becomes a process of elaborating that conceptual middle world to more adequately reflect in language the world we experience. But our adult recognition that the binary terms we begin with are not adequate representations of the complex reality should not lead us either to fail to recognize or deny their utility in the earliest attempts to grapple with areas of knowledge.

It might seem odd proposing the educational value of humour on the basis of it being one of our most fundamental meaning-making tools, derived from our earliest interactions with caregivers, then finding an important place in both establishing our social being and easing relationships with others. But our common understanding of its educational application seems restricted to it being simply a personality trait of some teachers who might use it to motivate students to learn. Little is said about its much more profound and important contributions to our developing understanding, for example in developing a richer grasp of language itself. That is, humour should not be seen as some educational incidental, but as an important tool of our meaning-making that itself should be a focus of our educational efforts—we should help students develop increasingly sophisticated understanding of humour and its possibilities.

The purpose of using jokes in teaching is to point out something that is blindingly obvious—young children enjoy a certain kind of joke, and humour is an important part of their lives, unless suppressed by adults for one crazy reason or another. Indeed, this observation seems to have generally eluded educators—at least, as evidenced by shelf-loads of educational textbooks that never mention it.

Most of the jokes young children enjoy play with language in such a way that, to get the joke, you have to recognize the language game being played; you have to see language as an object on which you can reflect. Language, very much a human behaviour, is one of these odd shared behaviours that make culture possible. Becoming conscious of it, and being able to reflect on it, are prerequisites to developing increasingly flexible language use, and that is prerequisite to a huge range of cultural attainments. Developing what is sometimes called "metalinguistic awareness," which involves seeing language as an object and not just a behaviour, is clearly tied to the later development of a wide range of literacy skills and to an enriched flexibility in language use in early childhood (Donaldson, 1968; Kummerling-Meibaue, 1999). So we would introduce a period in our school day for jokes, in which students would be helped and encouraged to tell jokes, and instructed and helped in inventing their own in small groups. Such activities would add significantly to their ability to shape narratives, to use language more effectively, and in a range of other important linguistic skills (Garner 2006, 2006). It might also make school considerably more fun. Because it is a tool that enables us to enlarge our understanding and pleasure in life, and because these are worthy educational goals, humour will be a consistent part of the educational program we are working towards.

CONCLUSION

By attending to the toolkit for meaning-making that comes along with the kind of bodies we have, and then observing how that toolkit blends into, and is changed by, the toolkit that comes along with an oral language, we have been led to a set of principles for primary education that are in some degree significantly unlike those that dominate our schools today. This approach inclines us to see primary aged children as engaged by abstract, emotionally-charged ideas, most especially when they are composed into story structure, and as using and benefiting from the educational application of binary opposites, the generation of images, humour and mystery. (Many more elaborate examples of using such tools in designing lessons and units for everyday teaching can be found at IERG, 2006 and in Egan, 2005.)

We take it for granted that teachers will be attentive to engaging students' senses in learning—something that Dewey emphasized continually. Our concern, however, is somewhat different and perhaps less straightforward. That is, much of what we consider conceptual activity in our students is tied in unexpected ways to their bodily experience. Attending to their bodily bases brings out principles of learning that seem to us inadequately recognized and practiced. Recognition of the emotional forces at play in stories, for example, leads us in the direction of re-thinking how to plan lessons and units in a manner that brings out the story in our topics rather than beginning exclusively by focusing on objectives; recognizing the role of image forming leads to paying more attention to locating the affective images in our topics, rather than attending largely to content and concepts; recognizing the importance of binary abstractions in children's ability to grasp new knowledge opens up new possibilities in teaching a wide range of topics; and recognizing the role of humour in adequate language development could transform the tone of classrooms and the experience of school for children.

These are just a few of the principles for early education that follow from taking more seriously our bodies and their roles in our intellectual education. For a simple initial trawl, trying to make what connections seem fairly apparent and relatively easy to see, we are led to a rather unfamiliar world of primary education. In our view, it is also one that makes much more sense than the experience children so commonly receive today.

REFERENCES

Bettelheim, B. (1976). *The uses of enchantment.* New York: Knopf.
Bowlby, J. (1969). *Attachment and loss: Attachment (Vol. 1).* New York: Basic.
Bruner, J. (1986). *Actual minds, possible worlds.* Cambridge, MA: Harvard University Press.

Call, J., & Tomasello, M. (Eds.). (2007). *The gestural communication of apes and monkeys*. New Jersey, NJ: Erlbaum.
Cassidy, J., & Shaver, P. R. (Eds.). (1999). *Handbook of attachment: Theory, research, and clinical applications*. New York: The Guilford Press.
Chomsky, N. (1968). *Language and mind*. New York: Harcourt Brace Jovanovich.
Cowan, N. (Ed.). (1998). *The development of memory in childhood*. New York: Psychology Press.
de Sousa, R. (1987). *The rationality of emotion*. Cambridge, MA: MIT Press.
Donald, M. (1991). *Origins of the modern mind*. Cambridge, MA: Harvard University Press.
Donaldson, M. (1979). *Children's minds*. New York: Norton.
Egan, K. (1978). What is a plot? *New Literary History, IX*(3), 455–474.
Egan, K. (2005). *An imaginative approach to teaching*. San Francisco: Jossey-Bass.
Ekman, P. (1992). Facial expressions of emotions: New findings, new questions. *Psychological Science, 3*, 34–38.
Fisher, R. (1996). *Stories for thinking*. Oxford: Nash Pollock.
Garner, R. (2005). Humor, analogy and metaphor: H.A.M. it up in teaching. *Radical Pedagogy, 6*(2).
Garner, R. (2006). Humor in pedagogy: How ha-ha can lead to aha! *College Teaching, 54*(1), 177–180.
IERG. (2006). Unit and lesson plans. Retrieved February 12, 2008, from http://www.ierg.net/teaching/lesson_unitplans.html
Kirchhoff, K., & Steven, S. (2005). Statistical properties of infant-directed versus adult-directed speech: Insights from speech recognition. *The Journal of the Acoustical Society of America, 117*(4), 2238–2246.
Klein, A. J. (Ed.). (2003). *Humor in children's lives: A guidebook for practitioners*. Westport, CT: Greenwood Press.
Kummerling-Meibaue, B. (1999). Metalinguistic awareness and the child's developing concept of irony. *The Lion and the Unicorn, 23*(2), 157–183.
Johnson, M. (1987). *The body in mind*. Chicago: University of Chicago Press.
Johnson, M. (2007). *The meaning of the body: Aesthetics of human understanding*. Chicago: University of Chicago Press.
Lakoff, G., & Johnson, M. (1980). *Metaphors we live by*. Chicago: The University of Chicago Press.
Mithen, S. (2005). *The singing Neanderthals: The origins of music, language, mind and body*. London: Weidenfeld & Nicolson.
Ohler, J. (2007). *Digital storytelling in the classroom*. Thousand Oaks, CA: Corwin.
Pinker, S. (1994). *The language instinct*. New York: Harper Collins.
Propp, V. (1985). *Theory and history of folklore* (A. Liberman, ed.). Minnesota, MN: University of Minnesota Press. (First published, Moscow, 1927).
Vygotsky, L. S. (1997). *The collected works of L. S. Vygotsky Volume 3: Problems of the theory and history of psychology* (R. W. Rieber & J. Wollock, eds.). New York: Plenum.
Vygotsky, L. S. (1981). The instrumental method in psychology. In J. V. Wertsch (Ed.), *The concept of activity in Soviet psychology* (pp. 134–143). Armonrk, NY: M. E. Sharpe.
Wertsch, J. V. (1991). *Voices of the mind: A sociocultural approach to mediated action*. Cambridge, MA: Harvard University Press.
Wertsch, J. V. (1997). *Mind as action*. New York: Oxford University Press.
Zipes, J. (1991). *Spells of enchantment*. New York: Viking.

Anne Chodakowski
Faculty of Education
Simon Fraser University

Kieran Egan
Faculty of Education
Simon Fraser University

SHANNON A. MOORE

SOCIAL JUSTICE AND EDUCATION IN "A WORLD FIT FOR CHILDREN?"

INTRODUCTION

Built upon the standpoint that equity in education is the cornerstone of all other human rights (Tomaševski, 2006a, 2006b; 2007), I argue that such an expression of social justice is bound to a 'World Fit for Children' (UNICEF, 2001; 2006; 2008). Simply put, a just world is a world fit for children, a world fit for all of us—its' point of axis pivoting upon the right to education as it enhances all other human rights (White, 2003). This paper establishes this argument by discussing equity, and the right to education within local-global discourse. Specifically, the narrative of this paper is informed by the author's participant observations at the UN headquarters in New York in 2002 and 2007 during sessions focused on the action plan 'A World Fit for Children' (UNESCO, 2002); along with Tomaševski (2006b) Global Report on The State of Education and Right to Education. It seems poignant to note that the midpoint to achieve the goals set out by a 'World Fit for Children' was marked over the last year. In addition, this paper is based upon the author's keynote address for the ISATT 2007 conference, which occurred on the seventh day of the seventh month of the seventh year of the new millennium. This day marked the exact midpoint for targets expressed by UN Millennium Development Goals (MDG)—and returning full circle, the MDGs reinforce the near global consensuses articulated in "A World Fit for Children" (White, 2003). By exploring connections among these international commitments, social justice and the right to education in this paper, a dilemma is uncovered: after affirming agreements developed under United Nations auspices how do we interpret these documents for the benefit of children and young people within their local realities?

Social Justice, Globalization and a World Fit for Children

As educational philosopher Clark (2006) suggests it is likely that we are all for social justice as it is difficult to imagine that anyone is seriously in favour of social injustice; yet, defining a just world in the context of global education remains highly contested ground (Apple, Kenway & Singh, 2005; Bloch, Kennedy, Lightfoot & Weyenberg, 2006; Burbules, Torres, 2000; Stromquist, 2000). Beyond ideological debates about the merit of globalization, our changing world of geopolitics, information exchange and commerce needs to be accounted for (Webber, 2002) because local cultures no longer exist in seclusion of the rest of the world (Beck, 2000). Accordingly, as a Canadian scholar I take seriously the challenge of defining a

J. A. Kentel and A. Short (eds.), Totems and Taboos: Risk and Relevance in Research on Teachers and Teaching, 17–29.

just world without essentializing notions from my Western Minority World standpoint. In light of this, I note my privileged academic position and my opportunity for reflection upon these notions when so many in this world do not have an opportunity to benefit from education at all. For instance, 100 million of the world's young people do not go to school and 2/3 of these young people are girls (UNESCO, 2007A). Given that the 2nd MDG is education for all and the 3rd MDG is gender equity, it is understandable that although progress has been made to achieve a world fit for children not a single MDG will be realized by the time-bound targets set in 2000. That is unless gender equity is meaningfully addressed because investments in women's rights will move children's rights and all the other MDG's forward (UNESCO, 2007B). Thus, a "double divide" is identified in which women's rights are linked to children's rights (UNICEF, 2007), and any advancement in global social justice means a change in the status of women systemically-globally-locally.

Still, through this paper, the author argues that commitments made by the global community under the auspices of the United Nations can inform definitions of a just world and action in service to local realities. This notion of reinvigorating local reality within a global context is captured in what Moss and Petrie's (2003) term "glocalization:"

> We can be global—with networks of communication and influence developing between different individuals, groups and communities who share certain interests and values—without being universalistic… 'children's spaces' can be linked together not only in a particular community, but also with 'children's spaces' in other communities in other countries and continents. (p. 170)

Furthering these points, the thesis of this paper emphasizes that the arena of education is a children's space, and potentially a decisive site for transformation from service to social justice in a world fit for all of us. Such a just world is fit for everyone and (White, 2003) and a space in which:

> All children get the best possible start in life and have access to a quality basic education, including primary education that is compulsory and available free to all, and in which all children, including adolescents, have ample opportunity to develop their individual capacities in a safe and supportive environment. (UNICEF, 2006, p. 4)

In a world fit for all of us, children have access to support to develop healthy minds and bodies, having access to their most basic birth rights as citizens of this world: nutritious food, clothing, shelter and health care. It is a world that "respects the integrity of children as human beings so they may survive and have opportunity to thrive—free from neglect and abuse, physical and sexual exploitation" (Torjman, 2005, p. 1).

Importantly, "A World Fit for Children" is not simply a slogan used by UNICEF but a plan for action that is built upon the UN Convention on the Rights of the Child (United Nations, 1989). The Convention on the Rights of the Child (CRC) is international jurisprudence and specifies that all children (individuals under the age of 18) have fundamental rights (UN, 1989). The existence of this convention is recognition that young people have special claims to protection due to vulnerability to abuse, neglect and disease and as such society should target resources to them:

> A rights framework can draw on international agreement among diverse societies about universal requirements for protecting children and promoting their well-being... An approach based on the UNCRC has other advances: rights are constituted in international law, and not merely dependent on the benevolence of well—intentioned adults. Rights also emphasize children's own stake in the conditions that promote their well-being, and that they must be consulted in matters that affect them. (Montgomery, Burr & Woodhead, 2003, pp. 2-3)

The CRC (United Nations, 1989) was originally approved by the UN General Assembly on 20 November 1989. Shortly after its adoption Canada became a CRC-member State by ratifying in December of 1991. The CRC has been ratified by 192 countries to date—the United States and Somalia being the only signatories that have not yet done so—positioning the Convention as the most globally accepted human rights document in history (Mitchell, 2000). As Mitchell (2007) discusses, since these terms have been committed to by 192 nations, CRC Article 42 is an important point of reference in relation to global human rights education and arguably its least ambiguous text. CRC Article 42 asserts that parents, adults, and the state have the responsibility to protect, maintain, and educate children and the public about, those rights—including the right to education. States that are signatories of the Convention are committed to implementing the CRC. The four guiding principles of the CRC commit states to ensuring children: (in all areas of their lives) do not experience discrimination (Article 2); have their best interests considered in all decisions (Article 3); are able to grow and develop safely and in the best of health (Article 6); and are able to participate fully and age appropriately as citizens in issues that affect them (Article 12). Thus, Articles 2, 3, 6, and 12 are the four core principles of the treaty for all signatories (Moore & Mitchell, 2007a, 2007b; Mitchell, 2007).

Furthermore, CRC Articles 28 and 29 (United Nations, 1989) are provisions that specify children's birthright to education:

- Recognize rights of all to compulsory/free primary, secondary education (CRC Article 28.1 a, b).
- Promote international cooperation to conform with this obligation particularly north/south (CRC Article 28.3)
- Education should be directed to developing full potential, including *respect for human rights* and principles of UN Charter (CRC Article 29.1 a, b)
- Also *respect* for culture, language, values of all nations; preparation to live in free societies in peace, tolerance, equality; respect for natural environment (CRC Article 29.1 c, d, e)

When CRC principles (Articles 2, 3, 6, 12) guide national policy and local practice dignity as a basic principle of human rights is reinforced and the relevance of the remaining principles and provisions (including education) of the CRC are heightened (Moore, 2008).

The UN Convention on the Rights of the Child (United Nations, 1989) echoes many of the principles articulated in the Millennium Development Goals and yet is unique among UN meta-narratives as it has been almost universally ratified (i.e.192 nations of approximately 212 nations globally have ratified this convention). This suggests global agreement as to what constitutes a minimum standard of life and liberty in a world fit for all of us: a framework for defining a just world that does not essential notions from a Western minority worldview since the CRC and MDGs were drafted from the contributions of over 180 nations around the globe (UNESCO, 2007b).

The Millennium Development Goals (MDGs) were derived from the UN Millennium declaration that was adopted by 189 nations in 2000. The MDGs are a framework for development and time-bound targets to measure progress in countries. These goals represent a global vision for a future with less poverty, hunger, disease, greater survival of infants and mothers, gender equity, better educated children and a healthier environment for all (UNESCO, 2007b). There are eight goals with a target of 2015 articulated by the MDGs that offer a focus for international cooperation and national action: 1. Eradicated Extreme Poverty and Hunger; 2. Achieve Universal Primary Education; 3. Promote Gender Equality and Empower Women; 4. Reduce Child Mortality; 5. Improve Maternal Health; 6. Combat HIV/AIDS, Malaria and other Diseases; 7. Ensure Environmental Sustainability; 8. Develop a Global Partnership for Development. These eight goals may be braided into a deeper understanding of the right to education: these MDGs show us that education is entwined with equity issues, poverty, hunger, disease as well as experiences of employment (Tomaševski, 2007).

Certainly, MDG 2 and 3 specifically articulate a commitment to achieve universal primary education and gender equity, and reinforce the central role of education if we aim to address our uneven globality (Schafer, 2005). Realization of education focused MDG's is only possible when preventable child and maternal deaths (MDG 4 and 5) and ravishes of HIV/AIDS and other preventable diseases are halted or reversed (MDG 6). Families, communities and nations states must address survival, ill health through the provision of safe sanitation and drinking water (MDG 7) for the education to take its place as every human's birthright. As discussed the right to education was established to protect children from injustices such as inhumane child labour but labour is indelibly linked individual, family and community survival in the context of absolute poverty (MDG 1). Impediments to realizing the right to education become more evident in the context of all the MDG's and the need for globalized cooperation (MDG 8) to address global inequity.

Some scholars in the arena of globalized education such as Lindahl (2006) question who might pay for the right to education for all: suggesting that the fiscal cost of such a birth right somehow is beyond what developed nations might have capacity to support. There is a straightforward response to this critique: the choice by some Western nations to finance military expenditures as opposed to building peace by building security locally (eradicating absolute poverty, gender inequity, death from preventable disease, and providing education for all). In fact, one recent estimate of the financial cost of the War in Iraq is two trillion dollars to date, a price tag that far exceeds what would be necessary to achieve all of the Millennium Development Goals:

> In other words, for a cost of $156.3 billion this year alone—less than a tenth of the total Iraq war budget—we could lift entire countries out of poverty, teach every person in the world to read and write, significantly reduce child mortality, while making huge leaps in the battle against AIDS, saving millions of lives...Then the remaining money could be put toward the $40 billion to $60 billion annually that the World Bank says is needed to achieve the Millennium Development Goals, established by world leaders in 2000, to tackle everything from gender inequality to environmental sustainability. (Kielburger & Kielburger, 2008, p. 1)

While recognizing that critics of United Nations may find this supranational organization modernist, essentializing and obsolete at worst, and perhaps utopian at best, I argue that the global consensus struggled for and represented in UN meta-narratives offer organizing principles that can tether our understanding of social justice and education in this ever change age of globalization. There are disadvantages and advantages to this globalization of childhood and it is difficult to reconcile uniform global standards such as the MDGs and CRC with larger issues of universalism and relativism. Central to preserving local cultural diversity and international democracy is flexibility within international organizations to promote new knowledge, new ideas, and take serious insights from children as citizens of the world (White, 2003).

Education as Birthright

> Education is not a static commodity to be considered in isolation from its greater context; it is an ongoing process and holds its own inherent value as a human right. (Muñoz, cited in UNICEF, 2008, p. xiv)

Considering our increasing global interdependence we may understand global education as both a response and a way of making meaning of our changing worldviews (Osler & Vincent, 2002). In fact, worldwide we find almost universal agreement that education, specifically free primary education, is a human right and represents a minimum standard of policy and practice for young people; yet, the experience of education globally is not equitable. An enormous gulf separates the statutory recognition of the right to education and the implementation of this right in national policy and local practice (Sweeney, 2006). For instance, to understand inequity in education one needs to consider that proportionally the number of young people in Western countries is small and with political voice funding for education is secured. Whereas, in Africa children are the majority of the population but many parents earn too little to pay tax, secure funding and experience political voice to ensure education as a right is protected (Tomaševski, 1999). Furthering this point of uneven globality, while "85% of primary school students make the transition to secondary school in Europe, Asia, North and South America, only a quarter of African countries achieve similar results" (Sheehan, 2007, p. xi). Indeed, if we achieve education for all, other human rights violations will be mitigated because the right to education is the key that unlocks all other human rights (Tomaševski, 2006b).

Dr. Katarina Tomaševski was renowned as the first UN Special Rapporteur for the Right to Education, her founding of the Right to Education Project (www.right-to-education.org) established in 1999, and her immense contributions to UN agencies concerning children and women's human rights. She was also notorious for being the first UN Special Rapporteur to request that her mandate on the right to education be discontinued because the focus of this role was the aspiration of the right to education rather than addressing education as a fundamental human right. She identified a core conflict in her role that may be summarized as the tension between economistic and rights-based education (Sweeney, 2006; Tomaševski, 1999; 2006a, b; 2007). Sadly, Katarina Tomaševski passed away just four months after the author met her at a human rights conference in Belgium (in 2006). At that time, Tomaševski was clear about her desire to have her work further disseminated and linked to projects the author had underway. Hence, her activism for education as a birthright and human rights scholarship are strongly focused upon here as was the case during the author's ISATT 2007 keynote address.

Tomaševski's (2006a, 2006b; 2007) commitment to uncovering the reasons for our global failure to uphold education as a basic human right reveals a pivotal shift from free to for fee—ergo, to the language of the free market and the role of the World Bank as a key architect of global education. This alternative vocabulary identifies education as a traded service through access to education rather than a right to a free public service (Sweeney, 2006). The World Band was originally conceived during World War II at Bretton Woods, New Hampshire, with the aim of supporting post-war reconstruction. Today, the overarching goal of the World Bank is poverty reduction (see http://web.worldbank.org); yet, among nations an imbalance is rampant among military expenditures, allocation for education funds and gender disparity in education. This situation exists regardless of international targets that have come and gone and UN metanarratives such as UN Convention on the Rights of the Child and UN Millennium Goals (White, 2003). In essence, the goal of Tomaševski's (2006b) final report entitled *The State of the Rights to Education World Wide. Free or Fee: 2006 Global Report* is to expose the global pattern of poverty-based exclusion from primary school visible in order to inform the intertwined global strategies for poverty reduction, dept relief and education. Primary education is the focus of her report because the reasons for declaring it a birthright eighty years ago remain unchanged today (Tomaševski, 2007).

As discussed, Tomaševski's (2006b) report is guided by the dictum 'free or for-fee' as it documents the laws policies and practices in 170 countries. It uncovers the impossibility of the World Bank advocating for the free public service of education because by definition the right to education will not make money: in fact, governments who export the service of education would lose billions of dollars if primary education was for free (Ibid). Obstacles to making education all encompassing, free and compulsory are enormous and reinforce Tomaševski

(2006b; also see http://www.tomasevski.net/) assertion that the World Bank should be debarred from education for the following six reasons:

- Top-down global central planning has supplanted bottom-up participatory design of education.
- Compulsory education as a free public service has been obliterated.
- Definition of free education has been distorted to disguise its real cost.
- Impoverished primary education cannot yield its assumed benefits.
- The absence of safeguards against human rights violations increases the debt burden of the victims and their children.
- Policies ought to be based on evidence, not opinions unsupported by facts.

The World Bank is argued by Tomaševski (2006b) to be the architect of global education policy, a power relationship that impacts local praxis. A central tension with this hierarchal relationship is ideological since any bank, by definition, is driven by economics not human rights.

The greatest repercussion for the top-down positioning of the World Bank is linkage of trans-national dept servicing to countries that default on the right to education (Tomaševski, 2006b). The World Bank has created a free-trade environment for education that mandates the exchange of so called 'fee free' education for national dept reduction. Through structural adjustment, funding is provided for free elementary education globally but national dept must be serviced first. Thus, public education is impoverished to enable poor indebted countries to continue servicing dept. Ironically, the right to education has been the cornerstone of international human rights law for more than 80 years—a safeguard against child labour and trade union freedoms. By excluding the right to education from the model of global access to education cycles of poverty and gender inequity are reinforced. Even if children have access to elementary education they will leave school by the average age of ten years old, an age that legally prohibits them from working, an age too young to impact the poverty cycle especially for girls. Children do not have the right to vote against these policies and that is why education is defined as birthright and protected by human rights law. Moreover, Tomaševski (2006b) documents cycles of oppression that are perpetuated at global and national levels when citizens are debarred from education, access to information about their human rights and the oppressions of national dictatorships. Indeed, poor education statistics instigate funding from the World Bank for countries with a record of violating human rights. This funding for elementary education can be channelled to increase military expenditure as the World Bank remains unaccountable to the question "is education free of cost or merely fee-free? , nor is there any corroborating evidence provided by the World Bank to support their policies and practices—the global community is simply asked to trust the veracity of the opinions put forth by World Bank officials that have converted education from a free public service into a freely traded service (Tomaševski, 2006b; also see http://www.tomasevski.net/).

The challenges articulated by Tomaševski (2006b) in her global report on the right to education point to the need for greater accountability to standards of practice that up-hold human rights law while being responsive to local diversity. Certainly, the World Bank's managerialist structure is a hindrance to the right to education while simultaneously having a mandate to serve the UN and global community. Accountability to UN meta-narratives begins with knowledge of their basic principles (Mitchell, 2007) among civil society actors—only then may the principles articulated in international law and policy be used as yardsticks for a local-global system of accountability (Moore, 2007; Moore & Mitchell, 2007a,b). Equipped with accurate knowledge, citizens may then lobby governing and non-government organizations for changes that reflect principles of human rights and social justice.

Words and Action: Social Justice and Education

Understanding education as a birth right and recognizing our already established commitments to international jurisprudence, under the auspices of the UN, brings us to a clarion call: the world doesn't need more laws or human right affirmations; instead, we need to up-hold the ones we already have (Kienge-Kienge Intudi, 2007). There is a gap between words and action, and real commitment when it comes to promises made to the world's children (White, 2003):

> Despite the… enormous emotional attachment most of us feel for children, adults do not seem to be creating societies in which children can genuinely flourish… We state regularly that children should 'come first'… but then proceed to organize societies without prioritizing, or even being conscious of, the distinctive needs of children. We value children highly in emotional terms but deem them 'useless' in any formal sense, excluding their contributions from measurements of work and production, and making them invisible in statistics, debate and policy-making. We may want to education children in freedom and democracy, but mostly they experience control and discipline. What is happening here? (Edwards, cited in White, 2003, p. 2)

Statistics collected for the past 40 years from UN organizations such as UNICEF provide tools to monitor the "State of the Worlds Children" and some progress has been made. In 2007, for the first time since statistics were gathered, the under five mortality rate for children dropped below 10 million a year—down from 13 million a year in 1990 (UNICEF, 2007a). The number of children not in primary schools is still staggering yet projected to drop to below 100 million, the lowest since statistics were recorded despite massive population growth (UNICEF, 2007a). UN organizations have influence, although often indirect—on the lives of individual young people. Of course, this impact could be much greater.

Many children do not survive, and many of the children that survive suffer abuse, neglect and a denial of their most basic human rights despite "unprecedented material abundance and technological progress" across the globe (White, 2003, p. 6). Certainly, the world is not on track to achieve Education for all (MDG 2) (UNICEF, 2007a). This leaves scholars and civil society actors with the challenge of developing a standpoint that moves from words and theory to action (White, 2003).

This time of globalization is a time of change that, directly or indirectly, shapes social contexts that in turn impact the lives of children and young people (White, 2003). Our challenge as educators and social scientist is neither to follow nor ride the wave of change (Weber, 2002); but, to lead and influence change by standing in solidarity with children. Human rights violations such as poverty are barriers to realizing education for all and necessitate a balance between universalisms and local plurality, diversity and difference, vulnerability and resilience. Notwithstanding these barriers, chief among impediments to the realization of education for all—education as a birthright, not a commodity to be given or taken away—are adults' attitudes towards children. Willingness on the part of adults to share power with children (Scraton, 1997) and recognize children as citizens could create space for young people to be agents of change and our main resources as we seek solutions (White, 2003).

A model is offered in Figure 1 with the aim of fostering a vital response to the challenge of actualizing a world fit for children in the context of social justice and education. This model illustrates themes woven throughout this paper: Education for All; Accurate Knowledge about Human Rights; Children as Citizens and Agents of Change, Adult Power Sharing in Solidarity with Children; Challenge Human Rights Violations.

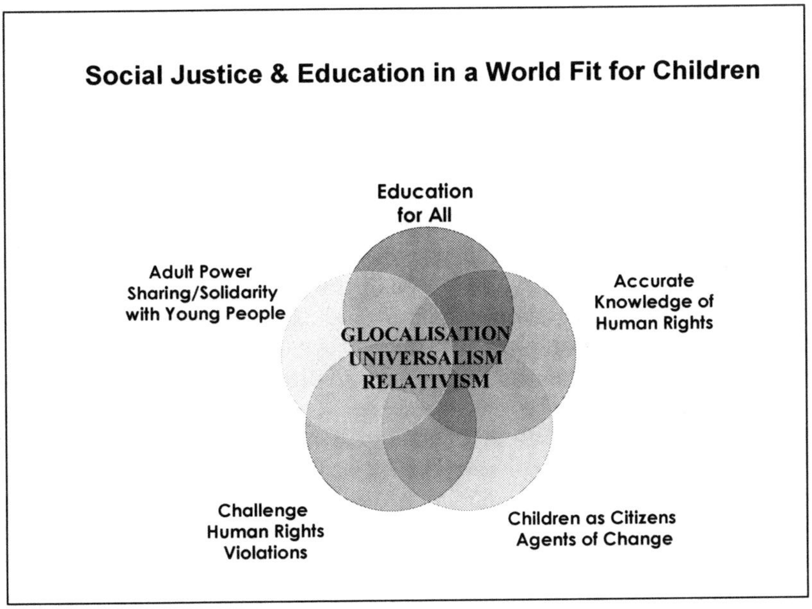

Figure 1. Social Justice & Education in a World Fit for Children

Final Reflections

Returning to the cyclical relationship between teaching and learning that Dr. Michael Kompf described during an address at the ISATT 2007 conference, I argue that civil society actors must engage human rights education with a willing ear to hear, act on, and learn from the experiences of children. Human rights often have a different meaning for the "generation that carries out the teaching and the generation that is learning, especially because of what the young are *not* taught" (Tomasevski, 2007, p. 165). From this frame of reference, it is possible to transcend debates about globalization and essentialist ontology and seriously engage social justice. Movement from words to action when UN meta-narratives are interpreted begins with accountability to adult-child power relations and promises already made to the children of the world.

As discussed in the introduction, the author was privileged to participate in high level meetings at the UN headquarters in New York focused upon children's rights and the action plan "A World Fit for Children" in 2002 and 2007 (United Nations, 2002; UNICEF, 2007). During the span of five years between these historic meetings the loss of momentum for children's rights felt palpable for the author; yet subtly infused into the processes and documentation recording these global gatherings. One can not discount the impact of the terrorist attack on the "twin towers" in New York which resulted in the Special Session on Children's Rights in 2001 to be delayed to 2002. This also marked a time when attention was focused on the "war in Iraq" and a new narrative "war on terror". These factors seemed to draw vitality away from previous commitments to build peace by building security, and taking seriously targets set forth in the Millenium Development Goals.

Still, during the opening of the UN's Special Session on Children, 8 May 2002, child delegates addressed the UN General Assembly for the first time in the history of this supranational organization. Gabrielle Azurduy Arrieta (Bolivia) and Audrey Cheynut (Monaco) spoke on behalf of the Children's Forum (UN Special Session on Children, 2002) and asserted that a world fit for children is a world fit for all of us. In this historical address, these young people described multiple forms of adversity, resilience and children's rights including their vision for the provision of education: "equal opportunities and access to quality education that is free and compulsory, school environments in which children feel happy about learning, education for life that goes beyond the academic and includes lessons in understanding, human rights, peace, acceptance and active citizenship. Mr. Longeni Matsi, a 14 year-old boy from Namibia, echoed the words of his colleagues in 2002. Longeni Matsi (UNICEF, 2007a) also represented the Children's Forum as he addressed United Nations General Assembly during a World Fit for Children +5 proceeding on December 11, 2007. He explained that our partnerships must extend our view beyond international cooperation and back to the voice and meaningful participation of young people. He emphasized that children and young people are not problems to be solved but essential partners as we search for solutions:

> … a time for honesty, real action and meaningful change, to end poverty and discrimination, to educate our children and fight disease. This is a time for us

> to come together. This is a time to listen to our words not only with your ears, but also with your hearts. There are no better people to consult on children's rights, than children themselves. Together, we can continue to build a World Fit for Us. (Matsi in UNICEF, 2007a)

This is an increasingly interdependent world and we are not in need of new goals or human rights conventions: the international human rights commitments discussed in this paper remain relevant yet beyond reach for many in our world community.

These texts, agreed upon by so many nations in our global community, are "sites of power" because they establish "narrative conventions, authoritative repertoires of interpretation and frameworks of argumentation and communication, they confer power upon preferred modes of speaking and judging, and upon certain ways of expressing moral and political subjectivity (Sevenhuijsen, cited in Moss & Petrie, 2003, p. 81). By recognizing the power within these texts and the real choice we have to share that power in solidarity with children, adults are more likely to be accountable to the promises already made.

In a closing address to the UN General Assembly in 2007, and speaking on behalf of the Children's Forum, Ms. Millicent Orondo, confirmed the need to move from words to action:

> It is no longer a question of what to do or how to do it, but of what is given priority… But what matters most to us are results. Children don't just want resolutions. Children want solutions. We don't want to hear any more good intentions; we want to see more actions. We are ready. Let us redouble our efforts. Let us together make reality of a World Fit for Children. (Orondo, cited in UNICEF, 2007b)

We must choose our priorities if we are going to realize our goals. As educators and actors in civil society we can build a more equitable world by mobilizing the power of our international jurisprudence while listening and acting on insights from young people. The right to education has been the central focus of this paper, a priority if we are to build a just world, because it is the cornerstone of all other human rights.

REFERENCES

Apple, M. W., Kenway, J., & Singh, M. (Eds.). (2005). *Globalizing education – Policies, pedagogies and politics*. New York: Peter Lang Publishing, Inc.

Beck, U. (2002). *What is globalisation?* Cambridge: Polity Press.

Bloch, M. N., Kennedy, D., Lightfoot, T., & Weyenberg, D. (2006). *The Child in the world/The world in the child – Education and the configuration of a universal, modern and globalized childhood*. New York: Palgrave/Macmillan.

Burbules, N. C., & Torres, C. A. (Eds.). (2000). *Globalization and education – Critical perspectives*. New York: Routledge.

Clark, J. (2006). Social justice education and schooling: Some philosophical issues. *British Journal of Educational Studies*, *54*(3), 272–287.

Kielburger, C., & Kielburger, M. (2008, January 21). How the Iraq war's $2 trillion cost could have been spent. *The Toronto Star*. Retrieved March 2, 2008, from http://www.thestar.com/printArticle/295870

Kienge-Kienge Intudi, R. (2007). The application of the International Convention on the Rights of the Child in Africa: When the law is tested by the reality. In A. Ang, I. Delens-Ravier, M. Delplace,

C. Herman, D. Reynaert, V. Staelens, et al. (Eds.), *The UN Children's Rights Convention: Theory meets practice. Proceedings of the International Interdisciplinary Conference on Children's Rights, 18–19 May 2006, Ghent, Belgium* (pp. 23–31). Mortsel, Belgium: Intersentia.

Lindahl, R. (2006). The right to education in a globalized world. *Journal of Studies in International Education, 10*(1), 5–26.

Mitchell, R. C. (2000). Implementing children's rights in British Columbia using the population health framework. *International Journal of Children's Rights, 8*(4), 333-349.

Mitchell, R. C. (2007). Towards a transdisciplinary model within child and youth rights education. In A. Ang, I. Delens-Ravier, M. Delplace, C. Herman, D. Reynaert, V. Staelens, et al. (Eds.), *The UN Children's Rights Convention: Theory meets practice. Proceedings of the International Interdisciplinary Conference on Children's Rights, 18–19 May 2006, Ghent, Belgium* (pp. 181–200). Mortsel, Belgium: Intersentia.

Montgomery, H., Burr, R., & Woodhead, M. (Eds.). *Changing childhood: Local and global.* UK: The Open University.

Moore, S. A. (2007). Restorative justice. In R. B. Howe & K. Covell (Eds.), *A question of commitment: Children's rights in Canada* (pp. 179–208). Waterloo, ON: Wilfrid Laurier University.

Moore, S. A. (2008). Rights based restorative practice evaluation toolkit. Minneapolis, MN: Center for Human Rights, University of Minnesota.

Moore, S. A., & Mitchell, R. C. (2007a). Rights based restorative justice: Towards critical praxis with young people in conflict with the law. In A. Ang, I. Delens-Ravier, M. Delplace, C. Herman, D. Reynaert, V. Staelens, et al. (Eds.), *The UN Children's Rights Convention: Theory meets practice. Proceedings of the International Interdisciplinary Conference on Children's Rights, 18–19 May 2006, Ghent, Belgium* (pp. 50–78). Mortsel, Belgium: Intersentia.

Moore, S. A., & Mitchell, R. C. (2007b). "Herstelrecht volgens de mensenrechtenprincipes" (or "Rights-based restorative justice"). *Het Tijdschrift voor Jeugdrecht en Kinderrechten (or TJK - Flemish Journal for Youth and Children's Law), 5*(4), 251–259.

Moss, P., & Petrie, P. (2002). *From children's services to children's spaces – Public policy, children and childhood.* London: Routledge/Falmer.

Osler, A., & Vincent, K. (2002). *Citizenship and the challenge of global education.* Wiltshire, UK: Cromwell Press.

Schafer, W. (2005). The uneven globality of children. *Journal of Social History, 38*(4), 1027–1039.

Scraton, P. (Ed.). (1997). *'Childhood' in 'crisis'?* London: Routledge.

Sheehan, P. W. (2007). Forward. In J. Butcher & L. McDonald (Eds.), *Marking a Difference: Challenges for teachers, teaching and teacher education* (pp. xi–xii). Rotterdam: Sense Publishers.

Somerville, M. A., & Rapport, D. J. (2000). *Transdisciplinarity: Recreating integrated knowledge.* Oxford: EOLSS Publishers Co. Ltd.

Sevenhuijsen, S. (1999). *Citizenship and the ethics of care: Feminist considerations on justice, morality and politics.* London: Norton.

Singh, M., Kenway, J., & Apple, M. (2005). Globalizing education: Perspectives from above and below. In M. Apple, J. Kenway, & M. Singh (Eds.), *Globalizing education – policies, pedagogies and politics* (pp. 1–29). New York: Peter Lang Publishing, Inc.

Stromquist, N. P. (2000). *Education in a globalized world: The connectivity of economic power, technology and knowledge.* New York: Rowman & Littlefield Publishers, Inc.

Sweeney, G. (2006, September 18–24). Tomaševski Book Review: A teaching aid on right to education. *Human Rights Features*, 9.

Tomaševski, K. (1999). *Education is not yet a human right.* Talk by the Special Rapporteur to the UN Commission on Human Rights. Oxfam, London. Retrieved February 28, 2008, from http:www. Katarinatomasevski .com/

Tomaševski, K. (2006a). *Human rights obligations in education worldwide.* Nijmegen, The Netherlands: Wolf Legal Publishers.

Tomaševski, K. (2006b). *The state of the right to education worldwide – Free or fee 2006 Global Report.* Retrieved February 29, 2008, from http://www.katarinatomasevski.com/

Tomaševski, K. (2007). Are we educating children as people with rights or just talking about it? In A. Ang, I. Delens-Ravier, M. Delplace, C. Herman, D. Reynaert, V. Staelens, et al. (Eds.), *The UN Children's Rights Convention: Theory meets practice. Proceedings of the International Interdisciplinary Conference on Children's Rights, 18–19 May 2006, Ghent, Belgium* (pp. 165–180). Mortsel, Belgium: Intersentia.

Torjman. (2005, September). A world fit for children: A Caledon commentary. Publication of the Caledon Institute of Social Policy. *Caledon Institute of Social Policy*, pp. 1–3.

United Nations. (1989). *Convention on the rights of the child.* New York: UN General Assembly.

United Nations. (2002). *Special session of the general assembly on children.* New York: UN General Assembly.

United Nations Educational, Social and Cultural Organization. (2007a). *Institute for statistics: Out of school children: How many are there and who are they?* Retrieved January 30, 2008, from http://www.uis .unesco.org/TEMPLATE/pdf/EducGeneral/OOSC-FAQ.pdf

United Nations Educational, Social and Cultural Organization. (2007b). *Institute for statistics: The MDG report.* Retrieved January 30, 2008, from http://www.uis.unesco.org/ev_en.php?ID=6941_201&ID2=DO_TOPIC

United Nations International Children's Emergency Fund. (2006). *State of the world's children 2007.* New York: UNICEF. Retrieved February 29, 2008, from http://www.unicef.org/sowc/index_37436.html

United Nations International Children's Emergency Fund. (2007a). *Opening statement by L. Matsi, the children's forum to the United Nations general assembly plenary session on the commemorative event of the special session/world fit for children+5, December 11–13, 2007, New York.* Retrieved May 4, 2008, from http://www.unicef.org/worldfitforchildren/index_41480.html

United Nations International Children's Emergency Fund. (2007b). *Closing statement by M. Orondo, the children's forum to the United Nations general assembly plenary session on the commemorative event of the special session/world fit for children+5, December 11–13, 2007, New York.* Retrieved May 4, 2008, from http://www.Unicef.Org/Worldfitforchildren/Files/Closing_Statement_Millicent_Orondo_13Dec07.pdf

United Nations International Children's Emergency. (2008). *A human rights-based approach to education for all. A framework for the realization of children's right to education and rights within education.* New York: UNICEF.

United Nations. (2006). *Millennium development goals report.* New York: United Nations. Retrieved February 29, 2008, from http://mdgs.un.org/unsd/mdg/Resources/Static/Products/Progress2006/MDGReport 2006.pdf

United Nations Special Session on Children. (2002, May 8). *Message from the Children's Forum, delivered to the UN General Assembly Special Session on Children by child delegates, Gabriela Azurduy Arrieta, 13, from Bolivia and Audrey Cheynut, 17, from Monaco.* Retrieved May 4, 2008, from http://www.unicef.org/specialsession/documentation/childrens-statement.htm

Weber, M. (2002, July). *Engaging globalization: Critical theory and global political change - alternatives: Global, local, political.* Retrieved March 1, 2008, from http://findarticles.com/p/articles/mi_go2624/is_200207/ai_n7087312

White, B. (2003, October 9). *A world fit for children? - Children and youth in development studies and policy.* Paper presented on the occasion of the 51st anniversary of the Institute of Social Studies: The Hague/ISS. Retrieved October 12, 2006, from http://www.iss.nl/news/Dies_Natalis_text_2003.pdf

Shannon A. Moore
Brock University

KEITH TRIGWELL

QUALITY TEACHING: SOME INSIGHTS FROM HIGHER EDUCATION RESEARCH

INTRODUCTION

This paper contains a summary of some of the research done in higher education teaching and learning contexts from which elements of high quality teaching have been characterized. The research is mainly from a relational student approach to learning (SAL) perspective, the early work of which is summarized in Prosser and Trigwell (1999). Some implications for teaching development and scholarship of teaching are addressed.

Most of the research described here is based on a relational model linking university teachers' approaches to teaching with students' approaches to learning, as represented in Figure 1.

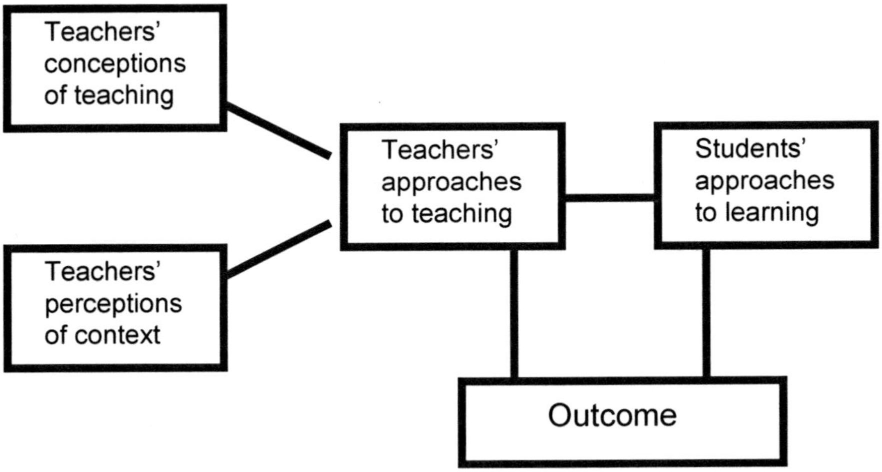

Figure 1. A relational model of the teaching/learning system

Factors associated with the variation in teachers' approaches to teaching are found in the teachers' perceptions of the teaching context and their conceptions of teaching. These four elements and the relations between them form the subject of the following sections of this paper.

J. A. Kentel and A. Short (eds.), Totems and Taboos: Risk and Relevance in Research on Teachers and Teaching, 31–40.

Students' Approaches to Learning

In the early 1970s in Sweden, Marton and colleagues developed new ways of studying the way students approached reading tasks, initially in Education (reported in Marton and Booth, 1997, and summarized in Marton, Hounsell and Entwistle, 1997). The focus of this research was on learning in the context in which learning would normally occur and the aim was to describe the variation in how the students learn, not from the point of view of the researcher, but from the students' own views of their approach. They found two qualitatively different student approaches to learning, now known as a deep approach and a surface approach to learning. Students who adopt a deep approach to learning are more likely to engage in learning that lasts than students who adopt a surface approach to learning (for a summary, see Prosser and Trigwell, 1999). An approach to learning is evoked by students' perceptions of their situation (a relationship between the context and the student) and so it is not fully either a characteristic of the student or the context. Students' approaches to learning do change with changing perceptions of their learning situations (Entwistle and Ramsden, 1983) and their perceptions can be changed by university teachers and administrators.

Definitions of approaches to learning also vary with the context of learning. The following descriptions are derived from several sources.

> The motivation associated with a *deep approach to learning* is to understand ideas and seek meanings. In adopting this approach students have an intrinsic interest in the task and an expectation of enjoyment in carrying it out. They adopt strategies that help satisfy their curiosity, such as making the task coherent with their own experience, relating and distinguishing evidence and argument, looking for patterns and underlying principles, integrating the task with existing awareness, seeing the parts of a task as making up the whole, theorising about it, forming hypotheses, and relating understanding from other parts of the same subject, and from different subjects. Overall they have a focus on the meaning in the argument, the message, or the relationships but they are aware that the meanings are carried by the words, the text, and the formulae.
>
> In adopting a *surface approach to learning*, students see tasks as external impositions and they have the intention to cope with these requirements. They are instrumentally or pragmatically motivated and seek to meet the demands of the task with minimum effort. They adopt strategies which include: a focus on unrelated parts of the task, separate treatment of related parts (for example principles and examples), a focus on what are seen as essentials (factual data and their symbolic representations), the reproduction of the essentials as accurately as possible, and rote memorising information for assessment purposes rather than for understanding. Overall they would appear to be involved in study without reflection on purpose or strategy, with the focus of that study being on the words, the text, or the formulae (Prosser & Trigwell, 1999, p. 91).

A number of studies have now confirmed that students' self-reports of their approaches to learning are related to the quality of their learning outcome as was originally reported by Marton and Säljö (1976). The results from one more recent study (Trigwell & Ashwin, 2003) at the University of Oxford, are shown in Figures 2a and 2b.

Figure 2a shows that students who achieve a First Class Honours degree report, on average, adopting deeper approaches to learning than students who have a lesser academic achievement. The reverse is true for students who report adopting more surface approaches to learning (Figure 2b).

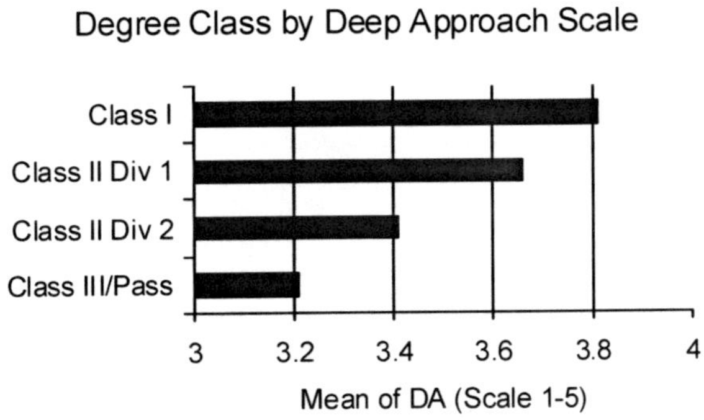

Figure 2a. Relations between learning outcomes (degree result) and deep approach to learning

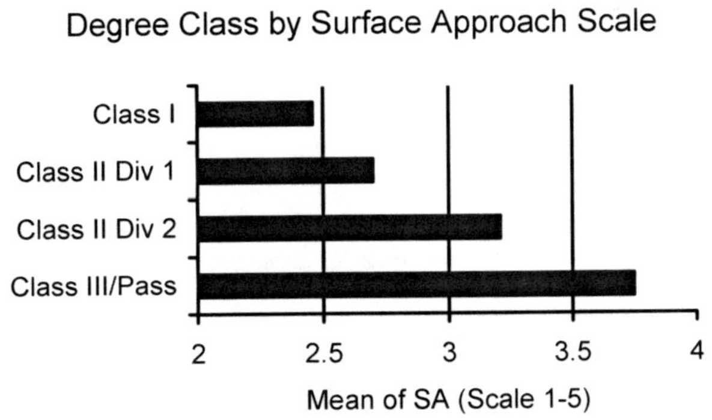

Figure 2b. Relations between learning outcomes (degree result) and surface approach to learning

Teachers' Approaches to Teaching

Similar qualitative variation is found in teachers' approaches to teaching. The following quotation from a teacher in London shows the extremes of the variation (in italics) and the relational nature of the phenomenon (perceptions of the environment evoke approaches to teaching).

> I find that I struggle when I am faced with an overloaded and technically complex area of the syllabus. I feel extremely pressurised to get through the material and sometimes find myself *emulating a transfer theory of teaching* whereby I simply repeat some of the rules and theories outlined in the lectures, simplifying them and ensuring that students have received all the information. It is a far more prescriptive and authoritative form of teaching than I am happy with. Within this format, and with demanding time pressures, there is little space for *the discussion that I deem so valuable*. I thus leave the class with a sense of dissatisfaction. (Portfolio of participant in the UCL CertLTHE, 2005)

Using a phenomenographic approach, Prosser, Trigwell and Taylor (1994) identified five qualitatively different ways in which science teachers experienced their teaching. At one extreme of this hierarchy is a conceptual change/student-focused (CCSF) approach in which faculty focus their attention on the students and monitor their perceptions, activity and understanding. Transmission is seen to be not enough. They assume students construct their own knowledge, and the task of the teacher is to involve the student, and challenge current ideas through questions, discussion and presentation. This teaching includes mastery of techniques, including those associated with transmission, but this is an empty display without learning.

At the other extreme, faculty adopt an information transmission/teacher-focused (ITTF) approach where they focus their attention on what *they* do (forward planning, good management skills, an armoury of teaching competencies, use of the literature, ability to use IT ...). They attempt to transmit the information about the curriculum on the assumption that students will learn from that process. That information is often complex and requires organisation and presentation skill.

Both approaches have been shown to be effective in teaching, but as a CCSF approach includes elements of an ITTF approach, and not *vice versa,* CCSF approaches are thought be more complete and possibly more effective (Prosser & Trigwell, 1999).

Using the results of the study referred to above, an inventory designed to measure qualitative variation in approaches to teaching: the Approaches to Teaching Inventory (ATI) was developed (Prosser & Trigwell, 2006; Trigwell & Prosser, 2004; Trigwell, Prosser & Ginns, 2005). Inventory items from each of the two approaches are shown in Figure 3. This questionnaire was used to study relations between learning and teaching approaches.

INFORMATION TRANSMISSION/TEACHER-FOCUSED (ITTF) APPROACH

Intention item: I feel it is important to present a lot of facts in the classes so that students know what they have to learn for this subject

Strategy item: I structure this subject to help students to pass the formal assessment items

CONCEPTUAL CHANGE/STUDENT-FOCUSED (CCSF) APPROACH

Intention item: I feel a lot of teaching time in this subject should be used to question students' ideas

Strategy item: I make available opportunities for students in this subject to discuss their changing understanding of the subject

Figure 3. Examples of Items from the Approaches to Teaching Inventory

Relations between Approaches to Learning and Approaches to Teaching

A study exploring the relations between teaching and learning has now been conducted (Trigwell, Prosser, & Waterhouse,, 1999a) and replicated at least three times (Kim & Branch, 2002; Kek, 2006; Trigwell, Prosser, Ramsden, & Martin, 1999b). The results from one study, which covered a broad range of disciplines and involved 55 large first year courses with feedback from 408 teachers and 8829 students in the classes of those teachers, are shown in Table 1.

Table 1. Correlation between teachers' approach to teaching and students' approach to learning variables

Variable	Variable			
	Deep	Surf	CCSF	ITTF
Deep approach to learning	-	-.22	.34*	-.15
Surface approach to learning		-	-.46*	.37*
CCSF approach to teaching			-	-.30
ITTF approach to teaching				-

Note. *p<.05, n=55.
CCSF Conceptual Change/Student-focused.
ITTF Information Transmission/Teacher-focused.
(Trigwell et al., 1999b).

When teachers report that their focus is on what they do in their teaching, when they believe students have little or no prior knowledge of the subject they are teaching, when they do little more than transmit facts so that students will have a good set of notes (ITTF approach), their students are more likely to adopt a surface approach to learning (R=.38). Conversely, when teachers report that they have the student as the focus of their activities, where it matters more to them what the student is doing and learning than what the teacher is doing or covering, where the teacher is one who encourages self directed learning, who makes time (in formal 'teaching' time) for students to interact and to discuss the problems they encounter, where the teacher assesses to reveal conceptual change, where the teacher provokes debate, uses a lot of time to question students' ideas and to develop a "conversation" with students in lectures (CCSF approach), their students are less likely to be adopting a surface approach (R=-.48) and more likely to be adopting a deep approach (R=.38).

Since one of the measured approaches to teaching is correlated more strongly with quality learning than the other, it can be used to define quality teaching. Teaching that is student-focused, that encourages self directed learning, that includes time (in formal 'teaching' time) for students to interact and to discuss the problems they encounter, that assesses to reveal conceptual change, that provokes debate, uses a lot of time to question students' ideas and to develop a 'conversation' with students in lectures, is good teaching. While recognising and rewarding good teaching in universities has been well researched (Ramsden, Margetson, Martin, & Clarke, 1995) these CCSF approach elements are often not included.

The foundations of the research perspective adopted in this research are continuing to be explored in the teaching context. Data on teachers' approach to teaching collected in Helsinki and Oxford (Lindblom-Ylanne, Trigwell, Nevgi, & Ashwin, 2006) show that the same teacher, in different contexts, reports adopting different approaches to teaching. This result is supportive of the relational bases of this perspective. Teachers can also change their approach to teaching over time. Academics at the University of Oxford who are participants in a Postgraduate Diploma in Learning and Teaching in Higher Education were asked to describe their teaching approach to a particular subject before and after completing the course using the ATI. The results of that study show statistically significant increases in CCSF scores and no significant change in ITTF scores over the year of the course. A similar result was found by Prosser, Rickinson, Bence, Hanbury, and Kulei, (2006) based on feedback from 393 teachers who had completed courses on teaching for university teachers in the UK. The changes in approach to teaching scores before and after doing the course are shown in Table 2.

Table 2. Approaches to teaching scores before and after doing a postgraduate certificate in learning and teaching

Approach	ATI score before	ATI score after	*p*
CCSF	3.37	4.17	<.001
ITTF	3.57	3.36	<.001

Note. N=393 (Prosser et al., 2006).

All these results indicate that the approach adopted by teachers to their teaching can be influenced, and if one (or some) approaches are preferable to others that they be the focus of teacher development.

Teachers' Perceptions of the Teaching Context

Trigwell et al. (1999b), in addition to studying relations between approaches to teaching and approaches to learning, have explored relations between aspects of teaching among their sample of 439 teachers. The sample was drawn from teachers across all areas typically taught in universities and, for analytical purposes, were organized into four groups–arts and social sciences; business/economics/law; science/engineering; and the health sciences. A factor analysis of approaches to teaching variables and five teaching environment variables (Teacher Workload; Class Size; Teacher Control; Student Characteristics; and Commitment to Student Learning) from a teaching environment questionnaire yielded one factor with the Conceptual Change/Student-focused approach variable loading positively with perceptions of an appropriate teaching workload, appropriate student characteristics, small class size and control of teaching. In the second factor, the Information Transmission/Teacher-focused approach variable loads negatively with perceptions of departmental commitment to student learning, and the control of teaching variables. No significant differences in these relations were found in the results for the four discipline groups. A more recent analysis (Ramsden et al., 2007) shows small correlations between these variables (Table 3), but the directions of the relations are all as expected (negative for ITTF and positive for CCSF).

Table 3. Pearson correlations between teaching context and approach variables

Context Variable	Approach Variable	
	ITTF	CCSF
Transformative leadership	-.04	.13
Collaborative management	-.13	.05
Support for student learning	-.22	.20
Class size	-.11	.10
Student characteristics	-.14	.18
Teacher control	-.22	.15

Note. N=439, Ramsden, Prosser, Trigwell & Martin (2007).

Quality Teaching & Scholarship of Teaching

The concluding section of this paper uses the idea of high quality teaching being about a student focus to reflect on the current attention being given to the scholarship of teaching. In *Scholarship Reconsidered: Priorities of the Professoriate*,

Boyer (1990) proposed a reconceptualisation of the activity of the university, arguing that it was best seen as embracing four distinct but interdependent and interrelated forms of scholarship: discovery, integration, application and teaching. Defined in terms of scholarship, he proposed, the activities of research and teaching could be put on a more equal footing. This way of seeing academic work appeared to offer the prospect of proportional and appropriate status for teaching alongside research and, through greater respect for teaching, increased potential for enhancing the quality of student learning.

Since that report, there has been considerable debate on what constitutes the scholarship of teaching. There has been, and still is, a focus on publication, but is it appropriate that expanded pedagogic content knowledge that reveals itself in scholarly publication for other teachers is the highest level of knowledge to which the teacher should be encouraged to aspire, rather than in effective reasoning that reveals itself in resonant acts of knowledge work with students? Another area of focus is reflection, but it is possible that a reflective scholar of teaching who develops teacher knowledge could be a fine reflector and a poor teacher. How would we know which they were? Knowledge development in the teaching community is not only a matter of quantitatively increasing what is known about teaching but also a matter of qualitatively enhancing the process of reasoning during teaching. If the scholarship of teaching is an integral part of high quality teaching, the relationship is not straight forward. What is needed is a conception of the scholarship of teaching that reflects the values embedded in existing conceptions of scholarship and of teaching, which focuses on the activity of teaching, and that accords student learning prominence.

In describing a model of the scholarship of teaching, Trigwell, Martin, Benjamin, and Prosser (2000) defined the link between teaching and the scholarship of teaching. To be scholarly is to be engaged in personal, but rigorous intellectual inquiry and development involving values such as honesty, integrity, open-mindedness, scepticism and intellectual humility. To be engaged in scholarship is to take that process, for scrutiny, into the public arena: It is to make transparent the processes and outcomes of scholarly activities. If teaching is about making learning possible, then the scholarship of teaching is about making transparent how learning is being made possible. If teaching is about collaborative meaning-making, then the scholarship of teaching is about making transparent how collaborative meaning-making is happening (Trigwell & Shale, 2004). Using this approach, the scholarship of teaching is directly linked to the act or processes of teaching, and to student learning.

An example of the scholarship of teaching in which the students are the focus might be a minute departmental discussion about an approach to teaching a course using student-focused teaching ideas from the literature to explain how the learning aims of the course might be achieved.

CONCLUSIONS

One way to define quality teaching is to describe qualitatively different approaches and to show that one (some) of those approaches is (are) more likely to lead to the desired (high quality) outcomes than others. Since conceptual change/student-focused (CCSF) approaches are more likely to lead to students adopting deeper approaches to learning, they can be considered higher quality approaches to teaching. In adopting this approach, teachers encourage self-directed learning, take time to discuss problems with students, assess to encourage conceptual change and encourage debate. This form of 'quality teaching' involves *a way of thinking* in which there is more of a focus on what the student is perceiving and doing, than on the teacher, and what the teacher is doing or the content he/she is teaching.

The ways of thinking which underpin a CCSF approach to teaching can also be used in leadership development (Ramsden et al., 2007) in course design, in planning student assessment, and in defining a student learning oriented direction for the scholarship of teaching: The scholarship of teaching is about inquiry that has, as the main focus, the facilitation and improvement of student learning.

ACKNOWLEDGEMENTS

Much of the original work described in this paper was conducted by the author in collaboration with Michael Prosser whose contribution is acknowledged.

REFERENCES

Boyer, E. L. (1990). *Scholarship reconsidered: Priorities of the professoriate*. Princeton, NJ: The Carnegie Foundation for the Advancement of Teaching.

Entwistle, N., & Ramsden, P. (1983). *Understanding student learning*. London: Croom Helm.

Kek, Y. C. (2006). *Individual characteristics, family, self-efficacy, curriculum, university and classroom learning environments, teaching approaches and teacher factors, learning approaches, and student outcomes in a Malaysian private university: A mixed research study*. Unpublished doctoral dissertation, University of Adelaide, Adelaide.

Kim, D., & Branch, R. M. (2002, April). *The relationship between teachers' approach to teaching, students' perceptions of course experiences and students' approaches to studying in electronic distance-learning environments*. Paper presented at the annual meeting of the American Educational Research Association, New Orleans, LA.

Lindblom-Ylanne, S., Trigwell, K., Nevgi, A., & Ashwin, P. (2006). Disciplinary differences in approaches to teaching. *Studies in Higher Education, 31*(3), 285–298.

Marton, F., & Booth, S. (1997). *Learning and awareness*. New Jersey, NJ: Lawrence Erlbaum Associates.

Marton, F., & Säljö, R. (1976). On qualitative differences in learning: 1. Outcome and process. *British Journal of Educational Psychology, 46*, 4–11.

Marton, F., Hounsell, D., Entwistle, N. J. (Eds.). (1997). *The Experience of learning: Implications for teaching and studying in higher education* (2nd ed.). Edinburgh: Scottish Academic Press.

Prosser, M., & Trigwell, K. (1999). *Understanding learning and teaching: The experience in higher education*. Buckingham: Open University Press.

Prosser, M., & Trigwell, K. (2006). Confirmatory factor analysis of the approaches to teaching inventory. *British Journal of Educational Psychology, 76*, 405–419.

Prosser, M., Rickinson, M., Bence, V., Hanbury, A., & Kulej, M. (2006). *Higher education academy report*. Retrieved August 31, 2007, from http://www.heacademy.ac.uk/research/FormativeEvaluationreport.rtf

Prosser, M., Trigwell, K., & Taylor, P. (1994). A phenomenographic study of academics' conceptions of science learning and teaching. *Learning and Instruction, 4*, 217–231.

Ramsden, P., Margetson, D., Martin, E., & Clarke, S. (1995). *Recognising and rewarding good teaching*. Canberra: Australian Government Printing Services.

Ramsden, P., Prosser, M., Trigwell, K., & Martin, E. (2007). University teachers' experiences of academic leadership and their approaches to teaching. *Learning and Instruction, 17*, 140–155.
Trigwell, K., & Ashwin, P. (2003, November). *Undergraduate students' experience of learning at the University of Oxford.* University of Oxford. Retrieved March, 2008, from http://www.learning.ox.ac.uk/files/OLCPFinal.pdf
Trigwell, K., & Prosser, M. (1996). Changing approaches to teaching: A relational perspective. *Studies in Higher Education, 21*(3), 275–284.
Trigwell, K., & Prosser, M. (2004). Development and use of the approaches to teaching inventory. *Educational Psychology Review, 16*(4), 409–424.
Trigwell, K., & Shale, S. (2004). Student learning and the scholarship of university teaching. *Studies in Higher Education, 29*, 523–536.
Trigwell, K., Martin, E., Benjamin, J., & Prosser, M. (2000). Scholarship of teaching: A model. *Higher Education Research and Development, 19*, 155–168.
Trigwell, K., Prosser, M., & Ginns, P. (2005). Phenomenographic pedagogy and a revised approaches to teaching inventory. *Higher Education Research and Development, 24*(4), 349–360.
Trigwell, K., Prosser, M., & Taylor, P. (1994). Qualitative differences in approaches to teaching first year university science. *Higher Education, 27*, 75–84.
Trigwell, K., Prosser, M., & Waterhouse, F. (1999a). Relations between teachers' approaches to teaching and students' approaches to learning. *Higher Education, 37*, 57–70.
Trigwell, K., Prosser, M., Ramsden, P., & Martin, E. (1999b). Improving student learning through a focus on the teaching context. In C. Rust (Ed.), *Improving student learning* (pp. 97–103). Oxford: Oxford Centre for Staff Development.

Keith Trigwell
University of Sydney

ROTATIONAL INERTIA

The funabulist most often carries a long and heavy balancing pole. This pole increases the rotational inertia of the artist, which generates more time to move his or her centre of mass back to the desired position directly over the wire. Rotational inertia, in sum, is the resistance of a body to a change in its rotational motion. As the body maintains its rotational motion, balance is achieved. This balance is integral to the equilibrist's perceived risk. Thus the pole acts as a base of support and in a figurative sense, a counter narrative in the act of risk taking. The papers in Part II embolden students, women, and unseen scholars by permeating the boundaries surrounding research on teachers and teaching and daring to bring back into balance the voices, which all too often, are unheard.

In the opening paper of Part II Elbaz-Luwisc et al. interrogate the barriers of multicultural living complicated by language, cultural diversity, and societal complexities. In *Life stories and the Development of a Multicultural Community of Women Educators* the authors dare to *dance with difference* thereby provoking cultural understandings through mutual goals of living and working together and a process of resonance. They candidly acknowledge the "provisionality and contingency of identity" vis-à-vis multicultural education.

In *Using Students' Voices to Change Teaching and Learning to Teach in Urban Schools: Studies from Three Teacher Education Programs*, Rust, Peterman, and Storz argue for substantive change in teacher education. Through an in-depth examination with teacher candidates in their respective universities the authors identify barriers to teacher education programs, which lead to broader and more nuanced understandings of the cultural and socio-economic complexities that affect children's learning. They close with a call for a shift in teacher education that moves towards collaborative and inquiry-based practice comprising a balance of student knowledge of self and others.

Mizukami and Masetto call into question the preparation of educators in higher education institutions. In *Professional Development of Higher School Educators* the authors present four challenges for transforming the frameworks for teaching in academia. This systemic shift, they argue, will foster the development of educational environments that will engage students in relevant learning.

In the final paper of Part II, Maryann Brown explores the transition from university to school teaching through the realms of narrative and autoethnographic inquiry. In *Welcome to the Real World, I Haven't Reached Those Dizzy Heights Yet: Reflections on a Transition from University Teaching to School Teaching,* Brown dares to play the academic game differently, thereby disrupting the conventional career flow of the scholar. Through her ingenuous self-examination she unveils the characteristics of care-full research and the care-full educator calling for a genuine nexus of theory and practice.

The effects of rotational inertia can be further magnified by lengthening the pole as much as possible and by weighting the ends. The pole must be centred when carried by the funabulist in order to prevent overcompensation and rotational motion. Through this process the lengthened pole acts as a stabilizer. The papers in this section are poignant examples of the need for researchers to broaden perspectives, maintain equilibrium in academic inquiry, and further bring into balance the subverted binaries of theory/practice, teacher/student, and self/other.

FREEMA ELBAZ LUWISCH, SHOSH KLEIN, HIAM NASSERALDIN, IDIT AVNI, IMAN AWADIYEH, DINA DAVID, AVIVA BEN HEFER, HANNA MORAG, TOVA SHAUL, FANY SHIMONI, AND CHAVA SIMON

LIFE STORIES AND THE DEVELOPMENT OF A MULTICULTURAL COMMUNITY OF WOMEN EDUCATORS

One of the main roles of teachers is that of passing on to students the language, conceptual categories and forms of discourse, which constitute society (Bowers, 1987). In a multicultural society, this task is obviously complicated by the diversity of languages, perspectives and discourses at play in the society. To carry out their educational role in a multicultural setting, teachers need to be able to draw on their own life experiences and identities, examining for themselves and then presenting to their students issues of diversity from a personal perspective. In the conflict-ridden situation of Israel, Jewish and Palestinian-Arab educators come to their work carrying a heavy baggage of historical memory, and with competing collective narratives which often impede mutual understanding and dialogue. However, the telling of personal stories has the potential to promote intercultural understanding. Through a process of 'resonance' (Conle, 1996), participants from diverse backgrounds can listen to and connect with one another's stories, examine issues closely, and experiment with claiming different voices as they reread and retell their own and others' stories. The study to be presented here explores the use of personal life stories as a vehicle for examining and developing multiculturalism in education, in the context of multiple and overlapping identities, conflict and narratives of exclusion that characterize the Israeli context.

Examining one's personal investments in multicultural education is never easy, because it requires one to acknowledge the provisionality and contingency of identity. Further, a public language in which the personal can be discussed critically is still lacking. The study reported on here seeks to contribute to the shaping of a public language adequate to this task, by focusing on the work of women educators who came together in a multicultural group to examine these issues in the context of their own lives and work.

BACKGROUND

Critiques of multicultural teacher education suggest that despite years of work we still lack knowledge on how to best prepare teachers to cope with diversity (Ladson-Billings, 1999; Zeichner, 1999), and practice often falls far short of its

J. A. Kentel and A. Short (eds.), Totems and Taboos: Risk and Relevance in Research on Teachers and Teaching, 43–57.

goals (Goodwin, 1994; Jordan, 1995; Cochran-Smith, 1995). Hoffman (1996) judges the discourse of multicultural education in the United States to be uncritical and insufficiently reflexive. She argues that this discourse draws on concepts of 'culture', 'self' and 'identity' that derive from an individualistic, Western-centric discourse. Eilam (2002) highlights the dilemmas encountered by Palestinian Israeli teachers who are educated in a western-oriented teacher education program and then return to teach in the traditional Arab-language educational system.

The conceptualization of multiculturalism in education has been undertaken from diverse perspectives (MacLaren, 1995; Giroux, 1992; Banks & Banks, 1993). From a philosophical vantage point Taylor (1994) emphasizes the notion of recognition as central to an understanding of relations between groups with differential access to power in society. What is missing or under-emphasized by these theorists, however, is the importance of taking a personal perspective in confronting issues of diversity. Nieto (1994) suggests that teachers need to "undergo a process of personal transformation based on their own identities and experiences… (and to) engage in a collaborative and imaginative encounter to transform their own practices and their schools" (175-6). Sleeter (2001) sees narrative research as useful because it "enables teacher educators to connect strategies or observations with examined life experiences and to communicate emotions." (238) Taubman (2002) also discusses the importance for educators engaged in multicultural and anti-racist education of examining their personal investments in their work. Among reasons for an avoidance of the personal, he points out that "to look at the personal, to begin to face the provisionality and contingency of identity, is to surrender the security of stable identities." Further, it is difficult to examine the personal because "we have yet to develop a public language to describe the personal that does not dissipate into psychologisms or unexamined narratives, or reduce our experience to some sociopolitical script" (p.99). This paper foregrounds the examination of personal narratives and perspectives by a group of women educators, and in doing so aims to contribute to the shaping of a public language adequate to the task of dealing with the personal.

Multiculturalism in the Israeli Context

Israel can be characterized as a deeply divided society in which relations between Jewish and Palestinian citizens are under constant tension (Al-Haj, 2002). Within both the Jewish and Palestinian communities, there are diverse sub-groups based on countries of origin (for Jewish Israelis), religion and forms of adherence to religion, social class and other characteristics, giving rise to multiple and overlapping identities. There is likewise a diversity of opinion, which results in lively and sometimes acrimonious debate, concerning the nature of Israel as a multicultural society and the prospects for multicultural education (Eden & Kalekin-Fishman, 2002). At the school level, however, policy is set and curriculum must be implemented without waiting for conceptual agreement. Studies have shown that the Israeli school curriculum fails to promote learning about the other (Al-Haj, 2002; Bar-Tal & Zoltek, 1989; Soen, 2002). Given this vacuum in official curricular treatment of multiculturalism, the task of teachers in classrooms is doubly significant: in addition to their everyday role in introducing students to new aspects of the discourse and culture, their role as 'curriculum makers' (Clandinin & Connelly, 1992) leaves room for them to adapt programs and elaborate their own multicultural curricula in the classroom.

Teacher Identity

In developing a pedagogy and curriculum adequate to the multicultural situation, one necessary resource on which teachers must draw is their own identity. Teacher identity is markedly shaped by the individual's biography and early educational experiences (Beijaard, Verloop & Vermunt, 2000; Nias, 1985); however, it does not follow that teachers cannot engage in questioning and thoughtfulness around issues of identity and the development of teaching practice (Britzman, 1991; Conle, 1996; Estola, 2003; Heikkinen, 1998). Recent studies, strongly influenced by the work of Bakhtin (1981), conceive of teacher identity as constructed in and through discourse. For example, Marsh (2002) illustrates the complex identities of a beginning teacher, identities which are seen as shaped by and within the different discourses that "swirled around her teacher education program," her school and classroom, and her personal life (p. 335). Elbaz-Luwisch, Gudmundsdottir and Moen (2002) draw on the ideas of Bakhtin to examine the multi-voicedness of teaching for practising teachers in different cultural contexts. Similarly, Coulter (1999) highlights the different discourses and voices at play in educational settings, and suggests that educational research should seek to generate dialogue among different voices. For this to happen, however, the teacher must become aware of the complexity of her own identity as a story constructed from diverse elements.

Narrative identity. The conceptualization of narrative identity rests on the idea that identity is narratively constructed; the stories we tell about ourselves over time, in various social and cultural contexts, play a formative role in shaping our sense of ourselves (Shotter & Gergen, 1989; Giddens, 1991). The connection between life and story can be seen as a hermeneutic relationship, each giving meaning to the other. MacIntyre (1984) stresses the importance of narrative, in producing the sense of "narrative unity" in life. Ricoeur (1991) emphasizes the role of "the act of plotting" in giving form to life and making its meaning explicit; he speaks of "life as an activity and a desire in search of a narrative" (1991, p. 434), and suggests that some episodes of our life may be seen as "stories not yet told." Both Ricoeur and MacIntyre remind us that we necessarily make use of tradition, and of the stories provided by the culture in developing our own narrative; thus, for Ricoeur, "we learn to become the narrator of our own story without completely becoming the author of our life" (1991, p. 437).

The work of Bakhtin, drawing on studies of the modern novel with its multiple story lines and many characters speaking in the voices of a diversity of social milieus, has been seminal in establishing the idea of narrative identity as multi-voiced. Bakhtin's theory sees the self as continually revisioned, and not only through the dialogues we hold directly with others: the voices of others are also sounded indirectly and come into play as equal partners in self-dialogues. Thus "the dialogical self knows itself through the responses of real, imagined, historical and generalized others." (de Peuter, 1998, p. 39)

This conception of self illuminates the multiple challenges facing teachers in a multicultural society: they need to first shape a workable personal and professional identity, and then draw on the resources of that identity and of their own life experience to adapt, develop and implement curricula and pedagogy that are adequate to the challenges of a multicultural environment. Bloom (1996) argues that the patriarchal, male model of the singular voice stigmatizes as weak or unhealthy any subjectivity which does not present itself as unified, strong and clear. Ribbens (1998) discusses the difficulties of studying and writing about personal experience and giving expression to "feeling voices." Bekerman (2002) stresses the pervasive, and often ignored, role of nationalism in shaping understandings of society and identity, particularly in the Israeli context. Thus, claiming a voice in a particular social, historic and cultural setting is not something to be taken for granted, but requires considerable effort (Gudmundsdottir, 2001). Lensmire and Satanovsky (1998), drawing on Bakhtin, explain the process of claiming voice as a "project" which "points to ongoing human labour that constructs and reconstructs our selves and our relations to others and the world" (p. 284). They see voice as involving three aspects: appropriation, social struggle, and becoming. The notion of *appropriation* emphasizes "the activity of the self in the face of cultural resources" (p. 284): knowledge is not passively acquired; rather, we must work to make sense of the phenomena around us using the language we share with others. The element of *social struggle* comes into play as we work to express our ideas in ways which will persuade our audience; often we must choose among multiple voices, taking a stand which positions us with certain audiences and against or outside others. The final element, *becoming*, means that in developing an internally persuasive voice we are engaged in growth and change, reconstructing the knowledge handed down to us, choosing what is useful for our current situation. These notions are particularly apt to describe what takes place as teachers engage in an ongoing process of identity development within the complex setting of the school system.

The Role of Storytelling in Multicultural Encounters

In the development of multicultural education in Israel, structured programs of encounters between Jewish and Palestinian Israelis have played a significant role for some years; only recently have these educational efforts been examined more critically (Bekerman, 2002; Maoz, 2002; Suleiman, 1997). Research makes it clear that just bringing people together is rarely sufficient (Abu-Nimer, 1999; Maoz, 2000), and practical arrangements are crucial. Courses that extend for a full year or intensive residential workshops, facilitation by two persons belonging to the Jewish and Palestinian communities respectively, the possibility of speaking in either Hebrew or Arabic, with translation, have all been found to be important. These arrangements, however, are difficult to provide within typical institutional contexts. It is also apparent that encounters must acknowledge and address wider political and economic issues, issues of identity and power (Bekerman, 2002). However, in most educational settings the addressing of such issues, however even-handedly, may be perceived by some participants as inappropriate to a professional context.

Meetings that are organized around various forms of storytelling have the potential to overcome some of these difficulties. In situations of cultural difference, it has been shown repeatedly that storytelling enables marginalized groups or individuals to claim the voices silenced by mainstream culture (McLaughlin & Tierney, 1993); hooks (1989) views storytelling as a way to "claim all the tongues in which we speak, to make speech of the many languages that give expression to the unique cultural reality of a people." Various formats have been developed for the use of story and narrative to promote teacher development in general, and intercultural understanding in particular. Conle (1996) describes the process of 'resonance' by which prospective teachers from diverse backgrounds were able to listen to and connect with one another's stories. Berlak (1996) provides an account of students learning about cultural difference through readings, film, classroom dialogue and, in particular, their own writing. Personal stories are rarely neutral with respect to past history or power relations in the present, so they allow these issues to be confronted, often indirectly; they also enable educators to experiment with claiming different voices as they reread and retell their own and others' stories in a multicultural group. Not least, they also facilitate the development of friendships among group members.

In recent work, telling and listening to one another's personal and family stories has enabled teacher education students to begin a process of 'restorying' their understanding of the 'other', examining the cultural codes which organize their lives as Jews and Palestinian Arabs in Israel, and trying out new forms of action on the basis of what they learned (Elbaz-Luwisch, 2001a, 2001b). As part of a larger study examining these issues, this paper focuses on the work of a small, multi-cultural group of women educators from diverse levels of the education system.

Understanding dialogue. The notion of dialogue is often used loosely in speaking about multicultural encounters. Theorists, however, have raised serious concerns. Hartley (2000) points out how often we do not say what we mean, fail to understand, or simply break off the attempt at dialogue without reaching shared understanding. For Hartley the idealized view of dialogue as "a neutral linguistic space wherein the conflict between voices is harmonised" (p. 82) cannot be sustained. Perhaps dialogue across difference requires what Bakhtin termed "living into", a process in which "one enters another's place while still maintaining one's own place, one's own outsidedness, with respect to the other" (Min, 2001, p. 10).

Typologies have been proposed for categorizing discourse in encounters; for example, Steinberg and Bar On (2002) suggest six categories: "ethnocentric talk, attack, opening a window, recognition of differences, intellectual discussion, and dialogic moment." However, a typology cannot account for the movement from one type of discourse to another, nor explain how 'dialogic moments' come about, or what enables participants to "live into" the experience of the other. Some approaches to conflict resolution (e.g. LeBaron, 2002; Mindell, 1995) suggest dialogue has to be understood holistically: conflict is not a negative phenomenon to be got rid of, but something that embodies and expresses meaning, and to understand it calls for intuition, imagination, and somatic knowing. Not surprisingly, these approaches rely on story and narrative.

Contested memories and the possibility of dialogue. In the Israeli context efforts at dialogue come up against the inevitable barrier of memory; the weight of historical memory carried by both Jewish and Palestinian participants, even if they themselves were not participants in the events, is heavy. Lentin (2000) uses the term "territories of silence" to refer to the many untold stories of the Shoah: survivors of the Holocaust were silent for many years because of the impossibility of narrating their experience, while society, and even therapists who treated survivors were often unable to hear their stories (Danieli, 1982). Still, it seems clear that telling the stories of trauma and loss can have both a therapeutic effect for the individual and an impact on learning (Crossley, 2000). Neumann (1998) discusses the impact on her personal academic work of the process of reconstructing the life stories of her parents, both Holocaust survivors.

The problematic of memory and storytelling is by no means confined to the Holocaust, though the unique difficulties of representation of Holocaust memory undoubtedly have an impact on any life story told in the Israeli context. Immigrants to Israel have found that their stories must be told in prescribed ways (Golden, 2001; Lieblich, 1992). The experience of the Palestinian community since 1948 has only recently begun to be heard in the public forum (e.g. Grossman, 1993). The Jewish and the Palestinian collective narratives of the events in 1948 are perceived to be in direct conflict; it often seems that each side negates the memory and narrative of the other (Gur Zeev, 2001). It is difficult to conceive ways of reconciling the collective narratives, but in the context of a small group, participants seem to draw on resources of creativity and generosity that enable them to accept and appreciate one another's personal stories and to raise and deal with difficult questions.

THE STUDY

The study described here sought to examine the use of personal life stories as a vehicle for learning about multiculturalism in education. Still ongoing, the study looks at issues of memory and storytelling in the context of multiple and overlapping identities, conflict and narratives of exclusion that characterize Israeli society. The focus is on the relevance of these issues for a pedagogy of border crossing and multicultural dialogue. The research aims to describe the processes of 'identity work' engaged in by participants in different settings (pre-service, in-service and in a collegial group of educators), to identify conditions and circumstances conducive to bringing about 'dialogic moments', and the constraints on dialogue among participants in different settings.

The study is of potential significance at the individual, inter-group and curricular levels. For participants, the opportunity to tell an important personal story, which is heard and validated by others, contributes significantly to both personal and professional development. In the group context, the significance widens as participants examine the various collective narratives at play in society. While collective narratives tend to be competing and contested, speaking in what Bakhtin (1981) termed an "authoritative discourse", participants in a small-group format are often able to work out ways of receiving, interpreting and understanding the personal narratives of colleagues from diverse backgrounds, by drawing on their own "internally persuasive discourses". The curricular significance lies in motivating teachers to elaborate ways of using personal stories in their teaching of diverse subjects, in their work as mentors of other teachers, and in their work as educators of new teachers, thus bringing multicultural perspectives into classroom curricula and teaching practice at all levels.

Description of the Study

As one element of a larger project, a small informal group of twelve Jewish and Arab-Palestinian women educators (all citizens of Israel living in the northern part of the country) was formed, based on a shared interest in telling their stories and listening to others. By design, the basis of membership in this group is not institutional or professional; rather, participation is voluntary and the format resembles other communal settings in which the women participate. Hence the choice of a women's group, in which it may be easier for some women to tell their stories openly. The group has met once a month for three hours for more than two years, and its meetings are continuing.

Data collection. The meetings of the group have been audiotaped, with written transcription to supplement the audiotaping. Transcripts have been prepared of all meetings. At each meeting, one participant told her story; transcripts were returned to participants who checked them for accuracy. After all the stories had been told, the participants engaged with the stories, responding in writing to selected passages, and a second round of storytelling began based on chosen themes. This process generated dialogue which continued in subsequent meetings and on email.

Analysis and interpretation. The materials collected are being analysed to identify major themes. The tools of narrative and biographical analysis (Clandinin & Connelly, 2000; Denzin, 1989; He, 2001; Mishler, 1886; Phillion, 2001) are drawn upon, as well as the Bakhtinian perspective presented above.

Main questions. The broader study seeks to respond to a number of questions. We ask ourselves what educators can learn from the process of writing, telling and retelling their personal stories in a multicultural group setting, and what particular meanings the participants derive from the encounter with colleagues from diverse backgrounds. We also seek to identify the main characteristics of the encounter, and to understand the role played by institutional and professional contexts, and by intervening events and circumstances, in fostering or impeding dialogue among educators from different backgrounds. In the present paper, we have chosen to pay particular attention to the group's collective story, and to the diverse voices that have come to expression within that story.

THE STORY SO FAR

The group of women educators is currently made up of eleven women, ranging in age from the twenties to the sixties. Two of the women are native Arabic speakers – one belongs to the Druse community, and one is a Christian Palestinian Israeli; the other women are Jewish, from varied backgrounds: four were born in Israel, five immigrated to Israel (three as young children, two others in their early twenties) from South America, India and Canada. Two women have doctoral degrees, two are engaged in doctoral studies, and three others are about to begin. The twelfth participant, who attended the first year of meetings, is from a Beduin background, and had just completed her bachelor's degree and teacher education diploma as the group began its meetings; due to changes in her work situation she was unable to continue participating in the group after the first year. The women work as teachers, teacher educators, teacher advisors and inspectors, and as researchers; most work in the formal education system, but one participant recently retired and works freelance as a teacher advisor, while another is involved in developing a consulting business. The women have a wide spectrum of talents: at least two write poetry (one in Hebrew, one in Arabic), several are involved in the educational uses of computers, one has written a children's book, and so on.

The group began meeting in November 2005. Two of the attendees at the first meeting did not continue because of time constraints, and two others joined soon after; the group has remained stable, except for one participant (mentioned above) who was unable to continue after the first year. At the introductory meeting, one participant volunteered to tell her story at the next meeting. This proved to be a significant starting point: in her twenties and having just completed teacher education, Samar told about her life with great candour and openness, and with rich detail that allowed all the listeners to connect to her story. Her story seemed to be one of those stories that demand to be told; it set a standard and opened wide a door for what was to follow.

For the next two and a half years, we continued meeting once a month. The meeting usually begins with some sharing about what has been happening since we last met; several times we began with a creative activity, such as collage. Then one of the participants tells her story, in whatever format she chooses. Many of the stories have been accompanied by photographs, objects or other materials. Sometimes these objects are simply presented alongside the story, illustrating various episodes; at other times objects, photos or topics written on slips of paper have been used to frame and organize the storytelling venture. All the stories have intertwined the personal and professional aspects of our lives, though in varying proportions and modes. Some stories have been told at critical junctures in the life of the teller: one participant told her story not long after the death of her father, another told hers soon after completing her doctoral dissertation, and one had recently learned of a serious health problem. In each of these cases, the critical situation served to organize the story in ways that might not have been chosen at another time in the teller's life. Despite their wide diversity, the way that all the stories were told reflected the openness and trust that had been established in the group.

At the end of the first year the group held a day-long meeting outside the university, in the pastoral setting of a kibbutz not far from Haifa. We began the day with a visualization that invited each participant to look over her own life's journey, and then drew pictures of our journeys and put them on the walls for all to share. After lunch we walked, quietly and single file, around the kibbutz, taking the time to reflect on whatever might arise for each of us. Over the course of the day, two participants told their stories, and then we worked in small groups to imagine the continuation of our journey as a group. The participants agreed that the journey of the group had been important, exciting and valuable for them; they mentioned qualities of wisdom, kindness, optimism and calm that had been manifested by other group members. They experienced a feeling of acceptance in the group that was liberating and inspiring, and they wanted it to continue. Still, they found it difficult to formulate the nature of this shared journey: one person wrote, "What is our goal? Where are we going together? I don't know … ", and another said, "All year I have been asking myself, what is this journey? What is its meaning for me?" It was agreed that we wanted to continue, to formulate some tasks for the group, to share our experience with other educators and to envision a product that we could work on together.

Throughout the day, the television set in the office of the centre where we were meeting carried breaking news of the kidnapping of two soldiers on Israel's northern border. The second Lebanon war ensued in the following days, and all the group members were affected in varying degrees: most live in Haifa or nearby towns that were under rocket attack; some group members had to leave their homes, and some had sons or other family members serving in the military. We kept in touch by phone and cursory emails, but the communication was sparse; the harshness of the events seemed to have silenced us. In September 2006, we met to share our experiences, letting out all the feelings, fear and sadness that we had not been able to express earlier. The bond we felt during this meeting was tangible; we raised a toast to the New Year just beginning, hoping that it promised better things for all of us and for the country and region of which we are a part.

Dancing with Difference

It is interesting that while the wider social and political issues appeared in our stories in a variety of ways, they rarely intruded into our interactions with one another. This was underlined at a meeting held in the spring of 2007 at the home of one of the participants, in Shefa'amer, a mixed Christian/Moslem/Druze town. As we basked in the early spring sunshine on a balcony overlooking the town, our talk was accompanied by the sounds of Friday prayers from the nearby mosque, broadcast over a loudspeaker. The melodies of the Moslem prayers provided a contrasting background for the observance of the customs of Easter and Lent (not least, a delicious meatless meal) in the home of our Christian hostess; the Jewish participants happily took time off from preparations for Passover which was to begin a few days later. As we discussed plans to expand our activities by starting several new circles of women educators, many other topics peppered the conversation. We discovered that some of us loved coriander (used in one of the salads), while others really hated it. Suddenly our hostess, Iman, disappeared into the kitchen, and returned to tell us that all of us, without exception, had eaten–and enjoyed–coriander in the falafel, which had quickly disappeared from the plate. Then, suddenly we found ourselves in the midst of a heated discussion about the reasons why many Israeli Arabs consider themselves Palestinians, and what the implications of this might be for Israeli citizenship and Jewish-Arab coexistence. Everyone talked at once as Shosh tried to explain what she found problematic about the designation "Palestinian Israeli", and Iman insisted on claiming both her cultural identity as a Palestinian and her civic identity as a citizen of Israel. Then, like the Moslem prayers which had just ended, the argument also came to a close (unresolved). We hugged and said our goodbyes, wishing one another good holidays. Just as we had differing views about coriander, yet all of us had eaten coriander in the falafel, so we managed to contain our diverse political views, holding them within the circle of our friendship and our commitment to living and working together. This way of 'dancing with difference' could indeed be seen as one of the defining qualities of the group's interaction.

This example also suggests that dialogue across differences does not necessarily proceed in a linear fashion according to definite stages. The six categories of discourse proposed by Steinberg and Bar-On (2002) could indeed be identified, but they did not necessarily occur in any particular order. Dialogic moments might occur upon recognition and acceptance of differences, as well as following the awareness of similarities; even something trivial, like the coriander, could give rise to a profound moment of dialogue. Like in the episode above, sometimes the dialogic moment was preceded by heated debate; then, unexpectedly, the disagreement would stop and participants would begin laughing together and sharing ideas. This suggests that the process of listening to one another's stories created a broad basis of understanding such that dialogue had become a concrete possibility, to be drawn upon at any time, even when views were in conflict.

On examining the life stories told by participants in the group, we found a complex pattern of shared and divergent themes. Family was an important theme that played out in different ways: participants told about influential family members, they talked about the connections between parenting and teaching, and about patterns that persisted across generations. Time was another theme: virtually all the stories connected past, present and future in varied ways. The centrality of learning and development was obvious: the women talked about their own growth and about their roles in the empowerment of others. In what follows we present and discuss some of the insights that have emerged from the discussion, writing and analysis of the stories. In particular, we will highlight the diverse voices that circulate in the talk about our lives and work.

Diverse Voices

The group discussion gave expression to our voices as concerned professionals, as mothers, daughters, partners, sisters and friends, as academics, and as community members. The diversity was apparent, but initially there was a reluctance to shift the purpose of the group away from the experience of telling, listening and responding to stories. (The group was originally formed as a discussion circle, not a research group.) However, new understandings and motivations began to crystallize as we realized that there were diverse views about the need for research. "We have something to say as a group of participants who have been studying ourselves; let's invest in analysing (the stories), and formulating some orderly insights," said one voice. An opposing voice held that "if we start to analyse, and write… we'll kill the circle. Why should we sacrifice the experiential process for a research product?" A few participants thought we could do both: the life of the group was not necessarily at odds with a research task. This discussion highlighted the way that we unconsciously perceived research and life as binary opposites. In struggling to find a definition of research that would suit us, that would not require us to sacrifice the vivid sense of connectedness that we experienced in our meetings, we were, in Bakhtin's terms, struggling to find a voice for ourselves as researchers. We wanted to appropriate a legitimate research voice, but not at the cost of losing the unique identity our group had shaped for itself.

Going further, we discovered additional distinctions, between doing and experiencing, between process and product. Idit commented, "The stories, and the activities, are different means of raising awareness, of inner reflection, and deep discussion that develops insights, both personally and on the group level. I'd like to continue to experience this through different means." This intense experience of a process was opposed to 'doing', which is more active which should lead to a 'product': "I have an expectation of something beyond this (the meetings), of breaking out, to make something of this: there should be some result, a new development." Another participant said, "About the group, I have a good feeling, of fullness; something surprising will happen. We're in a shared space; we should go forward to some joint creative work, something that goes beyond 'us'." Yet even as we contemplated doing creative work together – writing a joint paper or a book – there were voices (sometimes coming from the very same participants) that asked to continue our original process, telling and retelling our stories. As Dina said, "I'd like to touch the individual more. I'd like to meet with each one of you alone… I see the group as a gift." In these voices we can see the group members struggling with our understandings of ourselves: as educators and as researchers, we should be goal-oriented, should be able to create useful products for our field. At the same time, we recognize the intrinsic value of the experience of telling our own stories; it is an experience we want to preserve because it serves our own 'becoming'.

In referring to the group as a *gift*, Dina calls to mind the discussion in Davies and Gannon (2006) of the ethical reflexivity of the practice the authors refer to as 'collective biography'. Davies points out that "although collective biographies can be carried out with an end product in mind (a paper, a book), and can be carefully planned in advance, these organizational practices must operate in tandem with an openness to the unknown, and to the dynamic unfolding process through which a group of individuals work together to enable new insights to emerge from their collective work" (p. 184). The form of work presented by Davies, Gannon and their colleagues is not identical to ours, but the same considerations characterize our work. Davies speaks of the participation of students and colleagues in collective biography writing workshops as "a gift: a gift of their presence, their insights, their memories and their friendship;" (p. 185) she emphasizes the quality of listening and the art of being present as elements of the work that cannot be subsumed under a neo-liberal mentality, cannot be quantified or given a monetary value. Hence, like Dina, she views them as gifts. Although intangible and difficult to pin down, these qualities are self-evident to the group members and contribute directly to the methodology of our research; as Idit pointed out, "isn't it important to mention the qualities that were constructed over time like attentiveness, respect, acceptance, resonance, and so on–are they not part of our methodology?"

NOT YET AN ENDING

As the meetings of the women educators' group continue, we have learned that personal stories grounded in lived experience (Phillion, He & Connelly, 2005), particularly bodily experience, and in emotion, were the most powerful for us, and played an important role in facilitating our recognition (Taylor, 1994) of one another as unique individuals and as members of diverse groups. It was also apparent that *'resonance'* (Conle, 1996) with the stories allowed for connection and friendship to develop among the participants. Engaging the imagination (through poetry, exercises in writing or guided imagery, creating collages) has allowed us to transcend our limited understandings and create shared visions for the future. By attending to our stories and diverse voices, we seek to better understand our multicultural environment and to elaborate educational practice that fosters and promotes living well together.

REFERENCES

Abu-Nimer, M. (1999). *Dialogue, conflict, resolution, and change: Arab-Jewish encounters in Israel.* Albany, NY: SUNY Press.

Al-Haj, M. (2002). Multiculturalism in deeply divided societies: The Israeli case. *International Journal of Intercultural Relations, 26*, 169–183.

Bakhtin, M. (1981). *The dialogic imagination.* Austin, TX: University of Texas Press.

Banks, J., & Banks, C. A. M. (1993). *Multicultural education: Issues and perspectives* (2nd ed.). Boston: Allyn & Bacon.

Bar-On, D. (1998). Transgenerational aftereffects of the Holocaust in Israel: Three generations. In E. Sicher (Ed.)., *Breaking crystal: Writing and memory after Auschwitz.* Urbana & Chicago: University of Illinois Press.

Bar-On, D. (Ed.). (2000). *Bridging the gap: Storytelling as a way to work through political and collective hostilities*. Hamburg: Korber Stiftung.
Bar-On, D. (in press). Conciliation through story telling: Beyond victimhood. In G. Salomon & B. Nevo (Eds.)., *Peace education: The concept, principles, and practices around the world*. Mahwah, NJ: LEA.
Bar-Tal, D., & Zoltek, S. (1989). The reflection of the Arab and Jewish-Arab relations in readers. *Megamot, 32*(3), 301–331 (in Hebrew).
Beijaard, D., Verloop, N., & Vermunt, J. (2000). Teachers' perceptions of professional identity: An exploratory study from a personal knowledge perspective. *Teaching and Teacher Education, 16*(7), 749–764.
Bekerman, Z. (2002). The discourse of nation and culture: Its impact on Palestinian-Jewish encounters in Israel. *International Journal of Intercultural Relations, 26*(4), 409–427.
Berlak, A. (1996). Teaching stories: Viewing a cultural diversity course through the lens of narrative. *Theory into Practice, 35*(2), 93–101.
Bowers, C. A. (1987). *Elements of a post-liberal theory of education*. New York & London: Teachers College Press.
Britzman, D. (1991). *Practice makes practice: A critical study of learning to teach*. Albany, NY: State University of New York Press.
Carlsen, A. (2005). Only when I laugh? Notes on the becoming interview. *Teachers and Teaching: Theory and Practice, 11*(3), 239–255.
Clandinin, D. J., & Connelly, F. M. (1992). The teacher as curriculum maker. In P. W. Jackson (Ed.), *Handbook of research on curriculum: A project of the American educational research association* (pp. 363–401). New York: Macmillan.
Cochran-Smith, M. (1995). Color blindness and basket making are not the answers: Confronting the dilemmas of race, culture, and language diversity in teacher education. *American Educational Research Journal, 23*, 493–522.
Conle, C. (1996). Resonance in preservice teacher inquiry. *American Educational Research Journal, 33*(2), 297–325.
Coulter, D. (1999). The epic and the novel: Dialogism and teacher research. *Educational Researcher, 28*(3), 4–13.
Crossley, M. (2000). *Introducing narrative psychology: Self, trauma and the construction of meaning*. Buckingham & Philadelphia: Open University Press.
Davies, G., & Gannon, S. (Eds.). (2006). *Doing collective biography*. Maidenhead, Berks: Open University Press.
Denzin, N. (1989). *Interpretive biography*. Newbury Park, CA: Sage.
Eden, D., & Kalekin-Fishman, D. (2002). Multi-cultural education in Israel as a fulfillment of national ethos and political policy. In P. Pitkanen, D. Kalekin-Fishman, & G. Verma (Eds.), *Settlement policy and education in six countries*. London: Routledge Falmer.
Eilam, B. (2002). "Passing through" a western-democratic teacher education: The case of Israeli Arab teachers. *Teachers College Record, 104*(8), 1656–1701.
Elbaz-Luwisch, F., Gudmundsdottir, S., & Moen, T. (2002). The multivoicedness of classrooms: Bakhtin and narratives of teaching. In H. Heikkinen, R. Huttunen, & L. Syrjala (Eds.), *Biographical research and narrativity* (pp. 197–218). Finland: SoPhi Press.
Elbaz-Luwisch, F. (2001a). Personal story as passport: Storytelling in border pedagogy. *Teaching Education, 12*(1), 81–101.
Elbaz-Luwisch, F. (2001b). Understanding what goes on in the heart and in the mind: Learning about diversity and co-existence through storytelling. *Teaching and Teacher Education, 17*, 133–146.
Elbaz-Luwisch, F., & Kalekin-Fishman, D. (2004). Professional development in community: Fostering multicultural dialogue among Israeli teachers. *British Journal of In-service Education, 30*(2), 245–264.
Estola, E. (2003). Hope as work—student teachers constructing their narrative identities. *Scandinavian Journal of Educational Research, 47*(2), 181–203.
Felman, S., & Laub, D. (1992). *Testimony: Crises of witnessing in literature, psychoanalysis, and history*. New York: Routledge.
Giddens, A. (1991). *Modernity and self-identity: Self and society in the late modern age*. Cambridge: Polity Press.

Giroux, H. (1992). *Border crossings: Cultural workers and the politics of education*. New York: Routledge.
Golden, D. (2001). Storytelling the future: Israelis, immigrants and the imagining of community. *Anthropological Quarterly, 75*(1), 7–35.
Goodwin, A. L. (1994). Making the transition from self to other: What do preservice teachers really think about multicultural education? *Journal of Teacher Education, 45*, 119–131.
Grossman, D. (1993). *Sleeping on a wire: Conversations with Palestinians in Israel*. New York: Farrar, Straus, Giroux.
Gudmundsdottir, S. (2001). Narrative research on school practice. In V. Richardson (Ed.), *Fourth handbook for research on teaching*. New York: Macmillan.
Gur-Zeev, I. (2001). The production of the self and the destruction of the other's memory and identity: Israeli/Palestinian education on the Holocaust/Nakbah. *Studies in Philosophy and Education, 20*(3), 255–266.
Halabi, R. (Ed.). (2000). Identities in dialogue: Arab-Jewish encounters in Wahat as-Salam/Neveh-Shalom. Tel-Aviv: Hakibbutz Hameuchad Press (Hebrew).
Hartley, L. (2000, Autumn). Conflict not conversation: The defeat of dialogue in Bakhtin and de Man. *New Formations, 41*, 71–82.
He, Ming Fang (2002). A narrative inquiry of cross-cultural lives: Lives in China. *Journal of Curriculum Studies, 34*(3), 301–321.
Heikkinen, H. (1998). Becoming yourself through narrative: Autobiographical approach in teacher education. In R. Erkkila, A. Willman, & L. Syrjala (Eds.), *Promoting teachers' personal and professional growth* (pp. 111–131). Oulu: Oulu University Press.
Hoffman, D. (1996). Culture and self in multicultural education: Reflections on discourse, text, and practice. *American Educational Research Journal, 33*(3), 545–569.
Jordan, M. L. R. (1995). Reflections on the challenges, possibilities and perplexities of preparing preservice teachers for culturally diverse classrooms. *Journal of Teacher Education, 46*, 369–374.
Ladson-Billings, G. (1999). Preparing teachers for diversity. In L. Darling-Hammond & G. Sykes (Eds.), *Teaching as the learning profession* (pp. 86–123). San Francisco: Jossey-Bass.
LaCapra, D. (1998). *History and memory after Auschwitz*. Ithaca & London: Cornell University Press.
Lensmire, T., & Satanovsky, L. (1998). Defense of the romantic poet? Writing workshops and voice. *Theory into Practice, 37*(4), 280–288.
Lentin, R. (2000). *Israel and the daughters of the Shoah: Reoccupying the territories of silence*. New York & Oxford: Berghahn Books.
Lieblich, A. (1993). Looking at change: Natasha, 21, new immigrant from Russia to Israel. In R. Josselson & A. Lieblich (Eds.), *The narrative study of lives: Vol. 1* (pp. 92–129). Newbury Park, CA: Sage.
MacIntyre, A. (1984). *After virtue*. Notre Dame, IN: University of Notre Dame Press.
Maoz, I. (2000). Multiple conflicts and competing agendas: A Framework for conceptualizing structural encounters between groups in conflict: The case of a coexistence project of Jews and Palestinians in Israel. *Peace and Conflict: Journal of Peace Psychology, 6*, 135–156.
Marsh, M. M. (2002). The shaping of Ms. Nicholi: The discursive fashioning of teacher identities. *Qualitative Studies in Education, 15*(3), 333–347.
McLaren, P. (1995). White terror and oppositional agency: Toward a critical multiculturalism. In C. Sleeter & P. McLaren (Eds.), *Multicultural education, critical pedagogy and the politics of difference* (pp. 33–70). New York: State University of New York Press.
McLaughlin, D., & Tierney, W. G. (1993). *Naming silenced lives*. New York: Routledge.
Min, E. (2001). Bakhtinian perspectives for the study of intercultural communication. *Journal of Intercultural Studies, 22*(1), 5–18.
Mindell, A. (1995). *Sitting in the fire: Large group transformation using conflict and diversity*. Portland, Oregon: Lao Tse Press.
Mishler, E. (1986). *Research interviewing: Context and narrative*. Cambridge: Harvard University Press.
Neumann, A. (1998). On experience, memory and knowing: A post-Holocaust (auto) biography. *Curriculum Inquiry, 28*(4), 425–442.
Nias, J. (1985). Reference groups in primary teaching: Talking, listening and identity. In S. Ball & I. F. Goodson (Eds.), *Teachers' lives and careers*. Lewes: Falmer Press.
Nieto, S. (1999). *The light in their eyes: Creating multicultural learning communities*. New York: Teachers College Press.

de Peuter, J. (1998). The dialogics of narrative identity. In M. M. Bell & M. Gardiner (Eds.), *Bakhtin and the human sciences: No last words* (pp. 30–48). London, Thousand Oaks, New Delhi: Sage.
Phillion, J., He, M. F., & Connelly, F. M. (2005). *Multicultural education: Narrative and experiential approaches*. Thousand Oaks, CA: Sage Publications.
Phillion, J. (2002). Narrative multiculturalism. *Journal of Curriculum Studies, 34*(3), 265–279.
Ribbens, J. (1998). Hearing my feeling voice? An autobiographical discussion of motherhood. In R. Edwards & J. Ribbens (Eds.), *Feminist dilemmas in qualitative research* (pp. 24–38). London: Sage.
Richardson, L. (1994). Writing: A method of inquiry. In N. K. Denzin & Y. S. Lincoln (Eds.), *Handbook of qualitative research* (pp. 345–371). Thousand Oaks/London/New Delhi: Sage.
Ricoeur, P. (1991). Life: A story in search of a narrator. In M. J. Valdes (Ed.), *A Ricoeur reader: Reflection and imagination* (pp. 425–437). New York: Harvester Wheatsheaf.
Salomon, G. (in press). A narrative-based view of coexistence education. *Journal of Social Issues, 60*(2), 273–287.
Shotter, J., & Gergen, K. (Eds.). (1989). *Texts of identity*. London: Sage.
Sicher, E. (Ed.). (1998). *Breaking crystal: Writing and memory after Auschwitz*. Urbana & Chicago: University of Illinois Press.
Sleeter, C. (2001). Epistemological diversity in research on preservice teacher preparation for historically underserved children. *Review of Research in Education, 25*, 209–250.
Soen, D. (2002). Democracy, the Jewish-Arab cleavage and tolerance education in Israel. *International Journal of Intercultural Relations, 26*, 215–232.
Steinberg, S., & Bar On, D. (2002). An analysis of the group process in encounters between Jews and Palestinians using a typology for discourse classification. *International Journal of Intercultural Relations, 26*, 199–214.
Taubman, P. (2002). Facing the terror within: Exploring the personal in multicultural education. In C. Korn & A. Bursztyn (Eds.), *Rethinking multicultural education: Case studies in cultural transition* (pp. 97–129). Westport, CT & London: Bergin & Garvey.
Taylor, C. (1994). The politics of recognition. In A. Gutman (Ed.), *Multiculturalism*. Princeton, NJ: Princeton University Press.
Zeichner, K. (1999). The new scholarship in teacher education. *Educational Researcher, 28*(9), 4–15.

Freema Elbaz Luwisch, Shosh Klein, Hiam Nasseraldin, Idit Avni,
Iman Awadiyeh, Aviva Ben Hefer, Dina David, Hanna Morag,
Tova Shaul, Fany Shimoni, and Chava Simon
Faculty of Education
University of Haifa

FRANCES RUST, FRANCINE PETERMAN AND MARK STORZ

USING STUDENTS' VOICES TO CHANGE TEACHING AND LEARNING TO TEACH IN URBAN SCHOOLS: STUDIES FROM THREE TEACHER EDUCATION PROGRAMS

We come to this research as colleagues who, over the past three years, have been engaged in a collaborative inquiry focused on the preparation of teachers for urban schools. Our work has been guided by our theory that for our students who are by and large middle class, white women becoming an urban educator requires that they learn to walk in others' shoes. Such knowing requires both self knowledge (Britzman & Pitt, 1996; Korthagen, 2004; Rust & Orland, 2001) and knowledge of others (Gonzalez, Moll, Amanti, 2005), and, in the long run, we suggest that preparing preservice teachers for careers in urban schools will require substantive change in teacher education.

This paper tells the story of an assignment that opened a window on the complex process of learning to teach in urban classrooms. In broad strokes, it describes the assignment that we developed for use across the programs and then focuses specifically on one program as generally illustrative of the whole. Thus, the paper should be read as a draft report on the initial phase of our work with one program rather than as a comprehensive summary of our research activities.

THE ASSIGNMENT

We started by engaging our students in interviewing their students: Francine with preservice teachers of high school, Mark with middle school preservice teachers and Frances with elementary school teachers. Our intent was to help our students to develop an understanding of what Gonzalez, Moll, and Amanti (2005) describe as "funds of knowledge," that is, the ways in which "families develop social networks that interconnect them with their social environments (most importantly with other households), and how these social relationships facilitate the development and exchange of resources—including knowledge, skills, and labour—that enhance the households' ability to survive or thrive" (p. 73). We want our preservice students to learn about their students in these deeply informative ways. We, ourselves, wanted to similarly come to know our students. We theorized that our own practice as teacher educators could change as a result of what we might learn about and from our students and their students, and we were prepared to document such changes as part of our research.

J. A. Kentel and A. Short (eds.), Totems and Taboos: Risk and Relevance in Research on Teachers and Teaching, 59–66.

BACKGROUND

The teacher education program about which we write is one of two master's level, elementary preservice programs at New York University where Frances Rust taught until the summer of 2007. The program prepares students to teach in grades 1-6. Dubbed the "fast track" master's, it is conducted over the course of 4 semesters – two in one summer, two during the following academic year. The program enrols approximately 70 students a year who begin their course work in July and finish the following May. During the summer, preservice students complete 100 hours of participant observation in a variety of educational settings including summer school classes. They begin student teaching in the fall generally in lower elementary settings (grades 1-3); they continue in the spring usually in different schools than they were in during the fall and this time in upper elementary classrooms (grades 4-6). The program places most student teachers in public schools across the city. A handful of students are placed in local private schools.

Frances' course is one of 5 courses preservice students take in the fall semester, and it is one of three sections of the same course. It is intended as an integrating seminar that is concurrent with student teaching and designed to bring together all of students' course work with their experience in the field. Hence, readings and assignments draw on their work in other courses and are developed to support reflective action in the field. Course instructors meet together weekly so as to try to insure some uniformity of experience for the students across the program.

Drawing on research about the role of autobiography in the shaping of teachers' practice (Britzman & Pitt, 1996; Goodson, 1992; Korthagen, 1999; Lortie, 1975; Rust & Orland, 2001), Frances and her colleagues decided to begin the course with an assignment that would engage our students in interviewing their students and their cooperating teachers. However, the inquiry assignment did not stop with the interviews. Students were to use their interviews for themselves, too, and develop from the interviews both a portrait of the child and a self-portrait. They were, then, to compare the two and, in class, we were to discuss similarities and differences between their self-portraits and those of their students and then move from that to implications for teaching. They were also to develop a portrait of their cooperating teacher. These activities spanned the first four weeks of class.

Assignments that followed included a chapter on Development from Darling-Hammond and Bransford (2005), lesson plans developed with specific attention to the focal child, and observations. These assignments were designed to move students into crafting a case study of a child in their class. In the process, we hoped that these assignments would help to shape student teachers' interactions with their focus child in ways that were informed by conversation with the child as well as by readings and course work for this and other courses.

GETTING BENEATH THE SURFACE

The data of the interviews, the comparisons students made between themselves and the child whom they interviewed, their interviews with their cooperating teachers, and subsequent lessons containing adaptations for their focus child—these assignments taught Frances and her colleagues far more than they anticipated. For the purposes of this study, however, we will only focus on her class.

The Class

In its composition, the class resembled elementary teacher education programs around the country: Of the 19 women and one man in the course, six were from an urban environment, three were from rural environments, and the rest were from suburbs of large cities. Those from the rural and suburban areas reported little, if any, experience of cultural and ethnic diversity in their elementary and secondary schools. Six students were African American—all women. Of this group, five had grown up in urban environments and attended public schools. The majority of members of the class were recent college graduates. Three students were career changers. Three were parents—one of an infant, the other two of middle-school age children.

Most provided self-portraits that gave the information previously described and most chose middle class children who were in some ways like themselves. It was their comparisons with their focus student, however, that provided real depth on the student teachers and on the students whom they interviewed.

It was not unusual to learn from these comparisons how these beginning preservice students remembered themselves as elementary students:

> When I was X's age, I was very much like him. I completed my work always and forever responded to what was required of me. Additionally, I suffered from a processing disorder, which affected my comprehension of various texts.

From these comparisons, one learned about their struggles and strengths:

> Like me, she is unable to sit for long periods of time and usually gets out of her seat to move around the room… We both share a passion for fantasy books and enjoy riding our bicycles.

It was not unusual to read about how whole segments of their education came back to them in getting to know the child:

> Seeing her coming to school so well prepared reminds me of when my mother would send me to school over-prepared. She was very adamant about me doing well in school and wanted me to have the same opportunities as the other kids in the class. I was supposed to be at a different school in the southern parts of the Bronx, but my mother wrote to every politician in New York pleading for me to go to a better school in a different area. So when I see her sitting on the rug or at a desk listening attentively to the mini lesson or reading independently, I can't help but remember how I was the same way. Just like her, I would not reprimand my classmates for interrupting the lessons or causing disruptions. I was a spectator in the class. Luckily, I was not lost in the cracks like some students who are as quiet as might be.

The Children

The portraits of the children were richer than those of the preservice teachers. In class, Frances and her students developed the broad strokes of the interviews the student teachers would use with their students. Among those discussed were birth place, how the child got her/his name, siblings, languages spoken, places travelled to or favourite places to visit, favourite books, favourite toys/games/TV shows, favourite things about school, what the child would like to be when grown up. Of course, grade level was recorded and so, too, was school.

Of the 20 children chosen, 9 were girls—5 second graders, 4 third graders; 11 were boys—6 first graders, 3 second graders; one third grader. Most were children of the middle class though the schools that were chosen as field settings serve ethnically and culturally diverse populations of students.

Particularly interesting in their choices of students to focus on was the resemblances that they found to themselves. As previously noted, when the preservice teachers developed their comparisons of themselves and their focal students, their own self-portraits became richer. But they also seemed to have gained a deeper understanding of the children, too:

> Overall, I can see her potential, like my teachers recognized my own, and it is still very weird to me that I will be in the same position they were in–leading a class of growing minds.

> Identifying similarities has created a positive relationship between us.... Knowing her interests is important to providing appropriate activities that will engage her while also scaffolding her learning.

Only a few left this activity continuing to write about the child from the perspective of an observer. They clearly were beginning to think about the impact of such conversations for their teaching. As one of the student teachers wrote:

> So how can finding common ground with a child's interests and feeling authentic delight in her or his related strengths lead to building on those strengths to enhance a child's learning? This can happen in three ways. First, a child whose interests, skills, and delights are appreciated at school is going to have a stronger positive association with and attitude towards school in general. Second, through knowing a child's interests, a teacher can create links to them in crafting assignments... Third, a teacher can use her or his knowledge of each child's strength in pairing up children for group work to the benefit of both.

Knowing the child in the context of self also provoked a reflection on the schools in which the student teachers were doing their first of two semesters of student teaching.

The Schools

Students are placed across the City—Manhattan, Brooklyn, and the South Bronx. Like most teacher education programs, our effort in developing student teaching placements is to identify sites that will provide both models of good practice and hands-on experience in a broad range of socio-economic, cultural, and ethnic settings. The data of this small sample suggests that in some ways, the teacher education program is meeting its goals and in some ways, it is not even close to realizing them.

On the positive side, not a single student complained about the cooperating teacher. It was remarkable to read time after time of the broad experience of the teachers with whom these students were placed (anywhere from 6-25 years) and of the welcome that they received:

> I find her classroom library to be amazing and full of so many resources and options that would comply with many content standards.... She told me that she reads most of the books when given her theme before school starts and she gave me two of them to read so that I, too, may be prepared and have some better content knowledge of the topic. She is my ideal teacher.

Theirs were well-equipped classrooms and schools, and this came as a welcome surprise to many of my students:

> At my school, I feel that I have the space and freedom to practice teaching whether I fail or succeed.

Their concerns focused on having a mentor close by, on having other adults (particularly student teachers) in the classroom, on "forming a close relationship with the other staff members—the paras—as well as the students themselves." Only one expressed concern about classroom management. They found the schools, as one remarked, "very like my suburban elementary school." And therein is the rub: They were in settings that seemed both comfortable and familiar. Not one of Frances' students picked a child who was not a successful learner. Not one of Frances' students landed in a setting that made her or him question what Sarason (2001) calls the regularities of schooling.

SEARCHING FOR COMPLEXITY

The experience of Frances' students in these first weeks of their first semester of student teaching seemed to do little to get them into the complex weave of urban schooling. Though the assignment that she and her colleagues developed worked to get them engaging with their students as people and helped them in subsequent weeks to find ways to think about teaching and learning through the eyes of their focal student, it did not help them to stretch to finding a child who might challenge their experience of schooling. It did not lead them to a broader and more nuanced understanding of the ways in which culture, socio-economic conditions, and race come together to affect children's learning.

Frances noted that this is not the first time she has been confronted by the conundrum of helping middle class students who have themselves been successful learners open themselves to engaging with children whose experiences of school are very different from theirs, with children whose life experiences are unimaginable to them, with schools that do not remind them of the ones they attended.

This is not the first time that she heard the following sigh of relief:

> My situation is very different from most of my colleagues. A number of my classmates have been placed in non-lab, public schools and are faced with behaviours challenges every day. They have also encountered teachers who have a set curriculum they must follow. I hear that teachers in this situation almost feel pressured to cover the material and even overlook possible 'learning moments.' At our school, this almost never happens, the teachers have the freedom to cover what they want, whenever they want, and in any manner they want. It is hard to recognize where the children are developmentally because they are so cognitively advanced.

While Frances recognizes that the exercise of interviewing a child and engaging in dialogue with cooperating teachers and with colleagues in class enabled these students to begin to think about teaching and learning with the child in mind, she has come away from the experiment more convinced than ever that one course is not enough to raise consciousness of self and others. She and her colleagues found themselves working hard to find ways to accommodate students' assignments from other courses; after all, theirs was an integrating seminar. However, there were numerous barriers that often led to the students simply interpreting our assignments as "another thing to do."

Barriers to Integration

Frances and her colleagues were constrained by time and size. Theirs was a two-credit course, which met for an hour and 10 minutes once a week. They barely got time for community building activities. The size of the groups (at 20 Frances' group was the smallest) made it difficult to do the interactive work that can make a seminar so powerful.

They were constrained by the structure of the teacher education program. They did not have any systematic way to interact with course instructors many of whom were adjuncts. Nor did they have access to the student teaching supervisors. Thus, their informants regarding requirements from other courses and the field were the student teachers themselves.

The short duration of the fast-track program also became a constraint. Simultaneous with this first integrating seminar, Frances was teaching an integrating seminar for preservice masters students who were finishing up the other elementary master's program. Though the courses are identical in the two programs, this latter group had moved through the program over a period of two to five years. They had time to do their hundred hours of participant observation along with their foundations and methods courses. They did not come to their student teaching experiences until they were close to being finished with the program. There were only 11 of them. The contrast was stunning. All but one of this "slow track" group of teachers were deeply knowledgeable about and deeply committed to teaching in city schools. As Frances and the students worked together over the semester, they were able to carefully analyze their work in their classrooms using a variety of theoretical lenses including the impact of poverty, race, gender, and language on children's experience of schooling.

PLANNING FOR CHANGE

As we step back from this assignment, we note that the difficulties and conditions that Frances and her colleagues encountered are similar to those we have encountered in our own programs. Time, class size, programs taught largely by adjuncts, a lack of coherence across courses, and tenuous relationships with schools and with the field are issues that confront each of our programs. Thus, we have come away from this experiment more convinced than ever of the power and importance of thoughtful, interactive dialogue among teacher educators, their students, and the children and teachers with whom they work.

But we also come away troubled by the pull-away from a highly interconnected programmatic structure for teacher education that seems prevalent in many Research I Universities. As with good teaching in any environment, teacher preparation requires that we, teacher educators learn about and teach from our understandings of our students' funds of knowledge (Gonzalez, Moll, & Amanti, 2005). Further, it seems essential to us that we model the very practices that we want our graduates to use. If we create teacher education programs that are simply a menu of unrelated courses, our students cannot find themselves being "known" and they, in turn, may not extend the possibility to their students. Thus, little will change in schools.

If future teachers like our students are to embrace children whose lives and ways of knowing and expressing themselves are different from their own, it seems essential that teacher educators reshape the practice of teacher education in a variety of ways. Chief among these would be to place inquiry, action, and reflection (in that order) at the core of every program and, thus, as essential attributes and activities of every course. Such a move would enable our students to develop the capacity to learn continually from experience in school and beyond.

Dialogic interviews and conversations are only the beginning of becoming a researcher of teaching. They are essential first steps, but the ability to ask questions, to experiment using considered action, to step back and determine what to do next—this is power. This is what opening the door to "knowing" one's students should lead to. It is, as Clark and Rust (2007) have recently written, essential to "counteracting hope-depleting, pessimistic beliefs, and urban legends about urban public schools" (p. 11). Teacher educators moving toward collaborative, inquiry based practice could change the urban landscape by "knowing" their students.

REFERENCES

Britzman, D., & Pitt, A. J. (1996). Pedagogy and transference: Casting the past of learning into the presence of teaching. *Theory into Practice*, *35*(2), 117–123.

Clark, C. M., & Rust, F. O'C. (2007). *Feeding the good wolf: Urban teachers and action research.* Paper presented at the Annual Urban Ethnography Conference, Philadelphia, PA, February 23, 2007.

Darling-Hammond, L., & Bransford, J. (2005). *Preparing teachers for a changing world.* San Francisco: Jossey Bass.

Goodson, I. (Ed.). (1992). *Studying teachers lives.* New York: Teachers College Press.

Gonzalez, N., Moll, L. C., & Amanti, C. (Eds.). (2005). *Funds of knowledge.* Mahwah, NJ: Lawrence Erlbaum Associates.

Korthagen, F. A. J. (2004). In search of the essence of a good teacher: Towards a more holistic approach in teacher education. *Teaching and Teacher Education, 20*(1), 77–97.

Lortie, D. C. (1975). *Schoolteacher. A sociological study.* Chicago: University of Chicago Press.

Rust, F. O'C., & Orland, L. (2001, January). Learning the discourse of teaching: Conversation as professional development. In C. Clark (Ed.), *Talking shop: Authentic conversation and teacher learning.* New York: Teachers College Press.

Sarason, S. B. (2001). *Revisiting "The culture of schools and the problem of change."* New York: Teachers College.

Frances Rust
Erikson Institute

Francine Peterman
Cleveland State University

Mark Storz
John Carroll University

MARIA DA GRAÇA NICOLETTI MIZUKAMI AND MARCOS MASETTO

PROFESSIONAL DEVELOPMENT OF HIGHER SCHOOL EDUCATORS

Although the current Brazilian backdrop demonstrates that investments in the elaboration, implementation and assessment of educational public policies concerning teacher education have been made, it can also be said that more emphasis has been given to the initial and continuing teacher education processes of elementary, medium and high school teachers.

Higher education teaching is still an area in which initiative is weaker. Post-graduate programs in education, as a rule, receive professionals of different areas of knowledge. Those are usually professors from colleges or universities: teacher educators and other teachers who work with baccalaureates or with formative processes of liberal professionals. Even though there is great and constant demand for these professionals, there has usually been no space in post-graduate programs for the practice of teaching, or the systematized discussion of its specific aspects. There are no initial teacher education programs concerning the higher education teacher. Only a small part of the faculty that is involved with teacher education courses or programs has some kind of pedagogical preparation. Most of the higher education professors have never received any kind of pedagogical preparation (either pre-service or in-service).

Currently, there is an initiative from two public agencies–CAPES (Brazilian federal agency for higher education professional improvement) and CNPq (Brazilian federal research agency)–regarding the preparation of the higher education professor. It concerns a practicum to be developed in higher education institutions for a period from 6 to 12 months, by graduate students who receive scholarships.

Most initiatives, however, derive from the universities' own institutional policies, and even so, usually lack a formal explicit curriculum designed for teacher education, which lays out what the teachers involved are required to know and be able to do regarding the teachers at the receiving end–a requirement present in current educational public policies.

Thus, Brazil is currently going through a reform of higher education which involves critical analysis of the formative processes of different professions, as well as the establishment of curriculum guidelines for all courses. Most of these educational public policies are grounded on research related to how teachers learn to teach and how to develop themselves professionally. These reforms used to strictly encompass preschool, primary and secondary school education (K-11 or currently, since 2006, K-12), taking into account different regional and local contexts.

J. A. Kentel and A. Short (eds.), Totems and Taboos: Risk and Relevance in Research on Teachers and Teaching, 67–78.

More recently (2002 onwards), though, they have also started to include higher education teaching in the new national curriculum guidelines focusing on teacher preparation, certification programs, and baccalaureate courses. Higher education reforms involve critical analysis of the formative processes of different professions, as well as the establishment of curriculum guidelines for all courses. This is grounded on educational literature which emphasizes teaching and learning processes directed to the construction of knowledge, thus overcoming the obstacles presented by the transmission-reception model. College/university professors may well be considered the pillars of the new Brazilian reform of higher education.

In Brazil, as previously mentioned, conventional methods based on the transmission-reception model are dominant. Lessons are frequently set up as expository lectures, sometimes involving the aid of practical demonstrations as well as the supportive use of a variety of media. Content is conveyed through these expository lessons, and student development is measured by means of examinations that assess the memorization of facts, information, formulae and procedures. Teaching, in this way, is understood as the management of a group of techniques that are available for the teacher to use. The curricula are linear, sequential and compartmentalized. The sequence of courses is established so that courses related to the basic sciences are taught first, followed by courses on applied sciences, ending with the practicum.

The contents of each course are transmitted as if they were an autonomous block of knowledge, with the students left on their own to discover cohesion in the grouping of a series of blocks. Not infrequently, professors themselves do not know in what way the blocks fit together, since they're exclusively dedicated to their own block and unable to identify what kind of professionals they are supposed to be developing.

Institutional culture can also provide an obstacle for the use of methods, which favour the development of professional attributes such as autonomy, creativity, exchanges between peers, inquisitiveness, etc.–and much more so, if the institution is involved in research. What can be observed, however, is that individualism, competition and the isolation of teachers' work, may negatively affect the flourishing of teaching and learning processes compatible with the new guidelines for higher education. As previously mentioned, the majority of the faculties in universities have no pedagogical preparation (either pre-service or in-service). Usually these professors teach in exactly the same way they were taught, reproducing the same models of teaching to which they were subjected, and consider this process immune to questioning or change.

It can be said that innovation and alternative ways to prepare teachers for different modalities of teaching are the main objectives of the guidelines and the focus of this study, which seeks to offer an overview of conceptions, experiences and challenges underlying the Brazilian educational debate. Such conceptions take into account what the literature labels as the 'knowledge society', with its characteristics of spreading and deepening and socializing knowledge in real time through Information and Communication Technologies–ICTs.

Authors such as Drucker (2000), Senge (1996), Kanter (1996), and Shulman (1996, 1987), for example, present some important ideas to be considered when it comes to investigating the meaning of professional preparation and development including:, professors and students' needs, rethinking of the goals concerning citizens' education, the current state of knowledge in different fields, mastery of Information and Communication Technologies, the notion of lifelong learning, the implementation of decentralization in organizational processes of decision making, commitment of faculty with processes of change, the construction of partnerships, curriculum revision, the concept of "teaching as a community property" (Shulman, 2004), meaning actions engaging faculty and students in the development of new models and possibilities, the development of learning communities, acknowledgement, pf diversity as a cultural and pedagogical process, and the implementation of new methodologies which may be pertinent to new educational goals.

In many areas of knowledge, admission processes at universities emphasize research to the detriment of teaching. Institutional initiatives having the advancement of processes of professional development as a goal are as various as the number of institutions involved, since each institution conceives the formation of higher education teachers in a different fashion, and according to its own development plans.

Even so, a few universities, concerned with the quality of teaching and the peculiarities involved in the development of the future professionals that seek them out, have been undertaking initiatives in order to overcome the problems observed in Brazilian higher education. Many of these initiatives are very small and cover only the institution from which they came, or only a few of the majors offered within the institution. Some were born from experimentation regarding the implementation of new national guidelines for specific areas of knowledge.

REVISION OF SOME HIGHER EDUCATION CURRICULA IMPLEMENTING DIFFERENTIATED FORMATIVE PROCESSES, FOCUSING ON PROFESSOR EDUCATORS

Innovations in higher education usually comprise the introduction of new courses in the curriculum, for example, informatics in most programs, entrepreneurialism in business administration and economics, creativity in engineering, technology in most health-related programs, use of computers to gather information (Internet), project design, precision and safety procedures in labs, support to regular courses, creation of distance courses, formulation of the Institutional Development Plan and of the Pedagogical Project, and creation of a Local Assessment Committee, in accordance with the directives of the Ministry of Education.

What can be said about these innovations? Innovations in higher education are only those that promote changes that affect key points in its organization, such as innovations that attend to broader educational goals and encompass the promotion of skills (or human and professional competencies) and attitudes, instead of focusing only on the development of cognitive aspects.

Significant innovations affect curriculum organization and flexibility to address the demands of a new pedagogical project or new educational goals for higher education graduates. These innovations restore the role of courses as components of a curriculum, promote interdisciplinarity, replace traditional methodologies for new technologies that favour the attainment of diverse educational goals, motivate students to learn and be responsible for their learning, and introduce the power of new technologies (informatics, telematics, Internet etc.) that enable education beyond the classroom walls. In addition, these innovations re-examine the assessment process, the role played by the pedagogical mediator between the students and their learning, and encourage teamwork, partnerships and co-responsibilities. Ihese innovations prepare professors to take part in and commit themselves to the new projects and also support them during their implementation.

We have found innovative models that meet the aforementioned demands in some higher education programs in Brazil. For instance, a dentistry college in Fortaleza (Ceará State) has adopted a new curriculum for the preparation of dentist-surgeons, which is inspired by the medical education program of McMaster University, Hamilton, Ontario. This model has also been adopted by the Harvard Medical School for over 10 years with excellent results.

What does this project comprise and what are its strong and innovative points? It is based on self-directed instruction, emphasizing the kind of active learning that values ethics and sensitivity to patients' needs and concerns, promoting the students' capacity to seek new knowledge. It is a process of guided discovery and promotion of interactive learning in small groups: from the very first day students receive stethoscopes and begin their practical learning activities guided by a physician and professor.

Groups of 8-10 students and a coordinator-professor work together on one of the major themes of the medical program during 12 weeks. Each member of the group does bibliographical research and later discusses the newly gathered information with the other team members and coordinator. If necessary, specialists are invited to give more detailed explanations, to complement with information and solve problems. In addition to all this, all of the courses/subjects belonging to the curriculum concur to this major themes explored.

The courses/subjects are not taught in a juxtaposed or fragmentary way. Subjects are not taught or learned separately or because they are important per se, but because they have information and skills necessary to understand or explain a given health issue or disease as well its etiology, prevention or therapeutics.

Strategies are selected so as to promote student participation in debates, observation followed by discussion, reading, research and practical activities with patients, simulated activities, and discussion of cases after observing them through CCTV. There are no lectures to large classes.

The students study all year long. There are no tests or exams. The assessment process is on-going, Professors offer feedback on all activities performed by the students. It exists to help students to learn–not to find out what they have not learned. Contrary to other traditional systems where tension rises exceedingly during the period of exams, in this system tension is tolerable and continued, because students are expected (by other group members and educators) to work and bring information to the discussion meetings to promote the learning of the group. The feedback may come from the students themselves (self-evaluation), from group members (peer evaluation), and with educators and patients with whom the students interacted during their college years.

We have, also, some examples related to Medicine Preparation Programs. The curriculum has been totally redesigned within the regular medical program. The medical schools in Bauru and Marília (São Paulo State), Londrina (Paraná State), and the Public Health College in Fortaleza (Ceará State) have adopted Problem-based Learning (PBL) as their educational paradigm. PBL has been conceived not as a novel instructional methodology, but as a new curriculum paradigm, with a well defined curricular philosophy and with quite clear professional education goals. Its curricular philosophy proposes the development of self-directed learning in a collaborative learning context, from problems that are formulated by the program participants following explicit educational goals.

These problems indicate the curricular organization model, no longer determined by the courses/subjects, but by modules or cycles in which the basic sciences are taught in integration with the clinical courses. It intends to prepare health professionals with inquisitive disposition, lifelong learning habits, empathy towards patients, ability to articulate prevention and therapies, and sensitivity to social demands and policies in the health area.

This paradigmatic aspect of PBL should be highlighted, because in several papers, articles, experiences and discussions, only the methodological-technical aspect of PBL is addressed. The result is that PBL implementation projects in different areas and educational discussions focus more on technical issues about problem-writing, problem-solving steps, chronograms, time and content coverage than on the examination of the educational philosophy that supports these techniques,or the commitment to its goals for the training of teachers and students.

Since in our college and university programs it is more usual to seek technical resources in order to solve problems in a technical way only, the use of PBL, in many cases, has been reduced to a teaching method. The new paradigm has not been put into practice.

But PBL is not the only paradigm available. According to the actual implementation of professional preparation guidelines inspired by an epistemology of practice (Schön, 1983, 1987), which calls for for the examination of the practices engaged in by higher education professors in light of constructivist/cognitivist approaches as well as the socio-cultural ones, we have expectations that professionals of different areas who teach in colleges and universities will overcome the transmission-reception learning model and become aware of their educational practice. The aforementioned experiences are very important as they point to the possibility of innovation in higher education, including the empowerment of different professionals as professors.

SOME CHALLENGES TO BE FACED REGARDING THE PREPARATION OF HIGHER EDUCATION PROFESSORS

Some foci, related to the characteristics and roles of the teacher educator and the university professor in general, emerge from, and must be faced by educational public policies relating to varied processes of professional education in universities (e.g. Darling-Hammond, 2005; Bransford, 2005; Mizukami et al., 2003; Reali et al., 2007, Masetto, Vasconcelos, & Teixeira, 2004). All foci contemplate the urgency to overcome a usual transmission-reception model of teaching.

A Solid and Flexible "Knowledge Base for Teaching"

The importance of a solid and flexible knowledge base for teaching (Shulman, 1987), encompasses knowledge related to specific content areas, knowledge of formative school contexts, pedagogical knowledge, knowledge of the learning to teach processes, knowledge of educational public policies and of their underlying theories, and content pedagogical knowledge. This category also includes the importance of the adequate comprehension and use of the technologies of communication, and of information dealing with new ways of learning and construction of knowledge.

Such a solid and flexible knowledge base is invaluable for the professor to develop his or her functions, i.e. "learning to teach" in a variety of ways and to different types of students and within diverse educational contexts. Practice by itself is not enough to provide specific control of content in a satisfactory degree. It does not offer the knowledge base professors need in order to be able to teach and continue his or her process of learning and professional development. This knowledge base should involve specific content knowledge, here understood as the main axis of the knowledge base for teaching and the promotion of rich and flexible pedagogical reasoning processes (Shulman, 1987). The richer this knowledge base, the richer the processes of teaching and learning promoted by the university professor will potentially be.

The knowledge base here considered enables the comprehension of the interrelations between the contents of different curriculum components and the contexts of learning of students and professors, as well as the peculiarities of each area of knowledge and contexts. It must necessarily involve the knowledge of the learning to teach process, in different contexts. It also implies recognizing and putting to test professors' and future professors' personal theories and conceptions, either to reaffirm or alter those theories and conceptions. Another component of this knowledge base should be the knowledge of professional practice as an axis of the formative processes. This implies knowledge about the promotion of the learning to teach processes. In addition, considering the contributions of Shulman (1987), such a base must also contemplate the specificities of general pedagogical content, and the contributions and preconceptions of the students.

New Strategies for Professional Development

There is a need to construct and promote strategies for professional development, which are not invasive and which highlight the beliefs, values and personal theories of university professors. Among the strategies present in the studies we have analyzed, Problem Based Learning and Teaching Case Studies resulted in real success, and appear to be tools that overcome the limitations of the transmission-reception model in the promotion and investigation of the processes of learning.

Teaching cases, particularly, seem to be a powerful strategy for both the study of the professors' and professor educators' referential frameworks, and the construction and promotion of pedagogical content knowledge (Mizukami, 2002). The use of teaching cases (drawn from literature or the very writing of the cases) may allow the development of reflexive processes at different times and at degrees. Cases may also allow us to analyse the conceptions that are brought to surface and promote the understanding of specific learning in face of concrete situations of teaching and learning. The creation of situations that provide for processes of reflection-on-action, may help to establish different types of relations between theory and practice.

Shulman (1996) considers case based learning in professor education as a response to two central problems: learning through experience and the building of bridges between theory and practice. According to Shulman, to require professors and future professors to reflect over their own practice is a correct approach, though arduously demanding. The use of teaching cases as units of analysis would help in the organization of the reflection processes. Shulman likewise believes that a significant part of a professor's development is generic, consisting of general principles and maxims that can be broadly applied to a diversity of situations. Teaching cases would, in this process, consist of instances in which the specific artifacts of teaching (subject matter and situation) could be evaluated. Another issue pointed out by Shulman is the fact that teaching is an uncertain and unpredictable activity, meaning that it is difficult to make it rigidly conform to any formal theory, even even if this theory is responsible for the insights arrrived at by professors or students. Cases would have a function to fulfill whenever reasoning, discourse, and professional have to be addressed. They require analyses, attribution of meaning, and the construction of answers, improvised or otherwise, to the problems they propose.

> We do not learn from experience; we learn by thinking about our experience. A case takes the raw material or first-order experience and renders it narratively into a second-order experience. A case is the re-collected, re-told, re-experienced and re-reflected version of a direct experience. The process of remembering, retelling, reliving and reflecting is the process of learning from experience. (Shulman, 1996, p. 208)

It is in this context that Shulman contemplates the role of theory. He considers experience translated into narrative, brought together in a case, as a means to engage in an act of theory.

> The transformation of an experience into a narrative is itself an act of selection and conceptualization. In converting a first-order experience into a second-order experience through narrative, an author has chosen to frame an experience in a particular way, has placed that experience in more general terms. When the reader of a case connects that narrative to his or her own experiences, a second kind of selection has taken place.....It appears to be a

> characteristic of our species that stories explicitly breed yet other stories and, implicitly, the categories of analysis that connect stories to one another conceptually. Even in the concrete act of narrative, underlying theoretical categories emerge and often become explicit.
>
> There are four processes at work in learning from the writing and contemplation of cases. These are enactment, narration, connection (or recounting) and abstraction. Stories begin in the raw experience itself, are transformed into cases through narration, become part of a network of narratives through connections with other cases and both enrich and are enriched by theory when they are analyzed, interpreted and/or classified in the teachers' conversations. (Shulman, 1996, p. 209)

For Shulman (1996), the plot of each case must be developed around a plan, an incomplete intervention that gives room for surprises that interrupt the expected scenarios, and provide situations, in which the teacher may reexamine, rebuild, revise or reflect over his or her original plans, modifying them in some way. The essence of the case resides in the problem it carries, in the surprise element or failure experienced. It is precisely for that reason that it is considered educational.

> The practice of teaching, on the narrative view, is seen as constructed by teachers as they tell and live stories in their classrooms. Teaching stories are in part personal stories shaped by the knowledge, values, feelings, and purposes of the individual teacher. They are also collective stories shaped by the traditions of schooling in the setting where the teacher works, the social, cultural, and historical context within which the stories are lived out, and the rules and patterns of discourse that make particular forms of storytelling possible. (Elbaz-Luwisch, 2002, p. 405)

The Importance of the Construction of Communities of Learning Involving the Faculty

One of the greatest challenges involving universities is the construction and maintenance of a community of learning in the workplace, which provides the space for the construction and reconstructions of formative processes experienced during initial formation and professional practice.

Even though they consider elementary, middle and high schools, the analyses provided by Grossman, Wineburg and Woolworth (2000, 2001) offer invaluable contributions for higher learning institutions. From the recognition that there are many terms in literature related to such communities (communities of learning, communities of discourse, communities of learners, communities of teachers, school communities, communities of practice), the authors (2001) point out that these terms are used in relation to several theoretical frameworks seeking to answer how a community should work in educational environments. There are five common themes in theories related to communities: interdependence, interaction/participation, shared interests, the views of individuals and minorities, and significant relationships between the participants. According to Grossman and Wineburg (2000), little is known because:

> Studies of community typically examine already-formed groups. Consequently, we have little sense of how teachers forge the bonds of community, struggle to maintain them, work through the inevitable conflicts of social relationships, and form the structures to sustain relationships over time. Without understanding such processes, we have little to guide us as we try to create community (whatever it may mean!) in settings where it doesn't already exist. (p. 6)

Grossman, Wineburg, and Woolworth (2001) thus systematized the trajectory followed by a group in its process of transition to a community of teachers. Such a community, according to the authors, must be local, implying face-to-face interaction, dialogue, and trust as main ingredients for the construction of group cohesiveness. These communities are not easily or rapidly formed. They demand time, so that people build a history together and an actual "community of memory" in which public discussion by the members of the constitutional narratives of the group takes place.

A community of teachers may, in this way, be understood as a type of professional community that considers the multiple contexts in which teachers work. For the aforementioned authors, a professional community is also strongly connected to its students:

> For a group of teachers to emerge as a professional community, the well being of students must be a central consideration. According to this criterion for professional community, not all gatherings of teachers, even those in which teachers offer each other fellowship and support, constitute professional community. (Grossman & Wineburg, 2000, p. 13)

If we are to follow Grossman and Wineburg, not all groupings of teachers constitute a professional community. Two basic elements should be considered in a community of teachers: the improvement of professional practice and the belief that teachers are also students in their areas throughout their life. As such, they must grow in knowledge of the educational process, and be up to date in the production of knowledge in their specific areas. These two aspects related to the process of professional development of teachers do not always coexist harmoniously.

> The challenge in creating intellectual community for teachers in the workplace is to heed both aims simultaneously: to maintain a focus on students while also creating a structure for teachers to engage as learners with the subject matters they teach. This latter goal, in contrast to the former, has no school based tradition on which to build. Few examples exist of teachers successfully maintaining these dual agendas in the hurried context of the urban high school. (Grossman and Wineburg, 2000, p. 14)

This latter goal, is not traditionally backed within schools, and is consequently difficult to achieve.

Considering the collective and individual dimensions of learning, the authors defend the idea that a professional community of teachers requires that its participants engage in intellectual and social activities, including new ways of interacting with people. In the context of higher learning, there are fewer opportunities to interact with peers, with the exception of sporadic, topical exchanges, which do not involve regular experimentation. It is therefore difficult to share teaching and learning situations with other people in the workplace.

In the development of communities of teachers it is important to consider two kinds of knowledge distribution. The first one refers to the fact that some people know what others do not, and that collective knowledge surpasses individual knowledge. The second one refers to different ways of knowing. Here, what is distributed among participants are ways of reading, raising questions, making judgments, arguing, establishing exemplars, and representing knowledge.

The tasks of a community in the workplace demand new forms of social interaction. The characteristics mentioned so far are mandatory if the goal to be achieved is for the students of a classroom to also establish a community of learners.

"Inquiry as Stance"

The consideration of 'inquiry as stance' (Cochran-Smith, 2003) as the axis of the professional development of teacher educators and the university professor, must include a continuous and systematic investigation process in which all the participants question their assumptions and those of their peers. In addition participants must construct local and public knowledge as is pertinent and adequate to changing contexts higher education.

One expects the higher education professor to create formative situations that allow the construction of inquiry as stance related to specific and general educational processes. The teacher educator's formative processes should be products of shared conceptions related to those very processes, viewed both in narrow and broad fashion.This means that the process as a whole will be considered, within space and time limits, and in both local and amplified contexts.

The teacher educator's inquiry as stance is here considered as a formative tool par excellence (Cochran-Smith, 2003), involving the consideration of suppositions and values, professional knowledge and practice, school and higher education institutional contexts, and the private learning of teacher educators teachers and future teachers.

> Rather than inquiry as a project or an activity in teacher education, inquiry as stance is an intellectual perspective–a way of questioning, making sense of, and connecting one's day-to-day work to the work of the others and to larger social, historical, cultural, and political contexts. (Cochran-Smith & Lytle, 1999, in Cochran-Smith, 2003, p. 21)

> Inquiry as stance is distinct from the more common notion of inquiry as time-bounded project or activity within a teacher education course or professional development workshop. Taking an inquiry stance means teachers and student

> teachers working within inquiry communities to generate local knowledge, envision and theorize their practice, and interpret and interrogate the theory and research of others. Fundamental to this notion is the idea that the work of inquiry communities is both social and political–that is, it involves making problematic the current arrangements of schooling; the ways knowledge is constructed, evaluated and used; and teachers' individual and collective roles in bringing about change. (Cochran-Smith & Lytle, 1999, p. 289)

Such an investigative attitude demands constant analyses of formative processes (Cochran-Smith, 2003), which are possible only if:

- Different theories and educational proposals are known, in ways that a deeper and broader comprehension of the educational phenomenon and the teaching and learning process is acquired.
- Both objective and subjective, succinct descriptions of pedagogical practices in their multiple determinants and variables are achievable.
- Constant movement exists; theory-practice-theory
- Each community member has opportunities to become a...learner, a researcher, a seeker of new insights, and a poser of questions for which no one in the group already has the answers (p. 23), and where...teacher educators educate themselves and each other by regarding the work of others as generative but open to interrogation (p. 23).
- Local knowledge is generated. The construction of local knowledge is conceived as:

> a process of building, interrogating, elaborating, and critiquing conceptual frameworks that link action and problem-posing to the immediate context as well as to larger social, cultural, and political issues. The local knowledge we have conceptualized is not the same as 'practical knowledge', which others have described as how, when and where practitioners do things (Fenstermacher, 1994: Richardson, 1999). Rather the idea of local knowledge highlights the processes of knowledge construction as they are integrated with daily life in schools, programs, and classrooms and also how they are connected to larger social and political agendas. (Cochran-Smith, 2003, p. 24)

- It is manageable to work with certainties, uncertainties, dilemmas, problems, and the recognition that investigation is born from and at the same time generates issues that defy the system and involve learning and unlearning. (Cochran-Smith, 2003)

The four challenges here considered are highly promising in terms of modifying the current framework of teaching in colleges and universities, in ways to foster the development of educational environments which engage the students–the future professionals–in a constructive relation with their own profession and the specific knowledge related to it, as well as their continuous professional development throughout life.

REFERENCES

Cochran-Smith, M. (2003). Learning and unlearning: The education of teacher educators. *Teaching and Teacher Education, 19*, 5–28.
Cochran-Smith, M., & Lytle, S. (1999). Relationship of knowledge and practice: Teacher learning in communities. In A. Iran-Nejad & C. D. Pearson (Eds.), *Review on research in education* (Vol. 24, pp. 249–306).
Darling-Hammond, L., & Bransford, J. (Eds.). (2005). *Preparing teachers for a changing world. What teachers should learn and be able to do.* San Francisco: The National Academy of Education, Jossey-Bass.
Drucker, P. (2000). A nova sociedade das organizações. In R. Howard (Ed.), *Aprendizado organizacional.* Rio de Janeiro-RJ: Ed. Campus.
Elbaz-Luwisch, F. (2002). Writing as inquiry: Storying the teaching self in writing workshop. *Curriculum Inquiry, 32*(4), 403–429.
Grossman, P., & Wineburg, S. (2000, December). *What makes a teacher community different from a gathering of teachers*? (Research Report). University of Washington, Center for the Study of Teaching Policy.
Grossman, P., Wineburg, S., & Woolworth, S. (2001). Toward a theory of teacher community. *Teacher College Record, 103*(6), 942–1012.
Kanter, R. M. (1996). Líderes da classe mundial: o poder da parceria. In F. Hesselbein, M. Goldsmith, & R. Beckhard (Eds.), *O líder do futuro.* São Paulo-SP: Ed. Futura.
Masetto, M. T., Vasconcelos, M. L., & Teixeira, M. L. M. (2004). *Auto-Avaliação na Pós-Graduação. Teoria e prática.* Campinas: Papirus Editora.
Mizukami, M. G. N. (2002). *Learning from cases and bridging some 'theory-practice' gaps.* ERIC Education Resources Information Center. (ERIC Document Reproduction Service No. ED 477809).
Mizukami, M. G. N., Reali, A. M. M. R., Reyes, C. R., Martucci, E. M., Lima, E. F., Tancredi, R. M. S. P., et al. (2003). *Escola e aprendizagem da docência. Processos de investigação e formação.* São Carlos, SP: EdUFSCar, INEP, COMPED.
Reali, A. M. M. R., et al. (2007). Online mentoring: A Brazilian experience in teacher professional development. *Education Line*, EERA. Retrieved April 25, 2007, from http://www.leeds.ac.uk/educol/documents/160087.htm
Schön, D. (1983). *The reflective practitioner.* San Francisco: Jossey-Bass.
Schön, D. (1987). *Educating the reflective practitioner.* San Francisco: Jossey-Bass.
Shulman, L. S. (1987). Knowledge and teaching: Foundations of the new reform. *Harvard Educational Review, 57*(1), 1–22.
Shulman, L. S. (1996). Just in case: Reflections on learning from experience. In J. Colbert, K. Trimble & P. Desberg. (Eds.), *The case for education: Contemporary approaches for using case methods* (pp. 297–217). Needham Heights, MA: Allyn & Bacon.
Shulman, L. S. (2004). *Teaching as a community property. Essays on higher education.* San Francisco: Jossey Bass.

Maria da Graça Nicoletti Mizukami
Presbyterian University Mackenzie

Marcos Tarciso Masetto
Sao Paulo Catholic University

MARYANN BROWN

WELCOME TO THE REAL WORLD…I HAVEN'T REACHED THOSE DIZZY HEIGHTS YET

Reflections on a Transition from University Teaching to School Teaching

INTRODUCTION

I have left a position as a senior lecturer in a School of Education and I have returned to a secondary school as English curriculum leader and Curriculum and Professional Development Coordinator. In some ways this could be seen as a taboo or a step backwards. I prefer to see it as a planned career move. A research fellowship offered by the university has provided a natural bridge between the tertiary and secondary education worlds and has made the transition easier. I would like to see whether I can connect academic research and secondary classroom practice in some useful way. A belief in the importance of teachers enquiring into practice underpinned my teacher education work (Brown & McGraw, 2002). It has also informed my participation in practitioner research throughout my career. Recent doctoral work explored ways of learning in teacher education and led to a focus on the need for care in teacher research. Risk taking is a critical ingredient in learning. If we don't take risks we limit our own horizons. Having taken risks in research methods in the past, and having ventured into the challenging and creative realms of narrative (Clandinin & Connelly, 2000; Polkinghorne, 1988, 1995) and autoethnographic ways of writing about learning (Ellis & Bochner, 2000), I am excited about the possibilities that my career move has opened.

Traditionally, in Australia, education academics have taught for some time in schools before pursuing post-graduate study and a career as an academic. The career trajectory from lecturer to professor has been clear. The 'game' has had rules (doctoral qualifications, publication record, participation in professional bodies and so on). I think there are good reasons for playing the 'game' differently. The traditional path has led to interesting lives for researchers but it has not necessarily improved the experience of students or teachers. There has been tension around universities' relationships with schools and teachers – as played out in the frequent theory/practice divide debates (Korthagen, 2001; Loughran & Russell, 1997; Zeichner, 1999). The results of academic investigations have not always been disseminated to practitioners. Or maybe teachers have not 'heard'. Teachers are busy people and their focus is usually on their students. Often their own teacher education experiences have not been positive (Braiden, 1997). Anecdotally, academics have been viewed with suspicion or derision. Attributing blame is not useful. I am only interested in building bridges and connections between university and school, in helping teachers enquire and learn. I am keen to link research and practice more closely.

J. A. Kentel and A. Short (eds.), Totems and Taboos: Risk and Relevance in Research on Teachers and Teaching, 79–93.

Care in research of and with teachers is something that preoccupied me during the doctoral research. As I embrace the challenge of working with experienced teachers I am very conscious of the need to show care for them and their experiences. I sense a need to develop a model of enquiry into practice that incorporates care for individuals, their pedagogy and their content knowledge.

This paper is an exploration of my experiences in the first few months at school. It will be developed with a series of vignettes or stories of my personal experiences (identified by indented narrative), interspersed with discussion and background explanations of enquiry into professional practice and 'care-full' research. Narrative ways of writing help me explore in a personal way and provide a powerful way of learning (Connelly & Clandinin, 1990). Laurel Richardson's (2000) suggestion that we 'write ourselves into understanding' is a useful method for reflecting on the early months in my new role. I have not researched with any other teachers at the school yet. That will come later as we journey together. My approach is not conventional and boundaries are being challenged.

'WELCOME TO THE REAL WORLD'

> 'Here is my signed contract of employment,' I said tentatively as I handed the document over.
>
> 'Thanks. Welcome to the real world,' commented the administrative assistant. 'You know there won't be any administrative help for you now. Teachers don't get admin help.'
>
> Somewhat taken aback I responded defensively: 'Maybe teachers need administrative help, I know the university provided some admin help and it left lecturers with more time to do what they are meant to do- lecture and research.' I quietly left the room.
>
> Thoughts tumbled through my head. What real world? I thought my world was rather real. I know lecturers are accused of living in ivory towers. I know the press is constantly full of criticism of teacher educators and their lack of connection with what happens in schools. But then the press is full of criticism of teachers too. At the last ISATT conference I remember making a somewhat impassioned plea for educators not to be frequently cast as the 'devil'. I was tired of being part of a profession that was constantly criticised in Australia, despite our best efforts and commitment. I am still saddened by this.
>
> Accusations of not living in the real world have always bothered me. I have constantly sought ways to connect my professional practice with theoretical understanding and research.
>
> Still, I left that school office somewhat shaken. My decision to leave academia had not been an easy one. My fears were reinforced by this encounter.

Questions swirl. What is the 'real world'? Whose world is more real than any other person's? Don't we all just live in our own world and for us it is real?

'I HAVEN'T REACHED THOSE DIZZY HEIGHTS YET'

I attended the students' orientation day at my new school. Apprehension flooded my being. What was I really doing back here? It felt so strange, and yet so familiar.

So here I was back in a school, being introduced to my new form group for the coming year. The other form teacher was not new and I was happy to have her lead the proceedings.

'Hello, Year 8, my name is Ms .... and this is Dr Brown – I haven't reached those dizzy heights myself yet...'

I stopped listening, I was stunned. Almost six years of study had led me to the very recent completion of doctoral study. I had been engrossed in the learning journey and had engaged in the process so deeply. I certainly didn't see a post-graduate degree as reaching any 'dizzy heights'. For me it was a totally personal journey of discovery. I was exhausted and delighted when I finished.

Standing in a classroom with twenty-three interested, tentative students and one other teacher, I felt myself shrink. What was I doing here? What had that comment really meant? Was it pretentious to be known as 'doctor'? I would have preferred to be known by my first name, but this would not really be allowed.

I left as quickly as I could, thoughts swirling.

The doctoral work on the ethic of care and professional learning was high in my mind. Maybe I had my super-sensitive antennae working over-time because I was possibly committing a taboo. Leaving an academic career, a completed doctorate and a recent promotion to senior lecturer, could seem like career 'suicide'. I had misgivings myself. My reasons were complex but also logical. My university work took place in another town, an hour from where I lived. I had commuted for twelve years.

Another important motivation was that I felt I needed to work with school students and teachers again, to try to connect some of the things I had learnt and researched while teaching at university, to school life. Certainly I had visited many schools over the years while mentoring teacher education students and I had run various workshops with teachers. Occasionally I had felt a yearning to find out what was really happening in schools. Sometimes I was concerned when recent graduates contacted me with stories of the complexity and demands of their roles, the difficulties they were experiencing, the deep frustrations they felt. The doctoral research had highlighted the difficulty beginning teachers had finding time to reflect on their practice (Loughran, 1996; Brown, 2003, 2006).

TRANSITIONS...WHAT I NOTICE...THINGS HAVE CHANGED

Time is different. I have always enjoyed being busy and the challenge that some pressure provides. The idea of multi-tasking is invigorating. I have also always enjoyed thinking. As a university course coordinator I was flat out with administration, pastoral care and teaching. As an academic it was important to have thinking time and my one hour commute ensured that I had at least that time to think. I rationalized the travel by saying that the morning trip was for visualizing my teaching for the day or planning my research and the evening trip was for reflecting on the day and I consciously left the stresses of the day behind as I travelled. Obviously research requires more thought than this and I made sure there were blocks of time in my busy life for research and writing. I know I was frantically busy at university and I often felt that I could be doing three or four things with every minute I was at work - or at home.

I am surprised to find that school is even more frantic. We rush from class to class, meeting to meeting, yard duty, parent meetings and so on. So often I feel as if I am fighting to plan my teaching well. It must be my priority. It must!

Sounds are different. My world is totally invaded by noise. People want me or something from me all the time. Voices wash around me. Requests, orders, bells, questions, laughter, answers, denials, chatter. When I have a lesson off sometimes I put ear-phones in just so I can't hear the class next door. My old world had some quiet time. Driving time, writing time. I yearn for the hours spent sitting at my computer writing - gently tapping on keys, peaceful thoughts, hard thoughts, and quiet thoughts.

Thinking feels so rushed, so superficial. I yearn for depth. I attend so many meetings that are interesting and where important issues are raised. They all seem to require follow up work. I try, but I don't feel that I am able to give things the detailed consideration that they deserve.

Schools have changed. I teach in a privileged school. Laptops are present in all classes. The students are confident and happy using them. The technology feels like an integral part of my teaching. I am intrigued that students just use laptops as extensions of themselves. They personalize them and communicate with them. I remember earlier days of computers and laptops and the intense frustration when things wouldn't work or when no one seemed to know what they were doing. Now I can't imagine learning and teaching without all the technology.

The curriculum has changed too. New electives are offered, rich tasks are incorporated. Documentation and accountability requirements are much more evident than the past. In some ways this is a good thing as teachers can be supported by documentation. But I sense an underlying tension. This will require careful negotiation. My initial concern is that too much documentation will cut the creative edges off teachers' work. Teachers may lose their sense of personal efficacy, even pride and pleasure in their work if the requirements are too rigid, sanitized, homogenized. I know this is not the intention but those of us working in curriculum need to be mindful of these dangers.

Students have always been the reason I teach. I have been challenged by learning with them and exploring ways of helping them learn. I am somewhat relieved to observe that students are still interesting, funny, thoughtful, silly, smart, lazy, bewildered, organized, creative, challenging and all the other things they have always been. It is interesting to talk with them about the concerns they have and things they want to learn about. I grew up in the time when the nuclear threat seemed very real. I remember being deeply concerned that some idiot would end the world before I had a chance to grow up. Today's children are concerned about the environment, water, wars, poverty. Similar concerns–but different. As always I am so conscious of my responsibilities as a teacher.

Teachers are the same and different too. I am impressed by the pride they have in their work, in the commitment and industriousness of so many. I don't really want to generalize. I am reminded that some teachers will always be learners and some will not. I am constantly reminded of the emotional nature of teachers' labour (Brown, 2003, 2006; Hargreaves, 1998, 2002) and the pressure of time that they all feel. The intensification of teachers' work as described in the literature (Apple, 1986; Day, 1999; Kelchtermans & Ballet, 2002) is certainly evident.

My role has changed, of course. At university, course coordination was a busy, challenging, emotionally demanding, creative and totally engaging role. At school I have a leadership role in coordinating the English department and also coordinating the junior secondary curriculum. The roles are interesting and demanding and I spent the first term finding out about how teachers experience their work. The possibility of working to develop a culture of research and enquiry through curriculum and professional development leadership is very challenging and exciting. The bedrock of my own research and academic life gives me confidence and also respect for the complexity of the process.

I have changed. All through the university years I was conscious of constantly learning. I was invigorated by the academic reading and the lively conversations with students and colleagues. Research has become an integral part of my life. Writing has been a necessity and also a pleasure. I am a bit disoriented when I find no spaces in my day for these activities.

MY TOTEMS

My doctoral search included an exploration of teachers as enquirers into professional practice (Brown, 2003, 2006; Brown & McGraw, 2002). As part of the introduction to the research I clarified my beliefs about education. These beliefs, or my totems, for this paper, will be with me throughout my professional and personal life. Totem poles tell stories, using symbols. Written words are the symbols for my story.

This is Who I Am…

People matter. Without this fundamental belief there is no point in being involved in education. As a teacher, the students, colleagues, parents and others I work with matter in some way. They form part of my 'circles and chains of care' (Noddings, 2003) and as such our relationships are important. Successful relationships of any type rely on communication, good will, sensitivity to others and openness to learning.

Learning matters. There are an infinite number of ways to live and be. To me the idea of continuing to learn is central to living an interesting and rewarding life. Learning provides the possibility to empower people, to liberate people (Freire, 1998), to strengthen relationships and communities. Learning can be informal and formal, it can be structured and unstructured and it takes time.

Meaning matters. Making sense of our experiences is an important part of learning. As Dewey noted so long ago, experience alone does not actually mean much. The capacity to reflect on and learn from experience is what leads to personal growth (Dewey, 1938). Rogers (2002) in her analysis of Dewey's work, goes even further: "The creation of meaning from experience is at the very heart of what it means to be human" (p. 848).

Asking questions is usually, if not always, as important as finding answers. This is the heart of reflective practice (Schön, 1983; Loughran, 1996) and serves to connect the personal, the intellectual, the emotional and the social dimensions of learning in teaching and beyond.

Constructivist principles underpin these beliefs. The idea that each teacher has the ability, indeed responsibility, to construct his or her professional life thoughtfully, imaginatively, respectfully and creatively drove my thinking throughout the doctoral study. As I return to school, this feeling intensifies. It is another significant totem as I embark on the next stage of my professional life.

Teacher as Enquirer into Professional Practice

Professional learning has become an integral part of teachers' lives. For many teachers this is nothing new but for others it is. Sachs (1997) argues that teachers frequently focus so strongly on students' learning needs that they neglect their own. In times of rapid change and burgeoning information sources it is important for teachers to have the means to develop their own understanding of learning and teaching and the capacity to critique changes as they arise. We need teachers in the profession who can work with 'complexity and uncertainty' (Clarke & Erickson, 2003) and who can sustain their own engagement in the profession.

Enquiry into practice is not a new concept. Reid & O'Donogue (2001a) note that Dewey (1929) identified the importance of teachers studying the effects of their teaching on students' learning and developing a sensitivity to teaching being "an inherently non-routine behaviour" (p. 28). Hargreaves (2000) argues that it is critical for teachers to enquire systematically into their practice to "lift teachers out of the pre-professional prejudice that only practice makes perfect" (p. 167). Interest in enquiry into professional practice has gained momentum in recent years and Clarke & Erickson (2003) explore the rise of enquiry as a 'requirement' within current policy in the US, UK and Australia. They note: "...there is almost universal agreement that enquiry and reflection in and on practice are essential elements of the teaching profession" (p. 2).

Reid & O'Donoghue (2001a, 2001b) make a compelling argument for the development of an approach to teacher education based on enquiry. The argument centres on the fact that 21st century educators must work within a context of 'change, paradox and uncertainty'. They argue that educators are "engaged in the process of producing, as well as accessing, new knowledge. They are making their own meaning". Traditional ideas of teachers as transmitters of knowledge or skilled artisans are no longer relevant and "in contemporary times the complexity of the task of being an educator calls for deep professional expertise in a range of areas" (Reid & O'Donoghue, 2001b, p. 28). This idea is developed further:

> When educators use knowledge resources in their role as educators, drawing upon research, experience and formal and informal sources to make a professional judgment about some aspect of policy or practice, they are not simply transferring and applying this knowledge. They are critically engaging with this knowledge in use, addressing specific problems/ issues/ dilemmas in the context of their work, problem-posing and problem-solving, theorising, devising strategies, and implementing and evaluating these. That is, they engage in the process of making new meaning through the critical application in new contexts of knowledge resources they have accessed. (Reid & O'Donoghue, 2001a, p. 9)

The question of how schools encourage teachers to become enquirers into practice is what engages me at this time. Certainly there is an expectation of professional development within the teaching profession, and recognition that this is very important. The challenge is to make the professional development enquiry based, engaging and relevant for each teacher.

The actual interpretation of 'enquiry' can be seen at its most simple level as the act of asking questions. But it is more than this. Clarke and Erickson (2003) argue for enquiry as a central tenet of a profession. They identify teacher enquiry as "a generally agreed upon set of insider research practices that promote teachers taking a close, critical look at their teaching and the academic and social development of their students" (p. 3). Encouraging practicing teachers to adopt this approach requires careful planning.

The model adopted at the University of Ballarat supported the concept of teachers developing a disposition towards enquiry. It addressed the need to link theory and practice; to work in partnership with schools; for teachers to be reflective practitioners; to practice close observation and attention to students; to engage in learning and their own meaning making and for teacher educators to model acts of enquiry. The aim was to empower prospective teachers so they "have the knowledge, skills and dispositions to theorise systematically and rigorously about practice in different learning contexts, and to take appropriate action on the basis of the outcomes of this enquiry" (Reid & O'Donoghue, 2001a, p. 9).

In previous work I note: "On a personal level I wanted the course to encourage future teachers to be fully and actively engaged in their professional lives. I want their students to be the beneficiaries of teachers who are lifelong learners, actively involved in their own development and passionate about the teaching profession." (Brown, 2006, p. 12) In my transition to secondary school I am conscious of the need to maintain these ideals. I am excited about working with practicing teachers and my goal is to support these teachers on their professional journeys.

The motivation to develop as an enquirer will vary from person to person but there are some common elements. As Mitchell (2003) notes: "Teachers decide to engage in research for a number of reasons, but concerns about aspects of their own classrooms are almost always the most important" (p. 201). Teaching is an extremely rewarding career and it is emotionally and physically demanding (Hargreaves, 1998). There is no doubt that those teachers who are happy and engaged in the profession are a positive influence on their students. The idea of engaging teachers in a model of enquiry, "taking part in looking closely and by taking the time to notice, seeing so many other parts to learning and teaching…" (Cooley & Lugar, 2003, p. 32) is one that is appealing, interesting and offers many possibilities to teachers.

> A few weeks into school life and I reflect that it would be quite possible to forget I had ever been at university. Days pass by in a frenzy of activity. Certainly no one has asked me much about my university work or research. There have been some assumptions made: 'You must be crazy to come back.' 'You wouldn't know anything about writing reports now would you?' 'This might be a bit boring…' I don't say much in response. I am in my listening and observing stage! I suppose the teachers are working me out too, in some ways I am viewed with suspicion. I am conscious of being circumspect as we all negotiate the new relationships.

I had taught in the Master of Education program at the university for a number of years. I always enjoyed the opportunity to share professional conversations with educators from a range of backgrounds. Having undertaken post-graduate study whilst working full time I was very aware of the demands on teachers and the need to be sensitive to the professional and personal pressures they experienced. Post-graduate study in education does not hold the same status as in some other professions and frequently there are no tangible rewards. In many cases the study was a way for teachers to ensure they continued to be active learners. The cost of the courses is very high and we had had trouble finding ways to make the courses accessible. Occasionally the School of Education had talked about the possibility of introducing the Master of Education program directly into schools.

> Some email conversations with university colleagues suggest exploring the possibility of offering an M Ed to a group of teachers at my new school, with

> the possibility of the university providing support on-site, at school. It is an interesting opportunity. I am aware that some teachers I am working with are interested in post-graduate study.
>
> An opportunity at a staff meeting:
>
> 'Would anyone be interested in the possibility of studying a Master of Education through a university but using the school as your site of research? I don't know much else but please let me know if you might be interested.'
>
> Over the next couple of days eight people mention their interest. Most comments are prefaced by something like: 'I don't know how I would fit this in but I am interested…'
>
> A seed is sown.

I am immediately made aware of the vulnerability of teachers, even very experienced teachers (Kelchtermans, 1996). I have raised the possibility of study and clearly these people are interested, for whatever reason. But there is a tentativeness or diffidence in the enquiry. Teaching is emotional work, demanding work, consuming work. The idea of study is challenging, exciting and frightening. Perhaps the possibility of having a program brought to them is appealing. I haven't explored their motives yet. I am reminded of the work about care-full research (Brown, 2005, 2006) and so many aspects of that resonate in my new work. I need to work with these teachers care-fully as they enquire into aspects of their practice. What follows is an explanation of the idea of 'care-full' research. It is possible that some of the principles of care-full research that are described can be transferred into a care-full approach to supporting teachers enquire into their professional practice.

CARE-FULL RESEARCH

The idea of care-full research is one that developed over time. It needs to be understood in the sense of 'full of care'- hence my spelling. It developed from the feeling that some research seems to lack care for the participants and the data they provide is merely material for the researcher to use in any way he or she chooses. Care-full research clearly identifies the relationship between the researchers and participants as central to learning. It values the dialogue within the relationships (Ellis & Bochner, 2000) and supports the idea that research is something that should be 'useful' for both the researcher and the participant. Care-full research is respectful of what is shared and 'given' as data. It is attentive to the whole research process and it focuses closely on what is being said. It is tactful, thoughtful and reflective and as such has some larger purpose. Care-full research has pedagogical implications; it has the potential to transform the practice of the researcher and possibly the participants. It has its theoretical foundation in hermeneutic phenomenology and yet it springs from the heart and the mind. The idea of care-full research was developed with the image of the enquiring educator firmly in the front of my mind.

Care-full Research is Relational

At the forefront is the understanding that the researcher and the research participants are related through the research (Clandinin, 1986; Ellis & Berger, 2003). The relation from the researcher's point of view is one which is full of care in terms of wanting to learn, empathise, and hear the stories. Noddings (1992) outlines the importance of dialogue in moral education as a search for "understanding, empathy or appreciation…a genuine quest for something undetermined at the beginning". So care-full research develops out of conversations with participants and the relationship is central. The feelings and values of the participants are significant aspects in a relationship and they are important to consider when researching (Elbaz, 1983). Connelly and Clandinin (1990) explain this in relation to the shared construction of narratives, where "both practitioners and researchers feel cared for and have a voice with which to tell their stories" (p. 4).

The second part of the care-full relationship is with the data. On one level data can just be seen as words on a page or words on a recording. In another the words are jewels, gifts, bequests from the participants and as such they need to be treated with care. To read words 'care-fully' is to read with sensitivity. It is reading to understand more of the participants' lived experience (van Manen, 1990) and to honour the stories being told. Part of this includes avoiding making assumptions about what is said, or rushing to conclusions that might fit the research question but not the person telling the story.

From a personal perspective, I could not separate myself into the dispassionate researcher and I didn't really want to. Erkkilä and Mäkelä (2002) argue that a researcher "should not try to separate the emotional and cognitive aspects" of their work (p. 51).

I have wondered whether the relational sensitivity of care-full research only applies when the researcher has a prior relationship with the participants. I don't believe this is the case. In earlier research the same issues had arisen. In each instance the desire to honour the participants and to relate their stories honestly has been profound. In one awful situation I found a co-researcher grabbing sentences from transcripts and throwing them into a very neat and rigid analytical frame. Sadly that research did not ultimately reflect the depth of the emotions and experiences shared by the participants. It was just another piece of utilitarian writing.

Care-full Research is Respectful of What is 'Given' and 'Shared' as Data

Care-full research is embedded in respect for the participants and what they have shared. This links closely with the previous point in that respect can be construed as an aspect of care but it also highlights the participants' right to provide whatever information they choose. It is also informed by the understanding that:

> Just like literary stories, the personal stories we tell each other have thematic structures and artificial ends. In contrast our lives are complex, ongoing and incomplete. Many of our life histories cannot be integrated into a harmonious

> whole. Our identities are layered and laterally segmented... (van Manen, 1991, p. 23)

Beattie (1995) provided a useful insight into respect in research. She described how her own research with a teacher was actually enhanced by their mutual respect for the other's work: "We built on the initial trust and respect we had for each other and moved forward toward a greater understanding of the other and a greater valuing of each other as collaborative partners" (p. 123).

Care-full Research is Attentive and Focused

Care-full research is deeply attentive. Elbaz (1992) discussed attentiveness in relation to teachers' relations with children. She identified the aspect of attentiveness that relates to the ability to notice details, to watch for small signs of growth, to remember important bits of information at the right moment, to maintain "a sense of a children's complexity" (Ruddick, 1989, p. 426). These qualities of attentiveness are also relevant to a care-full approach to research. In conversations with research participants the researcher notices details, watches for change, remembers relevant information or connectors and always acknowledges the complexity of the individual lives being shared in the research (Diller, 1991).

Attentiveness in research conversations requires the researcher to focus fully on the interaction. It is not to be preoccupied with asking the next question, or pushing for a particular response. It is to listen very carefully to what is being said and to hear the subtle changes in a voice as a story is related. It is to carefully observe the person speaking.

Max van Manen (1991) provides an interesting perspective when he notes that "pedagogical understanding is sensitive listening and observing" (p. 83). In a way 'care-full' research could be seen as a natural development from the pedagogical understanding an enquiring teacher looks for.

Attentiveness also occurs after a transcript is produced and can be practised by people other than the original researcher. 'Care-full' reading involves holding a lens up close to the text: looking carefully for insights into the participants' experiences. Looking at the language chosen, the words selected to tell the story. The care-full reader is 'listening' carefully for details, for the sounds of the voices and the emotions being conveyed. The reader is attentive to the nuances within the text.

Care-full Research is Tactful, Thoughtful and Reflective

Care-full research is predisposed towards tactfulness as van Manen (1991) explained in detail the place of tact in teaching. I would argue that the same qualities he looked for in the tactful teacher should be found in care-full research. While van Manen's interpretation of care is narrow, I think his understanding of tact adds strength to the qualities that a 'care-full' researcher should bring to the research process. He discusses the concept of care in relation to tact:

> To be tactful is to be able to take other people's feelings into account. Tact is sensitive to delicate situations and having a feel for what they require… tact is the expression of thoughtfulness that involves the total being of the person, an active sensitivity toward the subjectivity of the other for what is unique and special about the other person. (p. 145)

'Care-full' research demands that the researcher displays 'active sensitivity' to the research participants as part of the research process and also when working with the data. This also requires a predisposition to thoughtfulness, which van Manen (1991) notes is the product of "self reflective reflection on human experience" (p. 127).

Max van Manen (1991) addresses the issue of tact in scholarship and interestingly he sees this as a "highly reflective human activity" practiced while reading and writing texts. In contrast, he sees tact in human interaction as something more spontaneous, more immediate. To me tact in scholarship can be the same as tactful action because it is "thoughtful, mindful, and heedful" and as van Manen himself notes: "Tact is the effect one has on another person even if the tact consists, as it often does, in holding back, waiting" (p. 127). Care-full research also requires the researcher to hold back and wait and to accept that developing understanding takes time.

Care-full research is reflective and reflexive. It stays in the mind of the researcher and questions about the process, the data, the relations and the writing compete with other everyday activities and thoughts. The research process can change and develop as the reflective thoughts become actions. The care-full researcher is naturally reflexive as they acknowledge like Shacklock and Smyth (1998) "that there are no privileged views on getting at the truth in the generation of research problems, processes, and accounts, because these things are, like the researcher, socially situated" (p. 7).

Care-full Research is Hermeneutic

Care-full research is essentially hermeneutic in that its central purpose is to find meaning or gain understanding from the research activity. There are elements of creativity, exploration, imagination even, in the process. The work in the field of hermeneutic phenomenology provides a useful framework here (Gadamer, 1989: Sharkey, 2001). The gaining of understanding is not seen as something that required a particular research method. Conversation is central to reaching genuine understanding.

Care-full Work with Teachers

In planning my day to day work with teacher colleagues I am conscious of the need to be respectful of their knowledge and experiences. The relationship I develop with them needs to be trusting and positive, with the hallmarks of a care-full practitioner. On one level it is easy because I have a naturally positive disposition and I am passionate about teaching. Leading change and innovation is invigorating. But I am aware that others are not necessarily like me. People teach for a host of reasons and earlier research explored the 'chip on the shoulder' that some teachers exhibit (Brown, 2006). Some started teaching at a time when it was one of few ways to get a bursary to university. Some have become disillusioned as the system has constantly changed. Some are simply tired and feel trapped. At the same time many teachers are enthusiastic and engaged even if they do feel overworked or under constant pressure. All teachers need to feel valued and supported and my role as professional development coordinator provides a good opportunity to do this. Conversations with teachers will help me appreciate their interests. Already some teachers have sought my advice or support for particular types of professional development. I am interested in developing structures to encourage sharing of professional learning experiences. The challenge is to provide opportunities for people to engage in deep professional learning without feeling as if it is another imposition on their precious teaching preparation and evaluation time. I am deeply conscious of the evidence that teaching has become increasingly intense and demanding (Apple, 1996; Fullan, 2001; Kelchtermans, 1996; Kelchtermans & Ballet, 2002).

The ethic of care (Noddings, 1992, 2003) must underpin whatever models of professional learning that are developed. My colleagues have now become part of my circles of care (Noddings, 2003). Their pedagogy and discipline knowledge need to be valued and possibly explored in their enquiry and research.

A meeting at the university in the Easter break…

> Some gentle enquiries come from former colleagues about my new job, and genuine interest from a number. There is astonishment from others as I explain that I am hoping to combine a secondary teaching career and an academic research profile. I am reminded of the 'rules of the academic game' and how limiting they can be. Education careers should not be divided into simple pathways if we are to have a genuine integration of research and practice.
>
> An interesting conversation ensues with some leaders around how we can develop the MEd study program. Teachers' views and interests will be sought via a survey. The possibility of reducing the high cost through scholarships will be investigated. I will explore the level of support available from the school.
>
> I return to school and further conversations. The possibilities of teachers exploring their own practice are increasingly interesting to them. The school administration is keen for some input into the proposed structure of the course. The program will begin in 2008 and I am looking forward to the learning journey. It is a privilege to be working with these teachers, and to maintain a connection with the university.

REFERENCES

Apple, M. (1986). *Teachers and texts: A political economy of class and gender relations in education.* New York: Routledge & Kegan Paul.

Apple, M. (1996). *Cultural politics and education.* Buckingham: Open University Press.

Beattie, M. (1995). *Constructing professional knowledge in teaching: A narrative of change and development.* New York: Teachers College Press.

Braiden, A. (1997). *Examination of the problems beginning teachers encounter*. Unpublished master's thesis, University of Ballarat, Ballarat, Australia.

Brown, M. (2003, June). *An exploration of the interconnection of emotion, intuition and reflection in 'becoming' a teacher*. Paper presented at the International Study Association of Teachers and Teaching Biennial Conference, Leiden.

Brown, M. (2005, July). *Connecting and caring: Towards a mentoring teaching profession*. Paper presented at the International Study Association of Teachers and Teaching, Biennial Conference, Sydney, Australia.

Brown, M. (2006). *Contemporary ways of learning in teacher education: Towards a deeper understanding of teacher learning*. Unpublished doctoral dissertation, University of Ballarat, Australia.

Brown, M., & McGraw, A. (2002). *Becoming inquirers into professional practice*. In A. Mander (Ed.), *Proceedings of the 30th Australian teacher education association conference. Brisbane, July 2002*. Toowoomba: Toowoomba Education Centre.

Clandinin, J. (1986). *Classroom practice: Teacher images in action*. Philadelphia: The Falmer Press.

Clandinin, D., & Connelly, F. (2000). *Narrative inquiry: Experience and story in qualitative research* San Fransisco: Jossey-Bass.

Clarke, A., & Erikson, G. (Eds.). (2003). *Teacher inquiry: Living the research in everyday practice*. London: Routledge Falmer.

Clarke, A., & Erickson, G. (2003). *Teacher inquiry: Living the research in everyday practice*. New York: Routledge Falmer.

Connelly, M., & Clandinin, J. (1990). Stories of experience and narrative enquiry. *Educational Researcher*, *19*(5), 2–14.

Cooley, M., & Lugar, C. (2003). Play(ing) > < living: Researching creative growth. In A. Clark & G. Erickson (Eds.), *Teacher inquiry: Living the research in everyday practice*. New York: Routledge Falmer.

Day, C. (1999). *Developing teachers: The challenges of lifelong learning*. London: Falmer Press.

Day, C. (1999). Researching teaching through reflective practice. In J. Loughran. (Ed.), *Researching teaching: Methodologies and practices for understanding pedagogy*. London: Falmer Press.

Diller, A. (1991). The ethics of care and education: A new paradigm, its critics and its educational significance. In A. Diller, B. Houston, K. Morgan, & M, Ayim (Eds.), *The gender question in education: Theory, pedagogy and politics*. Boulder, CO: Westview Press.

Elbaz, F. (1983). *Teacher thinking: A study of practical knowledge*. London: Croom Helm.

Elbaz, F. (1992). Hope, attentiveness and caring for difference: The moral voice in teaching. *Teaching and Teacher Education*, *8*(5/6), 421–432.

Ellis, C., & Berger, L. (2003). Their story/My story/Our story: Including the researchers' experience in interview research. In. J. Gubrium & J. Holstein (Eds.), *Postmodern interviewing* (pp. 157–183). Thousand Oaks, CA: Sage Publications, Inc.

Ellis, C., & Bochner, A. (2000). Autoethnography, personal narrative, reflexivity: Researcher as subject. In N. Denzin & Y. Lincoln. (Eds.), *Handbook of qualitative research* (pp. 773–767). Thousand Oaks, CA: Sage Publications Inc.

Erkillä. R., & Mäkelä, M. (2002). Face to face: Human dimensions in biographical interviews. In R. Hultinen, H. Heikkenen, & L. Syrjälä. (Eds.), *Narrative research: Voices of teachers and philosophers*. Jyväskylä, Finland: So Phi.

Fullan, M. (2001). *The new meaning of educational change* (3rd ed.). New York: Teachers College Press.

Gadamer, H. G. (1989). *Truth and method*. New York: Continuum.

Fullan, M. (2001). *The new meaning of educational change* (3rd ed.). New York: Teachers College Press.

Gadamer, H. G. (1989). *Truth and method*. New York: Continuum.

Hargreaves, A. (1994). *Changing teachers, changing times: Teachers' work and culture in the postmodern age*. London: Cassell.

Hargreaves, A. (1998). The emotional practice of teaching. *Teaching and Teacher Education*, *14*(8), 835–854.

Hargreaves, A. (1998). *The emotions of teaching and educational change*. In A. Hargraves, A. Lieberman, M. Fullan, & D. Hopkins (Eds.), *International handbook of educational change* (pp. 558–575). Dordrecht: Kluwer.

Hargreaves, A. (2002). Teaching in a box: Emotional geographies of teaching. In C. Day (Ed.), *Developing teachers and teaching practice: International research perspectives* (pp. 3–25). London: Routledge Falmer.

Kelchtermans, G. (1996). Teacher vulnerability: Understanding its moral and political roots. *Cambridge Journal of Education, 26*(3), 307–329.

Kelchtermans, G., & Ballet, K. (2002). The micropolitics of teacher education. A narrative-biographical study on teacher socialization. *Teacher and Teacher Education, 18*, 105–120.

Korthagen, F. (2001). *Linking practice and theory: The pedagogy of realistic teacher education.* Marwah, NJ: Lawrence Erlbaum Associates.

Loughran, J. (1996). *Developing reflective practice: Learning about teaching and learning through modelling.* London: Falmer Press.

Loughran, J., & Russell, T. (Eds.). (1997). *Teaching about teaching: Purpose, passion and pedagogy in teacher education.* London: The Falmer Press.

Mitchell, I. (2003). Why do teacher research? In A. Clarke & G. Erickson (Eds)., *Teacher inquiry: Living the research in everyday practice.* London: Routledge Falmer.

Noddings, N. (1992). *The challenge to care in schools: An alternative approach to education.* New York: Teachers College Press.

Noddings, N. (2003). *Caring: A feminine approach to ethics and moral education* (2nd ed.). Berkeley, CA: University of California Press.

Polkinghorne, D. (1988). *Narrative knowing and the human sciences.* Albany, NY: State University of New York Press.

Polkinghorne, D. (1995). Narrative configuration in qualitative analysis. In R. Wisniewski (Ed.), *Life history and narrative* (pp. 5–24). London: Falmer Press.

Reid, A., & O'Donoghue, M. (2001a, September). *Rethinking policy and practice in teacher education.* Paper presented at the Australian Teacher Educators' Association Conference, Melbourne, Australia.

Reid, A., & O'Donoghue, M. (2001b). *Shaping the future: Educating professional educators* (Report of the Review of Education). Adelaide: University of South Australia.

Richardson, L. (1994). Writing: A method of inquiry. In N. Denzin & Y. Lincoln (Eds.), *Handbook of qualitative research* (pp. 516–529). Thousand Oaks, CA: Sage Publications.

Richardson, L. (2000). Writing: A method of inquiry. In N. Denzin & Y. Lincoln (Eds.), *Handbook of qualitative research* (2nd ed., pp. 923–949). Thousand Oaks, CA: Sage Publications, Inc.

Richardson, L. (2001). Getting personal: Writing stories. *Qualitative Studies in Education, 14*(1), 33–39.

Rogers, C. (2002). Defining reflection: Another look at John Dewey and reflective thinking. *Teachers College Record, 104*(4), 842–866.

Sachs, J. (1997). Reclaiming the agenda of teacher professionalism: An Australian experience. *Journal of Education for Teaching, 23*(3), 264–277.

Schön, D. (1983). *The reflective practitioner: How professionals think in action.* New York: Basic Books.

Shacklock, G., & Smyth, J. (Eds.). (1998). *Being reflexive in educational and social research.* London: Falmer Press.

Sharkey, P. (2001). Hermeneutic phenomenology. In R. Barnacle (Ed.), *Phenomenology.* Melbourne: RMIT University Press.

van Manen, M. (1990). *Researching lived experience: Human science for an action sensitive pedagogy.* London, Ontario: Althouse Press.

van Manen, M. (1991). *The tact of teaching: The meaning of pedagogical thoughtfulness.* London, ON: Althouse Press.

Zeichner, K. (1999). The new scholarship in education. *Educational Researcher, 28*(9), 4–15.

Maryann Brown
School of Education
University of Ballarat

CENTRED MASSES

In one of his journeys across the falls, the Great Blondin paused in the centre and cooked for himself an omelette. His risk-taking acts were focused upon drawing attention to the unusual. This sort of precarious approach is one of the academic challenges that researchers face. Risk has its value; however, if one fails to centre, to bring to light balance in the field, one simply falls. The larger or higher the risk… the greater or longer the fall. The fear of disequilibrium or perceived contentment is perhaps why risks in academia are frequently overcome by more pedestrian approaches to the difficult questions. The papers in Part III ask difficult questions whilst struggling for stability in educational research.

In *Is There Light as Well as Heat? Teachers and the System* Olsen and Lang discuss the need for systemic reform. Through case studies in the European Union the authors uncover the tensions and challenges in enacting curricular and school restructuring. In doing so they bring to light the difficulties of balancing the role of the teacher in educational transformation.

Arnold and Kompf examine higher education as a commodity whereby stakeholders shield the uncovering of institutional goals. In *Transferable Academic Credits: Commodity or Albatross?* the authors question the authenticity of political agendas in attracting transfer and graduate students. They further challenge readers to take note of the absence of intellectual capital in North American higher education.

The inquiry enacted by Sanber and colleagues scrutinizes assessment practice in religious education. *Public Accountability, Religious Literacy and Student Learning* highlights the purposes of assessment in religious education and the need for further examination of religious literacy assessment practices.

In the closing paper of Part III Sue Moron-Garcia speaks to the relevance of pedagogic research. Amidst a climate of funding driven initiatives in a research-intensive university, *Talking Teaching: Engaging Engineers*, aims to create a space to build pedagogic research capacity.

To stay in balance while walking along a tightrope, the funabulist's centre of mass must remain directly over the wire. While stepping the foot is elevated and the centre of mass shifts slightly. Even the faintest deviation can disrupt the system of balance causing disequilibrium and an eventual fall. Thus, maintaining centre of mass in tightrope walking calls for intricate bodily awareness. Similarly, the researcher prepared to engage in risky inquiry must do so with awareness that any digression from centredness results in instability or at worst a complete loss of balance. The challenge then is to disrupt the tension that arises when one strives to maintain equilibrium while attempting the dangerous steps that move one forward.

JOHN OLSON AND MANFRED LANG

IS THERE LIGHT AS WELL AS HEAT?

Teachers and the System

SYSTEMIC CHANGE AS A LOCUS OF CONFLICT AND ILLUMINATION

If we want to understand why teachers act as they do, we ought to consult their purposes as they arise in particular settings. Those purposes allow researcher and teacher to see what the framework is that informs and directs those actions, including the moral grounds of the action. Those frameworks can be traced back to traditions of teacher practice. Case study brings those frameworks into view and such traditions, as Charles Taylor (1991) reminds us, have moral force but are not immune from change and improvement. While case studies often illustrate conflicts that arise when system plans conflict with teacher tradition (Olson, 2002), they can also illuminate the underlying principles on which teachers base their practice.

Behind what teachers say about adapting to change is a tension between wanting to change and to be successful, and protecting zones of security provided by well tried routines—routines often criticized by outsiders. Appreciating this tension helps us understand what teachers do and say about change. It is useful in this context to look at the OECD report, *Changing the Subject: Innovations in Science, Mathematics and Technology Education* (Black & Atkin, 1996). This report is a cross-case analysis 23 MSTE projects in OECD countries. As the authors said of the cross-case analysis:

> First, it is authentic. In drawing on the case studies we have let actors in their narratives speak in their own voices…out of their own preoccupations…. Secondly…[it] benefits from the restricted range of subjects… effective plans for any innovation in any subject must take account of the nature of and traditions of that subject and of its teachers…. Thirdly…[its purpose] is to give help…to the many kinds of people trying to respond to demands for change…. It addresses those who are innovating and those who have to work with innovations of others." (Black & Atkin, pp. 198-199)

These comments are by way of a critique of systemic reform. The authors note the dangers of systemic reform: "most current systemic views are through the telephoto lens…. [they involve] general responsibilities and weaken those closest to where educational services are actually provided" (p. 197). The reform process by implication would be strengthened were corrective feedback available.

J. A. Kentel and A. Short (eds.), Totems and Taboos: Risk and Relevance in Research on Teachers and Teaching, 97–111.

SYSTEMIC REFORM AND THE NEED FOR FEEDBACK

The problem with the telescopic view is that overly grand schemes may be set afoot leading to unrealistic expectations. Existing strengths and opportunities for improvement may be ignored due to the distant view. The challenge for systemic reform is to find some way of enabling curriculum makers and teachers to find common ground in selecting what should be taught in the school; the enacted curriculum. It is a common place that such a process requires collaboration (Strike, 1994); not so commonly agreed is the nature of this process. The need for collaboration amongst policy makers, teacher educators and teachers becomes most evident when schools are moving away from curriculum organization based on traditional subjects. The systemic approach to reform recognizes that schools are part of a complex system of expectations and that reform plans must recognize the diverse interests at play in any reform. The idea is that when all the parts are pulling together reform will happen.

The assumption is that the purposes for schools can be established, and that the technical means identified to achieve those purposes are known. It is a matter of everyone acting according to the plan. A good system if the plan is good. But how do we know the plan is good? We need to find out what teachers think of the reform—to ask those who have intimate knowledge of what happens when grand schemes are launched. What is needed in a systemic model of change is negative feedback. Teachers can and will in the future provide the negative feedback most often ignored and perilously so.

Most often teachers are left out of the power process that leads to the creation of policy and the search for positive feedback that is sought. But is positive feedback what is needed? The purposes of education are constantly evolving in dynamic ways, as are the means to achieve these purposes. What teachers can provide are insights into reform initiatives seen as experiments, which probe for the way forward. The process is much more like how traditions evolve than it is like radical shifts due to major breakthroughs. Teachers know what it is like to make the system work under conditions of duress. The systems they work in are subject to many stresses often due to funding problems but also often as a result of the related attempts to micro-manage the work they do. How can teachers be micro-managed when it is they who have to make sense and create coherence out of the contradictory demands of different stakeholders for what are often, in the end, controversial intended outcomes of reform?

Whatever the changes—draconian or Olympian—they challenge teacher survival and craft norms, and their relationship. Craft norms, which inhere in practice, and are often not expressed well, are often in conflict with survival norms, and the tension between them not recognized. Yes, teachers try to do their best, but in an imperfect world where shortcuts are taken. How are teacher's norms challenged? What can teachers tell us of those challenges? In what follows below we look at the Eudist project as a form of systemic reform, which takes into account the needs for teacher engagement in reform.

CASE STUDY OF SYSTEMIC REFORM IN THE EU: THE EUDIST PROJECT

The EUDIST project was funded by the European Union from 2003 to 2006. In this project teachers were offered a forum in which they could explore a number of issues related to curriculum development in science education. In these forums, called Curriculum Workshops, carefully chosen stakeholders clarified and learned from issues related to reform policies in the five participating countries: Germany, Austria, Spain, Sweden and Ireland. The upshot of these workshops was feedback to policy makers and researchers and to other teachers about problems of policy implementation in schools. This feedback gave rise to light as well as heat, as we shall see.

In those countries teachers face challenges to their practice posed by the advent of school reform policies. Such reforms involve departing from traditional ways of sequencing and teaching science subjects; for example: teaching and unfamiliar content in science courses; achieving new kinds of outcomes for science education; engaging students more in science and its role in society. What issues have arisen in these schools concerning the role of the teacher in school reform? What feedback to these cases provides that informs the systemic model of change? Let us turn now to such issues as identified in the cross-case analysis.

Organizing Subjects/Collaborating with Others

Subjects in secondary schools have been organized in schools to reflect the separate disciplines that exist outside the schools in universities. Units of time devoted to separate subjects remain stable over long periods of time and the perceived importance of subjects is reflected in the time assigned to them. What happens when teachers are asked to reform those subjects into new units of organization—often called integrated or interdisciplinary? In Austria teachers at the upper secondary level were faced variously with the task of transforming their work in science teaching into integrated units, teaching these in reduced amounts of time and linking these units to other subjects.

> The current autonomous organization of the upper grades comprises in part separate subjects labelled science. However, due to reductions on teaching time in the scientific subjects the desired learning outcomes are more difficult to realize than ever. While in the upper grades there is no longer mandatory teamwork, there is always some interdisciplinary work on certain topics. Unfortunately, in many cases, the curricula of the different subjects are not well harmonized, so that the only way of teaching interdisciplinary teaching is only to indicate lateral connections to other subjects. Especially in the field of scientific subjects a better cross-connection between the subjects would be possible with a more sensible structure of the curricula of the concerned teachers. The treatment of various scientific topics should be favoured. (Austrian Case)

In some senior high schools in Vienna integrated science is now one of the options open to students at the senior level. In one case school time devoted to science education in reduced by revamping the syllabus to retain essential topics and reduce overlap. In another case science is being taught in connection with social studies and language learning. Such policies prompt teachers to look at where and how their subjects fit and at the professional development implications of these new challenges and how those are met again at the school level.

Cross-case analysis showed that Teachers had concerns about departing from their well-established teaching routines based on familiar subject matter. They were also concerned about what they are expected to achieve—the learning outcomes common as part of systemic reform. These outcomes are used for evaluation purposes and for accountability. They are a form of supervision of teachers and can be perceived as a kind of intrusion.

> In School A, teachers developed a new integrated science programme (Science) for two years. The first two Science-classes began September 2004. Teachers said they needed support in developing integrated themes and for integrated science teaching and, in addition, support for coaching during the first year: "We have to be trained to develop materials for team teaching and in addition be supervised while working together. What we expect from our students we have to be able to do by ourselves."
>
> At School B, integrated science includes social subjects and especially language learning. This requires close co-operation with other teachers in the school and with schools of other countries. The teachers in this school said they needed to form a steering group with external moderators to help them manage the co-operation of so many teachers and schools in such a complex project. (Austrian Case)

The additional pressure here is that of team teaching. Not only do teachers have to adapt to new material they are working with others in new ways. A sense of the threats posed by this process can be seen in the reference to students. Teachers expect to model for their students methods of thought and inquiry as well as ways of working together. How can teachers expect students to work in teams if they do not know how to do it themselves? How can we be models for students when we do not know the procedures involved? This can amount to a very large frustration for teachers. Where in the systemic plan is the provision to deal with this or an awareness of it?

> At School C, teachers dealt with the reduction of lesson time in the syllabus for science teaching. They looked at the science curriculum to see if there were overlapping topics and thus to streamline the content to develop a "slim curriculum" without neglecting general education. The requirement to reduce the amount of time devoted to the subject in the curriculum has ramifications for other aspects of the teachers' work. Are these recognized in the planning?
>
> We can see here that teachers have to reassess what is important in their subject. This it appears has been left to them to do. They also have to apportion different aspects of the subject to different teachers. How is this to

> be done? The point here is not that these challenges arise but that they call for skills that teachers may not have developed well. And they make demands on time. When to meet other teachers to plan team teaching? When to organise the modules? Teacher views about the loss of teaching time capture their concerns.
>
> There is no time given for planning and performing subject integrated teaching in the timetable. Of course, this is a problem and a serious disadvantage for teachers' teamwork. Nevertheless meetings are frequent. Teachers have been learning to take advantage of common gaps in their timetables.
>
> The reduction of the number of lessons, which took place last March, is in our opinion, a step back in developing innovations in science teaching. In physics lessons student experiments are regular activities. These are supposed to be done even in the upper grades. Unfortunately, the current situation concerning reduction of weekly lessons in 2003 makes this more difficult. (Austrian Case)

This co-operation between the individual subjects can only be successful if the conditions are appropriate. This means sufficient time for conferences as part of regular working hours. It means availability of the necessary material and curricula adjusted to interdisciplinary lessons and arrangements for team-teaching. It means inservice training for teachers to promote interdisciplinary thinking. At present these conditions are not met and this hinders the realization of regular interdisciplinary education even though good ideas exist.

The opportunity to explore one's response to the demands of the policy with the views of others—a kind of reality check—was valuable the teachers said. The systematic review of these demands and their formal documentation provides feedback to policy makers about the effects on them of radical reshaping of the content and context of their work as subject specialists.

Progression of Learning/Discourse about Values

School subjects, integrated or not, start at some point in schooling and end at another. In between how is the learning to be sequenced? And what values are reflected in the different ways the subject is represented at different stages in its development. Do elementary teachers see the subject the same way as secondary? If there are differences how are they to be adjudicated? What form of discourse is needed? This was a problem that the schools in the Swedish study addressed. There four schools in the same school system represented different levels of schooling: one was a kindergarten, two were primary schools (six to thirteen years of age) and one a junior high school (13 to 16 years of age).

In the kindergarten and primary schools the focus is on the introduction of science-related activities, but the primary school is more focused toward the development of science related skills such as observation and concept development. The lower secondary school is introducing co-operation between civics and science, as a way of furthering student creativity, conceptual development in inclusive education. This diversity of school levels is a challenge to the setting of common aims and objects of collaboration. What they have in common is a need to see how the science they teach at different levels can be sequenced to improve what children learn.

The four schools decided to design a program of knowledge progression (concepts, skills in science from kindergarten to ninth grade (age 16). The proposed design would be being put to the teaching staff at the four schools for consideration, and eventually to other schools of the school district. Middle school teachers thus have to look at what students learn at elementary levels. How does the subject fit together? And again how can teachers from these different levels work together? Teachers agreed that a suitable topic to form the object of their thinking about how to engage in this reflection on subject progression was the topic of light. At an early stage of the project it was agreed, according to the case, that the aim of the work would be to effect empowerment of teachers in their work on curriculum in their schools.

The group met over two days to prepare a document to be presented to the respective schools which outlined an approach to teaching about *Light*. The group comprised teachers and principals, two resource persons who are doctoral students in curriculum science (didactic and educational science respectively), and three more researchers as external observers. The moderator was a Ph.D. student in educational science, proposed by the Coordinator and acclaimed by the deliberating group. The rules of discourse were those commonly followed by various popular movements in Sweden: trade unions, political parties, churches, and temperance sobriety organizations and the study circles of the various "bildningsförbund" (self-educational organizations). These group processes are a deeply ingrained part of the Swedish culture. The person chosen as moderator had been a churchwarden in her home parish.

> The debate soon became centred on the approach to learning; the learning outcome, in terms of the attained knowledge, was not approached. A polarization was discernible. One the one hand knowledge should be constructed with the perceptions of the students and their experiencing of phenomena as the point of departure—on the other hand, the formal requirement of the school system, and notably the higher grades were perceived as the guiding principle. (Swedish Case)

This tension between the mandated curriculum and its expression in learning outcomes and the orientation to the experience of the child is a common issue for teachers at different levels of the school system. Opportunity to engage with these issues amongst teachers from the different levels is not common. It is interesting that this issue became rapidly salient. According to the accounts of the deliberations amongst teachers, teachers of higher grades appeared to favour a discussion in terms of mental capabilities promoted and in terms of learning outcomes. This, rather than discuss the relevance of the subject matter, which seemed beyond debate. Meanwhile teachers of lower grades were questioning the relevance of the subject matter. A debate about the value of science was thus joined with non-specialist teachers asking difficult questions,

> Arising out of the deliberations about how to organize the progression of learning about light over the different grade levels—the progression learning—was the tension between the demand that learning goals be specified which can be understood as expressions of a bureaucratic perspective. Here the system is demanding the delivery of certain products. The perspective adopted by the teachers, on the other hand, is the perspective of Bildung: a careful coaching of the young person into the world of the grown-ups, which respects her or his unique way of experiencing the world. "So, we have the bureaucratic/technocratic alienated perspective, embodied by two researchers, and the perspective of the humanistic tradition embodied by the teachers." (Swedish Case)

Besides the tension amongst the teachers is one between outsiders and insiders. Outsiders were perceived to represent the demands of the political system, which makes curriculum. The teachers felt they represented the interests of children, as they perceive them in relation to their subject. How to resolve these tensions? The group decided to build in the contradiction in their thinking about subject progression so that it could be resolved in everyday work. Thinking about and planning for the progression of the subject meant the 7 to 9 grade teachers shouldered reconciling the two terms of the contradiction (working from the pupils, interest and working toward attainment goals). These were positions all the teachers were aware of and trying to reconcile.

However, according to the team leader team leader, this reconciliation did not occur. Rather, the conflict was smoothed away as was seen in the final document produced by the group. There the stages of learning about light at different grades were outlined in what we call the knowledge progression. The demands of content coverage, which concerned the senior teachers, were met. Meanwhile the responsibility of meeting the other requirements of the school system was delegated to the junior high school. Why was this decision made? Was it to concentrate on the subject matter at the expense of other more child-centred goals? According to the analysis of the case, a factor playing a role here might be the self-confidence of the primary school teachers and how they appraise their competence and independence as science teachers compared to the school principals and the senior teachers. The latter took a firm position in favour of the goals stipulated by the National Curriculum and the National Science Syllabus.

According to the case, follow up of the plans made in the workshop is dependent on individual teachers wished to work with pupils in a certain way. Change seems to have been effected on the level of the teacher not of the school. This may be due to the fact that there does not seem to be any support for these changes from the principal in any of these schools. This lack of concern in such curriculum changes may be due to the fact that science teaching is low on the priority list for Swedish schools. The main concern is student achievement measured by the percentage of those who pass in the three basic subjects: Swedish, Math and English must be as high as possible. The municipality has adopted a new policy, aiming at raising the average grade. Science is but a small part of this. So, one can conjecture that both the teachers and principals are more interested if our work was about numeracy or better skills at mathematical problem solving. The activity of Swedish school is not about improving science teaching and learning. It is about producing better average grades.

Thus the discourse was resolved in favour of the system requirements for learning outcomes based in subject matter requirements. Nonetheless issues to do with the value of science in the curriculum were raised and the elementary teachers had an opportunity to make their case. Having done this once, they might be inclined to do it again especially since they have seen the nature of the opposing arguments and have been able to see their limitations as they see them. Does the expression of voice here give rise to further stronger expression or resignation?

In Germany school support for school autonomy is a new trend in many of the Federal states. The purpose of such autonomy is to align more closely the practice of schools with the needs of teachers, students, parents, and the needs of the people living in the region. Since school autonomy is partially realized through local curriculum development, there is an increased awareness of the challenges schools face in developing such curricula. The workshops in Germany used an approach to inservice education developed by the Rhineland-Palatinate State. The workshop focus was on the competencies teachers need to develop when they collaborate in school improvement/innovation.

In the project schools a tradition of collaboration among groups of science teachers had already evolved. The teachers of these schools were all known as teacher leaders who had promoted school based curriculum activities in their respective schools. To provide a focus for collaboration teachers in four schools worked on a common theme, "water". This theme is a major unit in a countrywide project aimed at broadening the scope of science to encompass social issues and to engage students in discussion about these issues as well as in experimental activities.

At issue for the teachers was the problem of defining learning outcomes for interdisciplinary units like water. The broad scope of such a unit and its open possibilities means that teachers need to discuss how to structure such a unit for teaching. Such discussions raise issues about the planning process itself and so the teachers asked themselves, "How can we find agreement on what should be the outcomes of such a unit?" And once agreement on outcomes is reached, how can they be achieved?

Teachers were inducted into a well-developed inservice format, which they themselves did not create. They were required to assess their needs for inservice education in relation to a particular kind of task—creating teaching material for a thematic approach to science. At the same time they were to consider how their working together might advance the process of adopting standards for their work mandated by the state. And they had to consider what these tasks entailed, especially in relation to the assessment of learning. In other words how to cope both with formatting material in a new way and with making sure that this could be assessed effectively. This format derives from the systemic approach to school reform—an element in a larger reform plan. What did the teachers make of this process?

> The initial case study prepared by each participating school provided a brief description of the school, its demographic structure and its pedagogical orientation. During the workshop process, interviews were conducted with at least one of the participating schoolteachers and one person outside of the school who commented on the process. The information brochure provided to the participants comprised a variety of papers, school-based inservice education and school-development.
>
> Science teachers were involved in teaching an integrated science course. In order to focus their thoughts about the challenges this posed, they asked themselves a question about how to teach a particular topic and how to evaluate it. Teachers were concerned with very specific issues related to their competency, which appears to have been challenged by this kind of teaching/content. (German Case)

These background documents focused on the process of formulating teaching material—how the teachers might collaborate together; what effective groups were like. What rules were needed? These efforts as group process were related to the professional development needs identified by the teachers and the advisors. Teachers, on the other hand, were focused on the substantive issues in front of them. How to prepare teaching material for the demands of the curriculum they were teaching. As the case notes, subject development dominated the activities at the beginning of the project. Improvement of their own lessons was the focus of the teachers rather than developing skills in collaboration per se in the context of achieving standards.

This focus on the practical needs of the teachers remained over the length of the project. It seemed to have been the natural concern of the teachers even though they were encouraged to consider group process issues as time went on. It is not surprising that there would be such a focus. Clearly the demands of the curriculum concerned these teachers. Nonetheless the issue of standards was there.

According to the case, standards or student competencies became a major theme during the preparatory meetings. One of the reasons might have been the political context of reform and the other that many of the teachers were involved in the adaptation and enactment of integrated science in their schools. Teaching in an integrated approach needs a clear understanding of the difference between traditional conceptions of knowledge, competencies to solve science problems and competencies to connect science and everyday life.

Teachers were concerned about getting assistance for school-based development of science: specifically suggestions for how to conduct collaborative lesson planning and assessing student competency development. Teachers said the workshop would help them implement new projects in a school through collaboration among teachers who represent different conceptions and goals. According to the case, those organizing and advising the workshops mentioned the value of concrete products like the competency matrix for the work with science standards, individual work plans of the schools and a checklist for inservice education.

We see here an interaction between the requirements arising from school autonomy—learning to work in teams in order to achieve goals for learning established by the state—the standards—and teacher concerns to be able to produce specific and unfamiliar teaching material locally. This is a reflection of the same sort of issues that arose in the Swedish case.

This is an issue that arises for the reform of the way schools are organized and for those who have to plan teacher training to support such system changes. We see here a systemic approach at work. A new relationship between schools and central administrations is established and a plan for integrating teachers into this scheme is developed—teacher training for group work aimed at local material development and the achievement of standards. Teachers, on the other hand, are concerned about content specifics—indeed the very specific concern with teaching a unit on water. Present to them are other teachers who can act as resources for this new kind of teaching. Present also are the common thoughts about how to ensure that this material can be assessed effectively. Teachers are thus providing feedback to the system, helping us with very specific tasks that they face now that are not about process directly but implicitly require greater ability to work in groups. 'First things first' seems to be the message.

Systemic Reform/Teacher Voice

In Spain an important challenge for teachers is to see what their collective educational needs might be given the trends in school reform in Spain. Through discourse in workshops teachers have considered how their practices align with the nature of school reform in Spain and what the implications are for teacher education. Two teachers from each of four schools—who teach science at the primary or secondary level and have been involved in innovation—took part in the workshops. At the first workshop teachers became familiar with workshop procedures and each other. In preparation for the next meeting each teacher was asked to reflect on and write about his/her experience in curriculum innovation. The purpose of this document was to raise matters for discussion in the second meeting. These were: the work setting of the teacher; the school and the innovation; an account of the innovation (start pointing, methodology followed, changes observed, state of the art, future perspectives) as well as: a description of the teacher's role in the innovation; materials and products of the innovation; reflections about the qualities of the innovation.

In the second workshop, teachers, teacher educators and educational researchers participated in a discourse about the basic question for educational innovation: *"What are present and future benefits of school-based professional development in curriculum innovation?"* The task of the meeting focused on producing a common draft about the planning of school-based curriculum innovation that, from the teachers' point of view, promoted professional development.

Teachers discussed their experiences of a variety of reforms in science education and their role in these. In the workshop they analyzed their role in change and what made it easier to change or not. Emerging from this analysis was an elaboration of the notion of motivation in the change process. Teachers found that feedback during the change process was important—motivation during the change and not just at the beginning was an important support for change. As well, factors affecting and affected by change were seen as quite varied—changing one thing affected other aspects of work. In the workshop these more elaborate views about change and motivation emerged.

Some teachers, who had worked with an external advisor, mentioned that it was very important for them to see from the very beginning the applicability of the materials they were implementing. Teachers believed that some innovations are too theoretical and difficult to implement in practice. They do not want to be trained just at the theoretical level only, and they emphasize the importance of theory that has informed activities already successfully implemented in the school by educators.

Teachers here are commenting on how they perceive the process of systemic reform in their context. Motivation seems to be a word used to refer to the support and encouragement teachers need to sustain changes in their practice. Systemic reforms are often given strong initial support and attention, which tends to fade as time goes on. The teachers are left to deal with the details of the reform and as they saying goes "the devil is in the details" which is the point the teachers previously made. No reform is ready made at the outset and teachers are placed in the position of enacting plans, which have not been fully tested.

> Teachers want teacher educators and advisors to with them concerning the topics and format of the training to be received; to take into account the needs of the school and teaching staff. Teachers also recommend that inservice education be done during school time and not at the expense of free-time as it is usually the case. One important aspect that teachers mentioned was that there be established some measure of the pedagogical competence of teachers and that be considered in relation to promotion .After the series of workshops teachers asked for links to be established between them an policy makers, thus opening the door for teachers to be included in the planning of future intervetions. (Spanish Case)

Teachers commented as aforementioned on wide spread effects that reform has in all aspects of their work, effects that may not have been thought of in initial planning. It is not surprising that teachers want those effects to be recognized in the formulation of support that they need to implement the reforms or that they would like to be present in the planning process to advise on these matters.

As in the aforementioned case, in the Irish case we can see how teachers react to the implications of systemic reform, as they become apparent as time goes on. In this project teachers were asked to consider the demands posed to them by a new science syllabuses, especially the task of improving examination results through greater student motivation and a new assessment system. Teachers reflected on these issues in terms of the kind of professional development that they needed to cope. Teachers went beyond that question to consider what role they might play in the process of developing school reform itself, as we shall see.

Furthermore there were curriculum demands for completion of a mandatory set of science experiments. The method of assessment has changed. Instead of a written final examination, marks are divided between school assessment of mandatory experiments, a school-assessed project and a final written test. Teachers perceived these changes as a break with tradition. Science syllabuses had changed as well. The support services, teachers said, did not focus on teaching methodologies but on the nature of the content to be taught. They did not think they were getting the technical support they needed to implement the mandatory experiments and the use of data logging equipment involved. This has lead to a concern about how teachers can work together to meet these changes in the system and to the idea of teacher mentoring as a form of inservice education.

One response to these systemic requirements has been to establish a teacher mentor program. Teachers in the project were ones who had had experience of mentoring pre-service teachers. They were joined by other teachers who were interested in the idea of preservice and inservice mentoring as a way of coping with change. The teachers have found it useful to discuss the issues that concern them about the changes in the school system as well as considering the mentoring process. Thus two agendas are at work here: the systemic concern with mentoring and the teacher concern with specific aspects of their teaching responsibility.

> Teachers said that they wanted in service training to take place through dialogue and be more conducive to actual change in the classroom instead of the more traditional top-down type of presentation. They wanted there to be teacher representation in the syllabus design process to ensure the syllabus is more relevant to the needs of students and involve teachers from the beginning of the process. (Irish Case)

These appear to be references to the fact that the organization of science in the school had changed radically and that demands were being made that were difficult to meet—especially the demand to conduct mandated experiences when there may not be the equipment needed. Thus the dialogue about mentoring has led to issues to do with teacher empowerment that the idea of mentoring has fostered. Mentoring recognizes the contribution teachers can make to each other as professionals it also sets the scene for teachers to express their collective view about syllabus change based on that professional stance. Thus again we see the desire of teachers to give feedback to systemic reformers in the form of a critique about what needs to be attended to from the point of view of the teacher. Not what works but what doesn't work. [This is] the critical negative feedback that systems need.

HEAT AND LIGHT IN THE PROCESS OF SCHOOL REFORM

Teachers used the workshop setting to identify and assess the significance of the demands being made on them. What they said could be viewed as complaints about how well they are positioned to play their role in systemic change. The policies they were adapting to have explicit and implicit assumptions about the role teachers would play. The overall impression from these cases is that teachers were not well consulted in the formation of these polices. This must remain a hypothesis but on the face of it there is evidence of difficulties for teachers. At the same time teachers are identifying these issues and the effect they have toward them; they are also probing their role in change. While change agents may think teachers are to adjust and adapt, the teachers themselves have pragmatic issues to deal with as well as fundamental issues to do with the role of their subject, the value of schooling, and the ways and means of achieving goals in places like schools. These cases suggest that the assumption of a compliant role for teachers in change disregard the role they play in the didactics of schooling. To the extent that change policies disregard this role they are flawed.

How is this so? Strike (1994) argues in his discussion of discourses about schooling and reform:

> The attempt must be made to construct an overlapping consensus such that it can be agreed upon by people with diverse and perhaps incommensurable moral outlooks without posing irresolvable issue of conscience for them. [The question to be answered is] "What can we agree on, given ample time for debate, that allows us to meet in the commons and that does not require us to abandon those background convictions on which we differ?" (¶ 44)

Now Strike is talking about foundational visions about restructuring education. Nonetheless each time schools re-invent themselves to any degree; each time there is a movement for school improvement, moral issues arise and these finally need to be discussed in some sort of commons. Schools do not do their work through bureaucratic fiat. The workshop provides a commons in which to discuss the underlying issues at work in school improvements of any sort including those that involve teachers of science at different school levels as in this study. We can see an example of this commons in action in the Swedish case. Teachers, who took subject matter for granted, in an effort to protect that subject matter from criticism (and thus it might be argued their superior position in the debate), attempted to protect it by offering a gloss on it rather than a defence. Teachers in lower grades did not accept this gloss and asked that the subject matter itself be placed on the table. At issue here are basic questions about why teach science? Questions often glossed over by subject specialists. The workshops enabled such questions to come to the table.

In each of these cases teachers have discussed issues related to an existing reform policy including concerns about their capacity to cope with reform. The workshop was a forum to deal with issues related to change—a place to consider what reform means in practice. The policies governing reform, we have previously argued, will profit from the kind of feedback that teachers are providing. It is not easy for teachers to be critical. This is not normally expected of them; especially due to the hierarchical structure of schooling. The workshops provide a forum for teachers to research, analyze, document and discuss their work free of such constraint. They offer public space for teachers to see what underlying values are at work in their practice and that of others and where those values may diverge or converge. It is a forum to elaborate those values and debate them. Participants agreed to accept that they are equal partners with equal rights in the discourse who take one another as serious persons of equal value. Scientific jargon was replaced by language that can be understood by all of the participants.

Teachers brought with them the case study they had made of their school to the workshop. These were the outcome of an analysis of their situation in respect of reform activity. Their own experience became a text for discussion. This study formed one of the bases of the subsequent activity. These assessments provided a basis for discussing what the challenges were facing teaching in coping with school change at the school level. In these discussions certain issues arose which are emblematic of the issues that teachers face when they play a role in change. A central issue for professional development at the school level is: What skills do teachers need to participate in school improvement? This assumes that teachers have the scope to diagnose and remedy what takes place in the school. How much freedom teachers have to do this of course varies. As we saw in the Swedish case there is a tension between the demands of the established curriculum and the interest in reform of the teachers. How far can teachers go in changing what the school does?

In the Austria case teachers brought to the table a concern about what curriculum objectives hope to achieve and what really happens—perhaps a way of expressing some scepticism about the realism of curriculum plans. This critical frame of mind can be seen in the way these teachers defined their professional development needs—handling conflict was high on the list. The other central issue was that of assessment in integrated science. Teachers are quite familiar with assessment routines in the specialist subject. But assessment across subject matters and in relation to value issues commonly seen in integrated science courses raised PD concerns for these teachers.

Being able to hear other teachers express those concerns provides a context in which they can consider the implications of systemic reform for their work. It is not easy for teachers to question systemic plans especially in a climate, which promotes collective attachment to systemic goals. In a sense the workshop can act as a way of promoting valuable negative feedback in the context of system pressure. With out that negative feedback the system runs the risk of not correcting mistakes (Olson, 2002).

In the German case we see the value of teacher analysis of their own situation through keeping diaries and through a school based "audit" of issues for deliberation. The workshop promoted this kind of reflective stance towards the work of the school and suggests methods for gathering data about the school. The initial case study in each of the German schools worked well as a basis for the first meeting according to what the participants said.

We see also in the German case the strong emphasis on rules of discourse. The intent here was to create an awareness of the process of deliberation itself and its rational basis. The information brochure developed for the German workshop was an extensive review of the literature on school-based curriculum and professional development and on the methods of deliberative enquiry. Here we see a concern that warranted decisions are made not on the basis of power relations but in terms of an argued position. Now participants will come to the discussions with different ideas about what is really valuable in their work and the discussion process is aimed at encouraging those positions to be placed on the table.

This raises a further question, how will different stakeholders interact in the reform process. This is one of the main goals of the workshop approach—to set up conditions in which teachers and other stakeholders can establish the bounds of action and roles different people will play. Questions of expertise arise. Do teachers have the subject and pedagogical expertise to engage in school reform? The workshop approach opens this issue for discussion. In assessing school needs in the first stages, the teachers can test their capacity to do such work and in discussion with others test their perceptions. The workshop thus provides an arena in which to assess teacher capacity. Others present who may have detailed experience can then provide feedback which is itself part of the discussion. The egalitarian basis of the process ensures that power positions often associated with licensed expertise do not hold sway, as teachers are encouraged to defend their own assessments.

In this workshop process curriculum development and professional development are linked. The former supplies a context in which to consider how teachers can respond professionally. Participants prepare draft plans, which are considered in the light of their rationale in relation to curriculum value and in relation to teachers' capacities as they exist and as they can be developed. All followed a common approach to discourse and in all there was a firm attempt to adopt rules of discourse that would allow all the participants to be on an equal footing. In all cases teachers were called upon to assess their own work in each school before coming to the workshop. So a certain team effort was established before the meetings took place. That team effort was focused on an assessment of what was happening in the school, so already an inquiring approach to the work of the school was established. We can see the fruits of these inquiries in the issues that teachers raised and in the steps they took to disseminate their concerns and act on them.

REFERENCES

Black, P., & Atkin, J. (1996). *Changing the subject: Innovations in mathematics, science and technology education*. London: Routledge.

Olson, J. (2002). Systemic change/teacher tradition: legends of reform continue. *J. Curriculum Studies, 34*(2), 129–137. Retrieved March 13, 2008, from http://taylorandfrancis.metapress.com/content/3f4rj2l1h2xculma/

Strike, K. (1994). *Discourse ethics and restructuring*. Retrieved March 31, 2008, from http://www.ed.uiuc.edu/EPS/PES-Yearbook/94_docs/STRIKE.HTM

Taylor, C. (1991). *The malaise of modernity*. Toronto: Anansi Press.

John Olson
Queens University

Manfred Lang
Kiel University

CHRISTINE ARNOLD AND MICHAEL KOMPF

TRANSFERABLE ACADEMIC CREDITS: COMMODITY OR ALBATROSS

An earlier study, whereby a student hypothetically intending to relocate to another university contacted 25 institutions with questions about transferring academic credits, was followed up by asking questions at a higher administrative level. Findings from both inquiries are integrated to develop themes for this report. Overall, inconsistent and inflexible policies and practices were found that complicated mobility and represented disruptions and repetitions in academic experiences if an actual transfer were to occur. By way of providing context, discussions of commoditization and marketing from an institutional perspective are contrasted with an increasing consumerist trend among learners. Educational appropriation of name branding and customer loyalty concepts from business seems to have come full circle with next steps dictated by consumers of educational services. Educational learning needs and possibilities have been traditionally determined by available curricular and programmatic offerings of individual institutions. With the exception of facilities with direct field relations, universities tend to deliver a more abstract, theoretical and philosophical approach that assists deeper understanding. While some programs have practical or co-op experiences, graduates find that varying levels of retraining are often required once an applied field is entered. Protracted and non-applicable learning runs counter to a consumerist approach in a rapidly changing and mobile employment market where flexibility and an expedited sense of urgency to complete studies are often grounded in concerns over debt accumulation. While such market pressure has yet to be felt fully by many institutions, the emerging global marketplace for higher education has become a reality. Response strategies can be characterized as more insular than collaborative as most institutions opt for niche by name and reputation as might be portrayed by key performance indicators. The institutional Achilles' heel in these circumstances has to do with transfer credits between and among other institutions. Policies pertaining to transfer credits were less clear and equitable for students especially when contrasted with the clarity and quality of name and image branding and recruitment promises in globally redefined catchment areas.

INTRODUCTION

As the provision of educational services has become a marketable commodity, so has it become an albatross for providers and consumers of such services. Philosophers of old, educational and otherwise, argued that developing the capacity

J. A. Kentel and A. Short (eds.), Totems and Taboos: Risk and Relevance in Research on Teachers and Teaching, 113–128.

for deeper thought and reflection led to a better society and incrementally improved individual morality and quality of life. The advent of information and communications technology combined with fiscal restraints in education has instigated movement in orientation from the idea of further learning for the purpose of individual and social improvement to further education as a facilitator of improved financial circumstances and consumption ability. That further education is strongly linked to emancipation and improved quality of life is not a new argument and has been explored by many writers as a function of race, class, gender and geography in established and emergent societies. Rapid social movement by way of education seems to have led a shift from what Paulo Freire might have referred to as serial *conscientization* to progressive materialism. Cultural production is a complex process influenced by the intricate dynamics of globalization. The integral role played by further education includes the development of persons of responsibility who will fill the professions, lead in public and professional life and stimulate an intelligentsia that forms and informs circumstances for subsequent generations.

A consumerist loop has been created in the pursuit of further education in that consumption of qualifications is necessary to become a better consumer of material goods. Investment in this belief is evident as global demographic profiles of those seeking higher education have constantly increased in overall numbers since the mid-1990s. Increased numbers of educational consumers mean increases in the provision of educational services and providers such as public and private colleges and universities. The core issue explored in this discussion has to do with consumers' experiences of higher education as a loosely-coupled system (cf. Karl Weick).

For students the down side of transferable credits in higher education as a loosely-coupled system is expressed in a line of a popular song by singer-songwriter Tom Waits, "the large print giveth and the small print taketh away." This sentiment seems to apply as institutional policy regarding transferability of credits and articulation agreements between and among institutions make students the main casualties in a consumerist scuffle of branding and brand loyalty that has spilled over as a detriment to academic coherence, convenience and portability. University Admissions Offices perceive an intense competition for the brightest students in the most marketable programs. One of our themes has to do with universities as money-market managers in a "knowledge economy" that sanction, pre-package, and market curriculum and confer value by degree. With a quantity of universities abandoning their credit transfer systems entirely and others unsure of the cost and credits deemed as transferable, our questions lead to the perception, development and implementation of policy.

In order to understand institutional perspectives and subsequent rationale for transfer credit policy, in addition to other questions our most recent study asked for recommendations from those with power to influence university policy. Inquiries included what administrative units were responsible for determining credits viable for transfer, what changes were foreseeable, and who was served by these policies. We also asked, if given a globalizing hierarchy, would institutions ever consider opening transfer policy to a model like the European Union's Bologna Project? Twenty-five university presidents were contacted via letter, questionnaire, and telephone about procedures of transfer accreditation, the function it maintains within the University setting, and how feasible such practices are to students. Additionally, the Minister of Education for the province of Ontario, Canada, was asked for her level of satisfaction with university transfer systems at the provincial and national level and their performances, along with her knowledge of student discourse surrounding 'seamless education'.

BACKGROUND

This study has several parts and represents the beginnings of a larger long-term project. In Canada, education is the responsibility of each province, with the exception of First Nations schools, which are federally funded. Each province has a Ministry responsible for policy and funding for elementary, secondary and tertiary education. Each province has colleges, which primarily grant certificates and diplomas and universities that grant degrees. In the Province of Ontario a system of Colleges of Applied Arts and Technology (CAAT) was developed in the mid 1960s as a way of addressing the post baby boom needs of rapid growth in business and industry. Charters for several new universities were also granted during this time. While the CAATs had curricular expectations determined by the fields for which candidates were prepared, curricular mandates of universities were initially broad leading to a major and prerequisite for further professional preparation. University culture has traditionally consisted of alumni constructions of reputation and character as might be reflected through accomplishments or renowned graduates.

Rivalries between such institutions as Cambridge and Oxford, Harvard and Yale or University of Toronto and McGill open and close doors in professional and social life. Institutional allegiance traditionally afforded a measure of social reproduction in families and professions. In Ontario, post baby boom population growths and declines occur within an ever-increasing demographic curve. As such educational needs and goals have exceeded the capacity of existing institutional systems. Expansion and private enterprise are attempting to meet the demand. Growth coupled with reductions in financial transfers of government funding has caused rethinking about how accessibility can be married to quality.

Institutions are sites of knowledge production and education received certifies a certain level of competence. However, it seems that contemporary institutions are linked only by purpose, each playing out their own territorial game in trading "knowledged" goods. While *Education* is classified in the World Trade Organization as a serviceable product it seems that educated minds are not easily tradable items when considered from a branding and status perspective. For example, when universities are considered according to key performance indicators such as is reported in the popular press, overall quality places exceptional schools at one end of continuum, some in the middle, and low quality educational facilities at the bottom. While quality indicators assist choice of institution, the outcome of such an imaging process creates a persona, good, bad or otherwise, which the rated institution will either embrace and enhance or reject and defend, usually by attacking the ratings. Universities with low ratings face difficulties in attracting students, faculty and funding. Further to this, interactions in the higher education community carry the stigma of low ratings. The unwritten but known hierarchy of institutions in relation to each other is a reality at work daily in transactions among and between educational facilities in the trade of reputations. Those looking to transfer, seeking entrance to graduate programs, and applying to occupations in the work force with post-baccalaureate degrees feel invisible barriers in their decisions.

McLean's, a Canadian national magazine, ranks universities annually according to criteria mainly determined by reader interest, which is conducted independently of university input. The formation of impressions about individual facilities and their qualities and connections affects choice but lacks the breadth of information required to make effective and informed choices. Inter-institutional acknowledgement seems as strained in the business sector as it is at the study level and represents a disconnect between employment candidates and prospective employers. There exist layers of informed knowledge; agencies, faculty, and consumers have a stake in what education means and how it gets distributed and accepted within a society.

Critical consumers thus need a broader knowledge than just the key performance indicators listed on a website, some place in cyberspace, to make their future education decisions. The benefits and achievements of a certain program and school need to be expanded beyond a few generalizations posted on a mission's statement website. The tribulation that exists in the transfer of degrees and credits manifests itself in a modern triptych, each panel important in itself but when looked at on the whole the scheme/composition becoming much grander. Each panel flows over into the next as the eye moves to see the whole image; transferring between university institutions in undergrad turns to prerequisites and rudiment issues in grad program eligibility, carrying into the business field where degrees and qualifications come under scrutiny and challenge in terms of equivalency and accreditation.

METHODS AND STAGES OF INQUIRY

In an earlier study, one of the authors posed as a third-year university English major with excellent grades wishing to transfer to another institution. Questions regarding transfer policies and academic information were provided to twenty-five Universities along with the request for advice and assistance. The second phase of this inquiry involved contacting university presidents with questions about the origins and practices of transfer credit policy.

Data were collected via phone, e-mail, and letter with each University receiving a questionnaire by mail about transfer policies and the criteria used to determine and execute them. Institutions were informed of other research concerning the European Bologna Project, and the European Credit Transfer System (ECTS) explaining the accessibility of such transfer systems across borders. The topic of cited research was borderless education where members are cognizant of the impact of trade liberalization in higher education and the demands placed upon it within the global marketplace as explored by Knight (2002). Institutions were informed that the results yielded would be used as qualitative data surrounding transfer credits and policies across provincial, national, and international borders and used as research facilitating discussion into the future objectives and setbacks of seamless education. Results would be directly analyzed and discussed in the education field as a means of furthering discourse surrounding this area of tertiary education.

Questionnaires were to be completed by the President of each university regarding duration and details of existing transfer credit policy, administrative unit responsible and formal procedures in place to determine transfer accreditation. Questions were also asked about the level of customer satisfaction, meeting student needs effectively, and recommendations as to how the transfer system among universities could be improved. A final question concerned globalization and whether the institutions would consider opening their transfer system to something like the Bologna Project. Data allowed for insight into the discourse, terminology, and issues surrounding higher education at present, allowing a stage on which to critically dissect the current education boardroom as described by Noble (1998).

The study itself has acted as a form of increasing critical awareness of students about scholarship as a co-capital relationship as data analysis has led to exposing some harsh consumer realities. Student shopping of campus markets purely based on specifications and guarantees has become a reality. Buying one's education has become similar to the purchase of a home computer where the latest programs, flashy features, and extra upgrades are an all-consuming market but only available from the original source, or with tweaking and possible loss of performance, from a compatible supplier. In this economic interplay, where students have become their own market money managers, university institutions will be forced to play catch up regarding interchangeability in a society where crossing borders is an everyday reality. The contract prospective buyers receive needs to be treated as a contract if this is the corporate entity within which universities are choosing to operate. Such business transactions should fulfil the terms outlined and do so without sub-clauses making clear the meaning of one's education, and its worth, and appeal.

Lastly, those who will buy this product after it has been inspected and quantified as marketable good also need to be held accountable. The focus on student consumers needs to shift to consumers of the student and the student-as-product metaphors. The cost of one's education is not a factor for educational "retailers" as the corporate logo is argued to indicate worth. This represents a type of gift receipt education, where one is informed of the value of purchases made after they have been reviewed and checked for damage typifying recent inter-institutional education relations. In many jurisdictions the law now requires that goods be of merchantable 'quality' but for education it seems this does not apply and students are left figuring this small detail out in personal moments of crisis regarding debt and/or transferability.

Those who inform policy need to provide further more well-thought out responses regarding the functionality of the loosely coupled system in place as it does not serve those forced to consume at their disadvantage. The second portion of the study also included an inquiry directed to the Ontario Minister of Education with questions regarding how Ontario has fared in transfer systems. Questions addressed students' satisfaction levels as determined at the government level and where university institutions are currently determining their stance on the acceptance of degrees from non Administration of Universities and Colleges of Canada (AUCC) members. Other questions included: "Are you content with the way our university transfer system works provincially and nationally?"; "How do you think it functions and performs in an international setting?"; and "Do you have any recommendations as to how the transfer system among universities could be improved and what the consequences of those changes would be?"

Identifying and demanding major stakeholders consider the issues disturbing education in a global marketplace is focus of this study. From the institution to the governments that control it the voices of higher education have been collected and the need for a solution rendered. Out of this resolution a "buyer beware list" has been composed for patrons intending to utilize tertiary education and its goods. Treated as a commoditized item by institutions and employers, students need view education purchases for what they are: purchases. This means implying the same rules and policies to education as CDs and socks purchased at the local Wal-Mart. If the production of menial goods receives a guarantee of satisfaction, the production of knowledge defining selves and whole societies should be warrantee worthy.

RESULTS

The outcomes of this study yielded many more questions and issues concerning the nature of the transfer credits and of the university than were posed. Seventeen of twenty-five Universities (68%) responded to the questionnaire; however those who responded were others than the presidents to whom the questionnaire was sent. The questionnaire seemed to be a task to be juggled and handed off to various managers and secretaries throughout university faculties and admissions. University Presidents delegated the task to their secretaries, registrar, and other members that could be of any insight to the subject. It can only be assumed that the time required for completion (about 12 minutes) was an imposition, or they did not know enough about the policies to provide accurate information regarding their formation and operation. The only University president who responded directly was from the University of Liverpool to announce that he was passing the letter over to the Chief Operating Officer of the University of Liverpool.

Most universities did not even consider the issue of the president not providing answers directly as being problematic. Cornell University (USA) was the only institution in the study whose President's secretary called and asked "if it would be keeping with the study if she had an admissions officer fill it out" (Transcript record, March 30, 2007). The President did not have time as he was currently on a trip. Only one out of twenty-five universities considered this issue and asked how it might affect the research. Most universities seemed more concerned with their image, debating the answers they would be giving and how the respondents would be linked to what was written. A representative from the University of Western

Ontario exclaimed in a phone conversation, that before filling out the survey it was important to know if they would be "quoted or associated directly with the information they provided" (Transcript record, March 29, 2007). The answer was a quick and definite response that it would be. The secretary debated verbally over the phone and finally decided that they would participate even though this condition was something to be considered. Western has yet to respond to the survey.

Trent University (Ontario, Canada) was the timeliest through the office of the registrar who was informed and open about policies in place. Answers were well framed and thought through, unlike those of the University of Windsor (Ontario, Canada) whose respondent merely jotted yes and no answers to some questions leaving others entirely blank. Windsor initially made contact by phone during which the secretary designated to answer the questionnaire exclaimed that she was confused as her University would accept anything with a "C" or better from any undergraduate year, including third and fourth, as her institution is part of the Pan-American Protocol. Most interesting, however, is that this response conflicted with information gleaned from a previous study (Arnold, 2006), as a transfer query indicated that a student must complete a full year, that is ten senior level courses, before ever qualifying for a degree. Windsor may accept nearly all credits but candidates would need to spend a year of tuition at this institution before being qualified to graduate. Overall, Western's respondent seemed bothered to have been given the task to fill this questionnaire out and find answers to questions that were not readily at hand.

Regarding policy, data from all Universities responding, with the exception of Princeton (USA) and Syracuse (USA) had a place for transfer policies under general academic regulations in their Academic Calendar. Most stated that if their University offered the credit in question and a grade of 60% or better was obtained, transfer should not be an issue. The courses offered and the amount of credit granted become enmeshed in territoriality with the implicit argument that one university offers a more prestigious range of classes than the next. In illustration, the University of Toronto responded that their transfer credit policy reads:

> Acceptance of transfer credits by the University of Toronto shall be based on the recognition that, while learning experiences may differ in a variety of ways, their substance may be virtually equivalent in terms of their content and rigour. Insofar as possible, acceptance of transfer credit shall allow for the maximum recognition of previous learning experience in university level courses. Subject to degree, grade and program requirements, any course offered for credit by a recognized university shall be accepted for credit by the University of Toronto when there is virtual equivalency in course content (Transcript record, April 10, 2007).

Equivalency is the ambiguous wording that most universities seem to use as a means of escaping what truly does and does not get transferred. Even if institutions offered a similar course and degree the granting of the credit requested would have to be equivalent to their standards. Policies obviously exist but are subjective in rule.

Out of province Canadian institutions, University of Saskatchewan, McGill University, and Memorial University, all stated that they have had a transfer credit system for decades but state nothing about that changes that have occurred over that time period. Trent University's registrar was the only respondent to state that she did not know "how long the university's transfer system had been in place, to be honest. We have tweaked the policy a few times since I arrived in July 2000. We are currently in the process of reviewing the entire policy and we will be taking a revised policy through the appropriate academic approval channels in the fall of 2007" (Transcript record, April 15, 2007).

Syracuse University represented an un-integrated circumstance of mobile education as they stated in their response that, "No university wide policy exists as each of our colleges determines its own policies" (Transcript record, April 6, 2007) and that no policy had ever existed. More surprising was the statement made by Princeton University that currently they do not admit transfer students; "our transfer program was suspended in 1990 and is not likely to be reopened in the foreseeable future" (Transcript record, April 6, 2007). Even if students were willing to drop their credits and begin anew "once already enrolled in a college or university, he or she would be ineligible to apply to Princeton as an undergraduate or to begin again as a freshman" (Transcript record, April 6, 2007). If this university was not one's first choice for post-graduate studies then he or she will not be allowed to enrol. When an appeals procedure was questioned it was stated that there was none without any rationale provided. The issue was not to be "reopened in the foreseeable future" indicating an odd form of discord and dissention between higher education and the growing global economy.

The question of formal procedures for assessing credits represented a patchwork of styles. Universities responded that these decisions were typically made by recruitment officers or the registrar but did not provide reasons for why some credits were or were not transferable and what appeal procedures may look like. Windsor, Trent, and Syracuse University responded that for domestic files, the AUCC was used to determine transferability; however no mention was made about the way international files are assessed. Michigan State (USA) had another method guiding decision-making; "courses taught by institutions listed in the American Council on Education's "Accredited Institutions of Post-secondary Education", the I.A.U. "International Handbook of Universities", and the UNESCO online database http://www.UNESCO.org\iau may be evaluated. Procedures may vary from one faculty to the next" (Transcript record, 2007). McGill however had the most interesting response to this question stating that, "in general an assessment is made of the course content by the designated evaluator who could be at the departmental or faculty level" (Transcript record, March 30, 2007). A one on one approach seems to be more appealing; however, this is also extremely subjective providing no rationale for judgment.

The number of transfer credits able to be transferred averaged at 50% at most universities as credits could be transferred for students' first and second year of schooling (ten credit maximum). Michigan State was the only university that could say that there is "no limit in the number that can be transferred although there are limits on the number of credits that may count toward a degree" (Transcript record, March 30, 2007). Most universities stated that the residency component specified in their Academic Calendar must be met and would limit the number of transfer credits allowed at any one time. Universities had no problem transferring fourth year students to their institution, when questioned upon the year one would still be allowed to transfer, they just proclaimed that most (if not all) credits would not carry over. Students would have to complete a "do-over" for those years.

Although university administrators thought their transfer policies were accurate and descriptive, all provided cookie cutter responses to the questions of whether or not students were pleased with their system. Their responses indicated that they did provide access to all stakeholders and took individual needs into account but are continually looking for ways to improve. However, only one university followed up this statement with examples of improvement initiatives. McGill explained that "by and large our system does meet the needs of students. We are always working to improve our system. Our latest initiative has been to make equivalents as transparent as possible, posting known equivalents on our web site. This initiative is constantly expanding" (Transcript record, April 18, 2007). Allowing students to see for themselves the equivalency is a positive step in improving the systems currently in place. This initiative gives students a reference on which to fall back if they have questions or perceive injustices in the ways their evaluation has been treated. This online reference represents an option to which students do not currently have access to unless completing school in an institution enrolled in the British Columbia (CDN) transfer guide. Trent University gave the most informative opinion stating:

> In the past we have not been able to provide all of the transfer credit details to students prior to the start of classes. Various delays, including volume of transfer credit files and a longer than acceptable turnaround time in departments (due to various circumstances such as a new Chair starting his/her term on July 1, right in the peak of transfer credit requests) has resulted in students not knowing their exact transfer credit assessments until October or November (Transcript record, April 4, 2007).

Students beginning school still not knowing their assessment seems unfair and disadvantageous and seems a shared trait among institutions. When asked what changes could be made to alleviate tension Trent University responded that autonomous institutions make "the possibility for a 'system' to be adopted fairly remote" (Transcript record, April 4, 2007). Another issue had to do with equivalencies, e.g., full year versus half year courses, and the idea that while at most institutions introductory courses cover much of the same material, second year courses tend to represent faculty members' interests and concerns. For smaller institutions like Trent and Brock University these specialties would be the most difficult credits to transfer as larger and similar institutions would not offer them. The timing for release of grades is also problematic slowing down the processes and steps taken when switching universities. The Coordinator of Canadian Transfer Credits at the University of Saskatchewan, thought that communication was essential and that this could be done online so that all parties would have open access to information made available.

Communicating between and among institutions and stakeholders accounts for the most part how the Bologna Project in Europe came about. When study participants were asked their opinion of this convention, many institutions cited precedent attempts. Susan Salisbury of Trent University stated that, a few years ago, Ontario institutions attempted to put together an electronic database of equivalencies, so that prospective students could see what credits they might receive at another institution, but given financial and IT constraints at institutions, as well as the complexity of the transfer credit process, the system never came to fruition (Transcript record, April 4, 2007). Tracy Wood from the University of Toronto thought that the question was worth contemplation–"a good question, for which I have no answer. There seems to be much cooperation already amongst institutions in Ontario through the Baker Report in 1994. Subsequent to that was the Pan-Canadian Protocol on the Transferability of University Credit introduced by the Council of Ministers of Education of Canada (CMEC) in 1995 and was to be implemented by each University as of September 1995 to which the University of Toronto did not sign off (Transcript record, April 10, 2007). McGill stated that the issue was currently under discussion and the University of Saskatchewan remarked that they are very aware of the benefits of the Bologna Project, and are open to the project. They encourage transfer applicants from European countries, and give them fair and reasonable recognition and transfer credit upon their applications to undergraduate or graduate study. The study sparked interest in many respondents; the University of Saskatchewan and Trent requested to be mailed the results if they were able to be shared. No response was ever received from Ontario's Minister of Education.

DISCUSSION

Forming the Modern Triptych: Trade Amongst Universities

From the perspective of students ultimately concerned with the knowledge context at the university level, most interesting for understanding an intellectual infrastructure was the formation and development of control of knowledge through access and availability as a vehicle for learning. Most visible is the trend that sees tertiary education transformed through economics, which in turn brings about change in operations. The posted values of the University displayed in online mission statements and homepages seemed seldom in full harmony with operational values shown by disconnecting institutions' slogans and academic and administrative practices.

Universities' contribution to national gross domestic product is larger than the pulp and paper industry, the forestry and logging, and such prominent manufacturing industries as the motor vehicle, furniture or plastic product industries (AUCC, 2003). The university has become over the last two decades a significant site of capital accumulation. Trade in higher education services has grown over the last few years into a market estimated in 1999 at $30 billion worldwide (Association of Universities and Colleges, 2003). In Canada, most exports of education services currently take place through foreign student enrolment in Canadian institutions (AUCC, 2003). Canadian universities are a $16 billion enterprise. At the national level, the contribution of the university sector to the Canadian gross domestic product is comparable to many major industries (AUCC, 2003).

A change in social perceptions has lead to the systematic conversion of intellectual activity into intellectual capital, and thus the term 'intellectual property' has been defined by the WTO to classify such engagements (Noble, 1998). The automation of higher education has become a battle of commercialization (Noble, 1998). The products of Wal-Mart and Corporation Yale are currently hardly deferrable; each is assigned a merchandisable number for easy tracking and quality assurance. Ministries of Education need to consider why this has occurred and what to do with the information. At the very outset of this new age of higher education, the lines have already been drawn in the struggle, which will ultimately determine its shape (Noble, 1998). On one side are administrators and their myriad of commercial partners and on the other lies the core of education, students and faculty.

Panel 1: Recruitment Promises

Those involved in the higher education are taking responsibility for informing and changing the experience for those entering. The Toronto Star recently featured an article titled "It's Time to Weigh the Offers" with the opening disclaimer advocating that "research is crucial to picking the right learning institution for your feature career" (Thomas, 2007). Toby Whitfield, a first year business management student at Ryerson University, exclaimed that he knew what he wanted to do applying to university but had no idea where to go, choosing an institution based on the breadth of information he received and mere reputation (Thomas, 2007). The issue he found he should have considered was where this university was going to take him after the course, a question most students buying in do not consider. Choosing a program and institute should not be a binding contract but rather should work as the foundation for building and understanding what one wants to achieve and the right school in which to do so.

Tyler Charlebois, director of advocacy for the College student Alliance, a group serving Ontario's college and college-university students agrees. He states that picking a program should not mean locking yourself in. Twenty years ago the view was that if you started a program you finished it but it should be looked at as building a foundation to find the right fit (Thomas, 2007). Faculty has taken this tribulation as theirs to fix and the results are being made known. Sharron and Mike McIntyre, Professors of Business at Carleton and Queen's University, have started a program called University Matters and currently field questions forming a more educated education decision (see http://www.universitymatters.ca; Thomas, 2007). They encourage students to discuss their education with someone who knows the industry and all of the "unstated(s)" it embraces. They are using the art of advertising to sell knowledge of educational programs not just the programs themselves.

Panel 2: The Un-tradable Fully Trainable Grad

Upon applying to graduate studies one may feel that they have surpassed the field of transfer territoriality; however, the opposite occurs and instead the stakes are raised. With some applied degrees being considered terminal the employment skills focused upon are not intended as preparation for graduate and professional programs. There begins a discrepancy due to membership and who as a belonging member has the right to supply a worthy program for continued study. Most of undergraduate degrees in Canada are offered by traditional universities with membership in the Association of Universities and Colleges of Canada (Ministry of Advanced Education, 2007). This AUCC membership has over time become viewed as a *de facto* indication of the quality of an institution and the programs each offers. In the past it normally coincided with the authority to offer degrees under provincial legislation (Ministry of Advanced Education, 2007). However, most of the new applied and applied bachelor degrees are located in situations that offer degree programming that that are not AUCC members. This situation has become one in which different kinds of post-secondary institutions with and without AUCC membership are offering varying degrees that have not been well defined both in content and in equivalency standardization (Ministry of Advanced Education, 2007). Universities are punching out programs that offer new features but have not been linked in terms of their application to further educational studies. Students are being used as guinea pigs in product trials masquerading as courses (Noble, 1998).

The British Columbia Council on Admissions and Transfer state in their recent publication that some Universities have refused to accept graduates with different kinds of bachelor degrees into graduate and professional programs for a number of reasons: lack of knowledge about new degrees and their content/intent, concerns about the quality and rigor of applied degree programs offered, and questions about the appropriateness of applied degrees as preparation for further study (British Columbia Council on Admissions and Transfer, 2006). With an absence of national and regional accreditation processes, some Canadian Universities are using AUCC membership status of the institution conferring the degree as a factor determining whether a student is suitable for graduate studies acceptance (BCCAT, 2006). The problem lies in the AUCC not being an accrediting agency but instead an organization where universities benefit from public policies, communications, research, and advocacy roles (BCCAT, 2006). The situation is of particular relevance to Ontario, Alberta, and British Columbia students where the provincial governments have expanded access to baccalaureate applied degrees through the non-university post-secondary sector (BCCAT, 2006). Students' options for post-secondary studies become uncontainable and so too do the meanings given to programs taken. Upon application to graduate studies students are left with open promises only to be complicated further upon later entry into the professional world.

Panel 3: The Cog

With economic entrenchment being the primary concern of Universities at the present moment it seems that what occurs with one's degree status when they have attained their qualifications is too an issue of territoriality. Transferability of qualification has become awkward, with a degree from Harvard becoming the BMW of educational degrees and one from Iran being deemed a Lada. Upon receiving one's medical degree in Iran and coming to Canada to practice, doctors have been denied the right to do so. Dr. Shahab Khanahmadi, a graduate of the Tehran University of Medical Sciences, had worked as a family physician for two years (Cornwall, 2004). He also worked as an assistant in the university neurology department's clinical electrophysiology laboratory, studying diseases such as epilepsy. But in Canada, Khanahmadi has not been able to work as a doctor. Instead, he works only as an unpaid assistant to a neurologist and as a volunteer in a family practice (Cornwall, 2004). He has become trapped in a complicated bureaucracy that seems intent on shutting out foreign-trained physicians. Khanahmadi came to Vancouver in September 2001. Because his English is flawless, he aced the language tests—written and oral—that foreign-trained doctors must pass to practice in this country (Cornwall, 2004). He also passed a series of Canadian medical exams. This year Khanahmadi applied for a residency position under the Canadian Resident Matching Service (CARMS). He got two interviews but no position. Last year British Columbia had only six positions set aside in family practice for immigrant doctors.

The provincial colleges of physicians and surgeons, which grant doctors their licenses, require that after medical school, doctors complete a residency: at least two years of hands-on training, usually in a hospital. An American residency is treated on a par with a Canadian one, but residencies in other countries are not. Joan Atlin, executive director of the Association of International Physicians and Surgeons of Ontario, estimates that Ontario has between 2000 and 4000 immigrant doctors looking for a practice. They have a right to be assessed, and if found to be qualified, they should be allowed to practice their profession. Vancouver MP Dr. Hedy Fry, a medical doctor and the parliamentary secretary to Citizenship and Immigration Minister Judy Sgro, believes that we have to look at fast-tracking: "When do we start valuing foreign experience? Europe is ahead of us on this. You can be trained in Italy and work in the United Kingdom. We're lagging" (Cornwall, 2004). Like education in Europe professionals are able to transfer vocations by moving seamlessly between countries and governments under the jurisdiction of the European Union. Doctors in North America are given two options: start over or take more courses to reach the set standard. Looking across from that first admissions application out of high school to this final scene one can see how difficult and stumbling the academic composition can become.

RE-COGNITION

The Eye Moves to See the Whole

Much like trade in lumber, ore or other commodities, education will find that the obligation and enforcement of international standards for all participants will bring about full re-conceptualization of the ends, principles and practices that characterize circumstances of learning and teaching (Kompf, 2006). A universal paradigm needs to be fashioned; whether North America conforms to Iran or vice versa growth for all needs to occur. A collaborative resolution needs to be found versus competitive ends without means. There is an arrogance associated with the university and the way it defines itself. The way one defines oneself continually changes for as the background becomes larger events change to scale and so too must the measuring stick. If Harvard is representative of the top of the scale of standardization and Iran the bottom, an educational ISO that respects the individual institution needs to be implemented. Degrees function like the automobile industry, there is no sense investing in a propane-filled car if there is nowhere to fill it in the United States. The machine created may be great but if there is no way to push it then it is no longer deemed credible, much like the grad student himself.

Arbitrating deceptions of difference is the key to allowing interchangeable products to emerge in a leveling effect similar to that of the Bologna Project. If one drives a Lada and it suddenly needs a part where is one going to be purchased if the country in which it breaks down does not manufacture that car? If there will always exist more prestigious institutions then maybe the solution is layering degrees by specialization, the "McEd degree" not as worthy as the "degree plus". Employing a universal system for ranking institutions by quality of produced "knowledged goods" will have to be developed.

We need to reframe the definition of the university and account for the affordances in academics versus economics. The aims are different and upon buying in students only become aware of this after the fact. The successful graduate student is defined as one that is employable, making the aim of the university narrow in scope or at least in its utility. The post-modern university is one we would all like to think is engaged in producing people to produce knowledge: what has happened? Thomas Kuhn's (1972) explanation would be "shift happens." This shift occurs when the governing systems of organizations become informed from the outside and not from within. For example, we drive the car we have been taught to operate only to realize that is pollutes, at which juncture we must psychologically reframe the experience society has already framed for us. This is where the conundrum lies. We invest in the illusion we have been given until we see it as an illusion.

The modern definition of academics and the university serves special interests and will most likely be resolved as an economic issue rather than as academic one. Neil Postman (1993) discussed the furthering of knowledge as it has become marketable, schools engaging in competitive positioning and matters that have little to do with education. For example, the Faculty of Education at Brock University during the spring session of 2007 ran a slogan generating competition among faculty. It was questionable whether the chosen slogan itself as well as the contest was a declaration of interest in the issue of higher learning. Instead the exercise could be construed as "branding" and thus misleading: "Live life learning". Would a slogan be needed if members of the department were able to speak of their priorities without having to hide them behind a façade? Would institutions rather take away time from faculty teaching and research to cover up their "true selves" in favour of satisfying catchy phrases? Namely, phrases that often tell little of the programs a university offers but speak endlessly to the aesthetics and perception those in charge are so determined in presenting.

CONCLUSION

Deconstructing the domains of influence for higher education is to break it into bits as a means of determining the actions of the whole. There exists at this level of education competing interests and ideologies and it is important that they are reorganized as a means of seeing what one receives. These influences and constant creators of knowledge and practice are: the spiritual, emotional, economic, practical, and academic. Consumers of education need to know and attend to these cautions. Upon completion of this study there loomed a set of warnings that if written for others could change the helpless pattern repeatedly occurring. The following is a list of the top ten concerns that students should ask before writing a tuition cheque:

- Students enrolled in an applied bachelor degree with the goal of continuing their studies past the undergraduate level should confirm and check with the institution granting the degree about admissibility to other post-secondary institutions and the transferable worth of earned credits.
- Find out what your degree means and determine whether employers recognize the accreditation of the university and program you have attended.
- Online statements about available programs may be outdated. Make sure before deciding on a program of study you gather information surrounding how that program actually runs. What benefits and pitfalls does it contain?
- Secondary school guidance counsellors do not know a university as well as the students who have attended it or currently attend it. Ask questions before signing up as alumni seldom hide behind issues of policy.
- Economic gain is most universities' prime goal as they represent corporations in an ever-expanding marketplace. Most institutions do not care if students succeed. Projections for a set number of students to fail out of programs are made each year. Institutions get tuition and funding either way.
- Only you can make your education what you would like it to be. If it does not suit you find another outlet; take concepts you wish to learn that are not taught and engage them yourself.

The University classroom, the Wal-Mart superstore, and stockpiling Costco all communally exist as locations of trade; however, in trying to play in this globalized marketplace higher education has failed to anticipate and implement the rules of international game. In trades of 'intellectual capital' tertiary education has failed to give students a valid signifier of intellectual capital, that is, a representation or a paper of currency stating the development or value of their education. Where the European Union is engaging the voice of their consumer, North American Universities have failed to comply despite the corporate learning tools they have at their expense.

REFERENCES

Arnold. (2006). *The disparities and despair of transfer credit policies.* Paper presentation to Niagara University Crossing Borders Conference, April 03, 2006.

AUCC. (2001). *Joint declaration on higher education and the general agreement on trade in services.* Association of Universities and Colleges of Canada (AUCC). Retrieved January 3, 2007, from http://www.aucc.ca

Bienefeld, S. (2001). Retrieved from http://www.aic.lv/ace/ace_disk/Bologna/contrib/ESIB/WTO_GATS_intro.pdf

Bologna Process and Declaration. (1999). Retrieved from http://www.europa.eu.int/comm/education/policies/educ/bologna/bologna_en.html

Cornwall, C. (2004). Reader's Digest. *Why is Canada shutting out doctors: While millions of Canadians can't find a doctor, thousands of foreign physicians can't get a licence to practise.* Retrieved March 30, 2007, from http://www.readersdigest.ca/mag/2004/08/doctors.html

Knight, J. (2002). *Trade in higher education: The implications of GATS.* Retrieved March 15, 2006, from J Stor database.

Kompf, M. (2006). *The end of adult education in Finland.* Paper presentation televised to the universities of Helsinki, Oulu, Joensuu & Lapland, April 03, 2006.

Kuhn, T. S. (1970). *The structure of scientific revolutions* (2nd ed.). Chicago: University of Chicago Press.

Ministry of Advanced Education. (2007). *AUCC 2006–07 annual report.* Retrieved March 22, 2007, from http://www.bccat.bc.ca

Noble, D. F. (1998). Digital diploma mills:- The automation of higher education. *First Monday Online Internet Journal.* Retrieved February 2, 2006, from http://www.firstmonday.org/issues/issue3_1/noble/

Ontario Ministry of Education. (2005). *Ontario universities: Your gateway to higher learning.* Retrieved March 22, 2005, from http://www.edu.gov.on.ca/eng/general/postsec/univers.html

Postman, N. (1993). *Technopoly: The surrender of culture to technology.* New York: Vintage Books.

Thomas, E. (2007, Thursday March 29). It's time to weigh the offers. *The Toronto Star.*

World Trade Organization. (2005). *Frequently asked questions about TRIPS in the WTO.* Retrieved December 22, 2006, from http://www.wto.org/english/tratop_e/trips_e/tripfq_e.htm

Christine Arnold
Faculty of Education
Brock University

Michael Kompf
Faculty of Education
Brock University

SHUKRI SANBER, JUDE BUTCHER, TONY STEEL, GRAHAM ENGLISH, KRISTIN JOHNSTON, PAT O'GORMAN, BETH RIOLO & MARK RAUE

PUBLIC ACCOUNTABILITY, RELIGIOUS LITERACY AND STUDENT LEARNING

INTRODUCTION

In the past decade or so, a number of themes have gradually moved to centre-stage in the thinking, planning and practice of teachers and educational administrators in the English-speaking world. Terms such as outcomes, targets and benchmarking have taken their place in the register of education.

Many of these concerns flow from increasing calls for accountability from funding sources such as governments, from system authorities, from the media and from the public in general. They want to know what return might be expected from the investments made in education, and whether those expectations are being met. As a result, there is increasing attention given to assessment of student performance, and program evaluation.

In Australia numerous system-wide assessment regimes have been developed to assess students in basic literacy and numeracy skills at various points in their educational experience. In the state of New South Wales, for example, the Basic Skills Tests (BST) (basic skills test) in years 3 and 5; and English Language and Literacy Assessment (ELLA) and Secondary Numeracy Assessment Programs (SNAP) in years 7 and 8 have been used in both government and non-government schools.

Those educators involved in Religious Education (RE) have not been exempt from these trends and in Australia a number of Catholic diocesan school systems have implemented some form of system wide assessment of students.

There are several reasons for this. Firstly, in Australian Catholic schools there has been a strong desire to see Religious Education accorded similar esteem and credibility as that enjoyed by other subjects in the curriculum. As it is not part of the program of study prescribed by the State, and because it has not been assessed in the public domain, Religious Education has sometimes been treated as a 'soft' subject, especially when hard decisions have to be made about the allocation of scarce time and/or resources in the curriculum. Religious educators have seen assessment in religious education as a way of giving greater credibility to the subject.

Secondly, some parents also display certain ambivalence about the importance of Religious Education and this may be picked up by their children. If Religious Education incorporates a rigorous assessment process, parents and students may be

J. A. Kentel and A. Short (eds.), Totems and Taboos: Risk and Relevance in Research on Teachers and Teaching, 129–140.

helped to see its central place in the total educational experience of a student in a Catholic school and accord it a higher value.

Thirdly, teachers have seen the value of assessment in other subject areas in supporting teaching and learning and realized that it could and should offer similar benefits in Religious Education. Finally, Church officials have asked what return might be expected from the significant financial and human investments made by the Catholic community in its schools? Similar questions have also been asked by an increasingly vocal segment of the Catholic community. It is not unreasonable to infer that some of the initial impetus to move to diocesan testing may have been to respond to concerns such as these.

In the light of these factors, assessment has been increasingly viewed as a valuable strategy in Religious Education for the purposes of accountability and enhancing student learning.

ASSESSMENT IN RELIGIOUS EDUCATION

Religious Education in schools occurs in a variety of contexts, and with a variety of purposes. In Catholic schools in Australia religious education is part of the core curriculum studied by all students. It is often based on programs developed at a diocesan level and has a specifically Catholic character.

In this sense, religious education in Catholic schools is concerned with more than imparting knowledge about religion. It also serves as a medium of enculturating students into a Catholic understanding of life and the world, and inviting them into participation in the faith community.

Such a purpose suggests a broader horizon for assessment of competence and understanding about what it means to be Catholic, and how to participate in the heritage and life of the Catholic community rather than mere knowledge and its application. This is not to suggest any assessment instrument or procedure can or should measure whether a student 'has faith', a gift from God to be nurtured within the faith community. What can be measured, it is proposed, is the student's competence to engage with the faith community, its beliefs, traditions and practices.

Such an assessment initiative is the subject of this chapter. The Religious Literacy Assessment Project, a collaboration between the Wollongong Catholic Education Office (CEO) and Australian Catholic University (ACU) is one element of a larger initiative, Partners in Learning which came about as an outcome of the conversation taking place within Wollongong CEO and the schools of the diocese about the nature of literacy in general, and how literacy can best be fostered in schools.

Two major purposes of the Religious Literacy Assessment Project are: (i) to develop a practical assessment and reporting system that would help in gathering information about the process of learning in Religious Education; and (ii) to profile student performance in Religious Education at the end of Stage 2 of primary school (i.e. Year 4).

This placement of the assessment in Year 4 is important. It reflects the formative purpose of the Diocese's assessment, offering the opportunity to remedy gaps in learning while the students are still in primary school. This can inform the Religious

Education teaching so that it can be more focused and thereby more effective. This formative purpose contrasts with summative assessment such as if the assessment occurred in Year 6. In the latter case the assessment would be reporting on the end performance of students who will soon transition out of their primary school into high school.

With these foundational understandings the Religious Literacy Assessment Project was embarked upon.

CONCEPTUALISING THE PROJECT

A key strength of the Religious Literacy Assessment Project was the engagement of those in the field in its development from the very beginning. In this way the voices of those with significant responsibility for quality teaching and learning in religious education helped to shape the project.

In 2000 two think tanks were held, the first with the leadership group of Wollongong Catholic Education Office, and the second with fourteen selected RE practitioners, including some CEO personnel and teachers and RE Co-ordinators in schools.

Participants in the Think Tanks were invited into a number of activities:

- general discussion on applying a religious literacy framework to Religious Education, and suggesting what some expressions of religious literacy might be for particular stages in the primary school;
- responding to questions about the good news, hopes and challenges of Religious Education learning and assessment at the school level; and
- small group discussion on the good news, hopes and challenges of Religious Education learning and assessment at a diocesan level.

The information gathered from the Think Tanks was complemented by Case Study interviews held in four primary schools, one from each of the four geographical regions of the diocese. The schools were also representative of a range of other considerations including socioeconomic factors, school size and school type, such as schools that were well established, newer schools and those experiencing recent population growth.

Following discussion with teachers in staff meetings, researchers interviewed the Principal, the Religious Education Co-ordinator and teachers from Years 2, 4 and 6 in each school. These people were asked three questions:

- With your experience of teaching literacy do you think this concept and the methods that flow from it have anything to offer as an approach to Religious Education in schools?
- What would be the indicators that a student in the class you teach was religiously literate?
- Would you talk about what and how you can fairly assess in Religious Education classes?

Clear indications emerged from the Think Tanks and the Case Study interviews, that there was much good news about Religious Education learning and assessment as it was occurring in the diocese's schools, while nonetheless acknowledging some gaps in the understanding and process.

Strong themes of hope emerged in regard to both learning and assessment. For assessment some of the hopes were that assessment in RE would lead to better RE; that it be seen as part of the RE context; that it become integrated into the units of work; that RE be given the same importance as other KLAs; that it be relevant, and that a student's personal spirituality not be seen as under assessment.

Some of the challenges identified related to professional development of teachers, in particular supporting them to understand the purposes and usefulness of assessment in RE. Others were related to the importance of recognizing multiple domains of learning, and therefore utilizing multiple assessment strategies.

There was openness to the idea of applying the concept of literacy to Religious Education. A number of reasons were suggested: because of the many and diverse genres of literature and communication involved; the opportunities for integration; its potential for a more inclusive approach to students and the curriculum; and its relationship to culture.

The teachers were also able to offer indicators of religious literacy, in the forms of knowledge, skills, attitudes and behaviours of students. They also saw benefits in integrating the insights of literacy teaching and assessment in general, into religious education.

RELIGIOUS LITERACY AND THE RELIGIOUS LITERACY FRAMEWORK

In the light of these conversations 'religious literacy' was adopted as the framework for Religious Education assessment in the primary schools of Wollongong Diocese. So what exactly is religious literacy?

The term religious literacy refers to those literacies within the discourses of religion: the integration of reading, writing, listening, speaking, viewing, drawing, music, movement and critical thinking in recognizably appropriate religion-specific ways. In the case of Catholicism, the metaphor explicates the shared experience of participation in the Church.

Religious literacy is about understanding, participating and communicating. This understanding, participating and communicating happens between members of the group, between the group and its texts, and between the group, individuals and God. It encompasses knowledge, practices, strategies and skills for communicating within a Catholic community. In common parlance, being religiously literate requires children leaving a Catholic primary school to be able to communicate with and be at home in Catholic society, and religion in general.

The Diocesan Religious Education program is designed to help students:

- Gain access to and understand the traditions of the Catholic community, its story, its experience and its teachings;
- Make sense of everyday life experiences in the broader context of mystery, complexity, confusion and awe;
- Celebrate the traditions of the Catholic faith community with others; and
- Respond to the activity of God in their lives and in the whole of creation.

(Diocese of Wollongong Religious Education Curriculum, 2004)

As with other Key Learning Areas in New South Wales, the program is outcomes based. The outcomes have been grouped into three clusters:

- *Knowledge and understanding* of eight key concepts of the Catholic Community, namely God – Father, God – Jesus, God – Holy Spirit, Church, Prayer and Worship, Sacraments, Sacred Scripture, and Christian life.
- *Reasoning, and practical and social skills* essential for effective processing of religious communications and stimuli, including critical reflection, investigating and information gathering, analysing, interpreting and communicating, social and religious participation, and relating to God, self and others.
- *Attitudes and values* towards God's creation and presence, religious identity, spiritual heritage, Scripture, and Catholic tradition.

To reflect the role of Religious Education with respect to religious literacy in the Catholic tradition the research team developed a second set of classifications for religious literacy outcomes. These are:

- *Knowing the tradition* (knowledge and understanding outcomes);
- *Working with tradition* (reasoning skills), *applying the tradition* (practical and social skills), and
- *Valuing the tradition* (attitudes and values).

These four categories provided a basis for addressing the range of student outcomes associated with religious education.

To report upon the level of achievement of these outcomes by students, the following performance levels and their descriptors were adopted:

- *Developing*: in which student performance is largely within the outcomes for knowing the tradition and their responses are likely to suggest areas of knowledge and understanding that need more attention in the future.
- *Achieving*: in which student performance is occurs largely across the outcomes for knowing and working with the tradition.
- *Extending*: in which student performance occurs across the outcomes for knowing, working with and applying the tradition.

This reporting framework is simple in structure, informative and commonly used in reporting literacy standards in schools and is therefore familiar to teachers, students and parents.

METHODOLOGY – THE 'HOW' OF THE PROJECT

The research team, in consultation with primary teachers and religious education coordinators, expanded the Diocesan syllabus outcomes into more comprehensive lesson outcomes as an initial step in implementing the assessment framework for religious literacy. These lesson outcomes contained the targeted content and performance standards that can be easily translated into tasks which students could perform.

The instruments for assessing religious literacy were to be in two parts. The first, Part A, was to consist of a variety of selection type items and short-response questions while the second, Part B, was an extended task for which students could choose their own ways and modes of responding to the question.

In 2004, Year 4 classes in five schools were selected for the pilot implementation of the religious literacy assessment instrument. A Teacher Handbook was prepared with instructions for both Part A and Part B of the instrument. Part A was administered across five schools under standard assessment conditions on the same day, at same time and with the same set of instructions for teachers and students. Part B was completed by all Year 4 students in the pilot schools across a two week period.

Guidelines and marking criteria were developed to mark student responses for both parts of the religious literacy assessment instrument. These guidelines and criteria were trialled. The participating teachers participated in the trial and in the evaluation of the assessment process.

WHAT HAVE WE LEARNED FROM THE RELIGIOUS LITERACY ASSESSMENT PROJECT?

Analysis of the data gathered in the 2004 pilot program led to the development of a series of recommendations regarding both the religious literacy of students and the assessment instrument. Strong indications emerged of the project's value in assisting teachers to identify gaps in learning and how those gaps might be filled. Among other things, the recommendations indicated content areas needing further development and suggested teaching strategies to improve student performance.

Further recommendations about the assessment instrument proposed the continued use of Diocesan-wide assessment procedures (including Parts A and B of the instrument); affirmed the collaborative partnership of the project between the Catholic Education Office and Australian Catholic University; and proposed avenues for further development of the instrument and refinement of the marking and analysis protocols (Butcher et al., 2005).

Subsequently there have been two further implementations of the assessment, in 2005, 2006, and 2007 in all primary schools of the Diocese. Analysis of the 2005 data again identified strengths and weaknesses in the Religious Education learning of students and provided teachers with some clear indicators for future attention:

- Students performed well in their knowledge of the tradition particularly in the areas of: Saints, prayers and the events of Holy Week. More attention seems to be needed in the areas of the seasons of the Church's liturgical year and the sacraments. Students need assistance in recalling and re-presenting their knowledge in different formats such as presenting the correct sequences of the events. Attending to different formats is also applicable to students working with their knowledge of the tradition.
- Students worked satisfactorily with their knowledge of the tradition in the areas of: the creation story, Mary and the Annunciation, objects in the Church, parts of the Mass and the story of Zacchaeus. More attention seems to be needed in students' working with their knowledge of the tradition in the areas of: significance of the Mass, the Eucharist, commandments, and the Easter story. The analysis showed the importance of teachers developing explicitly students' capacity to work with their knowledge of the tradition across different terminologies and language contexts.
- A small number of students showed how successful students can be in articulating developed and well-founded reasons for their application of their knowledge of the tradition. The Diocese and individual schools are advised to

examine how much formal attention is given to students applying their knowledge of the tradition. For this outcome it is important that students are given appropriate scaffolding to develop their capacity to explain or justify their applications of the knowledge (Butcher, Sanber, O'Gorman, Raue, & Riolo, 2006).

The detailed reporting approach to the teachers and the Diocese indicates the formative nature of the Religious Literacy Assessment. By identifying strengths and weaknesses in students' performance, the reports indicate those areas of the curriculum needing further attention, and also suggest strategies to be adopted to address the gaps. This information informs the refinement of the practice of teachers and opens the way for significant improvements in student learning.

Following the successful implementations in 2005 and 2006 a number of recommendations were proposed for the continued use of the Religious Literacy Assessment data for formative and diagnostic purposes. These recommendations include, among others, The Religious Literacy Project Team work with schools on the analysis of their school data in order to:

- Use data to inform innovation and change;
- Inform the review of teaching practice and assessment in religious education;
- Challenge and influence pedagogy;
- Provide quality feedback;
- Focus on professional learning; and
- Reflect on the teacher as a leader of learning.

Part B continues to be developed and refined to:

- Explore more effective ways of showcasing and celebrating;
- Enhance student achievement and learning;
- Drive support for learning and teaching in the RE classroom; and
- Influence integration across a range of key learning areas (Butcher et al., 2006).

In addition to the focus on the content of students' performance, the assessment data also allowed analysis of student performance across the Diocese on the basis of factors such as gender, age, English speaking background, country of origin, church attendance, and literacy results on the Basic Skills Test (BST).

It was clear that there were statistically significant differences in students' performances with respect to the extent of use of English at home, their literacy performance as measured by BST literacy scores, church attendance and gender.

This type of data informs the quality of teaching and learning by indicating where additional attention needs to be focused in order to enhance the performance of those in the lower levels of achievement.

In each of the implementations of the Religious Literacy Assessment Project the teachers involved have been asked to complete an evaluation of the tasks and the process of the assessment. Their responses indicate a broad acceptance of the assessment process and an active engagement with it in terms of both their planning and teaching, and the administration of the assessment instrument.

The teachers' comments identified challenges or difficulties they or their students may have encountered, and professional insights they have come to, through participation in the assessment. The comments showed a depth of reflection on professional practice which has the potential to enhance significantly their teaching and in some cases already has done so. From such reflection and action, the learning outcomes of students will be improved.

In all of this an implementation – review – planning - implementation cycle of professional practice in assessing religious literacy has emerged which informs ongoing refinement and development of the Project, and contributes to its credibility among the various stakeholders.

CREDIBILITY OF THE RELIGIOUS LITERACY ASSESSMENT PROJECT

Four criteria were developed to evaluate the credibility of the Project. They are:
- Assessing the full range of student outcomes presented for religious education;
- Fostering the intrinsic role of assessment for enhancing teaching and learning;
- Serving the accountability requirements to stakeholders; and
- Being informed and owned by the stakeholders, and in particular, the teachers. (Sanber et al., 2005)

It can be plainly demonstrated that each of these criteria have been met in the Religious Literacy Assessment Project.

Assessing the Full Range of Student Outcomes

By addressing the four sets of learning outcomes identified earlier (knowing the tradition, working with the tradition, applying the tradition, valuing the tradition) the assessment has been designed to measure students' achievements in the major learning domains.

In collaboration with a sample of teachers and coordinators, a table is developed for specifying the extent of coverage of the different strands or concepts of the syllabus and the types of student outcomes to be emphasized in each of these strands. This specification of content and outcomes is represented as the percentage weighting assigned to each cell or element in the table (See Table 1).

Table 1. Specifying weightings to be allocated across assessment tasks

Key concepts	Knowing the tradition	Working with the tradition	Applying the tradition	Valuing the tradition	Total concept weights
Advent					10
Creation					15
Easter					15
Eucharist					10
Lent					10
Pentecost					10
Prayer					15
Relationships					15
Total processing weights	30	30	20	20	100

The table thus provided a framework, which assisted in generating assessment tasks that reflected the breadth of the curriculum and the depth of the treatment of its key concepts.

The range of different forms of assessment tasks in Part A such as multiple choice, matching and short answer questions involved students in a range of processes including recalling and/or recognising information, applying knowledge to new situations, and analysing situations from the perspectives of other people.

The open-ended nature of the extended task in Part B, and the option for students to respond and present their learning in a variety of modes recognizes the different learning styles among students and opens opportunity for creativity in the assessment process. This contributes to ensuring that the assessment is attentive to a broad range of outcomes.

Enhancing Teaching and Learning

Throughout this paper it has been shown that assessment of religious literacy has significantly enhanced teaching and learning in Religious Education. By providing clear evidence of students' learning and identifying gaps in that learning, the assessment informs the future practice of teachers to optimize learning outcomes for students.

This evidence-based professional activity is similar to that undertaken in other areas of the curriculum, and so serves the additional purpose of putting Religious Education on a similar professional level to secular subjects, thereby raising the profile and esteem of RE in the eyes of teachers, students and parents.

Beyond its value for informing planning and classroom practice, the assessment also provides information on teacher strengths and weaknesses in working with the curriculum. This is important in decision-making about professional development priorities for teachers in Religious Education.

Accountability to Stakeholders

Because the assessment provides objective data on student performance, it allows for evidence-based reporting to major stakeholders. In days gone by evaluation of the effectiveness of Religious Education was often anecdotal, relying on teacher perceptions and parental satisfaction. Others may have looked to Sunday church attendance as a measure of effectiveness. This approach is fraught with difficulty, running the risk of equating personal religiosity (or that of a family) with effective Religious Education. Also, for a number of complex sociological reasons church attendances in Australia continue to decline, even though the popularity of Catholic schools increases.

By providing evidence of student performance linked directly to the official Religious Education curriculum, the assessment provides evidence to the Bishop, the 'chief teacher' in the Diocese, and to the Catholic Education Office of the extent to which the curriculum's outcomes are being achieved.

The Religious Literacy Team prepares detailed reports of student performance on the religious literacy assessment tasks. Individual student reports are forwarded to the schools for presentation to the students' parents/carers. These reports provide information about the student levels of achievement for Parts A and B, an indication of their overall religious literacy performance on a continuum from 1-9 and the diocesan mean for comparison. The assessment of students' work for Part B was informed by a structured mark sheet and set of criteria. Sample work from each school was displayed at a central place and discussed by Religious Education Coordinators as a means of moderating the marking across the schools.

Comprehensive reports of the individual student's achievement and the school cohort's achievements were forwarded to each school. The school data included the distribution of student responses to each question, their achievement of the different indicators, and their performance levels. A comprehensive report on student performance was presented to the Diocesan Director and subsequently used as a basis for reporting to the Diocesan Catholic Schools' Council and the Bishop.

The annual review of the assessment process and data has informed the development and implementation of the assessment tools and procedures for the following year. The examination of the data across 2005 and 2006 informed the team's understanding of student performance across the different cohorts.

This assessment cycle of develop instruments, assess, analyse, report, and review is integral to the Religious Literacy Project. Differences in the performances of Year 4 students over different calendar years inform the schools' and system's understanding of changes or developments in learning outcomes achieved.

At a more local level, the assessment provides data to school communities and teachers about the performance of their own students, which can be compared with the mean performance of the Year 4 students across the Diocese.

The research team has relied upon anecdotal data from teachers and other stakeholders for reviewing the assessment process. Quantitative survey procedures need to be built into the feedback process, so as to access comprehensive data about the impact of the Religious Literacy Project upon teaching and learning at the levels of the student, class, school and system. Data are also needed about the perceptions of parents/carers regarding the student profile information they receive. Similar data are needed from the Diocese itself.

Informed and Owned by Teachers and Other Stakeholders

Finally, the credibility of the Religious Literacy Assessment project is illustrated by the fact that it was owned and informed by teachers and other stakeholders. From its very beginning the Project has been characterised by dialogue and collaborative activity, as this paper has clearly indicated.

Teachers saw the value of a literacy-based approach to religious education and emphasized the importance of principles and practices from literacy assessment being incorporated in assessment of students in religious education. While the research team did not interview parents, school staff reported how parents were appreciative of the emphasis on assessment in religious education (Butcher et al., 2002).

The research team had regular meetings with a core group of principals, religious education coordinators and teachers. They were involved in:

- The development of performance indicators and outcomes;
- Decisions regarding the placement of the assessment at the end of stage 2 (Year 4) of schooling, types of items and tasks; and
- Proposing the structure of the assessment package into Part A (with standardised administration and marking across the diocese) and Part B (school based with diocesan moderation).

The Director of Wollongong CEO and other CEO staff extended engagement with stakeholders beyond the groups who met with the research team. The Director had responsibility for keeping the Bishop informed. The Head of Religious Education Services was responsible for informing the Religious Education Committee of the Wollongong Catholic Schools Council and through that Committee the Council itself.

The priority given to stakeholder ownership by CEO, the core group from the schools, and the schools involved in the pilot study created a climate for open discussion and critique of proposals with the research team.

A PLATFORM OF HOPE FOR THE FUTURE

As this paper has demonstrated, throughout three successful implementation cycles the Religious Literacy Assessment Project has impacted very positively upon the teaching of Religious Education within the primary schools of the Diocese of Wollongong.

Because the Project is evidenced based, it provides teachers with concrete directions whereby they can enhance the teaching of Religious Education and improve the learning outcomes for students. This offers hope for continued improvement in the religious literacy of the students.

The assessment offers students the possibility of demonstrating competence in a variety of learning styles. It challenges them not only to gain knowledge, but also to work with, apply and value the religious tradition. This is a holistic vision of religious education and alerts students to the realization that religion and its practice are more than just 'knowing what you believe', so that they will see the connections between their faith and their everyday life. This offers the real hope that students will grow to become people whose religious literacy will inspire and equip them to make a positive difference in their world.

The language of the descriptors used for reporting student achievement is worth noting. The terms developing, achieving and extending carry no hint of pass or fail, but place students along a continuum, which recognizes current achievement and invites further development. This too is an expression of hope, since all students can be invited and challenged to continue to grow, even those who are already achieving at high levels.

Finally, the participation of those involved in the Religious Literacy Assessment Project–Bishop, CEO personnel, ACU research team, principals, coordinators, teachers and students - evidences a strong commitment to Religious Education and the development of religious literacy in Catholic schools. This is indeed a source of hope for the future of Catholic education and the Church, reflecting both a profound belief in the distinctively religious character of the Catholic school and a commitment to educational excellence and professional practice not only in the secular subjects of the curriculum, but also in that endeavour which sits at the heart of the Catholic school.

Religious literacy suggests a new way of conceptualizing the outcomes of religious education. Assessment of religious literacy provides the evidence upon which teacher practice may be enhanced and the learning outcomes of students improved.

The public accountability, which is being addressed through the Religious Literacy Project is focused upon informing the professional learning and development of teachers and enhancing student learning in Religious Education. Reporting upon the results of students' performances to stakeholders will indeed continue to be 'good news'.

REFERENCES

Butcher, J., English, G., Johnston, K., & Sanber, S. (2002). *Partners in learning. Assessment of religious literacy for primary schools*. Sydney: Australian Catholic University.

Butcher, J., Sanber, S., English, G., Raue, M., O'Gorman, P., & Riolo, B. (2005). *Assessment of religious literacy year four students. Pilot study. Joint project of Diocese of Wollongong Catholic Education Office and Australian Catholic University*. Sydney: Australian Catholic University.

Butcher, J., Sanber, S., O'Gorman, P., Raue, M., & Riolo, B. (2006). *Partners in learning religious literacy assessment project – Year 4, 2005*. Joint project of Catholic Education Office, Wollongong and ACU National.

Diocese of Wollongong. (2004). *Religious education curriculum: Primary content document*. Wollongong: Diocese of Wollongong Catholic Education Office.

Sanber, S., Butcher, J., English, G., Johnston, K., O'Gorman, P., Riolo, B., et al. (2005). Assessing religious literacy: Promoting credibility in religious education. In J. Clark & M. Maguire (Eds.), *Challenges for the profession: Perspectives and directions for teachers, teaching and teacher education*. Proceedings of the 12th ISATT International Conference, 3–6 July, Sydney, International Study Association on Teachers and Teaching, New South Wales, pp. 337–344.

Shukri Sanber, Jude Butcher, Tony Steel, Graham English and Kristin Johnston
Australian Catholic University National

Pat O'Gorman, Beth Riolo and Mark Raue
Wollongong Catholic Education Office

SUE MORÓN-GARCÍA

TALKING TEACHING: ENGAGING ENGINEERS

INTRODUCTION

The Engineering Centre for Excellence in Teaching and Learning (engCETL) is one of the seventy-four Centres for Excellence in Teaching and Learning (CETLs) created by the Higher Education Funding Council for England (HEFCE) in 2005. The CETL initiative was created "to recognize, celebrate and promote excellence by rewarding teachers who have made a demonstrable impact on student learning and who can enthuse, motivate and influence others to do the same" (Beaty, 2005, p. 9). It was intended to create some balance in a system where rewards (such as promotion and funding) are seen to be skewed in favour of those focusing on subject specific research rather than those engaged in learning and teaching and pedagogic research.

Staff associated with departments located in the Faculty of Engineering at Loughborough University, a research intensive university located in the English East Midlands, together with engineering-related departments in the other two faculties, the Engineering Education Centre (EEC) and the Higher Education Academy (HEA) Engineering Subject Centre put together a successful bid which won funding for the engCETL. This paper explains the origin and focus of the engCETL and the role of pedagogic research within this before going on to illustrate how engCETL is beginning to "acquire and utilise a capacity to draw in pedagogic research and evaluation and to undertake research into its own practice" (HEFCE, 2004, p. 2) in order to demonstrate impact. This is an account of my experience as an educational researcher employed by engCETL to develop the pedagogic research capacity of the Centre.

THE ENGINEERING CENTRE FOR EXCELLENCE IN TEACHING AND LEARNING (ENGCETL)

Origins

The engCETL evolved out of the Engineering Education Centre (EEC) which itself grew out of a support centre created by the Faculty of Engineering at Loughborough towards the end of 1997. This centre brought together staff already working within faculty departments to support learning and teaching, mainly through the development of learning technology tools. The aim was to create a critical mass of expertise and avoid duplication of effort. The Faculty committed to funding three core staff members and wrote the centre into its strategy, whilst making it clear that there was a need to bring in income to ensure longevity.

J. A. Kentel and A. Short (eds.), Totems and Taboos: Risk and Relevance in Research on Teachers and Teaching, 141–152.

The support centre bid successfully for various learning, teaching and learning technology funds growing and evolving into the Engineering Education Centre (EEC). During this time the Engineering Faculty also became the home of the Higher Education Academy's (HEA) Engineering Subject Centre (engsc). The HEA is a centrally funded national body in the United Kingdom (UK) with a "mission ... to help institutions, discipline groups and all staff to provide the best possible learning experience for their students" (http://www.heacademy.ac.uk/aboutus). The HEA provides support for the disciplines through its distributed network of subject specific centres. These are hosted by higher education institutions across the UK. In March 2005 staff associated with the EEC and the engsc formed a key element of the successful bid for HEFCE CETL funding.

Focus

The two-stage engCETL bid focused on addressing criticism of engineering education by various national reports. Issues raised included the lack of involvement of employers in the curriculum (Lambert, 2003) and found that a skills shortage was being created by "poor experiences of science and engineering education among students generally, coupled with a negative image of, and inadequate information about, careers arising from the study of science and engineering ..." and that "science and engineering graduates' and postgraduates' education does not lead them to develop the transferable skills and knowledge required by R&D employers" (Roberts, 2002, p. 2).

Therefore the engCETL focused on capturing the way industry input into the curriculum and student learning in order to make these processes sustainable and transferable. It was tasked with "build[ing] on the existing experience of the Engineering Education Centre (EEC) transforming a development and support centre to a research, development and support centre that is a beacon of excellence in learning and teaching" (Loughborough University, 2004, p. 1). Its goal is to be "recognised as the UK centre for excellence in the research, development and provision of engineering education through an active involvement with industry" (engCETL Strategic Plan 2007/8, May 2007).

A key aim for the engCETL is the development of "the pedagogy of engineering education and engineering employment" (Loughborough University, 2004, p. 10) and as such pedagogic research was listed in the bid documents as one of the seven strands of engCETL work alongside: Curriculum Design and Development, Learning Support, Student Impact, Industry Impact, Transfer of Practice and Evaluation. The roles of those who were expected to undertake the work (a post-doctoral researcher and three PhD students) were also listed, as were the initial research areas (the themes of excellence that characterise the engCETL: design projects, skills development for industry, sandwich placements, sponsorship schemes and work in resource development). The following section examines the challenges presented by a need to conduct pedagogic research.

PEDAGOGIC RESEARCH AT ENGCETL

The Pedagogic Researcher

I was employed as the engCETL's pedagogic researcher and right from the start I was told that pedagogic research was "central to what we do". However, it soon became clear that it was characterised and understood as a discrete area for work, rather than something that informs and underpins other work, and that it was a problematic concept for many of my colleagues working within the engCETL and some of the academics working with us. Typically I would be told that they did not understand what the term meant, what my role was and they could not say the word pedagogy; this despite many of them having previously attended an introductory workshop on pedagogic research methods. This reflected reported "sceptic[ism] about the benefits that can be derived from generic pedagogic research" (Loughborough University, 2004, p. 15) and anxiety arising from a change in the underlying unit's (the original EEC) purpose. My task was clear: I had to help both colleagues and academics see the relevance of pedagogic research to their work and explain how it should inform and underpin what we do. I began by trying to unpack what is meant by pedagogic research in order to relate it to what we and academics associated with us were doing.

Unpacking Pedagogic Research

Pedagogy is recognized as a contested term (Cannon, 2001) and for some andragogy (Brookfield, 1986; Knowles, 1984; Smith, 1996; 1999) is the preferred word in the context of higher education. While Stierer and Antoniou "define pedagogy simply as 'the processes and relationships of learning and teaching'" (2004, p. 277), Shirley Booth (2004) uses pedagogy to

> signify particular sorts of meetings between students, teachers and knowledge, where there is an intention to learn.... [and she intends it] to be less encompassing than "education" which can include institutions, political and professional regulations, and the needs and demands of society, as well as pedagogy. (p. 22)

The engCETL aims seem to encompass not only pedagogy but 'education' as explained in Booth's definition because of the link to professional qualifications and a desire to impact across the institution. The work is also highly contextualised within the institution and the focus that has been set: working with seven engineering-related departments across three faculties, with an industry focus. Nevertheless we stuck with the term pedagogic research at engCETL, perhaps because that is the term favoured by HEFCE, other funding bodies and the Research Assessment Exercise (RAE, see http://www.rae.ac.uk). An engCETL aim is to be returnable under a future RAE so the definition used by RAE documents is an important indicator of what is required. In the 2008 RAE pedagogic research in higher education (HE) is defined as:

- Research which enhances theoretical and/or conceptual understanding of:
- teaching and learning processes in HE;
- teacher and learner experiences in HE;
- the environment or contexts in which teaching and learning in HE take place;
- teaching and learning outcomes in HE;
- the relationships between these processes, outcomes and contexts.

Those wishing to submit are advised that:

> Reports of studies providing descriptive and anecdotal accounts of teaching developments and evaluations do not constitute pedagogic research. Pedagogic research is firmly situated in its relevant literature, and high quality pedagogic research makes a substantial contribution to that literature. (HEFCE, HEFCW, SFC, & DfEL, 2006, p. 8)

The key phrase in the RAE documents is "descriptive and anecdotal accounts of teaching developments and evaluations do not constitute pedagogic research. Pedagogic research is firmly situated in its relevant literature" (HEFCE, HEFCW, SFC, & DfEL, 2006, p. 8). Ashwin and Trigwell (2004) explain the nature of pedagogical scholarship and the place of "research" within this as a hierarchical relationship. Research is externally verifiable and contributes to public knowledge while other forms of investigation or scholarly activity contribute either to personal knowledge, being verified by oneself, or local knowledge and used to inform a group within a shared context and therefore verified by those within that context.

Prosser, during his tenure as Director of Research and Evaluation of the HEA, used Boyer's (1990) influential analysis of research and teaching in higher education to draw a distinction between pedagogic research as defined by the RAE and other "evidence-informed scholarship that can inform our understanding of, and help [...] to improve student learning experiences" (Prosser, 2005, p. 8). These other categories of scholarship were listed as: "investigations and evaluations, literature reviews and the scholarship of teaching and learning" (ibid.). All of them are described as evidence-based and informed by the literature, for example, "Investigations and evaluations [can] enhance our understanding of a local problem or issue, providing recommendations for policy and/or action firmly situated in the relevant literature" (Prosser, 2005, p. 8). This would describe much of the work being conducted at engCETL.

Sceptical Academics

For those of us in the pedagogic research community the importance of using the literature on teaching and learning to inform or reflect on practice (Brew, 2003; Ramsden, 1992) may be obvious. However many of our fellow academics remain to be convinced: they know they teach well, they can prove this with reference to student feedback, QAA teaching review scores, employer satisfaction and professional body endorsement (Loughborough University, 2004). From their point of view there are plenty of "good reasons" not to: workload related time pressures, an imperative to prioritise subject-based research in a research intensive university, unwillingness to change teaching that is working, innovation fatigue and perhaps more fundamentally, a perception that pedagogic research is not rigorous, serious research. While we know that "There is no one thing, not even a set of things, that research is" (Brew, 2001, p. 21), it is acknowledged that in pedagogic research we demonstrate rigour by explaining our methodological approach and the context of our enquiry so that others may judge for themselves, this often proves uncomfortable to those unfamiliar with social science methods (Canning, 2007). Unpacking what we mean by pedagogic research enabled me to identify some of the possible barriers to understanding, which facilitated later work, described in the following section.

Another difficult issue for academics working with engCETL is the realisation that pedagogic research can be messy and quite difficult to measure because it involves, among other things, the study of people, their actions and their perceptions, and as such "is infused with assumptions about the social world and is influenced by the researcher" (Burgess, 1984, p. 2). There are some tools and inventories that can help with measurement; for example the Course Experience Questionnaire (Ramsden, 1991) and the Approaches to Teaching Inventory (Prosser & Trigwell, 1999) and there are familiar research methods that can be used (for example questionnaires, interviews and focus groups). Any data that is collected needs careful interpretation and contextualisation to enable others to understand the methodological approach taken, that is, "the ways in which techniques, theories and processes [have been] developed by the researcher in relation to the experience of collecting, analysing and reporting data" (Burgess, 1984, p. 2). Academics more comfortable with a positivist paradigm or quantitative methods, like engineers, need help to conduct the more qualitative research.

BUILDING PEDAGOGIC RESEARCH CAPACITY

The key elements to building research capacity are understanding and engagement. A variety of strategies were employed at engCETL to aid understanding and increase engagement. This section explains how I endeavoured to explain "pedagogic research" to colleagues and academics and how increased engagement with pedagogic research was encouraged.

Explaining Pedagogic Research to Academics

The primary means of communication with potential academic collaborators is through the engCETL website: we need to find academics to work with and develop the evidence base of excellent practice. As engineers claim to be "practical folk" I adopted a practical, person-centred approach in seeking to explain pedagogic research to this audience by using a description of the type of work we were seeking to support, the RAE definition of pedagogic research and addressed the way in which this work could be carried out:

> When we talk about relating what the engCETL does to pedagogic research we mean grounding what we do in relevant teaching and learning literature. It is necessary, as a Centre for Excellence in Teaching and Learning, that we

> demonstrate awareness of and evidence for good practice that enhances the student learning experience. Any activities we undertake need to have a teaching and learning rationale, something we will discuss with and develop in collaboration with the person who proposes a piece of work.
>
> Doing pedagogic research means using various research methods to understand and enhance your teaching and your students' learning. It means being aware of 'the teaching and learning literature', that is, showing that you can relate what you do to what is understood by good practice; it is not necessary to agree with that literature, you could of course critically comment with reference to your own experience.
>
> The research methods used can be qualitative (e.g. interviews, focus groups) or quantitative (e.g. questionnaires) or a mixture of qualitative and quantitative. You may decide to draw from different methodologies (e.g. ethnography, case study, grounded theory, phenomenography, action research, activity theory) in designing your research and analysing your data. (See http://www.engcetl.ac.uk/research/pedagogic/).

The aim was to invite engagement with engCETL around the area of teaching and learning and to demonstrate that pedagogic research could also be categorised as serious, RAEable research. Academics who think they have examples of good practice they would like to share, those who are interested in undertaking some pedagogic research or any who would like to chat about what this might involve were asked to contact me at the engCETL.

My next task was to work with interested academics (to provide examples of how we could collaborate to conduct research and evaluation) and to help colleagues within the engCETL see how pedagogic research was relevant to them. The following sections illustrate how this has been attempted.

Making Pedagogic Research (and Evaluation) Relevant to Colleagues

Once more I adopted a practical, person-centred approach in order to make the idea of research and evaluation real for colleagues working in the engCETL. I was asked to develop a research and evaluation strategy so I began by trying to understand the legacy procedure (left over from the days of the previous centre, EEC) for working on projects and activities. One of the main areas of work was the development of learning technology tools for academics. These tools were usually portrayed as helping to save time and make life easier for the academics. The process or outcomes involved little or no thought about facilitating or enhancing the student learning experience, even though this may have been an outcome.

Using an action research model (McNiff & Whitehead, 2002; Wellington, 2000), typically adopted by those seeking to research into their own practice, I developed a framework to try and explain how research and evaluation could fit into what people were already doing as well as trying to emphasise the need to make sure that engCETL work focuses on the enhancement of teaching and learning. An action research approach, that encourages reflection on and the development of practice, fits well with the engCETL aim to change what is done, reflect and feed the findings back into the process of developing projects and undertaking activities.

Evaluation is listed in the engCETL bid documents as something that should be integrated into all activities and that all academics should be encouraged to do, with respect to their teaching (Loughborough University, 2004). While it is dealt with in a separate section of the bid document I see it as complementary to and allied to the pedagogic research activities, not least because of the focus on engineering education and the requirement to identify examples of good practice. Indeed the interplay between research and evaluation is something Baume writes about (2005) as an informative relationship and Bennett (2003) classifies it in terms of differences in intent, scope and agenda, among other things. The interplay between research and evaluation in the engCETL context is illustrated in Figure 1 where the research literature informs the intended objectives of projects or activities, and the methods used to evaluate their impact. The ultimate aim being that research outputs and ideas for future research should be generated from these activities.

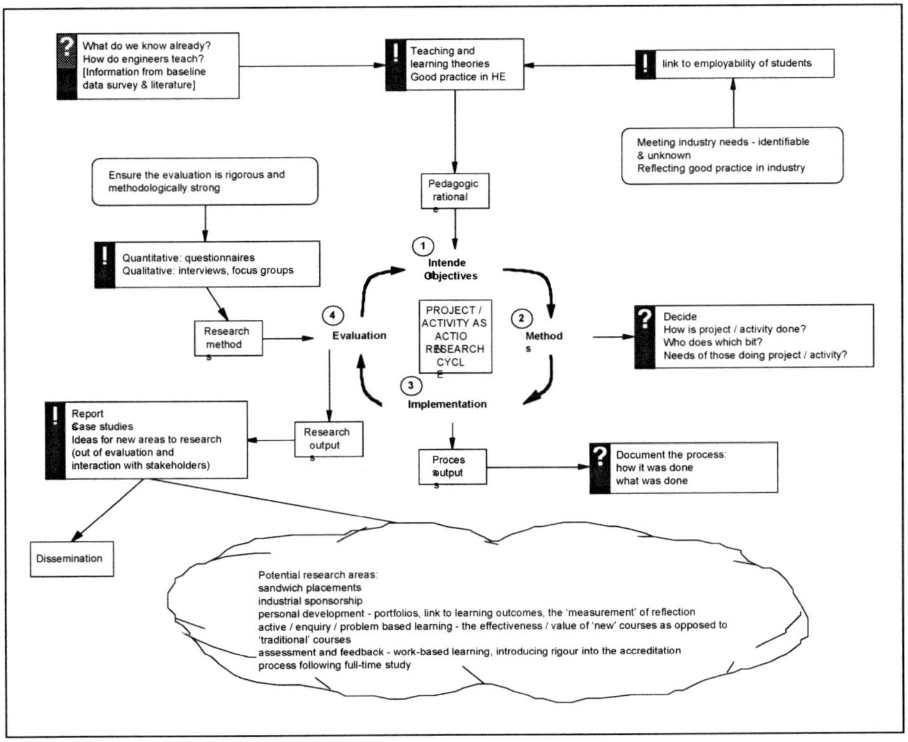

Figure 1. The engCETL draft research and evaluation strategy

The aim was to demonstrate that evaluation should be an ongoing, iterative process (in which case it is formative - the findings informing the next iteration or instance of activity or development), but that in some cases it is summative (particularly in the case of one-offs). Evaluation needs to:

- be informed by research - methods, linked to good practice identified in the literature;
- show that engCETL is delivering what it set out to and linked to the overall aims;
- show how teaching and learning practice is developing and good or innovative practice is transferring to other locations or impacting on other areas (departments or across the institution);
- should be embedded in all activities.

Increasing Wider Engagement with Pedagogic Research

Various strategies have been adopted, working closely with external consultants and interested parties from across the university, to increase engagement with pedagogic research. Academics who wish to investigate their practice and their students' learning are given support and advice and a seminar series provides a forum for people to share teaching and learning experiences and research into teaching and learning. There have been collaborations to write an educationally focused conference paper (Blanchard, Morón-García, & Bates, 2006) to evaluate the impact of a mini project award, to conduct an investigation into the use of a project allocation system and to collect student feedback on the use of electronic assignment submission (Gregory & Morón-García, forthcoming).

Four studentships have been funded in response to a call for interest to engineering academics. The studentships are focused on the exploration of engineering education topics (see the following section) that align with engCETL aims and objectives and brought in people who had not been involved with use previously. I worked with the academics who proposed topics and the engCETL pedagogic research consultant to develop the education focus of the studentships.

There was a fruitful collaboration with a colleague from the HEA engineering subject centre and the external pedagogic research consultant to conduct pedagogic research workshops for engineering academics (S. Morón-García & Willis, 2007). These workshops brought further academics from Loughborough (and other institutions) into contact and collaboration with engCETL and led directly to the development of pedagogic research resources targeted at engineering academics (pedagogic research toolkit, forthcoming) and further variations on the workshop for different audiences.

The engCETL funding of institutionally run academic practice awards and mini project awards for academics in associated departments provides the opportunity for more collaborations to capture practice and evaluate the impact of the awards (much as was done for a recent design and build activity, briefly outlined in the following section). Future sources of collaboration and engagement will arise from colleagues' work to support academics' use of the institution's virtual learning environment (VLE) and the social networking tool created by staff at engCETL to facilitate the sharing of teaching and learning knowledge and materials. This development arose out of an investigation into the potential use of a repository, similar to the one used for research outputs (see S. Morón-García, 2006). The quantity of work led engCETL to secure funding to create a second pedagogic research post (shared 50:50 with Professional Development, a central support unit where university-wide learning and teaching support for all staff is located).

Research Topics at engCETL

There are a large number of research projects underway at engCETL. These include funded studentship research as well as collaborative research conducted by named researchers in partnership with engCETL colleagues and academics from associated departments. The research areas have to align with the mission and aims of engCETL, so that they can provide an evidence base, demonstrate excellence and grow the capacity to conduct pedagogic research.

There are currently four funded students working in the following areas:

- the impact of work placements on transferable skills before, during and after work placements;
- the impact of sponsorship on students, academic departments and industry with the aim of developing sustainable models of effective practice;
- the development of a web-based Telelaboratory for Process Control Education with the aim of enhancing teaching and learning;
- an appraisal of the benefits of project-based learning in engineering education.

Other named researchers and collaborating colleagues are conducting or developing research in the areas of internationalisation, the accreditation of work-based learning, personal development portfolios, peer assessment (the use of technology-supported peer assessment) and the use of social software to facilitate the sharing and creation of teaching and learning knowledge and resources. These are in addition to my own investigations into the use of design projects in departments affiliated to the engCETL and the experience of students on work placements.

The design projects work also encompasses evaluation work carried out for a mini project holder. This involved an in depth evaluation of a design and build project with a focus on the observation of the conduct of the block and the collection of student feedback. The aim of the evaluation was to inform the development of a new part of the curriculum. The major part of this work is an investigation in to the use of design projects in departments affiliated to the engCETL. Academics are being interviewed to ascertain: the way design projects are taught, the rationale, the involvement of industry, the teaching approach adopted, their place in the curriculum, the assessment method(s) used and the collection and use of student feedback. The questions we are using to focus the study are:

- What role do design projects have in the curriculum?
- How do design projects involve industry in the curriculum?
- What approach to teaching is used by lecturers using design projects?

The student experience of work placements is being investigated in collaboration with a researcher located in one of the associated departments. We are examining the way in which higher education prepares students for the world of work, with particular reference to the work placement experience of engineering-related students at Loughborough University. The questions that bound this study are:

- How do students think the work placement enhances their learning experience?
- What are students expected to gain from a placement experience?
- How do students say departments prepare them for a work placement?
- What kind of work placement experience do students report they have?
- How could the work placement experience be improved according to students?

Once again interviews are the chosen method of data collection and part of the data has been written up elsewhere (S Morón-García & Powell, 2007).

CONCLUDING COMMENTS

Elsewhere we have characterised the process we are undertaking as a "change journey" recognising that "initially this might involve major diversions and engagement at a very low level, the key is to establish a relationship and to promote the benefits gained by those academics who do so" (S. Morón-García & Lamb, 2007, p. 23). It is clear from conversations with academics and colleagues that there is still a way to go in reaching a shared understanding of pedagogic research: what it is and how you do it. In particular we need to help those unfamiliar with this type of research to understand the language and terminology and we need to continue to explain the difference between teaching and learning methods, the methods we might use to research into teaching and learning and the role of pedagogic research in informing these.

The location and name of engCETL mean that there is a strong subject identity which has both a positive and a negative effect: it is a support centre that academics in associated departments can call on and there is strong support for the work from a team of "seconded academics" and senior faculty and department members. However, engCETL is also working within a culture that is "generally sceptical about the benefits that can be derived from generic pedagogic research" (Loughborough University, 2004) and it is noticeable that there is a reluctance to discuss and examine practice in some areas.

The various ways in which engCETL has tried to engage with people using a range of strategies, from learning and teaching focused calls for supported projects and funded studentships to building networks with other researchers and CETLs (for example, see http://www.eastmidlandscetls.ac.uk/pren/) and working with the engsc to run workshops on pedagogic research for engineering academics, seems to have started to generate more interest and awareness. In addition during the first year of operations there has been a focus on evaluation due to a need to examine the process and progress made in the early days of engCETL's existence rather than on research as defined by the RAE. This is something that will need to be addressed in the long term if engCETL is to contribute to the pedagogic research community and the pedagogic researchers are to achieve job satisfaction as members of the academic community.

This paper was presented initially as a way to describe a work in progress (the engCETL and engagement with pedagogic research) as well as the development of my own ideas as an early career pedagogic researcher. As it currently stands it is a record of the role of pedagogic research within the CETL programme in the UK, with reference to the experience in one particular CETL. It identifies the challenges faced by those charged with building pedagogic research capacity and indicates some possible strategies.

REFERENCES

Ashwin, P., & Trigwell, K. (2004). Investigating staff and educational development. In P. Khan & D. Baume (Eds.), *Enhancing staff and educational development.* London: Kogan Page.

Baume, D. (2005). *Research and evaluation: Closer allies than we might expect.* Paper presented at the Challenging the Orthodoxies 2005.

Beaty, L. (2005). *HEFCE CETLs booklet.* Retrieved April 23, 2007, from http://www.hefce.ac.uk/learning/tinits/cetl/final/brochure.pdf

Bennett, J. (2003). *Evaluation methods in research.* London: Continuum.

Blanchard, R. E., Morón-García, S. D., & Bates, M. R. (2006). *Converting the physical to the virtual: Providing a laboratory experience for distance learners in engineering.* Paper presented at the IV International Conference on Multimedia and Information & Communication Technologies in Education (m-ICTE2006).

Booth, S. (2004). Engineering education and the pedagogy of awareness. In C. Baillie & I. Moore (Eds.), *Effective learning and teaching in engineering* (pp. 9–23). London: RoutledgeFalmer.

Boyer, E. (1990). *Scholarship reconsidered: Priorities of the professoriate.* New York: The Carnegie Foundation for the Advancement of Teaching, Jossey-Bass.

Brew, A. (2001). *The nature of research.* London: Routledge Falmer.

Brew, A. (2003). *Theory, research and scholarship in relation to teaching: Issues and challenges.* Paper presented at the Improving Student Learning: Theory, Research and Scholarship, Hinkley, Leics.

Brookfield, S. D. (1986). *Understanding and facilitating adult learning.* Milton Keynes, UK: Open University Press.

Burgess, R. J. (Ed.). (1984). *The research process in educational settings: Ten case studies.* Lewes: Falmer Press.

Canning, J. (2007). Pedagogy as a discipline: Emergence, sustainability and professionalisation. *Teaching in Higher Education, 12*(3), 393–403.

Cannon, R. (2001). Pedagogy: A point of view. *Teaching in Higher Education, 6*(3), 415–419.

Gregory, K., & Morón-García, S. (in press). Electronic assignment submission, student behaviour & experience. *Engineering Education.*

HEFCE. (2004). Guidance notes for stage two CETL bids. In *CETL bidding process.* Retrieved January 15, 2007, from http://www.hefce.ac.uk/learning/tinits/cetl/guide/guide1.pdf

HEFCE, HEFCW, SFC, & DfEL. (2006). Generic statement. In *RAE 2008 Panel criteria and working methods.* Retrieved January 15, 2007, from http://www.rae.ac.uk/pubs/2006/01/docs/genstate.pdf

Knowles, M. (1984). *Andragogy in action.* San Francisco: Jossey-Bass.

Lambert, R. (2003). *Lambert review of business-university collaboration.* London: HM Treasury/HMSO.

Loughborough University. (2004). *CETL stage 2 proposal: Industry and employer linked Engineering Centre for Excellence in Teaching and Learning.*

McNiff, J., & Whitehead, J. (2002). *Action research: Principles and practice* (2nd ed.). London: Routledge Falmer.

Morón-García, S. (2006). *Rights and rewards: Attitudes towards the use of digital repositories for teaching and learning materials.* Loughborough: HEA Engineering Subject Centre.

Morón-García, S., & Lamb, F. (2007). The engCETL change journey: Encouraging engagement with pedagogic research. *Educational Developments, 8.1*, 23–24.

Morón-García, S., & Powell, A. (2007, September 5). *Working to learn – valuing placements.* Paper presented at the 15th Improving Student Learning Symposium: Improving Student Learning – For What?, 3–5.

Morón-García, S., & Willis, L. (2007, December). *Collaborating to engage engineers with pedagogic research.* Paper presented at the Society for Research into Higher Education Annual Conference 2007, pp. 11–13, Brighton, Sussex.

Prosser, M. (2005, Autumn). Supporting the student experience, a scholarly approach. *Academy Exchange*, 8–9.

Prosser, M., & Trigwell, K. (1999). *Understanding learning and teaching: The experience in higher education.* Buckingham: SRHE and Open University Press.

Ramsden, P. (1991). A performance indicator of teaching quality in higher education: The course experience questionnaire. *Studies in Higher Education, 16*(2), 129–150.

Ramsden, P. (1992). *Learning to teach in higher education.* London: Routledge.

Roberts, G. (2002). *SET for success.* London: HM Treasury.

Smith, M. K. (1996, 1999). *'Andragogy', the encyclopaedia of informal education.* Retrieved April 30, 2007, from http://www.infed.org/lifelonglearning/b-andra.htm

Stierer, B., & Antoniou, M. (2004). Are there distinctive methodologies for pedagogic research in higher education? *Teaching in Higher Education, 9*(3), 275–285.

Wellington, J. (2000). *Educational research: Contemporary issues and practical approaches.* London: Continuum.

Sue Morón-García
Loughborough University

BRAVADO

In order to increase challenge, The Great Blondin modified his initial walk through a range of risky increments. One of the most depicted feats was when he carried his manager on his back as he crossed the hazardous drop. To maintain stability the manager had to evenly distribute his weight while clinging to the shoulders of his carrier. What may have been overlooked in this accomplishment was the inherent contribution to solidity made by the other. The papers in this section give heed to the risks encountered by students and teachers and their contributions to relevance in research.

In *Lecturers' and Students' Attitudes Towards Technology in Lectures: No Taboos, More Thinking* the authors offer a comprehensive examination of the use of technology in higher education as a problematic totem. Bakioglu and Hacifazlioglu provide insights regarding technological constraints and further rationale for the development of critical thinking, reflection, and contextual awareness.

In the second paper of Part IV, Per Laursen offers a refreshing view of the theory/practice binary through the eyes of teacher candidates. *Student Teachers' Conceptions of Theory and Practice in Teacher Education* provides novel findings of student perceptions and views. This work is a poignant example of the potential of collaborative constructive inquiry and research design.

Šteh and Kalin provide insightful discourse in examining the intricacies of pedagogical and andragogical studies. In *The Changing Student Conceptions in Evaluating Teacher Effectiveness in Higher Education: Facing Challenges and Taboos* the authors question the inherent aura of educator superiority in higher education contexts and instead challenge readers to consider students as partners in the learning process.

AYSEN BAKIOGLU AND OZGE HACIFAZLIOGLU

LECTURERS' AND STUDENTS' ATTITUDES TOWARDS THE USE OF TECHNOLOGY IN LECTURES: NO TABOOS, MORE THINKING

Taboo, Totems and Technology appear to be counterparts in the era of globalization although those concepts seem to differ in terminology. A taboo can be placed on an object, person, place or word that is believed to have inherent power above the ordinary. This power called 'mana,' can only be approached by special priests. To give special distinction to special monuments in the life cycle, taboos are often declared at births, deaths, initiations, and marriages. Taboos are commonly placed on a clan an ancestral guardian, called the totem (Frazer, 1955). Technology being an obligatory issue in many fields penetrated into the world of education as a taboo or totem in some cases. The use of technology in classrooms has always been a problematic one for many reasons. There have been many discussions on the benefits of using technology in lectures. There is no doubt about using technology in a classroom setting; however its integration into the curriculum brings about several conflicting views.

Technology in the classroom seems to be a quiet revolution. Although many faculties still teach by means of traditional methods, many others are realizing the great potential of multimedia, the Internet, and other technology-based forms of instruction. Using technology in the classroom is beneficial because it:

- emphasizes active learning;
- responds to different learning styles;
- enhances collaborative learning;
- increases individualized learning and self-paced study; and
- encourages greater student independence (http://www.eriche.org/crib/technincl .html)

The rise of information technology introduces the possibility of new, individualized, cooperative, problem-oriented, student-centred and flexible learning approaches that have not been practically possible before. This has implications for the lecturers' role and "authority" particularly when many students are currently more computer-literate than their lecturers and where Internet, e-mail, public access databases, networking, and interactive programs provide fixed and enduring knowledge. Further, it is not difficult to envisage the role of the teacher changing from a deliverer of a fixed knowledge to a facilitator and supporter of student-centred learning. Learning becomes negotiated (Cohen, Manion & Morrison, 2000). However, this picture turns out to be a "dystopia", where the lecturer pretends to be addicted to the technology. Fabry and Higgs (1997) contend that

J. A. Kentel and A. Short (eds.), Totems and Taboos: Risk and Relevance in Research on Teachers and Teaching, 155–170.

technology has been shown to increase student perceptions of instruction's originality and creativity; on the negative side, there is a general discrepancy between the expected and the actual integration of technology into the classroom by educators.

Application of technology appears to extend into two main roads, either in the form of "obsession or resistance like a taboo" which similarly diverges in two contrary directions. On the one hand, it means 'sacred', 'consecrated', and on the other 'uncanny', 'dangerous', 'forbidden', 'unclean'. Instructional technology in this respect is perceived as a totem in the metaphorical sense, which is defined as an animal (whether edible and harmless or dangerous and feared) and more rarely a plant or a natural phenomenon (such as rain or water), which stands in a peculiar relation to the whole clan (Wikipedia, 2007).

This idea is in parallel with Freud's (1913) ideas on totem which is seen as the common ancestor of the clan; at the same time it is their guardian spirit and helper, which sends them oracles and, if dangerous to others, recognizes and spares its own children. Within this frame "taboos and totems" could be perceived from two dimensions; former lecturers perceiving technology as taboos and totems that must be used in every setting, latter lecturers denying the existence of innovative technology and perceiving it as hazardous. Both polarities are barriers to high quality teaching since creativity and interaction factors are disregarded. Within these limits, studies have emphasized social and cultural context, where information technology has shown to be determined by the culture of a country or organization. In cross-cultural research of Americans and Koreans it was shown that national culture plays a decisive role in the usage patterns of it (Kim & Kim, 2004).

There are many reasons why resistance to technology is experienced among the academic staff. Although the use of technology has many benefits for the educational system, it also creates a lot of burden both on lecturers' and administrators' shoulders. Lecturers' job descriptions are in a way redefined with this new approach, which alters the role of a teacher from one who spoon-feeds the student to a collaborative working partner. While helping the students to use technology in their projects, lecturers need to show competency in using it. Administrators, on the other hand, need to restructure their departments accordingly in order to meet the developments of the age.

Research, technology and academia are three so closely interrelated counterparts that the academic, whose main responsibility is to do research and transfer it to the student, cannot even start her or his research without using such magnificent tools. He or she needs to use technology again when relaying information to the students; therefore, the university should lead the way in technology to provide professional candidates with contemporary skills as lecturers. Furthermore, students need to use technology more than others in order to produce research and share knowledge. It is at this stage that technology should not be presented as a totem, rather, as a medium, which must be used.

The potential for using technology in teaching and learning provides new opportunities for higher education to meet the full constellation of students' needs. In this context, well qualified, dedicated faculty members are at the heart of education and are essential to defining and achieving what can be accomplished with technology. The rapidly changing pattern of student experience with mastery of technology application provides both great opportunities and challenges (Gilbert, 2005). Technology within this limitless border is attributed a new definition and applicability. Not only is it a means of learning but additionally a main vehicle serving for the quality of the management systems since educational and administrative benefits provided by the technology tools through which collaborative work and learning is maintained in the higher education.

Morrison (2003) foresees the future of higher education in US from a different dimension, in which classes will be harmonised with on line and in class instruction. Instructors will no longer rely on predominant mode of instruction; rather group and individual project-based learning will be the pedagogical form. Information technology in a way transforms the world of administrators, lecturers and students. On the other hand, despite research and testimony that technology is being used by an increasing number of faculties, the distribution of technological innovations for teaching and learning has not been widespread, nor has it become deeply integrated into the curriculum (Jacobsen, 2007).

METHOD AND SAMPLE GROUP

The purpose of this study is to determine the existing faculty learning culture created by the lecturers from the dimensions of technology based taboos and totems. In order to scrutinize both groups' perceptions towards the use of technology in their lectures, two questionnaires were devised. One of which was applied to 124 lecturers and 1410 students and was conducted at Marmara University at the Faculty of Education during the 2001-2002 academic year. To give more in depth understanding and updated data for the quantitative data, focus group discussions were conducted with three groups. PhD, Master and undergraduate students (N=39) constitute the study group. Three questions were discussed in three sessions as follows:

- Do lecturers' perceptions towards the use of technology differ in accordance with experience and age variables? To what extend is it reflected on the students' perceptions?
- What kind of attitudes exists in the culture of university atmosphere related to using technology as a totem and taboo?
- What kind of problems is reflected during lectures?

Transcriptions obtained via focus group discussions were analyzed by using content analysis and concept mapping.

FINDINGS

Demographic Findings

The details of the demographic data for the quantitative and qualitative study are as follows:

Quantitative study
Lecturers:
- 41% of the lecturers were female and 59% were male.
- 22% of the lecturers were below 30 years old, 34% were between 31 and 40, 21% were between 41-50, 20% were between 51 and 60 and 3 % were 61 and above years old.
- 15% of the lecturers were Professors, 8% were Associate Professors, 20% were Assistant Professors, 10% were Lecturers with PhD, 30% were Lecturers and 17% were Research Assistants.

Students:
- 52% of the students were female and 48% were male.
- 17.5% of the students were freshman, 28.8% were sophomore, 18.4% were juniors and 35.2% were seniors.
- 23.7% of the students accommodated in the dormitory, 34% stayed with their parents, 7% stayed with their relatives, and 35.3% stayed with their friends.
- 47% of the students stated that they had an opportunity to use computer whereas 53% did not.
- 37% of the students indicated that they had a chance to use the Internet whereas 63% did not.

Focus group/qualitative study. A total of 39 respondents constitute the study group in the qualitative part of the study as follows:
- 5 research assistants.
- 9 PhD students studying in Educational Administration department.
- 16 master students studying in Computer Instructional Technologies Teacher Education department.
- 9 undergraduate students studying in Computer Instructional Technologies Teacher Education department.

Lecturers' Attitudes Towards the Use of Technology Related to Experience and Age Variables

Comparative analysis revealed lecturers' differing attitudes towards using technologies in their classrooms related to experience variable. Meaningfulness was observed between lecturers who had 1-5 years of experience and lecturers who had 21 and above years of experience (U: 292,500; p=0, 01). Lecturers experiencing Career Entrance Phases appeared to be very keen on using technology in their lectures.

Mann Whitney U Test revealed the significance observed in the attitudes of lecturers towards the use of technologies in their lectures with regards to age variable. Lecturers 31 and below years of age indicated to have benefited from technology more than that of lecturers within the range of 51-60 and 61 and above age groups (U=161,000; P=0,000; U= 15,500; P=0,000). Similarly lecturers within the age range of 32-40 and 41-50 revealed significantly different responses when compared with the lecturers who were within the range of 51-60 years of age group

(U=212,500; P=0,012). Younger ones again expressed their positive attitudes towards using instructional technology. Such meaningfulness could be interpreted as a benchmark indicating a certain turning point where lecturers might begin to be less willing to use new alternatives and approaches in terms of teaching (Bakioglu & Hacifazlioglu, 2003).

As for the qualitative data, nearly all the students agreed on the impact of age variable on the successful use of technology. Five students indicated how resistance to technology appeared as a taboo for lecturers above the age group of 50. They all agreed that talent in integrating technology could be found only in few cases among the lecturers who were in the final phases of their careers and these were named as "exceptions".

Although age and experience variables seemed to be the most important reasons that affected lecturers' attitudes towards technology, there were other elements as well, which hindered the use of technology at universities. These constraints are listed in the following section.

Constraints in Using Technology

Table 1 reveals the constraints experienced by both lecturers and students in the questionnaires. These constraints were accepted to be the ones, which hindered the use of technology at universities. Lecturers and students believed that a great number of students in each class did not allow them to use computers in their lectures. Almost all the students pointed out that they did not have Internet access in their departments and could only use it either in the Internet cafes or at their homes. Nearly half the students had the opportunity to use a computer in their residences and fewer than half had a chance to use the Internet, which was again an indicator of the economic restrictions (Bakioglu and Hacifazlioglu, 2003).

Table 1. Constraints in using technology

Items	*Lecturers*		*Students*	
	Mean	Std	Mean	Std
Number of students in each class	4.45	0.82	3.74	1.22
Internet availability	----	----	40% yes	
Material availability	3.97	1.05	....	......
Limited economic opportunities for the lecturers	4.32	0.91	3.83	1.09
Teaching load of lecturers	4.25	0.89		
Total	N=124		N=1410	

Note. Resource: Bakioglu and Hacifazlioglu (2003). Lecturers' and Students' Perceptions Technology Use: Implications for Faculty Administrators, Proceedings of 12th Education Conference, 15-18 October, Antalya, Turkey.

These constraints could be presented as alternative reasons for lecturers' resistance to use technology, which will also be mentioned in the qualitative part. During the interviews, lecturers with administrative duties admitted that one of the reasons why all computers could not have Internet access was the poor communication infrastructure of the city. Faculty administrators could solve problems inside the buildings but were unable to overcome the obstacles related to the infrastructure. According to the research findings, even though lecturers held a positive attitude towards the use of technology in their lectures, they were unable to realize this most of the time because of the constraints created by either the faculties or the policy makers (Bakioglu & Hacifazlioglu, 2003).

Focus group discussions revealed similar concerns regarding the use of technology in lectures. Technologic competency was determined to be one of the main barriers indicated by the students in the group discussions (15/39). Lecturers' resistance to technology and incompetence serving as a hindrance was phrased by the students in the following words.

Resistance and Incompetence

> Lecturers do not seem very keen on learning how to use technology in their courses. This could be explained with their devotion to their habits. Younger ones are willing but the lack of technologic equipment appeared to be the main constraints (7/39).
>
> Lecturers who could be named as resistant to technology suppose technology as unnecessary. They have their formatted classical style and do not have the tendency to change it (6/39).
>
> Lecturers are scared of technology and this stops them to learn. Unfortunately they do not admit it (1/39).
>
> Most lecturers do not encourage students to prepare technology based assignments (2/39).

Lack of Inservice Training

The students in the group discussions mentioned the lack of inservice training courses as one of the main constraints. One third of the students (13/39) accepted it to be a necessary vehicle for high quality teaching and successful technology integration in courses. Students' views regarding this topic are given in the following statements:

> Most lecturers need to get in service training on the use of technology in their lectures.
>
> I do not think they are able to assess whether one needs to use technology in particular subject. Why do you use projector instead of overhead projector?
>
> In order to use multi media presentation, they need to have basic computer literacy skills. Both lecturer and students need to know that.
>
> During PowerPoint presentation, some fail to establish communication with students, participation of students remains limited.

> Some students have problems in expressing their ideas, establishing good communication. They have no assistance from the lecturer. This limits self-esteem.

Existing Taboos and Totems within the Faculty Culture in Terms of Technology Use

Taboos and totems were categorized into two groups as a result of the analysis of the transcriptions. Students' views regarding their lecturers' technology expertise and implementation were collected either as "resistance" or "addiction."

Technology as a taboo for addiction. Students indicated that in the era of globalization most lecturers fail in the mistake of feeling a sense of commitment to technology. In some cases this commitment appeared to be result in tragic cases where students feel themselves alienated in the classes. Such criticisms were put forward by nearly all of the students (36/39) during the focus group discussions:

> Lecturers all believe that presentations should be via PowerPoint otherwise it wouldn't be acceptable or the quality would be less.
>
> People believe that as they use technology the subject would be understood much better and the mission would be completed successfully.
>
> Some private schools use technology as a symbol for quality.
>
> Some believe that everything on the net would be correct and valid.
>
> They believe that every problem could be solved via technology and everything would develop easily.

Technology as a taboo for resistance. Findings of the study revealed that regarding the use of technology two contrary tendencies existed and were demonstrated by the lecturers. As opposed to the ideas of obsession, students emphasized a group of lecturers' resistance and avoidance towards the acceptance of new technologies. This attitude was also presented as a taboo in the metaphorical sense (20/39).

> Some lecturers perceive technology, which limits communication and integration in lectures.
>
> Some lecturers perceive technology as a tool which passives active learning among the students and the lecturers.

An interesting finding that appeared in this study was lecturers' reluctance to use instructional technologies to avoid making any mistakes while using the "so called precious tool". Nearly a quarter (8/39) of the respondents expressed lecturers' concern about using instructional technologies without causing any technical problems. The following view clarifies such anxieties:

Some lecturers feel tension on whether they could give harm to technologic equipment, because of lack of self-confidence.

RESULTS AND DISCUSSION

Technology within these borders serves as a manipulator in educational arena and has the power to create an artificial demand among the lecturers who lack creativity and talent in their teaching practices. Instructional technology has contributions and drawbacks as defined by Mackay (2003) with these words: "Every age has its peculiar folly".

Higher education professionals generally work in an information and communication technologies rich environment. There are expectations that the existence of technology benefits them, their students, and the overall learning environment, where these factors can be key in enhancing the capacity of the higher education teacher to engage positively, collaboratively and critically with the growth of learning technologies (Unwin, 2007). This is a key focus, which determines the quality of the course as well as the nature of the lesson content and implementation. Lecturers' expertise in using technology without converting it into a taboo depends on the lecturers' expertise and talent in both teaching and the use of technology. The questions arises in this circumstance is whether technology serves education, or education serves technology as it is emphasized by Kompf (2005). He indicates that the use of technology in everyday life as germinated in classrooms for a variety of well-intentioned but often misguided and wrong-headed reasons. The hopes, dreams, and drama that form the core issues arise from a deeper "who's steering the boat tension?"

This picture is quite similar to Freud's (1913) work conducted on neurotic patients, where he used the concepts of "projection and ambivalence". As in the case of King, he considers the two levels of functioning to be the "ostensible" (being honoured), and "the actual" (being tortured). In our study, students' views showed that some lecturers fall into this misconception and move in two opposite directions, accepting technology as good or bad without considering its pedagogic use. Schussler, Poole, Whitlock, and Evertson (2007) assert that it is necessary for lecturers to possess an understanding both of their students' academic and social needs as learners who are using technology and of the technology itself. Both components must be present for lecturers to integrate technology in classrooms effectively.

Although many cyberspace visionaries have asserted that technology inevitably brings decentralization and choice to the world, this analysis of institutional isomorphism suggests that the opposite might be closer to the truth. In order to use technology constructively, educators may have to reinvent it, reconceiving what it means to define an ontology, to standardize practices, and to fit modular components into a whole. At a minimum, it should be weighed as fully as possible towards the potential consequences of each individual standard (Agre, 1999).

In this study one PhD student categorized lecturers into three sub-groups depending on their technology competency levels:

- Traditionals: Lecturers who resist using technology.
- Semi-Traditionals: Lecturers who try to keep up with the trend for the sake of fashion.
- Professionals: Lecturers who believe that using technology is not the sole purpose but the means for high quality teaching.

Some graduate students in Education Faculty expressed their opinions such as:

> Some believe that technology hinders students to express themselves. Some believe that it is a luxury. Both could be solved with a good thinking and planning the lectures.
>
> We take the lecturer as a model and imitate whatever we observe in the courses.

These opinions highlight the importance of channelling "thinking" in the process of lesson planning and teaching. These categories all imply the hidden cultural beliefs of taboos where people totally devote or deny. It was observed in the group discussions that lecturers limit their level of integration and creativity in their courses either by depending too much on technology or avoiding it. This is summarized by the students as follows:

> Using too many slides force students to read and take notes rather than thinking and asking questions or making contributions during the course.
>
> Reading from power point slides does not mean teaching. Even though the teacher is not in the class you can play the sound as the background and give the course without any interaction.
>
> The belief that high technology would benefit the students and enrich the course content is accepted unquestionably by certain lecturers.

Similarly, undergraduate students' responses in a study by Hacifazlioglu, Sacli, and Yengin (2007) revealed the hidden power steering the lesson. This constraint created by the faculties is expressed by one of the students with these words:

> Administration should not insist on the use of technology. Lecturers should be given the initiative to decide whether to use it or not. Lecturers should also be careful when using technology and allowing themselves a space to manoeuvre within the class.

It might be concluded that most of the lecturers support student centred learning and autonomy via the Internet and technology but in practice they cannot fully achieve this aim. Results indicated that lecturers' attitude towards technology are affected by age and experience variables and the internal and external constraints which are inevitable. Furthermore unavailability of materials, equipment and support serve as barriers, which limit lecturers' use of technology (Bakioglu & Hacifazlioglu, 2003). Policymakers could help the lecturers overcome these constraints by providing them with ample time to design their courses. Similar results were found in another study (Wang & Holthaus, 1997), which also highlighted the need restructuring the educational computing courses. Anderson and Harris (1997) found in their studies that out of 300 lecturers, 45% reported the benefits of Internet for professional activities and 16% for personal and instructional activities. Seyal, Rahman, Noah, and Rahim (2002) confirmed the same hypothesis where half of his sample group considered the Internet as very important and even almost indispensable for their professional activities. A total of 79% stated to have used an Internet facility.

The use of the Internet was found to be significant when compared to other teaching related activities. Students in the focus groups (10/39) reported that lecturers were able to access studies in their related fields and this was reflected as a time and energy saving in their academic studies. However, such advantage does not guarantee high quality teaching in the course setting. Lecturers need to reflect their talent in integrating technology into the curriculum to maintain internalized learning among the students. Similarly, in the quantitative part of this study, 11-20 years of teaching experience was found to be a period of time when lecturers were more enthusiastic to try new challenges. Lecturers who had more than 30 years of teaching experience showed less interest in using technology. Qualitative data regarding this dimension supported this evidence as well. All the research assistants came to an agreement on the following finding:

> Lecturers prefer to use technology to make their teaching activities easier. Pre-prepared slides and transparencies are used for a long time without making any changes. Most of the experienced academics feel reluctant to alter their methodologies since they do not want to devote more time and energy. A dilemma occurs between the use of a new technology and sticking to the traditional values.

In support of this finding, the final 10-15 years of a career was determined to be the phase of greatest expertise in teaching accompanied by the potential for increased personal health and family concerns. Yet it may also be the time of greatest "conservatism" (Day & Bakioglu, 1996; Day, 1999).

Similarly, lecturers in Bakioglu and Hacifazlioglu's study (2001), significance was observed with regards to the experience variable. Lecturers who appeared to be in the career phases of "initiation and plateau," differed significantly from the lecturers who were on the disenchantment phase. The first 5 years were found to be the most accelerated period in lecturers' career in the mentioned study. The reason why this period of time was perceived as their most accelerated phase might be found in lecturers' sheer willingness to do research because of the satisfaction they receive after getting their degrees. This finding seems to overlap with the data obtained in relation to technology driven lesson planning and application. Lecturers' enthusiasm in using technology in the 11-20 and 21 and above experience group might also be interpreted in terms of career phases as it was previously scrutinized by Huberman (1995) and Day (1999) previously where the middle phases of the career cycle (7-18 years) were determined to be more diverse than earlier or later ones.

> This diversity will relate to career advancement, school culture and the way in which teachers respond to the well-established annually repeated cycle of students and colleagues which provides security but, may paradoxically, lack

> the variety, challenge and discovery of earlier years. It is a time when many teachers are likely to seek new challenges, either by taking new responsibilities in the same school or by moving school for the purposes of promotion. (Day, 1999)

A study by Hacifazlioglu et al. (2007) also supported this idea where experienced lecturers' first reaction towards the use of new technologies was resistance and phrased with these words: "We will definitely lose our credit and prestige!" In the aforementioned study, lecturers' first negative reaction was determined especially within the group who were 50 years and above. Yet it was mentioned that in a month's time, with the support of the orientation programs and training courses this sense of resistance was overcome.

In support of this finding Summers (1990) found that lack of knowledge and experience in the computing area is one of the most common reasons for lecturers' negative attitudes towards computers. Similarly, Yuen, and Ma (2002) asserted that lecturers generally resist using computers in classrooms, the development of lecturers' positive attitudes towards computers is considered to be a key factor in fostering computer integration and the enhancement of quality learning and teaching using computers.

Infrastructure, limited economic opportunities and heavy teaching burden were found to be the other constraints that prevent lecturers from using new technology. A well-planned programme would allow the lecturers to benefit from the use of it at a high level. This is particularly important in the developing universities where the infrastructure and economic problems are inevitable (Bakioglu & Hacifazlioglu, 2003). This result seems to contradict a previous study conducted at a foundation university, where physical conditions were perceived to be satisfactory at the faculties in our study. It was highly emphasized by the students in the in-depth interviews and focus group discussions that not every academic performed high levels of competency and expertise in harmonizing the technology with the curriculum. The ideal teaching related activities and such ideas were defined by the students in these words (Hacifazlioglu et al. 2007):

> We do not want to continue a lesson via a power point presentation. What we really look for is to interact with the lecturer, who skilfully manipulates all the dimensions of the learning process via technology. (3/7)

> I learn better with the sound of the "chalk," which is dictated into my brain. (2/7)

The reason why lecturers appeared to be reluctant towards implementing new technologies could be interpreted with the additional burden put on their shoulders, especially in the initiation phase of the new system. A study administrated on lecturers working at Foundation University revealed significance observed between the lecturers' title and the degree of difficulty experienced in the pre-teaching process from the basis of technical equipment. Lecturers reflected higher levels of concern about the pre teaching process while this was not seen as a problem for the research assistants. Lecturers holding doctorates did not mention it either. This could be interpreted as a reflection of the hidden hierarchical system established at faculties. The reason why the preparation process before the actual lesson was not seen as a concern could be explained with the job descriptions of the research assistants. Perceiving the preparation process as a part of their duty might cause them to be more pleased with the technology related preparation tasks (Hacifazlioglu, et al., 2007).

Findings revealed not only lecturers' positive attitude towards computer-assisted instruction but also the students' willingness. It could be said that to have a positive attitude towards technology does not contribute much to students' learning on its own but lecturers should be effective users of it and they should lead and encourage their students to use computers while preparing their projects, or in their autonomous learning, as well. Schussler et al. (2007) insist that lecturers must be first aware of how technology relates to their learning goals.

Globalization seems to affect every aspect of the academic life and technology in this context serves as the main vehicle to integrate the learner groups. In this circumstance, the use of computers and technology makes it necessary for faculties to formulate their own teaching policies. Otherwise it would be impossible to maintain standards both in terms of teaching and curriculum design. Although the use of technology has many benefits for the system in general, it also creates a lot of burden both on lecturers' and administrators' shoulders. It is at this point that technology is accepted or rejected as a taboo or totem from the dimensions of two career groups. Jacobsen (2007) suggests investigating why the integration of technology for teaching and learning is so appealing to some faculty and not to others especially in an era of globalization where the investment in instructional technology for higher education and the demand in distance education have been increasing.

Computer technology is currently used in the areas of research and development, communication, information access in libraries and all teaching and learning processes. This wide spectrum had been extended with the internationalization process. Lecturers' job descriptions are in a way redefined with this new approach, which alters the role of a teacher from one who spoon-feeds the student to a collaborative working partner. Administrators, on the other hand, need to restructure their departments accordingly in order to meet the developments of the age. From this perspective, written communication serves as a vehicle, which would pave the way for the integration process while creating a challenging setting for the lecturers and administrators during the pre-implementation process (Bakioglu & Hacifazlioglu, 2007a).

Students in Bakioglu and Hacifazlioglu's (in press) study conducted on 3500 undergraduates supported a view of satisfaction parallel to our study. In the aforementioned study, students who were better prepared academically and who devoted more effort to their studies, interacted more frequently with faculty members. It is neither in the mentioned study nor in our study whether this is because such students were more assertive in seeking out faculty members or whether faculty members invited students who performed well academically to make contact. Therefore, special importance needs to be attributed to research collaboration during the internationalization process. As it was previously emphasized, cultural exchange could be maintained not only through social integration but also through the academic projects, works and collaborations. Therefore higher education institutions involve the "quality culture" from many perspectives. As in the case of interaction with the faculty administration, academic staff has an important role to enable exchange students' integration. Technology within this internationalized frame serves as a facilitator in academic and social integration, which underline faculty administrators new roles rescued from certain taboos and limitations. In line with this idea Gilbert (2005) contends that as the trend continues for students from different locations, ages, and life situations to enrol in the same college course, faculty need training and support in using technology to identify and meet the range of students' needs.

Similarly, Christensen, Anakwe, and Kessler (2001) argue that there will be an increasing percentage of working college students (versus the traditional full time student) and these individuals have greater outside commitments that create barriers to "traditional" education. This idea is confirmed by Morrison's study (2003) in which he emphasizes the changing demographics and technology, which alter the context of higher education. Lecturers within this new perspective will see themselves as the designers of learning experiences for an increasingly diverse population with diverse needs and expectancies.

A compensatory relationship exists between academic and social integration in Mannan's study (2007), in which students' integration in the academic and social issues are differentiated with regards to their subject areas of studies and their years of studies.

Taking the size of investment in instructional technology for higher education, the increased demand for distance education, and the demonstrated effectiveness for some educational outcomes, it seems reasonable to investigate why the integration of technology for teaching and learning is so appealing to certain lecturers while others still resist it. The issue of using technology without turning it into taboos and totems could be maintained with the active contribution and commitment of the lecturer. Following phrases cited from Day's "A Passion for Teaching" (2004) summarizes the whole idea of passionate teaching, passionate teachers and in our opinion this is also valid for the lecturers:

> Passionately committed teachers are those who absolutely love what they do. They are constantly searching the more effective ways to reach their children, to master the content and methods of their craft. They feel a personal mission … to learning, as much as they can about the world, about others, about themselves – and helping others to do the same" (Zehm & Kottler, 1993, cited in Day, 2004).

RECOMMENDATIONS

Developing critical thinking should be the main target at the lectures, by reflecting provocative questions with the help of the technology when necessary. Internet surfing might widen students' horizons enabling them to ask provocative questions.

Interviews with the students revealed constraints experienced within the teaching process as technology is used in the lectures. Longitudinal studies could be implemented to examine the degree to which teaching objectives could be obtained by the lecturers as they use technology.

Internet connection, development of technical facilities to enhance the use of instructional technologies should be taken as faculty priorities. Interactive implications would sustain more effective lectures.

Teaching should be one by one interaction with students. This develops students' thinking, expands their horizons. Technology should be used if it is necessary depending the nature of the lecture content and viewed as a "tool" and a way to rethink curriculum and instruction.

Lecturers within this challenging setting need more support in terms of technology application and they should be given inservice training, which will meet the needs of each individual academic in preparing their lectures, thus enabling them to serve as ideal role models for their students especially for education faculties. Career phases regarding the age and experience variables should be used as an indicator when devising special support programs for the lecturers.

Leaders and faculty administrators should be engaged in an ongoing process of identifying appropriate technology applications and their educational uses that should be made available to all learners and lecturers.

Commitment to technology effectiveness should be maintained not only among teaching related activities but also administrative activities. Faculty should present a determined attitude towards sustaining continuous quality in the teaching and learning processes.

Students must access support services through which they could reach online resources, faculty access, maintain peer interaction and benefit from other advantages provided within the campus (Garson, 2007).

The effective use of technology needs to be related to how learners learn. As it was mentioned by the students in the study:

> Expecting technology to enrich the lesson and demanding too much from it could be seen as the projection of one's hopelessness not the technologies' fault.

Lecturers in this respect need to encourage creativity and critical thinking in their lectures through the effective and skilful use of technology. Goh, Dexter, and Murphy (2007) asserted that the idea of computer-mediated communication could promote critical among learners through internalization within a community of learners.

It is evident that critical reflection and contextual awareness lead to a learner view of course design and measured approaches to technology use (Burge, 1999). Like teachers, lecturers should put more thinking in their lecture planning and should question their teaching repertoire and renew it by not being a victim of the technology by thinking more about the taboos they have or the departments have. It should further be noted that critical thinking should be associated with problem solving skills going beyond computational mechanics to consideration of complex causal and value systems (Garson, 2007).

REFERENCES

Agre, P. E. (1999). Information technology in higher education: The global academic village and intellectual standardization. *On the Horizon, 7*(5), 8–11.

Anderson, S. E., & Harris, J. B. (1997). Factors associated with amount of use and benefits obtained by users of a state wide educational tele-computing network. *Educational Technology, Research and Development, 45*, 19–50.

Bakioglu, A., & Hacifazlioglu, O. (2003, October 15–18). *Lecturers' and students' perceptions of technology use: Implications for faculty administrators.* Proceedings of 12th Education Conference, Antalya, Turkey.

Bakioglu, A., & Hacifazlioglu, O. (2007a). Lecturers' perceptions of private university establishment standards and teaching quality. In T. Townsend & R. Bates (Eds.), *Handbook of teacher education in times of change*. The Netherlands: Springer.

Bakioglu, A., & Hacifazlioglu, O. (in press). *Integration as globalization in higher education.*

Burge, E. J. (1999). Using learning technologies: Ideas for keeping one's balance. *Educational Technology, 39*(6), 45–49.

Cohen, L., Manion, L., & Morrison, K. (2000). *A guide to teaching practice*. London : Routledge.

Christensen, E. W., Anakwe, P. U., & Kessler, E. H. (2001). Receptivity to distance learning: The effect of technology, reputation, constraints, and learning preferences. *Journal of Research on Computing in Education, 4*, 263–279.

Day, C., & Bakioglu, A. (1996). Development and disenchantment of head teachers. In I. Goodson & A. Hargreaves (Eds.), *Teachers professional lives*. London: Falmer Press.

Day, C. (1999). *Developing teachers*. London: Falmer Press.

Day, C. (2004). *A passion for teaching*. London: Falmer Press.

Eric Critical Issue Bibliography. (2002). *Technology in the classroom*. Retrieved from http://www.eriche.org/crib/ technincl.html

Fabry, D. L., & Higgs, J. R. (1997). Barriers to the effective use of technology in education. *Journal of Educational Computing Research, 17*(4), 385–395.

Frazer, J. G. (1955). *Taboo and the perils of the soul*. The Colombia Electronic Encylopedia.

Freud, S. (1913). *Some points of agreement between the mental lives of savages and neurotics: Totem and taboo*. Retrieved May 12, 2007, from http://www.mdx.ac.uk/WWW/STUDY/xfre1913.htm

Garson, D. G. (2007). *The role of technology in education*. Retrieved from http://hcl.chass.ncsu.edu/sscore/garson2

Grant, J. (2002). *Does integrating technology into curriculum increase student learning?* (ERIC Document Reproduction Service No. ED431006). Retrieved February 10, 2004, from http://ericae.ent/ericdb/ed431006.htm

Gilbert, S. W. (2005). *Integrating technology into higher education: Dangerous discussions, new conditions, old truths about faculty/professional development*. Retrieved April 6, 2007, from http://www.tltgroup.rog/ProFacDev/RationaleDangerousDiscussions.htm

Goh, W. W., Dexter, B., & Murphy, W. D. (2007). *Promoting critical thinking with mediated communication technology*. Retrieved January 11, 2007, from http://www.actapress.com/Paperinfo.aspx?PaperID=30018

Hacifazlioglu, O., Sacli, O. A., & Yengin, I. (2007, May 3–5). *Lecturers' attitudes towards the use of technology: alternative strategies for faculty administrators*. Paper Presented at the International Computer Education Conference, North Cyprus.

Huberman, M. (1995). *The lives of teachers*. London: Cassell.

Jacobsen, M. (2007). Teaching and learning with technology in higher education. *New Currents, 15*(2). Retrieved April 4, 2007, from http://www.ucalgary.ca/NewCurrents/VOL5.2/usingtech.htm

Kim, S., & Kim, S. (2004). The conflict over the use of information technology in South Korean schools. *Innovation, 17*(4), 363–375.

Kompf, M. (2005). Information and communications technology and the seduction of knowledge, teaching and learning: What lies ahead for education. *Curriculum Inquiry, 35*(2), 213–234.

Mackay, C. (2003). *Extraordinary popular delusions and the madness of crowds*. Great Britain: Harriman House.
Mannan, M. D. A. (2007). Student attrition and academic and social integration: Application of Tinto's model at the university of Papua New Guinea. *Higher Education: The International Journal of Higher Education and Educational Planning, 53*(2), 147–165.
Morrison, J. (2003). U.S. education in transition. *On the Horizon, 11*(1), 6–10.
Schussler, D. L., Poole, I. R., Whitlock, T. W., & Evertson, C. M. (2007). Layers and links: Learning to judge one more thing in the classroom. *Teaching and Teacher Education, 23*(5), 572–585.
Seyal, A. H., Rahman, M., Noah, A., & Rahim, M. (2002). Determinants of academic use of the Internet: A structural equation model. *Behaviour and Information Technology, 21*(1), 71–86.
Summers, M. (1990). New student lecturers and computers: An investigation of experiences and feelings. *Educational Review, 42*(3), 261–271.
Yuen, H. K., & Ma, W. K. (2002). Gender differences in teacher computer acceptance. *Journal of Technology and Teacher Education, 10*(3), 365–382.
Unwin, A. (2007). The professionalism of the higher education teacher: What is ICT got to do with it? *Teaching in Higher Education, 12*(3), 14–28.
Wang Y., & Holthaus, P. (1997, February 14–18). *Student lecturers' computer use during practicum*. Proceedings of the Selected Research and Development Presentations at the National Conversation of the Association for Educational Communications and Technology (ERIC Document Reproduction Service No. ED409879). Retrieved May 20, 2004, from http://ericae.ent/ericdb/ed409879.htm
Wikipedia. (2007). *Taboos and totems*. Retrieved March 9, 2007, from http://www.answers.com/library/wikipedia.cid-566250106

Aysen Bakioglu
Ataturk Faculty of Education
Marmara University

Ozge Hacifazlioglu
Faculty of Arts and Sciences
Bahcesehir University

PER F. LAURSEN

STUDENT TEACHERS' CONCEPTIONS OF THEORY AND PRACTICE IN TEACHER EDUCATION

ABSTRACT

This article presents the results of an interview study of student teachers' conceptions of theory and practice in teacher education. Student teachers often complain that theory in teacher education is not relevant to practice. This problem has probably grown worse during the last decades with the enhanced academic ambitions of many teacher training programs. However student teachers' reports about the problem are often expressed in clichés that are difficult for teacher training institutions to act upon. The purpose of this project has been to acquire a more precise and subtle understanding of the students' conceptions and their rationales. The empirical material of the project is qualitative group interviews with 34 students from five Danish teacher training colleges. The results show that student teachers view theory as a product of other persons' work and theorizing is not viewed as anything they do or can do themselves. Student teachers want primarily to learn to teach, not to reflect on teaching and therefore they want theories to be useful and to be 'tool-like'. Student teachers do not want recipes or manuals; they want freedom to develop their own way of teaching.

INTRODUCTION: HISTORICAL BACKGROUND OF THE THEORY-PRACTICE GAP

During the last decades the 'theory-practice gap' in teacher education has been widely discussed. Many student teachers experience problems about the relationship between 'theory' and 'practice' in teacher education and find 'theories' irrelevant to the development of teacher competences. However, 'theory' and 'practice' are vague terms and phrases like 'theory-practice gap' have become almost clichés. The purpose of this article is to answer the questions: What do student teachers mean by 'theory' and 'practice' and how do they believe that the relationship between theory and practice should be?

Seen in historical perspective the 'theory-practice gap' is a relatively new issue. The problem has not always existed and therefore it need not necessarily exist in the future. All through the long history of formal teacher education – in Denmark the first teacher training college was opened in 1791 – programs have been composed of two main parts, an academic part taking place at teacher training colleges or universities and a practical part taking place at schools. Seen from today's viewpoint it might perhaps be expected that the relationship between these two parts of teacher education always has been a complicated issue. But during the first century

J. A. Kentel and A. Short (eds.), Totems and Taboos: Risk and Relevance in Research on Teachers and Teaching, 171–182.

the relationship seems to have been considered to be rather straightforward: At the teacher training colleges students learned subject matter knowledge and principles and methods of teaching. At school they learned how to practice these principles and methods. Teachers both at college and in schools were supposed to be models the students should imitate (Braad, Larsen, Markussen, Noerr, & Skovgaard-Petersen, 2005).

At the beginning of the 20th Century this relationship became more complicated. The belief in the correct way of teaching was gradually replaced by the ideal that the professional teacher should master several or multiple ways of teaching and be able to choose among them according to the circumstances. Still the lecturers at teaching training colleges and the mentors at practice schools were supposed to function as models to be imitated by student teachers. And the relationship between theory and practice was viewed as a matter of application of theory. By the middle of the 20th Century the rational curriculum planning models brought with them a new concept of teacher competence based on professional rationality. Especially Ralph Tyler's *Basic Principles of Curriculum and Instruction* (Tyler, 1949) was influential. Teacher's competences were now understood as the ability to plan a course so that learning experiences and teaching methods resulted in the learning outcomes stipulated by the aims. The competent teacher could apply her knowledge of curriculum planning, the psychology of learning and so on to planning under various circumstances.

This 'technical-rationality' model (Schön, 1987) or 'application of theory model' (Korthagen & Kessels, 1999) became relatively quickly an object of both empirically and theoretically based criticism. Empirical studies of teacher socialization showed that practice seemed to be more important to teacher development than teacher education (Lortie, 1975) and studies of learning during field experience demonstrated that many theoretical conceptions were "washed out" from teacher education (Korthagen & Kessels, 1999). Other studies showed that student teachers' beliefs were difficult to change by direct intervention and 'applying theory to practice' so that teacher education had only modest effects (Tillema, 1998). Theoretically based critique noted that practical teacher competence was a result of personally and ethically based dispositions rather than standard models of 'rational' planning (van Manen, 1991).

'THEORY', 'PRACTICE', AND TEACHER COMPETENCE IN CONTEMPORARY RESEARCH

In 1983 two books were published that marked a new era in the conception of the role of theory and practice in teacher competence and teacher education, namely Schön's (1983), *The Reflective Practitioner* and Elbaz' (1983), *Teacher Thinking: A Study of Practical Knowledge.* Both books underscored that practical professional competence is not the result of applying theory to practice. Following this new tradition several concepts have been introduced to underline the practical character of teacher competence, for instance personal practical knowledge (Connely & Clandinin, 1990) and craft knowledge (Brown & MacIntyre, 1993).

Practical knowledge was seen as professional knowledge that is more specific and pragmatic than academic knowledge (Zanting, Verloop, & Vermunt, 2003). Studies of teachers' views on research and theory showed that teachers do not value academic research. Teachers tend to view academic knowledge as being neither practical, contextual, credible, nor accessible and they rely more on experiences of their own and their colleagues (Gore & Gitlin, 2004). Student teachers tend to share these attitudes; a study found the following statement of a student teacher to be typical: "Forget about theory, practice is all" (Hascher, Cocard, & Moser, 2004).

Overcoming this perceived gap between theory and practice in pre-service teacher education is a widespread endeavor (Westbury, Hansén, Kansanen, & Björkvist, 2005). Today's dominating view is that theory and practice should be integrated (Leinhardt, Young & Merriman, 1995). Reflection is often viewed as the way to achieve this integration. According to the integrative and reflective approach, student teachers are encouraged to construct their own philosophy of education integrating their experiences and personal practical knowledge with general theory (Shin, 2006). Several models of teacher education stress the continuing cycle of interplay between theory, practice and reflection as the way to promote changes in student teachers' attitudes and practices (Hill, 2000). Among the alternatives to the 'application-of-theory' is the constructivist (Kroll, 2004) or social constructivist approach that promotes students to develop grounded theories based on information gathered from the world of practice (Carlson, 1999). Another influential new model of teacher education is Fred Korthagen's 'realistic approach'. It is based on the insight shared by many teacher education researchers that students begin teacher education with rather persistent subjective theories of teaching. 'Reframing' of the students' minds requires much more than just presenting new theoretical frameworks to them. Instead the 'realistic teacher education approach' aims at the students having practical experience with ways of teaching that slowly can inspire new ways of thinking about teaching (Korthagen & Kessel, 1999; Korthagen, 2001).

Although the literature on teacher education and on theory and practice in education is enormous, only few research projects have focused on the student teachers' conceptions. Some authors have noticed that beginning student teachers expect to be told how to teach (e.g. Jong, Korthagen, & Wubbels., 1998; Loughran, 2005). The usual response from teacher educators and researchers confronted with this view has been that this expectation ought not to be met and that student teachers instead should learn how to reflect on teaching (e.g. Zanting et al., 2003, p. 207).

RESEARCH QUESTIONS

The aim of our project was therefore to reach a more subtle understanding of the student teachers' conceptions and preferences. We found it unlikely that there is nothing more to be said about prospective teachers' expectations of teacher education than that they want to be told how to teach. And we expected that the student teachers' expectations ought to be met with a more favorable attitude than telling them that they have to learn something else than they wished for.

Our research questions were:

- How do student teachers view teachers' work, competences, and teacher education?
- What are student teachers' concepts of 'theory' and 'practice' and the relation between them?

CONTEXT: TEACHER EDUCATION IN DENMARK

Danish teacher education takes place at 18 training colleges offering a concurrent-type program in which student teachers work with pedagogy, school subjects and internships throughout the program. The program is of four years' duration and includes teaching practice at a school for a total of 24 weeks, the organization of which is decided by the individual institution. The general outlines of the program are regulated by legislation: the duration, subjects, rules regarding the institutions and their management etc. The theoretical part of the program includes the following:

- Pedagogical subjects (theory of education, psychology, general didactics, school and society);
- School subjects: Danish or mathematics and three more main subjects must be chosen by the student.

The admission requirement for the teacher training program is an examination at upper secondary level. 1/3 of the students are men, 2/3 are women. About 55% of the students complete the program by the officially stipulated time of study, and 75% in total complete the program (http://www.uvm.dk).

METHOD AND MATERIAL

The research group (Karen Braad, Carsten Henningsen, Per F. Laursen, Bodil Nielsen, & J. Paulsen) decided to do semi-structured qualitative interviews (Kvale, 1996) as the obvious method to learn to know what 'theory' and 'practice' mean to student teachers. However, student teachers can often be heard uttering a certain repertoire of rather stereotyped cliché-like statements about 'theory and practice' in teacher education. Danish student teachers often say that 'theory is one thing, practice something else' or 'college and school are two different worlds'. We were interested in going beneath such statements and reconstruct the student teachers' thinking about teacher competence, how it can be developed and what role educational theory and practical experience might play. Therefore we decided not to introduce the words 'theory' or 'practice' to the student teachers during the interviews. Instead we asked the student teachers four broad questions in order to elicit their own thinking:

- What is demanded of a teacher today and what must a teacher be able to do?
- Where and how can you learn to do what a teacher must be able to do?
- Do you think that the teacher education program you are involved in will qualify you to become a teacher?

– If you could design a teacher education program according to your preferences what should it be like?

We decided to interview the student teachers in groups because we expected that students' conceptions of these fundamental issues are developed together with fellow students and therefore would be more validly expressed by a group than by single students. We interviewed 34 student teachers in 12 groups. The student teachers attended five of the 18 Danish teacher training colleges and they were interviewed at the colleges. Half the student teachers were first year students and the other half were fourth year students. The interviews lasted about one hour and were audio-recorded and transcribed.

The data were analyzed primarily by meaning categorization (Kvale, 1996, p. 196) aiming at identifying the student teachers' conceptual structure concerning teacher competence and the role of theory and practice.

RESULTS

We expected student teachers' conceptions of theory and practice to be subordinated to their general conceptions about teacher competence. We therefore analyzed the student teachers' conceptions beginning with the most general continuing to the more specific in the following order: teachers' work, teacher competence, theory and practice, and finally the relationship between theory and practice in teacher education.

Teachers' Work

The student teachers viewed teachers' work as very demanding and several of the first year students found it almost overwhelming after their first internship. Many of them were surprised to find that teachers have so many different things to do, that they must take care of many tasks simultaneously, and that many of the tasks cannot be planned in advance:

> A teacher must be kind of an all round person needing an eye on each finger and many fingers–in fact–needing to do all sorts of things. Not only socially and concerning subject matter; the teacher must be able to manage any unforeseen situation.

The student teachers viewed the task about the students' general social and personal functioning and their general social and personal development to be the most important in the daily work of teachers. In Denmark like in many other countries the public opinion these years stresses subject matter teaching and learning as the most important activity in school. The student teachers seemed not to have accepted this policy. Or, if they had, they tended to view a good social climate in the classroom and personally and socially well functioning students as preconditions that must be established prior to subject matter teaching and learning. Especially first year student teachers viewed subject matter instruction as something that can be done relatively easy if the social preconditions are established.

The fourth year student teachers had become more humble in relation to subject matter teaching and were not that sure that their competences would be sufficient.

Cooperation with parents was seen as an important and difficult part of teachers' work. Parents who are ambitious on behalf of their children as well as parents with social problems who do not care for their children were viewed as challenging:

> I had expected parents to interfere a lot. But I experienced the opposite – they simply didn't care about their kids. They did not support them doing their homework and the students didn't progress. It is a hopeless situation for a teacher.

Also the relations to colleagues were seen as an important aspect of teachers' work.

Summing up on teachers' work, student teachers viewed their work as complex and demanding and they found the relational and personal aspects to be the most difficult ones compared to subject matter teaching.

Teacher Competence

Talking about teacher competence the interviewees made a distinction between two main domains of competence: personal-relational competences and subject-matter-teaching competences. Official documents on teacher education in Denmark normally write about three main domains of teacher competence: subject matter knowledge, pedagogics and practical knowledge. The reason why students did not use these concepts seems to be that they viewed the personal-relational competences to be very important and this view is not reflected in official documents.

According to the student teachers you must have a basis of personal qualities before starting teacher education; the personal-relational competences can only to a limited degree be acquired in teacher education programs:

> Clearly, it is the human being behind that is most important.

The most important personal quality is to be committed to working and being together with children:

> You can't learn to care for kids. This is something you have to make clear to yourself before you become a teacher. I mean, you don't become a doctor if you can't stand seeing blood.

It is important to be able to perform and to lead a large group of children also under chaotic circumstances. And it is important to be able to take an interest in all the children regardless of their personalities or behavior. A teacher should be able to evoke respect from her students and to be regarded as a natural and trustworthy authority. Precondition for this is that the teacher shows the students her respect.

Some of the student teachers, especially from the fourth year, were quite explicit and detailed in their specification of the personal qualities demanded of a teacher: The teacher must be enthusiastic, ambitious, sincere, tactful, extrovert, empathic, and a good communicator. The teacher must consider her job as a kind of calling. If the teacher shall be able to make the students learn with enthusiasm she must invest herself personally in the teaching. A teacher must be interested in her students not only as learners but as persons. She must familiarize herself with the lives of her students outside school and she must also be willing to let her students know something about her own life outside school. Still, she must be able to draw a line and avoid the relations to students becoming as private. According to the student teachers a teacher must be able to show her caring for each student and she must be able to relate herself to each individual student and not only to the class as a group. Students with emotional or social problems are great challenges, especially because they evoke many unexpected problems in class needing the teacher to improvise. To mediate conflicts between students and between parents and school is another important competence.

Student teachers tended to view the necessary personal qualities as a matter of personality rather than professional competence. On the basis of these qualities relational competences can be developed in teacher education according to the student teachers, primarily in internships:

> I do believe that it is when you are in practice and relate to the real kids that you learn. It is difficult coming into schools, always, but it is getting easier each time. You learn something and you bring something with you home and you can say: Now I have got this experience.

Being together with children is indispensable if the student teachers want to learn how to relate to them. A lot can be learned by studying mentors and fellow student teachers but the core of relational competence can only be learned by practicing as a teacher relating to children. Still, something can and should be done about relational competences at college. Psychology-courses can give a basic understanding of children's reactions and personality. The student teachers thought that the colleges should supply them with more tools to develop relational competences and the student teachers believed that training in managing relations should be done in college. Some of them mentioned role-playing as a method.

Besides the personal and relational competence student teachers considered the ability to teach subject matter to be the other main part of teacher competence. This part is judged to be more simple and easier to master than the personal and relational aspects:

> It is important to make yourself visible, it is obvious. That's why I thought: 'OK, first of all'. Then subject matter teaching can follow.

The first year students simply expected the college to give them the necessary qualifications whereas several fourth year students were far from sure that they would have acquired the necessary qualifications by graduation.

The student teachers wanted the college's courses in the school subjects to be close to common practice in schools concerning both content and method, although of course at a higher level. According to the student teachers analysis of lesson plans and accounts of teaching cases are valuable activities in college courses. They also enjoyed analyzing textbooks and other teaching material used in schools.

They criticized that several college lecturers do not have sufficient updated knowledge about teaching in schools.

Basically the student teachers believed that subject matter teaching is learned in the same way as the personal and relational qualities: by practicing in schools. The student teachers did not consider the college courses to be useless but they clearly preferred them to mirror practice in schools and to introduce tools to master the teacher's challenges.

Summing up on teacher competence, the student teachers view personal and relational competences and being able to teach subject matter as the main parts of teacher competence. They find the personal-relational aspect of the job to be the most complex and demanding. Both aspects of teacher competence must be learned primarily in practice according to the student teachers.

Theory and Practice

The student teachers used 'theory' in several different senses:

- subject matter content in school subjects;
- tools and methods to be used while teaching and managing the class;
- educational and psychological views on for instance learning and human nature.

Common to these different senses was that the student teachers viewed 'theory' as a kind of existing product which they could come to know from their lecturers or from textbooks and which they thereafter should be able to use in 'practice'.

None of the interviewed student teachers ever used 'theory' about their own activity or about the products of this activity, e.g. their own analyses and reflections on their teaching. To them 'theory' was something that is produced by others ('theorists') and which is valuable if it can be used by student teachers and teachers.

'Practice', on the other hand, is something which they themselves should become able to do. 'Practice' was used about activities in schools, especially about what the teacher does in the classroom working with students. Sometimes the student teachers also used 'practice' about the planning of teaching and about cooperation with colleagues or parents. The interviewees never used 'practice' about developmental or researching activities.

According to the student teachers a theory is good if it can be used in practice in schools and can help teachers and student teachers manage their job. Compared to this ideal the interviewees mentioned three problems about the relation between 'theory' and 'practice' in teacher education:

- The teacher education program does not introduce a sufficient amount of tools and methods.
- The lecturers teach theories but do not care about how the theories should be used in practice.
- If lecturers talk about ideas about practice these ideas are often too theoretical and to distant from the daily life in school.

An interviewee said about the insufficient promotion of tools:

> I lack tools. After the summer holiday I'm going be a teacher of Danish and when I arrive in a class to teach Danish how do I find out if some students are dyslexic? How do I bring about flow in classroom activities? How can I vary my teaching? I think I lack a lot of tools to do things like that.

Several of the interviewees said on their own initiative that they were well aware that currently it is not possible to give any recipes or manuals showing in detail and step by step how to teach:

> I think that you can get some tools. Then it is up to you how to use them. You can modify things so that you can use them yourself. I don't think that 'how to do it' can be delivered to you. But you can get some tools and then you can choose how to use them.

Even if it was possible to use recipes they preferred instead to develop their own style of teaching and to develop kinds of teaching adapted to the circumstances and the students. They feared that the personal and relational qualities in teaching which they valued so much would be destroyed by recipes or manuals.

Summing up on 'theory' and 'practice,' the student teachers see 'theory' as made by 'theorists' and used by teachers. 'Practice' is done by teachers in class. A good 'theory' is like a tool helping teachers to manage their job. 'Theories' introduced in teacher education programs should leave open the possibility to develop teaching adapted to the persons involved and to the circumstances.

CONCLUSION

The research questions of this study were:

- How do student teachers view teachers' work, competences, and teacher education?
- What are student teachers' concepts of 'theory' and 'practice' and the relation between them?

Based on the interviews it is relatively easy to answer these questions because the interviewees were explicit and outspoken and almost all of them shared the same basic conceptions and attitudes.

Student teachers view teachers' work as complex and demanding and they see the personal and relational aspects as especially important. Therefore teacher competence is conceived primarily as a matter of personal qualities and relational competences and only secondarily as a matter of being able to teach subject matter. Teacher competence is primarily acquired by practicing in schools and college courses should support this by introducing tool-like theories.

Student teachers view 'theory' as products made by 'theorists' and 'practice' as something they should become able to do themselves when teaching and managing classes. A good theory works like a tool helping teachers to master their job. Because the personal and relational aspects of teaching are so important 'practice' cannot be guided by recipes or manuals. Instead the teacher should be able to improvise and to develop teaching adapted to the persons involved and to the circumstances.

DISCUSSION

To put the conclusion of this study simple and provoking: Teacher education programs want students to learn how to reflect on teaching but students want to learn how to teach.

Especially in the beginning of the process of becoming a teacher student teachers do primarily focus on their own classroom behavior (Burn et al., 2003, p. 325). Why not simply try to meet the needs of the student teachers and supply them with ideas, suggestions, guidelines and tools about how to teach and how to develop their own way of teaching?

It might be argued that teachers' way of teaching is strongly influenced by their values and beliefs and that it is impossible for teachers to develop new ways of teaching unless they reflect critically on their values and beliefs (Tatto, 1999). It might further be argued that professional teachers ought not to be 'consumers' of other peoples' theories, but should be co-constructors of the profession's theoretical-practical knowledge (Sweeny, 2003). Of course the ambitions of teachers' professional development should not be any lower than that. But it seems legitimate and fully understandable that students in pre-service teacher education are more concerned about learning the basic craft of teaching and prefer theories that are helpful in mastering this challenge.

Teacher training should of course not be reduced to skill training in the classroom. An obvious response to the expressed expectations of student teachers however is to promote a kind of reflective apprenticeship continuum ranging from imitation to exploration and gradual expansion of the reflective process throughout the period of teacher education (Smedley, 2001). Student teachers' development towards teacher competence is complex and varied (Sendan & Roberts, 1998) and student teachers are concerned about being able to develop their own way of teaching adapted to their students and to the circumstances. As pointed out by recent research on the development of the concerns of student teachers they are not totally unwilling to reflect (Burn et al., 2003; Guillaume & Rudney, 1993).

Teacher educators have feared that teacher education would be turned into a totally school based enterprise following the classical apprenticeship model (Hill, 2000). However, this will not be the result of meeting the student teachers' needs. Student teachers want to develop their own way of teaching instead of following recipes and they are motivated for reflection but the reflective component should be based on student teachers' self-expressed concerns and questions (Guillaume & Rudney, 1993). Student teachers do not want teacher education to become totally practical and free of theory and they do not want any simple recipes for teaching. They just want theory to help them learn to teach.

REFERENCES

Brown, S., & McIntyre, D. (1993). *Making sense of teaching.* Milton Keynes: Open University Press.

Braad, K., Larsen, C., Markussen, I., Noerr, E., & Skovgaard-Petersen, V. (2005). *- for at blive en god lærer. Seminarier i to århundreder.* [*- to become a good teacher. Teacher training colleges through two centuries.*] Odense: Syddansk Universitetsforlag.

Burn, K., Hazel, H., Mutton, T., & Everton, T. (2003). The complex development of students-teachers' thinking. *Teachers and Teaching: Theory and Practice, 9*(4), 309–331.

Carlson, H. L. (1999). From practice to theory: A social constructivist approach to teacher education. *Teachers and Teaching: Theory and Practice, 5*(2), 203–218.

Connely, F. M., & Clandinin, D. J. (1990). Stories of experienced and narrative inquiry. *Educational Researcher, 19*, 2–14.

Elbaz, F. (1983). *Teacher thinking: A study of practical knowledge*. New York: Nichols.

Gore, J. M., & Gitlin, A. D. (2004). (Re)visioning the academic-teacher divide: Power and knowledge in the educational community. *Teachers and Teaching: Theory and Practice, 10*(1), 35–58.

Guillaume, A. M., & Rudney, G. L. (1993). Student teachers' growth toward independence: An analysis of their changing concerns. *Teaching and Teacher Education, 9*(1), 65–80.

Hacher, T., Cocard, Y., & Moser, P. (2004). Forget about theory – practice is all? Student teachers' learning in practicum. *Teachers and Teaching: Theory and Practice, 10*(6), 623–637.

Hill, L. (2000). Theory, practice and reflection: A pre-service primary mathematics education programme. *Teachers and Teaching: Theory and Practice, 6*(1), 23–39.

Jong, J. D., Korthagen, F., & Wubbels, T. (1998). Learning from practice in teacher education: Processes and interventions. *Teachers and Teaching: Theory and Practice, 4*(1), 47–64.

Korthagen, F. A. J., & Kessels, J. P. A. M. (1999). Linking theory and practice: Changing the pedagogy of teacher education. *Educational Researcher, 28*(4), 4–17.

Korthagen, F. A. (2001). *Linking practice and theory: The pedagogy of realistic teacher education*. New Jersey, NJ: Lawrence Erlbaum Publishers.

Kroll, L. R. (2004). Constructing constructivism: How student-teachers construct ideas of development, knowledge, learning and teaching. *Teachers and Teaching: Theory and Practice, 10*(2), 199–221.

Kvale, S. (1996). *Interviews: An introduction to qualitative research interviewing*. Thousand Oaks, CA: Sage.

Leinhardt, G., Young, K. M., & Merriman, J. (1995). Integrating professional knowledge: The theory of practice and the practice of theory. *Learning and Instruction, 5*, 401–408.

Lortie, D. (1975). *Schoolteacher: A sociological study*. Chicago: University of Chicago Press.

Loughran, J. (2005). Knowledge construction and learning to teach about teaching. In Beijard, Meijer, Morine-Dershimer, & Tillema (Eds.), *Teacher professional development in changing conditions* (pp. 27–41). Dordrecht: Springer.

Schön, D. A. (1983). *The reflective practitioner. how professionals think in action*. New York: Basic Books.

Schön, D. A. (1987). *Educating the reflective practitioner*. San Francisco: Jossey-Bass.

Sendan, F., & Roberts, J. (1998). Orhan: A case study in the development of a student teacher's personal theories. *Teachers and Teaching: Theory and Practice, 4*(2), 229–244.

Shin, S. J. (2006). Learning to teach writing through tutoring and journal writing. *Teachers and Teaching: Theory and Practice, 12*(3), 325–345.

Smedley, L. (2001). Impediments to partnership: A literature review of school-university links. *Teachers and Teaching: Theory and Practice, 7*(2), 189–209.

Sweeny, A. E. (2003). Theory and practice in science teaching. *Teachers and Teaching: Theory and Practice, 9*(2), 107–132.

Tatto, M. T. (1999). The Socializing influence of normative cohesive teacher education on teachers' beliefs about instructional choice. *Teachers and Teaching: Theory and Practice, 5*(1), 95–118.

Tillema, H. H. (1998). Stability and change in student teachers' beliefs about teaching. *Teachers and Teaching: Theory and Practice, 4*(2), 217–228.

Tyler, R. (1949). *Basic principles of learning and instruction*. Chicago: University of Chicago Press.

van Manen. (1991). *The tact of teaching: The meaning of pedagogical thoughtfulness*. Albany, NY: SUNY Press.

Westbury, I., Hansén, S.-E., Kansanen, P., & Björkvist, O. (2005). Teacher education for research-based practice in expanded roles: Finland's experience. *Scandinavian Journal of Educational Research, 49*(5), 475–485.

Zanting, A., Verloop, N., & Vermunt, J. D. (2003). How do student teachers elicit their mentor teachers' practical knowledge? *Teachers and Teaching: Theory and Practice, 9*(3), 197–211.

Per F. Laursen
Department of Curriculum Research
Danish School of Education, University of Aarhus

BARBARA ŠTEH AND JANA KALIN

THE CHANGING STUDENTS CONCEPTIONS IN EVALUATING TEACHER EFFECTIVENESS IN HIGHER EDUCATION – FACING CHALLENGES AND TABOOS

INTRODUCTION

Background: University of Ljubljana and the Courses in Pedagogy and Andragogy

The University of Ljubljana, the largest and oldest of the three Slovenian universities (approximately 60.000 students) defined itself recently in its mission statement as "an institution striving for excellence in research". The absence of mentioning "excellence in teaching" was observed even in 1996 by a group of international experts in the CRE Auditors' report (Institutional Audit of the University of Ljubljana). The promotion criteria for university teachers are still based primarily on the quantity of their scientific production. Nominally, 25% of the weight is to be given also to the candidate's pedagogical qualities, but those are mainly reduced to writing textbooks and successful mentoring of MA and doctoral students. Lately also the *student's voice* is being included into promotion procedures. A report on teaching quality, written by students, is a mandatory part of promotion documentation. In the last five years also standard student questionnaires have been widely used as a basis of this report.

To what an extent do university teachers strive to improve the quality of their teaching? Do they think about how to activate students during lectures? To what extent do they think about the ways in which they influence students–not only from the point of view of the content they transmit, but through their approach, attitude, methodology, demands and assessment? While it would surely be interesting to find out the teachers' perspectives, the present paper limits itself to the students' responses to some of these questions.

The Faculty of Arts is the largest member of the University of Ljubljana, with 8.000 students and 550 employees, of which there are 230 tenured teachers. The faculty comprises 21 departments, which are relatively independent units with quite different histories. Overall, there are 31 courses of study offered. One of the biggest and oldest departments is the Department of Pedagogy and Andragogy. The graduates of the department are trained to research educational theory and practice from pre-school to adult education. They gain the competences needed to develop educational science and resolve issues related to management in education. They also work in educational counselling, teach pedagogy and andragogy, and run educational activities of various types in schools and other institutions.

J. A. Kentel and A. Short (eds.), Totems and Taboos: Risk and Relevance in Research on Teachers and Teaching, 183–197.

There are approximate 600 students at the Department every year. The undergraduate course in pedagogy and andragogy can be taken as a single subject or combined with one of the numerous other courses within and outside of the Faculty of Arts. There is also a variety of postgraduate courses.

Most of the classes offered take the form of lectures, with more seminars in years 3 and 4, but only few exercises in some subjects. The obligatory two-week school based practice period also takes place towards the end of the course. Students often say that they need more practical experience. Group visits to schools and other institutions are therefore a valuable component of the programme.

Conceptions of Knowledge Teaching and Teacher/Student Roles

All students entering university have had years of experience in education, and their mental models are more or less coherent systems of conceptions about: knowledge and learning, themselves as students, and learning goals and tasks. the students' conceptions of roles and responsibilities of participants in the teaching/learning process. have already been formed (Vermunt, 1993). With these mental models and learning orientations—personal goals, motives, expectations, doubts—they enter various learning situations and then interpret them accordingly. These interpretations and the students' repertoire of learning strategies determine how the students will use various learning strategies and act in certain situation, which in turn determines the quality of their learning process and resulting knowledge. The teacher's assessment criteria and the students' self-evaluation of learning effectiveness have a reverse effect on the students' mental models of learning and learning orientations. We are therefore interested in the messages we as teachers send to our students and the effect these have on their existing conceptions of knowledge, teacher and student roles and, indirectly, on the quality of the learning process and the resulting knowledge (Biggs, 1999).

The study is grounded in modern cognitive-constructivist notions of knowledge, learning and teaching, which stress the dynamic nature of knowledge and its constant construction and reconstruction. *Constructive learning* thus refers to active (re)construction of knowledge; it is an attempt of building richer and more complex memory representations. Vermunt (1993) stresses the importance of the student's own activity; in constructive learning, the learner actively constructs their own knowledge through a deep approach to learning and self-regulated learning activity. We need to transcend the traditional conception of knowledge in the sense of final truths that can be accumulated and transmitted to others. Simons (1997) in his meta-study of papers on constructive learning lists six key features of constructive learning on which there is a high degree of consonance between different authors. Constructive learning is:

- An active process: the learner's mental activity is crucial for him/her to arrive at certain meanings;
- A constructive process: in a narrow sense this means the connecting of a new piece of information with others in order to understand more easily both that particular information and the entire complexity of the subject matter;

- A cumulative process: in each new learning cycle we depart from previous knowledge and build on it;
- A goal-oriented process: learning will be successful if the learner is aware of at least some general goals he/she wants to achieve and has appropriate expectations concerning the achievement of learning results;
- Diagnostic: the learner keeps track of his/her learning and results;
- Reflective: rethinking the whole learning process.

Of course we cannot expect students to always be engaging in the same quality and quantity of mental activity. Sometimes their previous knowledge is quite limited and students need to focus on detail and certain processes. There is also nothing wrong with occasionally following the learning process without a specific learning goal in sight, and it is also impossible to constantly monitor and reflect on one's own learning. However, it is important that these processes occur in students' learning and that teachers understand their significance for a successful introduction of constructive learning and learner training with their students.

Quality of Learning and Teaching

All these characteristics of constructive learning can have a certain indicative role when we consider the quality of our own learning or teaching (depending on the role we play) and plan our next steps which should lead us to quality results—deeper insights into particular phenomena, comprehension of their interdependence, the ability of critical judgment ... and after all to a student who has mastered a specific knowledge and competences (an image of a graduate). Again and again we must ask ourselves, what kind of knowledge and competences have been achieved by our students. Researchers have shown that students at a higher education level often do not make any qualitative progress in their conceptions of essential phenomena in the area of their studies (Dahlgren, 1978; Brumby, 1979; Dahlgren, 1984; Gardner, 1991; Gibbs, 1992; Nightingale & O'Neil, 1994). Questions which we put to students are mainly quantitative and only rarely reach beyond the matter which can be memorized in an unreflected manner. Students acquire surface characteristics of core phenomena and the matching expert terminology which often hides their misunderstanding of phenomena, while they never achieve a deeper understanding of these phenomena. In the present research we ask ourselves, among others, what are students' conceptions of knowledge, teacher and student roles—essential conceptions in the expert area of their studies? On the other side we ask ourselves whether we create conditions which would lead students to higher quality learning and to acquiring high quality knowledge.

Nightingale and O'Neil (1994) stress that high quality learning will emerge in the following cases:

- When a student *is ready (cognitively and emotionally) to face learning tasks*: it is necessary to obtain a proper degree of imbalance between demands and capabilities, between the difficulty of teaching contents and previous knowledge, so that students are prepared to accept a certain learning task as a challenge.

- When a student *has reasons for learning*: students naturally perceive reasons for learning in achieving good marks and passing exams, so it is very important to plan an evaluation which will encourage them for high quality learning (when it is not memorizing which is primarily expected from them, but rather higher levels of knowledge). Yet the motivation should not be only external, but also inner—a need to explain and find reasons for particular phenomena, to develop certain skills, which in turn capacitates us/enables our better performance and participation. To achieve this we must build on previous students' experience and ask them to apply them in new learning tasks, to find the core problem by themselves as well as its applicability, to let the new knowledge become relevant for them personally.
- When a student will *clearly link the previous knowledge with the new knowledge*: the authors specifically state that they do not support the assumption that "students must first get a certain basic knowledge and then…" They rely on Gibbs (1992), who maintains that without existing conceptions it is impossible to make new conceptions meaningful; therefore it is essential to include the existing knowledge and experience in the learning process. He also stresses the importance of a well structured and organized knowledge, for which an active linking process of students is important.
- When a student becomes *active* during the learning process: it is reasonable to assume that nobody can be completely passive during the learning, but there exist considerable differences in the activities of students. On the one hand there are activities like dictation taking, a detailed learning of explanations from the notes, definition of formulae and their reproduction; on the other hand there are activities demonstrating a student's involvement in the learning process: problem-solving, search of important data with the aim of obtaining particular answers, group work…
- When the *environment will offer a student a suitable support*: the authors maintain, that by this we first think of support programmes to develop particular learning skills and strategies as well as various counselling methods. But we should also bear in mind how to achieve a better flexibility by means of a more open learning and by planning possibilities for cooperative learning. The general climate in the whole society is important as it is not stimulative for students if they are constantly related to as illiterate or incompetent or if they are told that what is taught at school is merely a theory.

AIM OF THE STUDY

The main goal of the present study was to uncover how students of pedagogy and andragogy interpret various messages and demands of their university teachers and whether four years of undergraduate studies bring about any changes in the students' conceptions of knowledge and student/teacher roles. We were especially interested in factors, which according to students' opinions had an influence on changing their conceptions. The paper presents the answers of our study to the following research questions:

- What conceptions of knowledge and student/teacher roles do students of pedagogy and andragogy possess? Are there differences between 1st and 4th year students in this respect?
- Do the second year and pre-graduation students feel that their conceptions have changed through the years of their schooling? If not, why not? If they have, what were the changes? Are they able to articulate and explain these changes?
- How complex are the students' explanations of the changes in their conceptions?
- What, in students' opinion, are the key factors that led to the changing of their conceptions of knowledge and learner/teacher roles?
- What is the second year and pre-graduation students' perception of the pedagogical and andragogical studies?

METHOD

The research was carried out in two phases: we had questionnaires completed in May 2006 and proceeded with interviews in March 2007. Questionnaires were presented to 74 students of pedagogy and andragogy at the Faculty of Arts in Ljubljana; a half of them in their first and the other half in the fourth year of their studies. The participating students mainly attend classes frequently, a half of them are fairly satisfied with their studies and 34% is neither satisfied nor dissatisfied; their average exam grade is 7.7 (in our assessment system the highest grade is 10 while the lowest passing grade is 6).

The questionnaire included multiple choice items, scales, open-ended questions and unfinished sentences. Based on the students' answers to the open questions we formed preliminary categories. Then we compared the groupings with the theoretical concepts and, for some items, with the classifications validated in previous research. This formed the basis for our categories. The data was processed with the help of SPSS for Windows in which we used a range of statistical procedures.

The aim of the interviews was to deepen our insight into the question whether the students' conceptions of knowledge and student and teacher roles have changed and whether students are able to articulate and explain these changes. For this purpose we made a random choice of 6 second year students and 6 pre-graduation students.

RESULTS AND DISCUSSION

Conceptions of Knowledge, Teacher and Learner Roles as They Are Revealed by Results Obtained from the Questionnaires (Šteh & Kalin, 2006)

Our primary inquiry was aimed at revealing the students' conceptions of knowledge, which we inferred from their answers to the question, "*What, in your opinion, is the gist of knowledge?*" The students' conceptions were divided into the following four categories, listed from lower to higher order, whereby the higher order conceptions still contain elements of lower order conceptions.

Quantity and durability of knowledge (17.6% responses). In this category we included very general responses, in which students mostly stressed that learning means retention, not forgetting something right after the exam is over.

Use (27%). Within this category students mostly stressed practical applicability of knowledge.

Understanding (39.2%). This category includes responses by those students who stressed the importance of understanding learning matter.

Seeing things differently (16.2%). This category of conceptions clustered around the idea of a shift of perspective, of viewing a phenomenon from different angles and critically evaluating one's knowledge. These changed views can of course also lead to development of personality—to greater independence and competence, but only two students mentioned that.

The results show that only half of the students (55.4%) have higher order conceptions of knowledge, with only a small percentage talking about shifting perspectives, knowledge construction and development of personality.

Besides that 35% of the students have *no real control of their own learning*, 28.4% of them rely on the quantity of studying they have done, and only 36.5% on understanding. We can conclude that most students cannot regulate their own learning and rely on surface strategies such as the amount of time spent studying (Vermunt, 1993). Simons (1997) would say that most students do not learn actively and constructively, because monitoring and reflection of one's own learning process are two of the key features of constructive learning.

A further aim of our study was to see if there are differences in student conceptions of knowledge between different years of studies, that is whether these conceptions change during the four years of studies, but there were no statistically significant differences between the responses of the 1st and 4th year students. It is true, however, that there is such a relationship between the year of studies and exam readiness according to the Kullback 2Î test (2Î (3, N = 74) = 7.94, p = .047): in the 4th year there are fewer students who don't know if they are ready to take an exam (2.7%) as compared to 13.5% in the 1st year. In the 4th year there is also a somewhat higher percentage of students who rely on their feelings and quantity of studying to judge how ready they are (20.3% as compared to 17.6% in the 1st year) and more students who judge their readiness by understanding (23% : 13.5%). These differences, however, are not big and we wonder whether they imply that teachers do not send the students enough messages about the importance of understanding subject matter or that these messages do not interact with their existing conceptions of knowledge and learning and thus have no effect on their learning. It is likely that teachers invest too little effort into developing various learning strategies and helping students become independent learners. Related to that, of course, is the question of how teachers conceive of their own roles—is developing students into self-regulated learners one of a teacher's tasks at all?

In categorizing responses about the role of the teacher we used a classification of conceptions developed by Fox (1983) specifically for teachers in higher education. This classification is more detailed than the two types of teaching styles distinguished by Kember and Gow (1994): transmission of knowledge and encouraging learning. However, students' conceptions were quite undifferentiated—only a few exhibited higher-level conceptions by saying that the teacher plays a role in encouraging a student's personal growth. The students' responses to the question about the role of the teacher were thus divided into the following three categories, listed hierarchically.

Transmission of knowledge and subject mastery (39.2%). Within this category, students stress that the teacher has to be a skilled lecturer, to provide clear and engaging explanation, be systematic and exhibit mastery of his/her subject.

Shaping the students (37.8%). This group of conceptions portrays a teacher who makes an effort to teach and motivate but retains a dominant role.

Activating students (23%). In this category, students stress that the teacher should actively involve the students in the learning process, encourage them to express their ideas and opinions, and take these into consideration.

How the students defined their own role:

Receiving knowledge and learning (41.9%). Within this category students mostly said that it is a student's duty to attend classes and try to gain from them as much as possible and diligently learn what the teacher demands.

Involvement (29.7%). In this group, students go beyond mere listening to lectures, making notes and diligent memorizing to learning activities that indicate more mental activity.

Taking initiative and responsibility (28.4%). This category shows that students see their role to also involve taking initiative and responsibility and care about their personal growth.

The students' responses show that only a small percentage of them take responsibility for their own learning—*8.1% expressed the highest-level conceptions of the teacher and student roles*. What is especially worrying is the fact that there is no statistically significant difference between 1st and 4th year students in this respect. Teachers seem to be sending them messages corresponding to the traditional role of the teacher who primarily has to explain everything very clearly and show mastery of his/her subject matter, and the traditional role of the student who has to learn the subject matter in detail and prove that in an exam.

A statistically significant connection has been found between students' conceptions of knowledge and conceptions of their own roles (2Î (6, N = 74) = 14.33, p = .026): most students who exhibit lower level conceptions of knowledge tend to also see their own roles as being "the diligent student", while those who conceive of knowledge as understanding tend to see themselves as being active, participating, taking initiative and responsibility. It is interesting that the responses of the students who see learning as changing one's views are dispersed.

Our aim was to obtain a deeper insight into the question whether the students' conceptions of knowledge and a student and teacher roles have changed and whether students were able to articulate and explain these changes. The following text presents reflections excerpted from the interviews taken with twelve students, randomly selected from the group which had completed questionnaires, and who are second year or pre-graduation students in 2006/07 study period.

Deeper Insights in Conceptions of Second Year Students

It proved that three second-year students clearly express their conception of knowledge in terms of critical thinking and changing of views, they understand a teacher's role in encouraging independent learning with learners and also their own role in assuming initiative and responsibility. All three students clearly describe their changes of conceptions:

> Well, I feel that before I was oriented only in mastering data and facts, that later on I gradually felt a certain need that essentially I should have stepped over that barrier once and for all. Slowly I began to feel that such learning of bare facts without a certain background or without proper thinking could lead me nowhere and didn't have any effects at all. So I gradually came to understand that by starting to think about something, the point is that doing this the knowledge can actually become interesting and useful for yourself. (Person A)

> Especially during the study period, when it is an issue of a completely different teacher and learner role… that a teacher is not only the person who lectures about a subject matter and a student who learns it. (Person C)

This student stresses in particular that a learner role is not to "photocopy" certain knowledge, but to conceive meaningful connections, to critically evaluate, not to believe everything a teacher says.

> My conception of knowledge keeps changing.... in order that I will truly be able to use it.... This conception changed a lot—I used to learn only to pass an exam. (Person D)

The student stresses that her conception of learning did not change, that even during her primary schooling she learned mathematical principles by herself; she stresses that private tutoring is a mixed blessing, since a learner has to find their own answers.

The importance of different—good—teacher role models in previous education already is set out by Persons A and C, and her own learning experience by Person D: "I had studied the subject matter by myself and I truly came to understand." Persons A and D set out the importance of good learning experience at the faculty, with teachers who demand a more active and independent role from them. Person C expounds the importance of lectures and discussions, since we teachers constantly prompt them to think about it.

One of the students (Person B) expresses her conception of knowledge in terms of understanding; a teacher is still the person who must motivate, even force students to work and to encourage them to go slightly beyond the limits of their capacities. Her learner role is perceived in terms of importance to do something on one's own initiative, to address a problem etc. She crystallizes a view, that you can achieve more durable knowledge if you do the work yourself; this view was prompted to by her independent seminar work as part of her study obligations. Another important experience was an independent presentation—a teaching lesson she held at a secondary school.

Two students (Persons E and F) express their conception of knowledge in terms of understanding; they expect a teacher to motivate, activate, while still stressing the importance that he/she systematically covers the subject matter, shows what is important, "hammers particular things into their heads" ... They see their own role in participating, yet it is sometimes hard to take the initiative. It is noteworthy that none of them describes clear changes in conceptions, but they both expose, how much easier it is now for them to assume the teacher role and they are aware how difficult and responsible their work is. This is stressed also by Person B. Person E expounds her preparations for mature exams as important experience which influenced her—self-discipline is important, you can't learn anything the last minute. She stresses her being more mature now, that studying has not influenced her significantly, and that more practical work and communication were necessary. Person F stresses the meaning of study contents and expounds significant experience during their studies, when more active participation was expected from them: they defined the scope of previous knowledge; active participation at practical work and educational programme planning.

All six students are *critical of teaching within the study process*—that there is too much lecturing, where teachers give lectures without actively involving students. Students would like their teachers to encourage them to express their own views and to ask questions. They wish more practical work with their active participation and more practical experience. They are particularly critical of evaluation—they say that teachers often require only a reproduction.

> I somehow feel we still stick to material in manuals, which we simply have to master in the end. This annoys me a bit, because it looks as a slightly downgrading attitude toward students as if we weren't able to do any better. That is, by learning the easiest way you master one definition and you present it at the exam. You show it to the teacher who, in turn, is satisfied. Essentially I think, that studies should be based on different principles with more reading and above all more understanding, not with learning by heart, which prevails as far as I experience now. (Person A)

> Tests could be formulated to ask about your opinion on a subject, based on particular theories. You should essentially relate to some sort of knowledge, but with your own thinking included. (Person C)

For us the teachers an important message which these interviews reveal is that students want to be actively included into the teaching and learning process and that we often underestimate them, as one of the students pointed out:

> Not encouraging us is a major sign of a bad teacher. The point is that students can do a lot, although it sometimes seems that they are not aware of that, still students can contribute a lot and give many new pieces of information. It might be that we have not been burdened (in inverted commas) with all possible data yet and are able to disperse the flow of our thoughts in different directions…

Deeper Insights in Conceptions of Pre-graduation Students

Pre-graduation students gave rather dispersed answers to questions about conceptions of teacher role: two see it in transmitting basic knowledge and in training for the future profession (Persons J, K), three (Persons I, L, G) stress the importance of forming students, where a teacher should animate students, be dynamic, build on a dialogue with students during lectures and also design the work with students outside the lecture room (visits of institutions, case-study, constant connecting theory and practice etc.). Only one pre-graduate student exposed the importance of activating students (Person H):

> The role of a good teacher during the studies is to challenge you, to awaken curiosity in you, and to provoke you to speak up. [Also,] that you upgrade previous knowledge and open yourself to the new. (Person H)

It may be wise to think about the message of one pre-graduate student who stressed:

> During the first and second year there are mainly lectures, so we don't have to think a lot, while during the third and fourth year we had more independent thinking and questioning. I think that in the beginning we thus developed a habit of coming to lectures and listen. In my opinion we became a bit lazy. (Person J)

Therefore the first year study experience is very important in terms of the role a teacher assumes, as in this way a student role is determined and often even fatally marked for the whole study period. Three of the students stressed the importance of student participation (Persons I, K, G).

> Our role is mainly in participating at lectures, in getting actively involved, that you speak about themes, get information about them from colleagues, try to obtain as much knowledge as possible. In presenting seminar papers you demonstrate the theme as attractively as possible, out of responsibility towards your colleagues. It is important that you try to present your ideas. (Person I)

Three of them (Persons H, L, J) exposed how important it is for a student to take the initiative and assume responsibility. Two of them (Persons H, L), stress that it is not enough for a good student to comply with minimum requirements of a study programme, on the contrary, important are student's initiative and their own activities to upgrade the matter presented at lectures. One of the students particularly stressed that at the beginning she scrupulously attended lectures and fulfilled her obligations, while later in her studies she called herself a learner, because she developed a deeper interest in the subject, as she felt herself becoming a part of the science she studied and became generally interested in its matters without the feeling of "being obliged" to do it (Person J).

> You take your obligations as an opportunity to discover something new, that you really get to know the profession you decided for.... that you realize during the process that teachers and students essentially work for the same purpose, and gradually realize that professional cooperation between both is possible. (Person H)

> The role of a student is primarily in making most of the opportunities, given during the educational process. To finish studies. To absorb as much knowledge as possible. So to say, to take a maximum advantage of a teacher if he/she wants to. If it is in his/her interest to absorb maximum knowledge a teacher possesses. And above all to get trained in practical work. And as a private consideration—to progress, to develop personally, to learn discipline. (Person L)

In view of their knowledge conceptions we conclude from their answers that two students (Persons J and K) stress the importance of understanding and practical use of this knowledge in actual problem situations. Four students (Persons G, H, I, L) give answers which tend to stress a changed view of matters, their own increased independence, a comprehensive value of knowledge and an ability to convey knowledge to others.

> When I interconnect facts of a subject, I become aware of my knowledge… When everything gets interrelated, when I essentially don't see connections any more, but everything is one ultimate matter, and everything becomes, so to say, one tree trunk with different branches. Then everything becomes one. (Person G)

It is interesting that in this case a grade becomes secondary—the student maintains she does not care if she gets an excellent grade for her knowledge; the most important for her is to be able to combine the knowledge and use it also in future.

> The knowledge is essentially that with your knowledge you give something to the society… It is essential to do something in your life. It is you useless if you enter your professional life without knowledge, you must offer something to the society, your employer and to yourself. Even if you have an employment, I think that you must upgrade your knowledge every single day, build it up, participate at seminars. (Person I)

> Knowledge is essentially that you know how to use it so as to benefit you and others. Its use is demonstrated in problem-solving, improving the quality of one's life on the earth, the financial situation, helping others, conveying knowledge, developing something new, developing a particular science and profession in general. (Person L)

All interviewees except one student (Person I) refer to changed conceptions of knowledge, teacher and student roles during the studies. One pre-graduation student expounds that relation to teachers became more and more personal (particularly, if compared to study programmes where 400 students enrol yearly). The other four report on many aspects of changes with their very complex interdependence—from a better understanding of teachers to different conceptions of knowledge, understanding the whole education system and the possibilities they have as counselling staff or teachers.

One of the students particularly stresses the importance of mutual knowledge- and awareness-building. During her study years she discovered her ability of knowledge-building in dialogue and in communicating with teachers:

> A teacher is not an unapproachable person, but somebody who can help me and with whom I can discover, maybe also for the teacher him/herself, some unknown matters. The fact that I can discover, to build up knowledge. (Person H)

A changed conception related to consultation hours was stressed twice – namely that gradually they become a *place of dialogue*, where you can come as a student and you are welcome; where you may ask and get an answer, where you can form your knowledge in a dialogue with the teacher. The first year they went to consultation hours only to get their grades written down. According to them this was influenced by a shift in understanding their role, but also by a process of getting closer to teachers during studies and by teachers' readiness, openness to dialogue and by students' sincerity in seeking knowledge (Person H). During those years teachers become not only lecturers but also mentors, partners in dialogue, as exemplified in:

> You perceive a teacher not only as an authority, but also as a person. It is not an ideal person. But you understand better their reacting. And also yourself … we come here, when we are twenty, we haven't gone through our development yet. Mental development. It is natural to change. The attitude to ourselves and to the study changes in years. It has changed with me. You are not so superficial any more, you want to know more and to gain more. The first year you only want to pass. (Person L)

The pre-graduation student expounded a turning point which marks the 3rd year. First two years have more theoretical subjects and those which support the pedagogical science in an interdisciplinary approach to phenomena. In time the studies get more and more specific, they deepen, "slowly you get aware of the essence of the studies, which wouldn't have been possible without obtaining a wider theoretical basis during the first two study years" (Person L).

Among key factors in the study programme which contributed to the shift of conceptions a study practice was mentioned three times, together with peer discussion at seminars (in particular at a week-end seminar), where dealing with practical cases and their explanations take place, basing it all in theoretical concepts and knowledge. Practice and visits to schools and various institutions were mentioned twice, where students actually met with educational practice and saw, how particular novelties work in reality. Two pre-graduation students exposed their experience in preparing seminar papers and their presentation – from preparation of contents to activating colleagues and designing a presentation – in this way they acquired skills of deeper understanding of the subject matter, writing of expert texts, a critical approach (comparison between different standpoints and opinions of different teachers), presentation, an improved self-confidence in presenting their knowledge. One student was specially influenced by a teacher who did not allow taking notes of lectures till they understood the lecture contents; this will in future accompany all her work as a teacher.

Outside the faculty one of the pre-graduation students stressed the importance of experience she gains in holding various workshops for children, when she constantly verifies her activities with theoretical assumptions, for example, she asks herself, "Was it proper to react this way?" (Person K); another student stressed intensive work on herself, on self-understanding and her reactions in the process of preparing for marriage and in her work with scouts, where her knowledge can be concretized when she prepares materials for scout leaders (Person H).

Another interesting answer was that pedagogy, as a humanistic science (according to this student's opinion) and with its contents, influenced the formation of specific personal characteristics of an individual:

> The contents of the studies influence you. If you read something, then you see clearly, what is right and what is not. During studies you develop certain empathy towards people. A social sense develops. A lot. During studies of natural sciences it cannot develop as much as in programmes of social studies. Here this attitude is very important. How much work we put in communication, interaction among people. This way a person changes, also intimately. For the better, I guess. You see that you must work with a person to benefit you and him/her. (Person L)

CONCLUSIONS

Students have a lot to tell us about the quality of the studies if we care to ask them. The question is whether we are prepared to listen to them or whether their reactions may prompt us to profound changes in our own teaching when we are convinced of our indisputable superiority. I think that we should seriously consider students' statements, not to underestimate that they want a more active role themselves and that our duty is to make this possible—that we create circumstances where they can actively participate in the study process as our partners. We can sum up the interview analysis that students were significantly influenced by the learning experience, which allowed them to have a more active and independent role.

To what extent the existent taboos can be shaken by a reflection of a second year student in her assignment presenting a critical analysis of an article on active learning and teaching:

> With almost no practical work and mostly dull lectures I experience a great contradiction between teachers' words, our reading assignments, the words we have repeat over and over (what we perceive as active learning, what is modern—efficient teaching…) and the actual activities of most teachers. What we read in all these articles and what we learn about how teaching/learning should proceed is in my opinion still a taboo theme in our department and the faculty as well. Then how can we become initiators and operators of active learning? Shall we know how? Or will we only talk about how good it would be to put these methods into practice?

The answer is complex and multi-layered—in view of a teacher's direct work with students, organization of studies, promotion criteria for university teachers etc. In pursuing the goal of *excellence in teaching*; however, a lot of change and effort is still needed. The first step at a personal level is to perceive students as partners in the learning process—also in search of higher quality studies. As Nightingale and O'Neil (1994) put it: when we start thinking of students as active participants in the learning process, sharing their experience with a teacher, or as partners in the learning process, we will more easily keep focused on creating circumstances which lead to quality learning.

REFERENCES

Biggs, J. (1999). *Teaching for quality learning at university: What the student does.* Buckingham: SRHE & Open University Press.

Dahlgren, L. O. (1984). Outcomes of learning. In F. Marton, D. Hounsell, & N. Entwistle (Eds.), *The experience of learning* (Chapter 2). Edinburgh: Scottish Academic Press.

Fox, D. (1983). Personal theories of teaching. *Studies in Higher Education, 8*, 151–163.

Gardner, H. (1991). *The unschooled mind. How children think and how schools should teach.* New York: Basic Books.

Institutional Audit of the University in Ljubljana. (April, 1996). *CRE auditors report.* Geneve.

Kember, D., & Gow, L. (1994). Orientations to teaching and their effect on the quality of student learning. *Journal of Higher Education, 65*, 58–74.

Naghtingale, P., & O'Neil, M. (1994). *Achieving quality learning in higher education.* London: Kogan Page.

Simons, P. R. J. (1997). Definitions and theories of active learning. In D. Stern & G. L. Huber (Eds.), *Active learning for students and teachers: Reports from eight countries OECD* (pp. 19–39). Frankfurt am Main: Peter Lang.

Šteh, B., Kalin, J. (2006). *The messages university teachers send to students about knowledge and teacher/students roles.* Paper presented at the European conference on educational research, University of Geneva, 13–15 September 2006. In *Education-line*. Retrieved March 13, 2008, from http://www.leeds.ac.uk/educol/documents/158113.htm

Vermunt, J. D. H. M. (1993). Constructive learning in higher education. In J. K. Koppen & W. D. Webler (Eds.), *Strategies for increasing access and performance in higher education.* Amsterdam: Thesis Publishers.

Barbara Šteh
Faculty of Arts
University of Ljubljana

Jana Kalin
Faculty of Arts
University of Ljubljana

INNER BALANCE

Whilst traveling, the tightrope walker encounters balance from within, using focus, concentration, inner calm, and a continual correction of movement. The wire acts as a base of support. With each step, the wire shifts making it extremely challenging for the equilibrist to maintain balance. The lower extremities, namely the feet, are the lone body parts making contact with the wire yet act as the mechanism for holistic bodily equilibrium achieved through the body's core. The four papers in this final section examine the significance of equilibrating educational research with equity as a core value.

In the opening paper Leisa Desmoulins critiques cultural incongruence and racism discourses of schooling for urban Aboriginal students. She further examines the contextualization of indigenous identities and oppression of Aboriginal populations. *E/raced: Aboriginal Youth and Public Schooling* calls on readers to both recognize and problematize racist subtleties that exist in schools and cities with Aboriginal peoples.

Nissilä utilizes transformative learning theory to examine the perspectives of mature teacher candidates. *Towards Equity and Self-Discovery in Teacher Education: Development of Pedagogical Thinking Among Second and Third Career Student Teachers* speaks to the interconnectivity of a balanced self-image and equity between persons, environments, and cultures.

In the third paper of Part V, Jason Ellis questions, *The Digital Divide in Special Education: Where Do My Students Fit In?* Through a careful examination of assisted technology and technological infrastructures in schools, the author reveals the complexities and challenges for educators working with students with special needs. He further explicates the need for administrative plans and policies, which permit accessibility and teacher involvement in decision making.

The final paper, *Information and Communications Technology and the Infusion of Social Justice from a Global Perspective in the Elementary Classroom: A World of Possibility*, O'Sullivan uncovers the ways in which students and teachers think differently. He identifies the disconnectedness youth encounter when confronted with global problems and makes insightful linkages between the technological revolution and progressive global education.

When the funabulist crosses the wire so little of the body, merely the soles of the feet, is in contact with the base of support. Learning to counteract the rotational motion and gravitational pull takes skill, courage, relentless practice, and commitment to the process. Such is the task of the academic who engages in risky, yet forward moving research.

LEISA DESMOULINS

E/RACED: ABORIGINAL YOUTH AND PUBLIC SCHOOLING

> *The classroom is where our future well-being, both economic and social, is being forged. It is where we will discover whether our model of diversity passes or fails.* (E. Greenspon, 2007)

The editorial comment above puts a strong onus on schools for well-being and economic success in communities and amongst groups of peoples. This model of diversity, in cities such as Thunder Bay, is played out as Aboriginal peoples negotiate social and institutional borders and often face discrimination and racism in their participation in city life (Haluza-Delay, 2002; McCaskill, Fitzmaurice, & Desmoulins, 2007); at the same time Census Canada reports a growing and youthful Aboriginal population (McCaskill et al., 2007). Two recent local studies looked at Aboriginal peoples' relationships with the city and found themes of racism, culture and identity, class differences, and transition and basic needs supports required for youth. Local youth workers reported that education was the largest challenge facing Aboriginal youth in Thunder Bay (McCaskill et al., 2007).

These studies did not fully engage youth within public institutions such as high schools. Through these community-based studies and within the literature I began to notice overlapping linkages between knowledge, culture, race, and subjectivities. These studies and conversations in the community led me to ask how cultural and racial theories, research, and practices of education shape how we think about Aboriginal youth and schools and conversely how Aboriginal youth identify with and subsequently engage and/or disengage with school.

These gaps and linkages informed this study's two research questions: (a) how do students in a public high school identify themselves, and (b) how do they negotiate their racialized, classed, gendered and cultural identities within public schooling. These questions are embedded within the school and the multiple subjectivities created by discourses of urban Aboriginal peoples and public schooling. By subjectivities I mean the personal views and beliefs of individuals about identity as well as the views and beliefs that have emerged through the literature and research about identity. For individuals, these constructions of identity are "shaped by society as it is constructed in relationship with others based on differences of race, class, and gender" (Ward & Bouvier, 2001, p. 6).

Scholars from two academic discourses, the cultural incongruence and racism discourses have focused their research on Aboriginal youth in high schools and have influenced educational theory and policy-making. Discourse as a concept combines language and practice, what people say as well as what people do (Hall,

J. A. Kentel and A. Short (eds.), Totems and Taboos: Risk and Relevance in Research on Teachers and Teaching, 201–212.

1997). Discourses establish "the parameters for thought and action; the conceptual and classificatory models for understanding the world; and for the questions that may be posed and the possible answers that may be produced" (Yon, 2000, p. 12-13). The discourses and how they frame the problems and practices of culture and identity in education often serve to depoliticize and dehistoricize the differences and inequalities of education. Discourses can promote particular conceptual models as taken-for-granted ways of knowing while promoting the status quo. For example, findings of cultural differences causing academic failure require no vesting of power in the classroom, schools, or education systems. Yet these concepts of culture, identity, and equity collide and elide with one another, particularly for racialized students.

In this paper I define the terms I use followed by an abbreviated critical review of the cultural incongruence and racism discourses of schooling for urban Aboriginal students. Next, I provide the methodological framework for the study. Although multiple themes emerged from the research, in the next section of this paper I discuss the theme of racism from the study. Finally, I provide conclusions about how racism works within schools and in the context of the city.

TERMINOLOGY

Identities

Hall (1997) defines identities as "multiple, contradictory, relational, and always in process: they embody both possibilities and limitations on how individuals understand themselves and each other and ultimately how lives are lived" (p. 37). These terms 'relational' and 'multiple' provide language about identities as contextualized within socio-cultural political locations: relational in terms of power relations and inseparable from connections to race, ethnicity, class, and gender; and multiple as being related to many contexts and identifications. Lakota scholar Hilary Weaver (2001) defines indigenous identities as "a composite of many things such as race, class, education, region, religion, and gender" (p. 240). Weaver's (2001) identity is a fusion of multiple aspects of social location that incorporate cultural identity as one's identity in relation to his or her culture. Weaver (2001) and others brings subjectivities and representations into considerations of identity (Absolon & Winchester, 1994; Lawrence, 2003; Restoule, 2004; St. Denis, 2002).

Contextualized/relational identities. Indigenous scholars (Absolon & Winchester, 1994; Restoule, 2004) have used a self-defined, relational, situational, and contextualized approach, that is, identity as the intersection of race, identity, identifying, representation, or as interactional constructs. For these scholars, the constructs of identity are contextual and self-defined by respondents. Absolon and Winchester (1994) note that "when we set out to understand and describe identity we have to build constructs that are inclusive of all, or we may contribute to a subtle form of 'ethnic cleansing' by defining narrowly who is and who is not part of the community of Aboriginal people" (n.p.).

Performative identities. To look at identities contextually embeds them relationally within global and specific histories and places, known as 'performative identity' (Dei, 2000; Hall, 1996; James, 2003; Yon, 2000). McCarthy (1995) defines performative identity "in terms of the effects of political struggles over social and economic exploitation, political disenfranchisement, and cultural and ideological repression" (p. 263). Hall (1996) situates performative identity saying that it is "produced within specific historical and institutional sites, within specific discursive formations and practices, and by specific enunciative strategies" (p. 4). Performative contexts highlight and make explicit existing power relations and the relations of race and culture to identity and agency within social locations.

Mi'kaq scholar Marie Battiste (n.d.) speaks to decolonization of existing education laws, policy, and structures based on racial or cultural superiority. This study considered the theoretical and practical space to 'challenge the colonial education project' for *everyone* within education. And what is the relationship of this challenge to identity? Métis scholar Bonita Lawrence (2003) asserts that "[f]or Native people, individual identity is always being negotiated in *relation* to collective identity, and *in the face of* an external colonizing society" (p. 4). Lawrence proposes that "decolonization must involve deconstructing and reshaping how we understand indigenous identity" (p. 3). If, as Battiste (n.d.) asserts, the decolonization project is actually two-pronged—as deconstruction plus reconstruction—then in the vesting of power decolonizing strategies may have applicability in challenging colonial education by considering racism and identity and reconstructing alternatives. Thus, identity relates to race, indigenous nationhood, and culture through both identifying and representations. Representations of indigenous peoples, while beyond the scope of this paper, relate to racial perceptions, knowing the 'Other' and racism, discussed below.

Race, Racialization, Racism

Race. The meaning of the term race is not fixed but has different meanings depending on the context (Dei & Calliste, 2000; Fleras & Elliot, 2003; Haluza-Delay, 2002; James, 2003; St. Denis & Hampton, 2002). For example, James (2003) notes that race has been used to refer to many differing meanings, viz: 1) lineage; 2) subspecies; 3) ethnic groups; 4) religions; 5) nationalities; 6) minority language groups; 7) blood groups; and, 8) people from particular geographic regions (p. 37). Race is also is used to refer collectively to distinct indigenous nations (Fletcher, 2005). Usages of 'race' differ with no singular, definitive meaning. The changing nature of race allows for its elusiveness (Dei, 2000; Henry & Tator, 2006; James, 2003). That is why scholars refer to race as a socially-constructed process (Dei, 2000; Henry & Tator, 2006; Omi & Winnart, 2005; St. Denis & Hampton, 2002). It is not scientifically real but the social construction of racial differences has real socio-political and material consequences through racialization and racism for groups and for individuals.

Racialization. A social system of inequalities whereby categories of the population are constructed, differentiated, inferiorized, and excluded based on race. Skin colour is a prevalent classification because it is visible (but not the only one) (Haluza-Delay, 2002; Henry & Tator, 2006; Sixkiller Clarke, 1994; St. Denis & Hampton, 2002) and racialization processes are historically and locally contextualized (Haluza-Delay, 2002; Sixkiller Clarke, 1994).

Racism. Scholars examine the performative impact of race because "as a concept or an idea [race] does not signify inferiority or superiority" (Dei, 2000, p. 14): racial superiority is enacted through cognitive imperialism in general and specifically transmitted through "institutional and social practices that create and sustain injustice and inequality…" (Dei, 2000, p.14). Many scholars acknowledge a typology of racism including individual, institutional or systemic, and cultural racism (Fleras & Elliot, 2003; Haluza-Delay, 2002; Henry & Tator, 2006; James, 2003; Laroque, 1991; St. Denis & Hampton, 2002). These forms are distinct although linked; these types of racism work concurrently within cities and schools.

REVIEW OF LITERATURE

Scholars often use conceptual models of race or cultural identities (St. Denis, 2002; Ward & Bouvier, 2001): the discourses follow.

Cultural (in)Congruence Discourse

The concept of culture and identity for Aboriginal youth and schooling has been a Canadian discourse since the 1967 release of the Hawthorne report. Hawthorne (1967) examined "*schooling and its adequacy*" (original emphasis, part II, p.6) from the perspective of "making schools better for the unhappy or failing Indian child" (part II, p. 7). Hawthorne (1967) outlines cultural dissonance theory and then defines cultural dissonance as 'a discontinuity of experience' affecting scholastic achievement. Cultural incongruity factors included: early socialization, shelter, food, clothing, and objects (e.g., toys and books) and psychological factors (e.g., verbal nature, parent interest, discipline, and routines for learning). Hawthorne (1967) concludes that schooling forces a choice for Aboriginal children "between being an Indian or an Indian "White" (p. 126).

Hawthorne's (1967) study set the theoretical ground for future cultural in-congruence studies that has remained fundamental to educational research literature (Demmert, 2001; Deyhle & Swisher, 1996) with studies predominantly "using a cultural framework for the analysis of schooling and Aboriginal children, parents, and communities" (Deyhle & Swisher, 1996, p. 117). Researchers have investigated an array of research topics to explore Aboriginal students' failure—differences in the home environment, parenting style, communication styles, learning styles, and cooperative rather than competitive orientations—and found cultural incongruity.

Racism Discourse

This discourse focuses on the production of knowledge, subjectivities, and social relations as it relates to racism in society and its socio-cultural organizations. This discourse theorizes that dominant discourses about schooling are constructed as neutral for everyone and that educational discourses and studies depoliticize and dehistoricize the effects of schooling for racialized students and thus negate the need for theories of racism. St. Denis and Hampton (2002) note that particular to schools forms of racism directed against Aboriginal and Indian students or teachers "has not received scholarly or systematic attention" (p. 5) (Huffman, 1991; Ledlow, 1992; Sixkiller Clarke, 1994; St. Denis, Bouvier & Battiste, 1998; St. Denis, 2002). Scholars attribute this lack of scholarly attention to denial of racism in schools (Deyhle, 1995; Henry & Tator, 2006; Laroque, 1991; Ledlow, 1992; Sixkiller Clarke, 1994) and the effectiveness of cultural discourses to replace racial discourses (Laroque, 1991; St. Denis, 2002; St. Denis & Hampton, 2002).

Despite the denial and the lack of scholarly engagement of racism in education, researchers note that cognitive imperialism (Battiste, 1998; Smith, 1999) and racism (Haluza-Delay, 2002; McCaskill et al., 2007; Ryan, 1998) occurs within schooling. Scholars have noted experiences of Aboriginal students in public schooling (Deyhle, 1995; Laroque, 1991; Reid, 2001; Ryan, 1998; St. Denis & Hampton, 2002). Racism in schooling include the following sources: relations with/treatment of students; rejection, blaming, and stereotyping (via texts, curriculum, and teachers/ administrators); marginalization to racial harassment/incidents; attitudes and expect-ations of teachers and administrators; Eurocentrically-focused curriculum and representations; and, assessment, streaming/expectations, and discipline (Deyhle & Swisher, 1996; Henry & Tator, 2006; Laroque, 1991; Ryan, 1998; St. Denis & Hampton, 2002). Other scholars found individual, institutional and cultural forms of racism in public schooling antithetical to Aboriginal students' success (Cleary & Peacock, 1998; Deyhle, 1995; Fletcher, 2005; Silver & Mallet, 2002).

Both the cultural incongruity discourse and the racism discourse have found that Aboriginal students do not succeed in public schooling. The two discourses differ in that each approach provides radically different explanations for Aboriginal students' failure. Both discourses have shown inattention to the other within the research and within schooling.

Cultural Congruence and Racism

Few researchers (e.g. Fisher & Campbell, 2002; Grantham Campbell, 2005; Ryan, 1998; St. Denis, 2002) have studied racism with cultural incongruency. Scholars found that culture and identity are not experienced homogenously and that cultural congruence may undertheorize Aboriginal youths' academic success (Deyhle & Swisher, 1996; Ledlow, 1992; Reid, 2001; St. Denis, 2002). These researchers conclude that cultural incongruity articulated with racism better theorizes Aboriginal youths' engagement and alienation with schooling.

METHODOLOGICAL FRAME

Personal Locatedness

My self-identity—who I am, where I am, and how I connect to the discourses and practices of identity research—also inform my research. My positionality at the borders is explored below.

For the first half of my life I lived as a White middle-class child, youth, and then woman. My father's grandparents came from the Ukraine to western Canada through an offer of land for farming. My mother's grandparents came from Alsace in Europe, settled in America as Pennsylvania Dutch, and later immigrated to Canada. Both parents have genealogical books tracing their families back to the Old Country and their routes to their current home. I read these books growing up.

I have lived the second half of my life as a White, middle class woman. In 1984 I gained Indian status through marriage. A year after I gained Indian status, my sister-in-law lost her Indian status, also through marriage. These events marked the first time I had considered race and its relationship to culture, and marked my initial (conscious) bumping up against the borderlands. These legislative representations, that seemingly cross racial boundaries without consideration for identity or culture, have provoked me to consider the historical, social and political contexts that made these situations possible. I choose to maintain an outsider/insider (playing on Smith's (1999) insider/outsider) belonging to the urban Aboriginal community through personal relationships and community-based research work.

My bordered identity informs this research work via my social location, data analysis, research interpretations, and worldview. It also informs the methodological frame I used for this work.

Methodology

The methodology focused on "culture and identity without subverting the material and structural forces of inequality and discrimination" (Saukko, 2003, p. 156) using a conceptual framework of border theory (Anzaldua in Reuman, 2000) and border pedagogy (Giroux, 2005) and multiple methods used in the study.

Border theory. In an interview with Reuman (2000) Anzaldua explains that

> … in a multicultural society, we cross into each other's worlds all the time. We live in each other's pockets, occupy each other's territories, live in close proximity and in intimacy with each other at home, in school, at work. We are mutually complicitous--us and them, white and colored, straight and queer, Christian and Jew, self and Other, oppressor and oppressed. We all of us find ourselves in the position of being simultaneously insider/outsider… [But] the future belongs to those who cultivate cultural sensitivities to differences and who use these abilities to forge a hybrid consciousness that transcends the "us" vs. "them" mentality... (n.p.).

Border pedagogy. Giroux's (2005) border pedagogy calls for dialogue between various discourses for educators to become border crossers "engaged in an effort to create alternative public spheres" through zones of cultural difference. These alternative public spheres are potential sites to deconstruct how racism is manifested and then, by using Battiste's (n.d.), two-pronged approach, reconstruct schooling to consider Aboriginal youth's success.

Methods. I began the study by inviting youth who self-identified as Aboriginal students as well as teachers and administrators at a local high school to participate in a qualitative study from November 2006 to February 2007. In the study I used a variety of methods with student participants—interviews, PhotoVoice, letters, and group discussions and interviews—and interviews and discussions with teachers and administrators to investigate the interlocking relationships of race, culture, and identity with schooling. Lutrell (2005) explains PhotoVoice, using student's photography, to "represent the everyday conditions which shape their lives from their perspective...to provide clues to their concerns and identities" (p. 2). I also used students' photographs to provide a conversation gateway for talk about identities and identifying in interviews.

DISCUSSION

In this study I set out to investigate identity and culture, and yet racism pervaded students and teachers' discussions. Study participants' interviews and discussions demonstrated personal, cultural, and institutional components of racism within the school. Cognitive imperialism (Battiste, 1998) as interlocking ideological, socio-political, and material oppression of Aboriginal peoples is also considered here as a component of educational racism. Finally, everyday racism (Laroque, 1991) manifests itself in many and sometimes small ways through "glances, gestures, forms of speech, and physical movements" (Henry, Tator, Mattis, & Rees, 1995, p. 47) which are often difficult to name due to their subtlety and the absence of any reference to race. Examples of these components of racism are discussed below. All names are pseudonyms.

Individual Racism

Student had differing experiences and perceptions of racism. All of the eight student participants had recently experienced individual forms of racism in the city. Isabel, Emmett, and Jade related recent separate 'drive by racism' incidents. Lorraine described drive-by racism through her experiences of, noting that it happens "all the time" (interview, 30-01-07):

> Lorraine: "We always get called bogans or stupid Natives or other bad words but I don't know if I'm allowed to say them." [laughs]
>
> Leisa: Oh, you don't have to say them. [laughs] And that's here at school?

Lorraine: Here and out of school. Once in a while. Not really in school. Because they know I'll confront them. Outside of school though either in a car or if there's lots of people.

Leisa: Uhuh. They're in a car and you're walking. Is that when it happens?

Lorraine: I'm walking and they're in a vehicle driving (interview, 30-01-07).

Emmett and Jade added that passengers in cars and busses also threw objects at them. Although respondents to Haluza-Delay's (2002) study and McCaskill et al.'s (2007) study spoke to individual racism as derogatory comments and violence against them, Lorraine, Emmett, Isabel, and Jade described a spacialized and contextualized form of racism while getting around the city.

The confidence that Lorraine showed above in confronting racial talk and behaviours at school may be related to the school's zero tolerance policy: when racial incidents occur, students and teachers can ask school administrators to intervene. For example, Ella described an incident in the high school and explained that it was resolved quickly when she brought the incident to school administrators.

Ella: And then I talked to, whatever it's called, Student [pause]

Leisa: Student Services?

Ella: Yeah, they had a talk with her and she never bugged me after that. Now we're good friends (interview, 23-01-07).

One teacher participant, Mary, described one of her student's recent racial incidents. The anecdote also illustrated the school's zero tolerance policy on racist incidents. Mary said "[s]o I asked her if she had taken it up with the principal or [name of counsellor] or whatever. She goes "Yeah, I mentioned it and I think that the student was called to task. It's [bogan] a very slang racial term" (interview, 21- 12-06). The racialized term "bogan" was mentioned by Lorraine (above) as well as by respondents in Haluza-Delay's (2002) study of racism. Bogan is an example of a localized term used by Whites to convey racial superiority.

These students and teacher used the school's zero tolerance policy on individual racism when situations arise. Few student participants reported individual racism occurring in school which contradicts the findings from Haluza-Delay's (2002) and McCaskill et al.'s (2007) studies finding schools one of the top three social locations where participants' experienced racism in Thunder Bay.

Everyday Racism

Everyday racism was less commonly cited by students, perhaps due to its elusive nature. Jade and Isabel spoke to it occurring in school. Isabel described everyday racism with some hesitancy. She was certain that it existed and yet she struggled over the subtlety of the racism. Isabel asserted that

Sometimes I feel like, I don't know, sometimes I feel like I do see it. But they just don't say anything about it, but maybe they just think about it. But I

> don't know if it's just me thinking it but sometimes I can read people's faces and their eyes. Maybe I think I do. That's the kind of impression that I get. Even with my math teacher. There's just something about him/her that scared me and I didn't like it. S/he made me feel, s/he made me feel like I didn't deserve to be there, I didn't deserve to be in that class. I wasn't smart enough or something. That's the kind of feeling that I got off of him/her. Or s/he intimidated me. (interview, 08-02-07)

Isabel questioned her own perceptions, "I don't know if it's just me thinking it..." yet remains convinced that she is being 'paintbrushed' racially. She explained that "[w]hat they call paint brushing people, paint brushing everyone with one colour" (interview, 13-12-06) leads to everyday expressions of racism towards her by teachers and others in the school. Isabel's hesitancy related to expressions, impressions, and the ability of the teacher to make her feel that she didn't belong without the teacher needing to reference race.

Cognitive Imperialism

Battiste (1998) explains that

> Cognitive imperialism is a form of cognitive manipulation used to disclaim other knowledge bases and values. Validated through one's knowledge base and empowered through public education, it has been the means by which whole groups of people have been denied existence and have had their wealth confiscated. Cognitive imperialism denies people their language and cultural integrity by maintaining the legitimacy of only one language, one culture, and one frame of reference. (p. 17)

In December two students, Isabel and Lorraine, were taking a biology course. Both students raised the dissection class in interviews: each student had a different way of coping with their own perceptions of cognitive imperialism in science. In an interview Lorraine told me that she rarely skips classes, but she couldn't go to Biology class. She told me that she skipped biology to avoid dissections, but she later returned to school to attend the last period of the day (interview, 14-12-06). Isabel attended the dissection class, but she's quite conflicted about it afterwards. She told me that

> Today, playing around with the rat, I felt wrong doing it, because it's disrespecting an animal. I didn't want to sit there and do it, cause that one of the things I care about. What this world has. (interview, 13-12-06)

In Lorraine and Isabel's examples cognitive imperialism related to the concept of dissecting animals. Isabel used the term "playing around with the rat" to describe dissecting it. Both students are conflicted between attending classes and being required to "disrespect an animal."

A biology teacher participant, Heather, talked about her previous teaching experiences and successes in a remote First Nations community. Heather mentioned the structural changes to scheduling and schooling that she believed, based on her experiences, would assist Aboriginal students to succeed in secondary school, especially students coming from remote communities (interview, 09-01-07). Heather showed no awareness of the cultural imperialism of the science curriculum mentioned by Lorraine and Isabel. This unawareness speaks to a singular frame of reference (Battiste, 1998) that makes cognitive imperialism invisible to those teachers perpetuating it.

CONCLUSION

Thus, participants illustrated how racism exists in the city and within a public high school. Study participants provided examples of personal, everyday and cultural components of racism had recently experienced. One of the reasons that racism, particularly cognitive imperialism may not be discussed in the literature is perhaps that researchers and teachers, like Heather, are not aware of the dissonance that Aboriginal students may face. These experiences impact on student success within schools. Schools can have policies prohibiting individual forms of racism but the more insidious forms such as the cognitive imperialism experienced by students in this study impact upon student success. Addressing these unconscious forms of racism is needed for decolonization to occur.

REFERENCES

Absolon, K., & Winchester, T. (1994). *Cultural identity for urban Aboriginal peoples: Learning circles synthesis report* [CD-ROM]. Ottawa: Libraxus. Available: For seven generations: An information legacy of the Royal Commission on Aboriginal Peoples, 1997.

Battiste, M. (n.d.). *Can cultural based education cure the educational failure of modern education towards Aboriginal students?* Retrieved July 17, 2005, from http://www.usask.ca/education/people/battistem/pdf/diversity.pdf

Battiste, M. (1998). Enabling the autumn seed: Toward a decolonized approach to Aboriginal knowledge, language, and education. *Canadian Journal of Native Education, 22*(1), 16–27.

Cleary, L., & Peacock, T. (1998). *Collected wisdom: American Indian education.* Boston: Allan and Bacon.

Dei, G. (2000). Towards an anti-racism discursive framework. In G. Dei & A. Calliste (Eds.), *Power, knowledge and anti-racism education: A critical reader* (pp. 23–39). Halifax, NS: Fernwood Publishing.

Dei, G., & Calliste, A. (2000). Mapping the terrain: Power, knowledge and anti-racism education. In G. Dei & A. Calliste (Eds.), *Power, knowledge and anti-racism education: A critical reader* (pp. 11–22). Halifax, NS: Fernwood Publishing.

Demmert, W. G. Jr. (2001). *Improving academic performance among Native American students: A review of the research literature.* Retrieved October 10, 2004, from http://www.ael.org/pubserv.cfm

Deyhle, D. (1995). Navaho youth and Anglo racism: Cultural integrity and resistance. *Harvard Educational Review, 65*(3), 403–436.

Deyhle, D., & Swisher, K. (1996). Research in American Indian and Alaska Native education: From self-determination to assimilation. *Educational Researcher, 22*, 113–194.

Fleras, A., & Elliot, J. (2003). *Unequal relations: An introduction to race and ethnic dynamics in Canada* (4th ed.). Toronto, ON: Pearson Education Canada Inc.

Fletcher, S. D. (2005). Aboriginal people and stories of Canadian history: Investigating barriers to transforming relationships. In C. James (Ed.), *Possibilities and limitations: Multicultural policies and programs in Canada* (pp. 34–56). Black Point, NS: Fernwood Publishing.

Giroux, H. (2005). *Border crossings: Cultural workers and the politics of education*. New York: Routledge.

Grantham, C. M. (2005). *Recasting Alaska Native students: Success, failure, and identity*. Unpublished doctoral dissertation, Stanford University, California.

Greenspon, E. (2007, April 14). The editorial. *Globe and Mail*, p. A2.

Hall, S. (1996). Introduction: Who needs identity? In S. Hall & P. duGay (Eds.), *Questions of cultural identity*. Thousand Oaks, CA: Sage Publications.

Hall, S. (1997). *Representation: Cultural representations and signifying practices*. London, England: Sage Publications in association with The Open University.

Haluza-Delay, R. (2002). *A community of acceptance: Respect for Thunder Bay's diversity*. Retrieved December 4, 2006, from http://www.thunderbay.org (under publications).

Hawthorne, H. B. (1967). *A survey of the contemporary Indians of Canada: Economic, political, educational needs and policies, Volume II*. Ottawa: Indian Affairs Branch.

Henry, F., Tator, C., Mattis, W., & Rees, T. (1995). *The colour of democracy: Racism in Canadian society* (2nd ed.). Toronto, ON: Harcourt, Brace & Company, Canada.

Henry, F., & Tator, C. (2006). *The colour of democracy: Racism in Canadian society* (3rd ed). Toronto, ON: Harcourt, Brace & Company, Canada.

James, C. (2003). *Seeing ourselves: Exploring race, ethnicity and culture* (3rd ed.). Toronto, ON: Thompson Educational Publishing Inc.

Laroque, E. (1991). Racism runs through Canadian society. In O. McKague (Ed.), *Racism in Canada* (pp. 73–76). Saskatoon, SK: Fifth House Publishers.

Lawrence, B. (2003). Gender, race, and the regulation of Native identity in Canada and the United States: An overview. *Hypatia*, *18*(2), 3–29.

Ledlow, S. (1992). Is cultural incongruence an adequate explanation for dropping out? *Journal of American Indian Education*, *31*, 21–36.

Lutrell. (2005). *Framing childhood: Visual imagery and image-making's role in training educators*. Retrieved September 23, 2005, from http://www.gse.harvard.edu/news/features/luttrell01012005.html

McCarthy, C. (1995). The problem with origins: Race and contrapunctual nature of the educational experience. In P. McLaren & C. Sleeter (Eds.), *Multicultural education, critical pedagogy, and the politics of difference* (pp. 245–263). New York: Albany State University of New York Press.

McCaskill, D., Fitzmaurice, K., & Desmoulins, L. (2007). *Urban Aboriginal task force: Thunder Bay report*. Toronto, ON: Ontario Federation of Indian Friendship Centres.

Reid, C. (2001). "Magpie Babies": Urban Aboriginal students, identity, and inequality in education. In A. Ward & R. Bouvier (Eds.), *Resting lightly on mother earth: The Aboriginal experience in urban educational settings* (pp. 19–36). Calgary, AB: Detselig Enterprises Inc.

Restoule, J. P. (2004). *Male Aboriginal identity formation in urban areas: A focus on process and context*. Unpublished doctoral dissertation, University of Toronto, Ontario.

Reuman, A. (2000). Coming into play: An interview with Gloria Anzaldua. *MELUS*, *25*(2), n/p.

Ryan, J. (1998). Understanding racial/ethnic stereotyping in schools: from image to discourse. *Alberta Journal of Educational Research*, *44*(3), 284–301.

Saukko, P. (2003). *Doing research in cultural studies: An introduction to classical and new methodological approaches*. Thousand Oaks, CA: Sage Publications.

Silver, J., & Mallett, K. (2002). *Aboriginal education in Winnipeg inner-city high schools*. Canadian Centre for policy alternatives. Retrieved September 23, 2005, from http://ius.uwinnipeg.ca/pdf/aboriginal-education.pdf

Sixkiller Clarke, A. (1994). *OERI Native American youth at risk study*. Bozeman, MO: Montana State University (ERIC Document Reproduction Service No. ED373951).

Smith, L. (1999). *Decolonizing methodologies: Research and indigenous peoples*. Dunedin, NZ: Zed Books Ltd.

St. Denis, V. (2002). *Exploring the socio-cultural production of Aboriginal identities: Implications for education*. Unpublished doctoral dissertation, Stanford University, California.

St. Denis, V., & Hampton, E. (2002). *Literature review on racism and the effects on Aboriginal education*. Minister's National Working Group on Education of Indian and Northern Affairs Canada. Retrieved September 23, 2005, from http://www.sfu.ca/mpp/aboriginal/colloquium/pdf/Racism_and_Abo_Education.pdf

Ward, A., & Bouvier, R. (2001). Introduction. In A. Ward & R. Bouvier (Eds.), *Resting lightly on mother earth: The Aboriginal experience in urban educational settings* (pp. 5–15). Calgary, AB: Detselig Enterprises Inc.

Weaver, H. (2001). Indigenous identity: What is it and who really has it? *American Indian Quarterly, 25*(2), 240–255.

Yon, D. (2000). *Elusive culture: Schooling, race, and identity in global times*. New York: State University of New York Press.

Leisa Desmoulins
Faculty of Education
Lakehead University

SÄDE-PIRKKO NISSILÄ

TOWARDS EQUITY AND SELF-AWARENESS IN TEACHER EDUCATION

Development of Pedagogical Thinking Among 2nd and 3rd Career Student Teachers

Although authoritarian pedagogy is by no means uncommon today, it is no longer the ideal and dominant practice that it was earlier. Today the ideal teacher is often seen as a servant of knowledge and learning, an initiator of learning processes wishing that students establish their identities on established systems of knowledge, know-how and practice. On one hand, this aim seems very desirable, but on the other hand, we can see that the students who allow themselves to be colonized by their teacher's knowledge may become subjects on that field and may not maintain their personal identities. In the worst case they become emptied of their own identity-bearing beliefs, knowledge, values, ideals, and key concepts. Thus students such as "women, minorities, and others who have significant identity components that are devalued by, or incompatible with, the teacher's system, or with the more general educational or cultural system of which the teacher's system is a part, may resist learning because to learn would be to sacrifice crucial identity components" (Bracher 2006, p. 92). To ensure equity in educational contexts student teachers should be encouraged to establish their identities on self-discovery, self-awareness, self-efficacy, reflected knowledge and the appreciation of others, on the side of know-how and practice.

PERSPECTIVES IN SECONDARY AND TERTIARY TEACHER EDUCATION

Modern, often humanist-constructivist pedagogies, acknowledge the needs of both teachers and students to become aware of their personal identities, and to construct them on certain ideals and values. Rather than offering students and teachers new identity components directly, the nature and origin of students' and teachers' own identity components should be first made understood, as well as the consequences of these components and the source of alternative identity components that they might embrace or pursue. The aim is not to change persons but to provide them with the opportunities to change and develop according to their identity needs (Bracher 2006; Nissilä 2006, pp. 180-197).

The research of teacher education in general has often focused on teacher processes, such as teacher knowledge and beliefs about teaching, practical arguments underlying their action repertoire, and their conceptions of learning, teaching and their personalities (Calderhead, 1996; Doyle, 1990; Kagan, 1990; Schön 1983;

J. A. Kentel and A. Short (eds.), Totems and Taboos: Risk and Relevance in Research on Teachers and Teaching, 213–228.

Shulman, 1987). Teacher personality and conceptions exert a great influence on student engagement. The question is also of personal features like intelligence (rational, emotional and spiritual; cf. Csikszentmihalyi 2006, p. 306; Goleman, 1999) and empathy. Teaching is an ethical endeavour, and to be ethical, teachers need empathy. It starts from understanding the role of the Other in us all (Kristeva, 1992).

RESEARCH CONTEXT, DATA GATHERING AND ANALYZING

In accordance with the purpose of seeking out elements of teachers' professional growth, the present phenomenographic study aimed at explaining the individual and shared experiences and conceptions of learning a new profession, developing a new professional identity and a way of thinking in pedagogical contexts. The data was collected during 1998-2004 from adult, academic, vocational student teachers (N=289). Their reflective essays concerned their school memories and experiences of learning and teaching. The more closely analyzed material was produced by 50 randomly chosen student teachers representing various fields of science, 36 females and 14 males, having the average age of 42. The analyses were made by the qualitative content analysis method.

Vocational teacher education is provided for persons with master's or doctoral degrees, and in a few cases persons with bachelor's degrees, along with at least three-year work experience in their fields of discipline. The education is given in multi-disciplinary groups. The research group consisted of prospective and present tertiary (university) and secondary level teachers as well as skilled specialists, with or without experience in teaching. They all strove for general pedagogical qualifications, which in Finland, are attained either in the so-called vocational higher teacher education units after graduation and work experience or before graduation in the subject teacher programs arranged by educational faculties of universities. The latter is offered mainly for younger students who are not included in this study. Both programs score 60 ECTS (European Credit Transfer and Accumulation System) and give equal qualifications.

EDUCATING THINKERS

In general, *thinking* means "the act or practice of one that thinks, formulating in mind, a way of reasoning, judgement, believing, supposing or occupying oneself mentally." Thinking at the teaching level refers to the possession of higher order thinking skills or critical thinking skills, as they are often called. Cognitive psychologists have investigated human performance acquired over many hours of learning and experience in various diverse domains. The data revealed differences in the competency levels resulting from the interaction of knowledge organization and information processing (Patel, Groen & Fredriksen, 1986).

While much is known about the cognitive skills of good thinking, there may be scarce information about the dispositional elements that support their use among student teachers. If teacher educators have knowledge of them, it can help foster critical thinking skills in the student teachers. What are the skills they should acquire in order to gain "membership" of competent educational discourses?

Firstly, understandings of knowledge as a 'commodity' are typical of what are termed 'reproductive' conceptions of learning, while constructivist conceptions of learning involve applying what the teacher has said to existing knowledge so that the knowledge is transformed in some way.

Secondly, one difficulty in thinking concerns the negotiation of 'voices' in both spoken and written texts An academic text contains many voices, for example of authorities, of authors in relation to other voices as soloists and of the lecturers. When the student teachers have to produce their own intentions, their own texts, to 'sing their own songs', they should be able to distinguish between the different voices (Bakhtin, 1981; Boughey, 1995).

Thirdly, academic student teachers have generally the understanding of writing as a process that generates new learning rather than one that reproduces other people's old texts. What is intuitively perceived of writing is confirmed by research showing that the act of writing is indeed an act of generating or creating learning (Murray, 1980; Emig, 1983). In accordance with this view many student teachers stressed active learning during their teaching practice, suggesting written assignments as a way of reporting what their students had learned:

> I try to enhance active and autonomous knowledge acquisition by connecting written exercises to tasks, which make students find solutions by themselves. (Female, PhD)

Thinking as a mode of communication produces either spoken or written language. The previous may show a lack of contextualization and a failure to make propositions follow from one to another in a linear fashion. The need to make the links explicit for the reader, on the other hand, accounts for the claims of a writer to have a sense of audience. To be a good writer, the student teacher has to move from an oral to a literate mode of communication. Sometimes symbols, illustrations and concept charts can make thinking both logical and visual, as is stated in the following quotation:

> As a visual person I tend to draw figures and tables, so I wanted to draw a figure of the orientation basis, which I should have simplified a bit more. However, my insight was that it is a very useful tool through planning to implementation. (Female, MSocSci)

Robert Ennis defines *critical thinking* by saying that it means, roughly, reasonable and reflective thinking focused on deciding what to believe or do. In doing such thinking, one is helped by the employment of a set of critical thinking dispositions and abilities that can serve as a set of comprehensive goals (Ennis, 1996).

Critical thinking is also essential as a tool in inquiry. It is a liberating force in education and a powerful resource in one's personal and civic life. Critical thinking is the skilled and active interpretation and evaluation of observations and communications, information and argumentation (Fischer & Scriven, 1997), as is the case in the following reflection on the feedback:

> It is difficult to evaluate one's human relation skills. I got, however, positive feedback from both students and the tutor teacher. They praised the atmosphere of my lessons as very accepting and open. We had a deeper conversation on that with my tutor teacher. According to her my natural and democratic attitude towards students was the basis of atmosphere. (Female, MEdSci)

Researchers in general see critical thinking as a direct positive force in building democratic society in all its levels and forms, which is one of the social tasks of school organizations as well. Some studies show *the* tendency towards developing critical attitudes in meeting different aspects of society and information. Taken in a positive way, they contribute to developing teacher thinking as well. Reynolds (1997) and Mingers (2000) emphasize the word `critique` and define it as the critique of rhetoric, of tradition, of authority and of knowledge. Critical thinking in this sense is often silenced in schools. The following quotation tells of an opposite attitude:

> I do not think I was mistaken to favour passive learning. I tried to evade it consciously. Criticalness was given space. I accepted the students' opinions and expressed my argued views whether they were similar or deviating. (Female, SocSci)

According to Mezirow's conception of critical thinking, the teacher is expected "to foster leadership and effective participation in others" to the extent that he/she becomes less necessary to the "self-directed learning process" (Mezirow, 1990, p. 363). The control of the learning process should reside in the student so that successful pedagogy is measured in terms of the student's increasing independence and self-motivation. Critical self-evaluation is thus necessary in this process.

Pedagogical thinking is here defined as decision-making based on the personal belief systems and as a result of combined rational and intuitive thinking. It becomes concrete in planning, implementation and especially in the situations, which demand immediate reaction (Shulman, 1986, 1987). The term knowledge, in the connection of *personal knowledge*, does not refer to an objective, scientifically proven knowledge base, but to teachers' individual constructions. A distinction between objective and personal knowledge is that, 'formal knowledge' is generated by educational researchers and 'practical knowledge of teaching' by teachers as the result of their experience in the classroom (Fenstermacher, 1994). The following examples of pedagogical thinking show how they appear in unexpected situations:

> The students were perplexed somehow, because all became silent. The next move would be mine. I understood well that the situation could escape from my hands, and I felt rather helpless for a time. Nothing like this was planned! However, I was able to handle the issue in a way that the person who had told the sensitive history did not feel sorry for her openness, and the other students were relieved. (Male, BSocSci)

Pedagogical thinking appears also in the ability to plan and carry out learning sequences and to choose evaluation methods that are successful and practical from the viewpoint of learning, students and community, as in the following:

> I am interested in planning different courses. Along with it I have taken pains in preparing them as well as possible straight from the start. Although all the themes I have taught have not been within my special mastery…. I have, however, learnt that, actually, with the smaller amount of information that I bring to the students, I will get better results. (Female, MSocSci)

The research data in studying teacher thinking and teachers' tacit or personal, practical knowledge are from 'narratives' or 'teacher stories'. The term tacit refers to the kind of knowledge that is implicit and hard to articulate. It is often described as situated (Berliner, 1992; Brown & McIntyre, 1995; Carter, 1990; Connelly & Clandinin, 1990; Elbaz, 1983; Schön, 1983). Schön (1983, 1987) originated the terms 'reflection-*in*-action' and 'reflection-*on*-action'. The former indicates the knowledge of professionals as demonstrated in their actions, maybe as reactions, the latter referring to the process of reflecting on their actions in order to broaden their knowledge. When used for planning, the third type of reflection could be named 'reflection-*for*-action'. Thus, Schön distinguished between knowledge and reflective thinking. Knowledge is a state and reflection is a process by which knowledge can be acquired, adjusted and expanded. The notion of reflection has greatly influenced the education of prospective teachers and professional development of already certified teachers.

In this study the terms 'practical knowledge' and 'personal knowledge' are used of all teachers' cognitions, such as declarative and procedural knowledge, beliefs and values that influence their pre-active, interactive and post-active teaching activities.

The idea of *transformative thinking* is that teachers should not unload new information on learners in a blind hope that they will absorb it, but that the learners must instead transform their previous knowledge and skills into something new. It promotes the idea that learners, or student teachers in this study, have to be encouraged to sharpen their critical thinking skills in order to be able to transgress epistemological limitations. They should be helped to see boundaries, whether personal or social, as constructed and move beyond them. This movement both empowers and transforms the learners.

Transformative learning is most likely to occur when student teachers become personally engaged and perceive the subject matter to be directly relevant to their own lives. Understanding the diversity of learning and finding new meanings to their previous experiences are keys to enhancing the engagement. Learning process is individual, content and context specific. Teaching at its best is igniting transformative learning (Boyd, Myers & Gordon, 1988; Mezirow, 1995; Talvio, 2002; Taylor, 1989). The following quotation reports of the feeling of change after teaching practice:

> In the beginning my self-confidence towards succeeding in teaching practice was very weak. The period made me assured that I will be able to work as a teacher…. The period was both professionally and personally significant. During the previous years in my job (as a social worker) I met difficulties,

> which greatly ruined my professional and personal self-confidence. (Female, MSocSci)

Transformative learning theory according to Mezirow (1998) exposes the centrality of experience, critical reflection and rational discourse, which are based on psychoanalytic and social theories. For learners to change the specific beliefs, attitudes and emotional reactions (=meaning schemes), means that they must engage in critical reflection on their experiences, which in turn leads to a perspective transformation. It is "the process of becoming critically aware of how and why our assumptions have come to constrain the way we perceive, understand, and feel about our world; changing the structures of habitual expectation to make possibly a more inclusive, discriminating, and integrating perspective; and finally, making choices or otherwise acting upon these new understandings" (Mezirow 1991, p. 167).

Mezirow has been criticized for his emphasis upon rationality (Cranton, 1994; Taylor, 1989). A new view of transformative learning as an intuitive, creative process has emerged in literature, based on analytical (or depth) psychology and represented for instance by Boyd (1988) and Cranton (1994). They consider the process of discernment central and call upon such extra-rational sources as symbols, images and archetypes to assist in creating a personal vision or meaning of what it means to be human. Thus transformative andragogy draws on the realm of interior experience, one constituent being the rational expressed through insights, judgements and decisions; the other being the extra-rational expressed through symbols, images and feelings.

Transforming thinking in teacher education presupposes awareness of *mental models* in thinking and giving attention to their transformation. Mental models are deeply held internal images of how the world works. They limit us to familiar ways of thinking and acting. That is why the discipline of managing mental models is vital for educating teachers. Mental models can be simple generalizations or complex theories. What is most important to grasp is that they are active—they shape the way how people act, because they affect to what they see and observe.

In teachers' work, the most predominant models of thinking are the conception of learning as well as human and epistemic conceptions. *Learning conceptions*—whether they are behaviouristic, constructivist, humanistic or other applications of learning theories—influence teachers' often intuitive choices of material, learning plans, teaching methods and evaluation. The behaviouristic learning conceptions, which were earlier dominant, do not always bring good memories to student teachers, when they recollect their school days:

> In the secondary school... being successful was learning by heart.... don't remember any positive learning experience from that time. School succeeded in killing my joy of learning. Since that time in my mind there is hovering a sense of worthlessness, feeling stupid. This feeling afflicts me sometimes even today. (Female, MEdSci)

> After graduating from the senior high school, I started to prepare for the entrance examination of the law faculty....I felt very disappointed after

> noticing that I had nearly reached the required level. Afterwards . . . I think that the tasks, which needed applications and analyses, were not successful. They needed real deep processing of information. My understanding of the written text stayed on too superficial a level to be applied in practical problem solving situations. (Female, MEdSci)

When observing the lessons in secondary and tertiary learning contexts, the notions of student teachers varied. The next quotation tells of the tertiary school of health and social care in which, the psychiatric department excluded, behaviouristic approach was emphasized:

> The contents of teaching are explained shortly and concisely, in the behaviouristic way. More comprehensive reflection is regarded as negative. In psychiatrics there prevails interaction and humanistic attitudes. (Female, MSc)

The justified demand of mastering the substance knowledge is primary among teachers and student teachers. A tutor teacher`s deficits in her mastery of the substance matter were revealed, as is written in the following quotation:

> The teacher of... wind instrument playing should know profoundly the physiology of breathing and, more widely, the physiology of the whole person to be able to teach it to the students. This claim, at least when I myself am concerned, starts from knowing oneself and how one acts when breathing. If the teacher has never thought of and reflected on these questions, he/she can't teach them to anybody. (Male, MA, Music)

Disciplinary knowledge is vital for teachers, connected with appropriate learning conceptions. Constructivist and experiential learning conceptions seem more attractive to the student teachers than traditional teacher-directed lessons. It is expressed in the following quotation:

> In the department where I observed lessons the official learning conception is constructivism. PBL is carried out according to a Dutch model.... In the lessons, which I observed I thought that the way of learning was that of learning-by-doing, constructivism in fact. (Male, PhD)

Behind these actions there are *human conceptions*, which are in general connected to teaching methods. A teacher can see his/her student, for example, as a 'tabula rasa' to whom the contents of lectures can be transferred, or an independent, autonomous individual able to develop and build the constructs of knowledge himself/herself when given guidance and care. If a teacher has the behaviouristic conception of students, or he/she has not thought of his/her mental models at all, he/she acts in the way that is reported by the student teacher in the following quotation:

> My tutor teacher had a very different view of teaching and treating students from that of mine, which allowed me to consider whether my view is the only

> and right one.... I don't, however, accept the teacher swearing at the students or underestimating them. (Female, Engineer)

If the teachers do not appreciate their students as autonomous persons able to develop, they can't obviously expect any good outcomes either:

> You succeed in getting to university (technical faculty), if not, you have to be satisfied with getting to university of applied sciences, and it is seen in the student learning. Many teachers complained of the weak quality of the student material. (Female, MSc)

More than negative examples of teacher attitudes there were observations of teachers who were really engaged in student centred approaches. It made a student teacher to formulate her own views as well:

> My conception of meaningful learning made me choose collaborative learning as the teaching method. It emphasizes humanistic conception of learning and human beings. (Female, B of Catering and Food Processing)

Epistemic conceptions should be in harmony with the aims and methods of teaching, as well as with learning and human conceptions. Today knowledge is understood, not as a reproduction of given ideas or facts, but as a tool in solving problems, understanding the phenomena behind observable issues, and even making inventions and innovations. In the following quotation a student teacher reflects on her epistemic conceptions:

> Traditional school learning serves the aim badly. Traditionally we think that transferring knowledge is primary and takes place before learning. Teaching that is separated from the contexts of information produces inert knowledge. This kind of knowledge can be used in school contexts as in tests and exams, but it can't be applied to the complicated problem solving situations of working life or everyday life.
>
> The prospective teachers should be well aware of their preconceptions of learning and teaching, of their human views and epistemic choices, before entering the teaching profession. (Female, MA)

Transforming the conceptions is the aim of teacher studies. Transformation of learning and thinking is difficult to notice, if student teachers do not write in their learning diaries regularly. In other words reflective practices increase reflective skills and also form the basis of observations of development.

REFLECTIVE SKILLS

How to foster transformative learning in teacher education? Should it be approached as a consciously rational process or as a more intuitive and imaginative process? Both the rational and affective, feelings and emotions as a means of reflection should be emphasized, as was already stated in the connection of pedagogical thinking.

Systematic *individual reflection*, as it appears in the quotations on earlier pages, helps the student teachers become aware of themselves as persons and professionals, and become more daring to see themselves realistically. A learning journal will serve the purpose well, since in reflective practice the experiences are not always possible to be reflected on the spot. While a learning journal allows later reflection, it also prevents too hasty evaluation of the experiences, which might lead the person astray. No actual learning or change in attitudes and assertiveness in emotional intelligence would then take place. The learner would lose a lot of valuable information without note-taking.

Habermas (1984) sees reflection as a process in which the person becomes conscious of the contexts and the influence of social and ideological stresses and limitations, which were earlier taken for granted. By being aware of them he/she can control their influence. For instance, through inquiry orientation towards the working situation a teacher can become more conscious and professionally more independent, as is expressed in the following:

> I must leave time for creativity and developing new approaches in the future. (Female, MBA)

Student teachers have also come to understand the necessity of reflective practice based on real experiences in a teacher's work as well as of the complex nature of practice involving whole persons in complicated and ambiguous situations:

> Reflection is often connected with the use of rationality and intelligence. Learning takes place, however, often through non-rational processing. Since personality is an entirety, making use of emotional area in the learning process is important. In the world of science people know that in rational and empirical acquisition of knowledge also intuitive and emotional solutions are needed. (Female, PhD)

Experiences without reflection (reflection-on-action) hardly teach anything. Reflection-in-action can be seen sequential or intertwined with the journal practice. Learning this skill means practising interactive (between earlier reflection and the present situation) and interpretive skills on the spot in solving complicated and indefinite problems. In other words, it appears as "reading" the situation in a new way, trying perhaps new actions, in a new framework. It is thus not reflection in the traditional meaning, but is based on earlier reflection and situational sensitivity, and is sometimes called reaction rather than reflection (Eraut, 1995).

Max van Manen (1995) recognizes the inappropriateness of the image of reflection-in-action when "life in the classrooms is contingent, dynamic, everchanging… [and] situation-specific" (p. 39), and so allows for reflection, which is contemporaneous with action only in the most qualified and circumscribed sense. He introduces the notion of 'pedagogical tact' in which perceptiveness, understanding and feelings are instantly realized in action. He further believes that the practice of teaching possesses integrity in its own, and that being a professional involves more than the possession of technical skills (van Manen). The same conclusion appears in the following quotation:

> Pedagogical theory knowledge that we have studied this year are: planning, implementation and evaluation of teaching as well as some special areas of teaching, but the holistic view of teachership and teaching is created and formed only along working experience. (Male, Engineer)

Critical reflection presupposes individualization of learning to constitute new perspectives into emotional and aesthetic experiences in life and work (Boud et al., 1985; Mezirow, 1991).

An earlier research showed that changes also implied cooperation with colleagues. Thus, besides personal, also collective tacit knowledge and making it conscious is understood to be significant (Nissilä, 2004). In working communities this kind of reflection cannot be compelled but is worth fostering. In *collective reflection* or collective dialogue there should be free and creative exploration of complex and subtle issues, a deep listening to one another and suspending one's own views (Senge, 1990). Team learning thus involves learning how to deal creatively with the forces opposite productive dialogue (Argyris, 1992).

Collaboration for professional development means sharing power and mutual interaction. It presupposes common aims and interests, collective responsibility and coherent needs. It means a challenge to teacher culture. Reflection in this change means an interactive process between earlier experiences, actions, personal theorizing and understanding theories. Its significance is in gradual construction of personal and shared collective knowledge and meanings as well as in making implicit things explicit. The students often refer to collegiality or the lack of it in their reports. The following experience is positive concerning both collective reflection and consultation:

> As a student teacher I was taken along in all activities. I felt I was welcome. I felt that I was in a unique situation, when I was allowed to observe and learn from another teacher and her teaching. I discussed with the students about their experiences in on-the-job learning, and I could hear many interesting stories on how working life teaches. (Female, B of Tourism, Catering and Food Processing)

In reality, things can be complicated. Beliefs are often deep-rooted and persistent. A significant issue in change is how a student teacher views his/her professional identity, what kind of teacher she/he wants to be. Or the problems may be even more complex: the student teacher may be enthusiastic in his/her discipline (mathematics, science, languages, etc.) and finds his/her inspiration in this rather than in building and maintaining a relationship with learners. The problem may also be a limiting self-concept interfering with the development of a number of personal qualities. To get the process of identity development moving, it is not enough to reflect only on the environment, behaviour and competencies, which form the outer level but to try also to understand the lived experiences and give meanings to them. The inner level is also to be recognized and reflected on. The so-called onion model (Dilts, 1990; Korthagen, 2004) shows that the inner levels of reflection (beliefs, identities and missions) determine the way an individual functions on the outer levels (environment, behaviour and competencies), but there is also a reverse influence.

TEACHER IDENTITY

Experiences do not only increase knowledge, but also touch and change personal identity. It is often social identity, which undergoes changes, seldom the core identity.

An individual's self-concept is his/her perception of himself/herself. It contains perceptions relating to the standards of characteristics such as traits, competencies, values, beliefs and attitudes that the person has internalized. These internalized standards make up who the person is, and will influence how he/she interprets stimuli and behaves in response to them. The cohesive forces within personal identity are *values*. Conceptualizing values as a core element in identity leads to understanding the cohesion among a person's various *social identities*. Values illustrate how a value-based conception of personal identity influences the formation of a role identity (Hitlin, 2003). Role (social/situational) identities in turn form the so-called *sub-identities*. The following quotation from a student teacher tells of the notions of the pressure on the engineering students' social identities in the building site:

> The nonverbal culture of the building site appeared in swearing, spitting and acting roguishly. I suppose it was an effort to hide one's weakness in the cold, heavy and demanding working site, in snowy and frosty circumstances.... There was also a certain relationship between the 1st and 3rd year students: the younger ones were elbowing and the older were stuck-up. When orders were given to the students, they had minimal expressions and gestures, maybe to seem uninterested. Obviously it meant lack of motivation and rebellion against the authorities. The hierarchy in building sites is strong. (Female, Engineer)

According to the social identity theory a person has not one "personal self," but several selves that correspond to widening circles of group memberships. In school contexts a kind of collective identity prevails, as a tutor teacher explained:

> The atmosphere is relatively bad and it influences the attitudes and the way of commitment: he himself is not as committed to his work as he had earlier been. (Male, MSc, repeating his tutor's words)

On the other hand there is a quest for positive distinctiveness, i.e. people understand that, although as members of a group they are defined as "we", the definition of "I" is also possible. Though it may be either positive or negative–depending on the situation–isolation from others is criticized by a student teacher:

> The teacher seems to be an independent entrepreneur in his/her classroom. I wonder where the collaboration and shared expertise were left–in the haste of daily duties? (Female, MEdSci)

The same student teacher writes of her role, which differs from that of permanent teachers:

> The role of the student teacher during the practice period is favourable in the sense that then he/she has a person nearby whose duty is to point to problematic features and give comments, to exchange ideas of the situations etc. This kind of collegial support every teacher needs–from time to time. In his it seems, however, to be too well true the supposition that when you are a "qualified" teacher, you are to get along by yourself. (Female, MEdSci)

It is obvious that collective experiences in school communities shape the teachers' social identities and roles. Some researchers (e.g. Deleuze & Guattari, 1987) are concerned with how identities are constantly 'becoming', how they are constantly redefined. The following excerpt describes the need and wish of development and, consequently, the shift of identity from that of a social worker to a teacher:

> I have a long work experience in the social field, and am used to theorizing practice. Still, I find many developmental tasks for myself, before I am an expert in teaching.... I am uncertain in front of the group, and I can't necessarily react in the right way in problematic situations.... I am afraid of periods of silence, although I understand that thinking and reflecting need time and space.... Especially, I find it difficult to be with young and lively students. Adult groups seem easier. I don't think too highly of my skills. For that reason, I am open to feedback and able to make use of it. (Female, MSocSci.)

The quotation suggests the incompleteness of professional identity and a *dynamic identity construction*. It emphasizes the affective character of the process by providing meaning to experiences. Thus not only are emotions central to identity formation, but we have to understand their roles in the multiplicity of emotions, which are likely to be experienced.

There is reason to believe that *specific self-views* influence people's cognitive responses to, for example, success and failure in life, while the *global self-esteem* influences people's emotional responses. Thus specific self-views would predict what a person will think about his/her performance, but global self-esteem would predict how he/she will feel about the performance (Dutton & Brown, 1997).

Working self-concept activates identity by defining the standard to which a person compares himself/herself. The specific domain in it is triggered from social or physical contexts or recent experiences and they can be even contradictory to each other (Ruohotie, 2004).

The working self-concept consists of three components: (a) self-views, (b) possible selves, and (c) goals and standards/ideal self-images (Lauriala & Kukkonen, 2005; Lord, Brown, & Freiberg, 1999). *Self-view* tells how a person sees himself/herself in a certain context when comparing demands and capacities.

Possible self defines what a person might be or become in the light of future expectations and fears. Although future-oriented, possible self-image has a connection with the present and appears in motivation, activities and affections:

> I want to walk with my students a passage of life together; spending time for it does not mean wasting time. I would like to be more flexible... A good teacher is courageous; I am such, too, but that kind of courage is still too hidden in me. (Male, MSocSci.)

Goals and standards direct information processing and also have a connection with motivation and self-regulation. They create an ideal image of what is to be attained:

> I learnt, however, how small I am and how much I have to learn about pedagogical things and building houses. I suppose I will never be fully competent, but by practising I will perhaps move forward. (Female, Engineer)

The *control system* regulates the emotional state and motivation by comparing the feedback and the relevant standards with each other and reacting to the possible discrepancy (Ruohotie, 2004). The writer quoted above goes on to explain about her increasing self-esteem and self-efficacy:

> (Being a female engineer) I won the boys' confidence gradually, when I was able to explain things to them. I also noticed that they put me on trial by asking difficult questions, and the attitude was that "you tell now as you are supposedly a building engineer." (Female, Engineer)

Recent interest in how the *teacher's self* is constructed and re-constructed through social interactions has shown that teacher identity requires the connection of emotion with self-knowledge (Kelchtermans, 1996; Little, 1996; Nias, 1989; Zembylas, 2003). The construction of teacher identity is in essence affective and dependent on power and agency. Self-transformation pays attention to both the multiplicities and complexities of teacher identity and the place of emotions. Emotions are indispensable for rationality. Change in perspective happens through a combination of emotion, cognitive thought and the unconscious and is connected to experiences, their reflection and the system of giving meanings.

PROMOTING PROFESSIONAL AWARENESS AND IDENTITY INTEGRATION

When starting their pedagogical studies, the 2nd or 3rd career student teachers see the teacher's profession mainly as having sufficient professional competence ("doing certain acts well"), having a positive and rightful attitude towards the students as well as showing good interpersonal skills, situational sensitivity, self-esteem, and knowledge of teaching contents. After gaining experiences in teaching and reflecting on them, they specify the components of teacher identity in a more conceptual, and thus in a more flexible way. The emphasis is moved from single acts (what the teacher is able to do) to aims, targets, values and principles. The higher the relevance of the experiences, the more likely they are to aid involvement, motivation and enthusiasm (Nissilä, 2006).

Insight into student teachers' interactive cognitions and ways of thinking in pedagogical interaction is valuable and of great additional importance, because it provides information that would not otherwise emerge. It is partly reflections on what was taught and written during earlier phases of teacher education, but on the other hand it is something that they have created themselves based on their theoretical knowledge of education, on their biographies and on their experiences of school and teaching.

Creativity is central in connection to inventiveness and innovation. Teacher qualities are needed to deal with conflicting elements while acting in a teacher's role to satisfactorily resolve the many dilemmas arising spontaneously in the teaching situation, to improvise and seize the moment in the teaching situation to optimize learning, and last but not least, to cope with constraints.

Creative teaching is defined as having four main properties: innovation, ownership, control and relevance. As a matter of fact, they are the criteria known from the theories of autonomous learning (Nissilä, 1993, 2002). Ownership of knowledge means learning for oneself. For that reason personal awareness and its gains should always be reflected upon. Creative learning also means internalizing knowledge and transformation.

Control of the learning process should reside with the owner. It means that creative learning and teaching does not necessarily need outside control, but the owner's self-control through collegial reflection should be enough. Relevance, again, means that student teachers strive to construct knowledge that is meaningful within their frame of reference. If knowledge conveyed to them is relevant to their concerns, and reflects their societal and cultural knowledge, it is easily internalized and developed into personal knowledge.

When the process of teacher education presented in this research is examined from the perspective of development towards transformative teachership, the findings show how the teacher's work is complex and connected to many groups of interest holders. The dialogue between persons, environments and cultures is constantly shaping and reshaping the participants' personalities, cognitive and metacognitive capacities, emotions and social competences. The dialogue is also needed for defining the relationship between equity and self-awareness. A balanced self-image promotes equity.

REFERENCES

Argyris, C. (1992). *On organizational learning*. Cambridge, MA: Blackwell Publishers.

Bakhtin, M. (1981). The dialogic imagination. In M. Holmquist (Ed.), *The dialogic imagination*. Austin, TX: University of Texas Press.

Berliner, D. C. (1992). The nature of expertise in teaching. In F. K. Oser, A. Dick, & J. Patry (Eds.), *Effective and responsible teaching: The new synthesis* (pp. 227–248). San Francisco: Jossey-Bass.

Boud, D., Keogh, R., & Walker, D. (Eds.). (1985). *Reflection: Turning experience into learning*. London: Kogan Page.

Boughey, C. M. (1995). The UNIZUL writing respondent programme: An alternative to writing centre. In *Proceedings of the Annual Conference of the South African Association for Academic Development*. Bloemfontein: University of the Orange Free State.

Boyd, R. D., Myers, & Gordon, J. (1988). Transformative education. *International Journal of Lifelong Education, 7*(3), 261–284.
Bracher, M. (2006). *Radical pedagogy. Identity, generativity, and social transformation.* New York: Palgrave Macmillan.
Brown, S., & McIntyre, D. (1995). *Making sense of teaching.* Buckingham: Open University Press.
Calderhead, J. (1996). Teachers: Beliefs and knowledge. In D. C. Berliner & R. C. Calfee (Eds.), *Handbook of Educational Psychology* (pp. 709–725). New York: Simon Schuster Macmillan.
Carter, K. (1990). Teachers' knowledge and learning to teach. In W. R. Houston (Ed.), *Handbook of Research on Teacher Education* (pp. 291–310). New York: Macmillan.
Connelly, F. M., & Clandinin, D. J. (1990). Stories of experienced and narrative inquiry. *Educational Researcher, 19*, 2–14.
Cranton, P. (1994). Self-directed and transformative instructional development. *Journal of Higher Education, 65*(6), 726–744.
Csikzentmihalyi, M. (2006). *Kehittyvä minuus. [Developing identity.]* Helsinki: Rasala kustannus.
Deleuze, G., & Guattari, F. (1987). *A thousand plateaus: Capitalism and schizophrenia.* Minneapolis, MN: University of Minnesota Press.
Dilts, R. (1990). *Changing belief systems with NLP.* Cupertino, CA: Meta Publications.
Doyle, W. (1990). Themes in teacher education research. In W. R. Houston (Ed.), *Handbook of Research on Teacher Education* (pp. 3–23). New York: Macmillan.
Dutton, K., & Brown, J. (1997). Global self-esteem and specific self-views as determinants of people's reactions to success and failure. *Journal of Personality and Social Psychology, 73*(1), 139–148.
Elbaz , F. (1983). *Teacher thinking: A study of practical knowledge.* London: Croom Helm.
Emig, J. (1983). *The web of meaning.* Portsmouth, NJ: Boynton Cook.
Ennis, R. H. (1996). *Critical thinking.* Upper Saddle River, NJ: Prentice-Hall.
Eraut, M. (1995). Schön shock: A case for reframing reflection-in action? In *Teachers and Teaching, 1*(1), 9–22.
Fenstermacher, G. D. (1994). The knower and the known: The nature of knowledge in research on teaching. *Review of Research on Teaching, 20*, 1–54.
Fischer, A., & Scriven, M. (1997). *Critical thinking: Its definition and assessment.* Norwich, UK: Centre for Research in Critical Thinking, University of East Anglia.
Goleman, D. (1999). *Working with emotional intelligence.* London: Bloomsbury.
Habermas, J. (1984). *The theory of communicative action, volume one: Reason and the rationalization of society.* Boston: Beacon Press.
Hitlin, I. (2003). *Psychology of perception.* Retrieved March 13, 2008, from http://www.discover-your-mind.co.uk/1d-perception.htm read
Kagan, D. M. (1990). Ways of evaluating teacher cognition: Inferences concerning the Goldilocks principle. *Review of Educational Research, 60*, 419–469.
Kelchtermans, G. (1996). *Teacher vulnerability: Understanding its moral and political roots.* Cambridge Journal of Education, *26*, 307–324.
Korthagen, F. A. J. (2004). In search of the essence of a good teacher: Towards a more holistic approach in teacher education. *Teaching and Teacher Education, 20*(1), 77–97.
Kristeva, J. (1992). *Muukalaisia itsellemme. [Strangers to ourselves.]* Helsiki: Gaudeamus.
Lauriala, A., & Kukkonen, M. (2005). Ammatillisen identiteetin rakentuminen harjoittelusituaatiossa. [Building Professional Identity in Practice Situations.] In P. Väisänen & P. Atjonen Kohtaamisia, *ja kasvun paikkoja opetusharjoittelussa. [Encounters and growth in teaching practice.]* (pp. 91–108). Joensuu: Joensuun Yliopistopaino.
Little, J. (1996). The emotional contours and career trajectories of (disappointed) reform enthusiasts. *Cambridge Journal of Education, 26*, 345–359.
Lord, R. G., Brown, D. J., & Freiberg, S. J. (1999). Understanding the dynamics of leadership: The role of follower self-concepts in the leader/follower relationship. *Organizational Behaviour and Human Decision Process, 78*, 167–203.
Mezirow, J. (1990). How critical reflection triggers transformative learning. In J. Mezirow et al. (Eds.), *Fostering critical reflection in adulthood. A guide to transformative and emancipatory learning* (pp. 1-20). San Franisco: Jossey-Bass.
Mezirow, J. (1991). *Transformative dimensions of adult learning.* San Francisco: Jossey-Bass.
Mezirow, J. (1995). Kriittinen reflektio uudistavan oppimisen käynnistäjänä. [Critical reflection triggering transformative learning.] In J. Mezirow et al. (Eds.), *Uudistava oppiminen. Kriittinen*

reflektio aikuiskoulutuksessa. [Transformative learning. Critical reflection in adult education.] (pp. 374–397). Helsingin yliopiston Lahden tutkimus-ja koulutuskeskus.
Mezirow, J. (1998). On critical reflection. *Adult Education Quarterley, 48*(3), 185–198.
Mingers, J. (2000, June). What is it to be critical? Teaching a critical approach to management undergraduates. *Management & Learning, 31*, 2.
Murray, D. M. (1980). Writing as a process: How writing finds its own meaning. In T. R. Donavan & B. W. McClelland (Eds.), *Eight approaches to teaching composition* (pp. 3–10). Urbana IL: National Council of Teachers of English.
Nias, J. (1989). *Primary teachers talking: A study of teaching and work*. London: Routledge.
Nissilä, S.-P. (1993). *Kielenopettajan oppimiskäsityksen tausta. [The roots of language learning conceptions]*. Oulun yliopisto: Kasvatustieteellinen tiedekunta. Lisensiaatin tutkimus. [University of Oulu, Faculty of Education. Licentiate Study.]
Nissilä, S.-P. (2002). Pratique reflexive et besoin dáutonomie dans la formation des enseignants. In A. Camilleri (Ed.), *Inroduction de l'autonomie de l'apprenant dans la formation des enseignants* (pp. 11–19). Strassbourg: editions du Conseil de l' Europe.
Nissilä, S.-P. (2004). Reflection for staff and faculty development. In A. Kolmos, O. Vinther, P. Anderson, L. Malmi, & M. Fuglem (Eds.), *Faculty development in nordic engineering education* (pp. 133–150). Aalborg: Aalborg University Press.
Nissilä, S.-P. (2006). Dynamic dialogue in learning and teaching. Towards transformation. In *Vocational teacher education*. Acta Universitatis Tamperensis 1179. Retrieved March 13, 2008, from http://www.acta.uta.fi/teos.phtm/?10698
Patel, V., Groen, G., & Fredriksen, C. (1986). Differences between students and physicians in memory for clinical cases. *Medical Education, 20*, 3–9.
Reynolds, M. (1997). Towards a critical management pedagogy. In J. Burgoyne & M. Reynolds (Eds), *Management of learning: Integrating perspectives in theory and practice*. London: Sage.
Ruohotie, P. (2004). Minäkäsityksen ja–identiteetin muuttuminen johtamisen tavoitteena. [Change of self image and self identity as the aim of management.] In M. Tuominen & J. Wihersaari (Eds.), *Ammatti ja kasvatus. Ammattikasvatuksen tutkimuksia vuonna 2004. [Profession and Education. Research Results of Professional Education in 2004.]* (pp. 185–197). Hämeenlinna: Tampereen yliopisto.
Schön, D. (1983). *The reflective practitioner: How professionals think in action*. New York: Basic Books.
Schön, D. (1987). *Educating the reflective practitioner: Toward a new design for teaching and learning in the professions*. San Francisco: Jossey-Bass.
Shulman, L. S. (1986). Those who understand: Knowledge growth in teaching. *Educational Revie, 57*(1), 1–22.
Shulman, L. S. (1987). Knowledge and teaching: Foundations of the new reform. *Harvard Educational Review, 57*, 1–22.
Senge, P. (1990). *The fifth discipline*. New York: Doubleday/Currency.
Talvio. (2002). Tutkimus opetustyössä–kuka, mitä, miten ja miksi? [Research in teaching–who what and why.] In P. Kansanen & K. Uusikylä (Eds.), *Luovuutta, motivaatiota tunteita. Opetuksen tutkimuksen uusia suuntia. [Creativity, Motivation and Emotions. New Trends in Educational Research.]* (pp. 151–172). Jyväskylä: PS – kustannus.
Taylor, C. (1989). *Sources of the self*. Cambridge: Harvard University Press.
van Manen, M. (1995). On the epistemology of reflective practice. In *Teachers and Teaching, 1*(1), 33–50.
Zembylas, M. (2003). Interrogating teacher identity: Emotions, resistance and self-formation. *Educational Theory, 53*, 97–127.

Sade-Pirkko Nissila
School of Vocational and Higher Teacher Education
Oulu University of Applied Sciences

JASON BRENT ELLIS

THE DIGITAL DIVIDE IN SPECIAL EDUCATION

Where Do My Students Fit In?

INTRODUCTION TO THE RESEARCH & LITERATURE REVIEW

This research sought to understand special education teachers' experiences and interpretations of the digital divide as manifest in the disparity of technology access and technology resources in schools for students in special education services. From this inquiry, emergent themes developed, marked by rich descriptions of the quality of barriers that special education teachers confront in attempting to integrate assistive technology, for students with disabilities, into academic instruction. Thus, the principal research question for this study was: What are special education teachers' lived experiences related to the digital divide?

The Merriam-Webster's online dictionary (n.d.) provides a general definition of accommodation as "something supplied for convenience or to satisfy a need" (¶ 1). In special education services, Smith, Polloway, Patton, and Dowdy (1998) delineate educational adaptations as "changes in the manner in which students are taught . . . they include changes in instruction, assignments, homework and testing" (p. 40). Within this framework of adaptation comes the concept of educational supports for interventions such as assistive technologies (AT).

Bryant and Bryant (2003) discussed the importance of assistive technology accommodations in the lives of individuals with disabilities by focusing on aspects of independence and academics. Assistive technology for individuals with disabilities is viewed as a means to achieve independent living that otherwise would not be possible without its use. Scherer (2004) noted the importance of the feeling of connectedness to academic and social aspects of school that students can achieve from effectively using assistive technology in and out of the classroom. Hasselbring and Glaser (2000) note that assistive technology "can enable even those students with severe disabilities to become active learners in the classroom alongside their peers who do not have disabilities" (p. 102). It is clear that assistive technology can prove to be an important mode of accommodation in an academic setting and thus it is of no surprise that AT has been written into several acts of legislation over the years.

School districts are required under law to provide appropriate assistive technology to students with disabilities when it supports their acquisition of a free and appropriate public education (Individuals with Disabilities Education Act, 1997). In order to support the inclusion and participation of students with disabilities in regular education classrooms, all Individual Education Plans developed for children identified as needing special education services, must indicate that AT has been

J. A. Kentel and A. Short (eds.), Totems and Taboos: Risk and Relevance in Research on Teachers and Teaching, 229–240.

considered to provide meaningful access to the general curriculum (Individuals with Disabilities Education Act, 1997). More specifically, the Individuals with Disabilities Education Act indicates that assistive technology devices and services must be made available to a child with a disability if required as a part of the child's: (a) special education, (b) related services, or (c) supplementary aids.

Many assistive technologies are computer based; they necessitate access to computers to work. This access to technology infrastructure may be influenced by the digital divide in who gets access to technology in education. Hendrix (2005) noted that:

> Computers are becoming common tools in schools, often viewed as a democratic panacea despite the costs involved and despite the fact that the majority does not have access to computers and/or the Internet; this creates a digital divide for students, in which some are 'more equal' than others. (p. 63)

Schools serve an essential role for students who access computers from only one location. Although nearly all schools and classrooms have computers, most provide severely restricted access to the students and teachers (Bronack, 2006). In light that the digital divide has traditionally been associated with inequities in access related to race (Fairlie, 2004), gender (Cooper & Weaver, 2003), and social class (Cleary, Pierce, & Trauth, 2006), this research attempts to observe the digital divide through the lens of disability.

METHODOLOGY

In order to identify the experiences of special education teachers in Preschool to grade 12 (P-12) education, the researcher was not interested in confirming an existing theory, but rather, in the process of knowledge construction that can emerge from the interaction between researcher and participants. Therefore, a naturalistic or constructivist inquiry was determined to be the most appropriate mode of inquiry for this study. Further, because of the uniqueness of the participants' experiences within the school setting as both preservice and inservice special education teachers, a qualitative methodology best served the purpose of this study by providing the researcher with "depth of meaning and richness of understanding" (Erlandson, Harris, Skipper, & Allen, 1993, p. 30) of the participants' experiences.

Participant Selection

This study analyzed the phenomenon of the digital divide experiences of pre-service and in-service special education teachers in P-12 education. In order to seek the essence of the experiences of these teachers, a sample of six special education teachers (three pre-service and three in-service) currently engaged in graduate studies at a university in northwest Ohio, and concurrently teaching students with disabilities in P-12 institutions were recruited to participate in this study.

Sandelowski (1995) noted that, "a common misconception about sampling in qualitative research is that numbers are unimportant in ensuring the adequacy of a sampling strategy" (p. 179). The researcher must be weary that sample sizes may be "too small to support claims of having achieved either informational redundancy or theoretical saturation, or too large to permit the deep, case-oriented analysis that is the raison-d'etre of qualitative inquiry" (p. 179). Thus, the determination of an adequate sample size in qualitative research is "ultimately a matter of judgment and experience in evaluating the quality of the information collected against the uses to which it will be put, the particular research method and purposeful sampling strategy employed, and the research product intended" (p. 179). As such, sampling for this study was terminated upon the sixth interview as the researcher believed that the quality of information collected had sufficiently met the purposes of the research intentions.

This research used a style of purposeful sampling referred to by Creswell (2005) as homogeneous sampling, principally due to the fact that the pool of participants held "membership in a subgroup that has defining characteristics" (p. 206). In the case of this research participants were pre-service or in-service special education teachers, engaged in graduate studies and currently working as teachers or performing student-teaching in P-12 schools.

Further, Lincoln and Guba (1985) explained that purposeful sampling has four characteristics: (a) emergent sampling design, (b) serial selection of sample units, (c) continuous adjustment or focusing of the sample, and (d) selection of the point of redundancy. In order to satisfy these requirements participants in this study were not identified *a priori* (as a result of a random selection). The School of Intervention Services (SIS), at the participating university in northwest Ohio, indicated possible participants at their institution. A list of potential participants was generated from class rosters of the academic years of 2004/2005 and 2005/2006 of EDIS 647, kept by the secretarial staff. The SIS administrative staff indicated possible individuals using the following selection criteria. Prospective participants: (a) were currently enrolled in a graduate program of study in special education, (b) had successfully complete coursework in assistive technology for intervention specialists (EDIS 647), and (c) were currently working as special education teachers or engaged in the student-teaching portion of their degrees in northwest Ohio. Prospective participants were contacted by the SIS secretarial staff by e-mail. Individuals whom were interested in participating in the study were asked to contact the researcher directly (by phone or by e-mail).

The SIS secretarial staff e-mailed a recruitment script to a total population of 78 students who fit the recruitment criteria. Of the 78 e-mails sent, only one e-mail was returned from the institution's mail server as being undeliverable. The script was e-mailed out by secretarial staff on three separate occasions, separated by two-week increments. Six individuals volunteered to participate in this study by directly e-mailing the researcher.

Data Collection

A face-to-face, individual in-depth interview was the main mode of data collection for this study. Lancy (1993) discussed the importance of obtaining information in the interview process, but simultaneously being wary of not constraining the interviewees' responses to a predetermined framework. By letting participants stray from guiding questions, the interviewer allows participants to possibly bring forth their conceptualization of the phenomena.

Open-ended questions were used during the interview process in order to facilitate the exploration of the emic perspective. Patton (1990) stated that truly open-ended questions allow the participants to respond in their own terms. Furthermore, he (1990) suggested that open ended questions do "not presuppose which dimension of feeling or thought will be salient for the interviewee . . . which] allows the person being interviewed to select from among that person's full repertoire of possible responses" (p. 296). Individual interviews were approximately 30-60 minutes in duration. The researcher requested permission to audio-tape the interviews to ensure accuracy of the participants' responses. Transcriptions were made from the audio-recordings, which were, in turn, shared with participants through a member-checking process to ensure credibility of data. In this manner, participants reviewed both their constructions within the interview and the researcher's interpretations of their constructions and were asked to make commentary on the material. As Morrow and Smith (1995) pointed out, within this context, participants had the opportunity to become analysts of their own data.

FINDINGS

Emergent Themes

Two themes emerged from the data that were relevant to the digital divide in special education: *Access to Existing or Shared Resources* and the *Distribution of Resources.* The theme of *Access to Existing or Shared Resources* was used to cluster responses that focused on issues such as time lags in having assistive technology resources set up or installed in their classrooms, hierarchies to access, and sharing of assistive technology resources within schools. The theme of the *Distribution of Resources* focused on how materials were distributed throughout the school and particularly, the difference between materials provided to special education classrooms compared with regular education.

Access to Existing or Shared Resources

Some participants noted that they had little access to technology in their classrooms and to shared technology. Amy observed that there was not a shared laboratory environment in her school, and thus, had to use what little resources she had available to her in her classroom. Elle observed not even having basic resources such as appropriate lighting in her classroom: "I would love to have technology. I can barely get basic technology, like light bulbs" (Elle, 115-116).

Participants also noted stigma related to special education and gaining access to technology. Elaine noted "it's like pulling teeth to get the librarian to lend [technology] out. Especially, unfortunately to the special education classrooms because they see my students as fairly irresponsible and are afraid one of the kids will break it" (Elaine, 29-32). Of great concern is that stigma, of students in special education being perceived as irresponsible, which may have led to a hierarchy of who gets access to technology in schools. Diana observed this hierarchy in stating:

> Yes, they had a couple of computer laboratories, and they had projectors, and they had a couple of Smart boards, and so they had a lot of technology but the access, we didn't have a lot of access to it. So that was a problem. It was all for more the general population and we came last in the pecking order for access to it. (Diana, 35-38)

Mary noted a similar belief that "the general education classrooms got up and running [with their technology] before we did. They were the priority to get access" (Mary, 28-29). Elaine noted experiencing a similar 'pecking order' to gaining access:

> There has been times I've had a schedule that my kids are going [to the computer laboratory] and then somebody else needed it more and they had more students to take and so the kids went down there and she sent us back to the room. I think that those resources [are important]. A lot of kids have computers at home, but only probably half of my kids do, so anything we do using assistive technology has to be done at the school just because they don't have access [elsewhere]. (Elaine, 188-192)

In this instance Elaine notes both a hierarchy to getting access as well as noting the importance of school provided access to children who may not have such resources at home.

Mary described her students' access to assistive technology as being non-existent. She observed that the computer lab scheduling at her school was:

> Another thing where special education was different . . . . The other teachers all were in a lottery to pick their laboratory times. We did not have a laboratory time at all. Even though there were blocks of times where we had consistent groups of students and we could have used it, we were not able to have a laboratory time at all. (Mary, 113-117)

Elle described that the lack of assistive technology resources in her classroom had lead her to use computers in other teachers' rooms:

> The kids have to go to different rooms to use computers because we don't have enough. So let's say the fourth graders are going to [use] computers, like there's twenty kids in a regular fourth grade [class], so it's there time to do [computer work] at 10:00 that morning, maybe two kids would go to room 104, two kids would go to room 105, four kids would go to room 106. Everyone is divided up. (Elle, 124-127)

In this case, access is dependent on other teachers' willingness to allow Elle's students to use their general technology resources for assistive technology purposes. This, having to negotiate access to the technology resources, shows a discrepancy in distribution and access to resources associated by a digital divide.

Distribution of Resources

The theme of the distribution of resources held, within it, several different facets of barriers to assistive technology integration. In general, participants believed that special education was "getting skipped over" (Amy, 234-235) in the distribution of resources. For instance, Elaine discussed the disparity of some teachers being very privileged in receiving technology while others went with little or none. She observed:

> I do know that there's one teacher who has a smart board in our building; he teaches chemistry and physics. I don't know how he got it, whether it was some kind of grant. I'm not sure what the circumstances are other than he has it and nobody else, to my knowledge, has ever used it. (Elaine, 237-241)

This conception contrasts greatly with Elaine's depiction of what assistive technology her students have access to, in stating, "We kind of get the old [computers]. You know, when people retire theirs because they're so slow and then we get them. We would never get new laptops in a special education room" (Elaine, 44-46). In fact, Elaine noted a stigma to special education; that students are being *housed* rather than *schooled*, so the logic thus follows 'why bother providing resources?' She observed: "My boys just get called to haul the old stuff out, when, you know, that they figure we're not doing anything anyway so they ask the guys to haul stuff to the dumpster even though we have a class" (Elaine, 66-68). She clarified further, in noting that school staff believes that:

> Other than looking up dirty pictures [special education] kids aren't going to use [computers] for anything anyway. So let's give it to the kids who are going to go on to write term papers or do something wonderful with their lives. So I think we're just kind of the bottom of the totem pole as far as what we get and it's unfortunate because I feel like my students probably have a greater need than a lot of the others. (Elaine, 266-271)

Mary described a very similar belief in a stigma associated with special education. When asked to speculate as to why special education was not provided with sufficient resources she replied that:

> I don't want to think that it's a lot of things like they just don't care as much about those kids or they don't expect those kids to go out and be successful and give back to the school in ways that other kids can and that the parents aren't as influential maybe. No one ever made any comments. There were just things, like I saw things that other teachers got that special education didn't. At open house, very few people came down to the special education room. They went to their home rooms and stuff like that. (Mary, 127-132)

Elaine also noted a hierarchy, or pecking order, as to the distribution of technology resources. She observed:

> I think we kind of get whatever's left over. The technology laboratory gets the nicest computers, followed by the library, followed by the regular [education] teachers that teach journalism, yearbook, or English and then when they get the new computers we are asked if we need anything that isn't being used anymore. (Elaine, 119-122)

Diana also noted a similar belief that a hierarchy existed in technology services in stating, "the general classrooms got first priority. I think our technology guy gave first priority to the general education classrooms and teachers . . . and when he had finished all of those, then he would address our issues" (Diana, 180-182).

Participants showed confusion and frustration at the disparity in the distribution of technology resources. Elle observed that, in her school, "some rooms did [have more resources]. I noticed some rooms had more computers in them but they were the regular classrooms. I didn't really understand that" (Elle, 23-24). Similarly, Diana observed the disparity in noting how non-special education classrooms continued to receive technology resources while her resource room went without: "They already had three or four [computers] and we still didn't have any" (Diana, 187). She discussed her frustration further in noting that "we were supposed to get a computer. . .in the beginning of the year we were supposed to get one but it never showed up" (Diana, 65-66). Elle noted her frustration in the following rationalisation:

> It seemed to me that the people who needed the most access to technology, and new technology the most, had the least . . . . They had more computers in the room and I didn't have a light bulb and I had children who had visual impairments and who could have used a computer to have things enlarged and read to them. I couldn't get a computer; I couldn't get a light bulb. (Elle, 29-33)

Elaine also described her frustrations at the disparity of the distribution of resources in her school in observing that:

> People talk about how important [technology] is, you know, heading in the right direction. We're in a technological world and I kind of think 'put your money where your mouth is' because they tell us that we are supposed to do it and then they don't give us the tools to do it. (Elaine, 309-312)

From this logic, Elaine described an incident in which she tried to secure more funding for her students to provide them with more access to technology. She noted:

> I started checking the assistive technology box [in their IEPs] because I heard that you can get more grants if you do. I was cautioned against doing that because then we [the school] would have to provide that [technology] for them [students] so I was told not to do that because then we're obligated to provide what they need. (Elaine, 234-237)

Elaine, in this instance, noted her belief in the importance of having access to assistive technology, but her beliefs and good intentions were easily quashed by her school administration's commitment to budgetary obligations.

In trying to procure more resources for her students, Elle started to inquire into funding with her school's administrative body. She noted:

> I could never get a straight answer on [access to funding for AT] because I would talk to my special education supervisor because I knew that there had to be money coming in because my kids had special needs and so I knew they were getting certain funds from the state. I had kids who had autism and they got somewhere between $20,000 and $40,000 a year but when you would ask for the money to get even something as basic as a special book or a reading series the money was never there and I know that I was not being paid $40,000 per kid. Nobody could explain where the money was and I never got it. (Elle, 36-42)

Amy noted "I see differences" (Amy, 228) in the distribution of resources but she felt that it was not based on different expectations or attitudes toward students in special education services. Rather, she felt it was more about "[how] the school is trying to get the most bang for their buck" (Amy, 229). She noted that when purchasing assistive technology materials for individuals with disabilities, by nature, the technology must meet that individual's specific needs. As such, with "mainstream people you get a better price, you get more bang for your buck because you are not buying such a small quantity" (Amy, 232-233). In any manner, participants felt that assistive technology resources had not been managed and distributed in a uniform way throughout schools, with special education taking the lowest priority in the distribution.

DISCUSSION

The discussion section addresses the principle research question for this study; what are special education teachers' lived experiences related to the digital divide? The following areas are discussed, in terms of current research literature, to draw a context from the emergent themes as related to (a) technology infrastructure and (b) special education perceived as lesser education in schools.

Technology Infrastructure in Schools

Since participants in this research noted not being involved in the planning for technology in schools and not privy to budgetary information they began to harbour feelings that these issues were being hidden from them by administration and thus actively questioned the inequitable distribution of technology resources. They perceived that other professionals within their school buildings had been provided more resources which brought forth feelings of frustration and anger. Means (1998) noted that technology infrastructure is often envisioned as the first step in successfully integrating technology into instruction, and as such, "large applications of public funds are likely to focus on infrastructure improvements, often with a formula for 'equitable' distribution of resources across all districts, schools, or classrooms" (¶ 6). Means subtly observed that there may not be much equality in a formula of equitable distribution of resources. As such the disparity of the distribution of technology resources within schools may be seen as another of the "complex factors that shape technology use in ways that serve to exacerbate existing education inequalities" (Warschauer, Knobel, & Stone, 2004, p. 562).

This frustration, over the disparity of resources, lead participants to a state of learned helplessness, in which they felt that there was no longer a point in attempting to request or procure assistive technology as their voices would not be heard by administration. In light that participants could not secure school funds and procure dedicated assistive technology for their own classrooms for their students to use, they were faced with having to share the current technology infrastructure within their schools. Sharing technology resources was noted as being a difficult process for the participants. They noted that access to shared computer laboratories was highly competitive in schools and they had to rely on the willingness of other teachers and school personnel in order to provide access to their students. Williams, Coles, Wilson, Richardson, and Tuson (2000) noted a similar trend in studying barriers to Information and Communication Technologies integration in schools in Scotland. They observed that a substantial barrier to successfully integrating technology into general instruction took the form of obtaining access to shared technology resources. In the current research this access issue was further confounded in that participants observed a hierarchy of access in which special education was perceived as last in the pecking order. This is a vivid example of how the disparity of access to technology resources helps fuel the digital divide in special education services. As Hendrix (2005) notes, within this example of technology access, some students are clearly denoted as 'more equal' than others. This leads to a discussion of the perception of special education.

Special Education Perceived as Lesser Education in Schools

Participants noted that they perceived that special education was treated as lesser education in schools. For instance, Elaine discussed that her students were frequently asked to haul garbage out of the school during instructional time by other teaching professionals and administrators. Similarly, this perception was put further askew by participants witnessing a disparity between both access to existing technology resources in schools and the distribution of new technology resources.

It appears that a certain stigma surrounds special education. Hiebert, Wong, & Hunter (1983) observed that teachers had negative perceptions of, and low academic expectations for, adolescents with learning disabilities, and further that, parents of adolescents with learning disabilities had lower academic expectations for their children than did parents of normally achieving adolescents for theirs. This effect many stem from a larger stigma associated with disability in general.

It is commonly believed that "negative evaluations of people with intellectual disabilities abound in society" (Craig, Craig, Withers, Hatton & Limb, 2002, p. 61).

Green, Davis, Karshmer, Marsh & Straight (2005) further clarified the issue of negative evaluations in stating that:

> People with disabilities... are generally perceived to possess traits that others do not want to acquire. Others may consequently feel sadness and pity in the presence of individuals with disabilities and these feelings can further interfere with the shared meanings needed for ordinary social interaction. Seeking to avoid these feelings, others may even avoid individuals who possess the difference they dread. (p. 202)

As Baker and Donnelly (2001) noted, "such perceptions result in barriers that divide the 'worlds' of children with and without disability" (p. 72). Stigma also has a large effect on self-perception and academic performance. Children with less negative perceptions of their learning disabilities have been found to have higher achievement scores, perceive themselves more positively in terms of intellectual and behavioural competence, and feel more socially accepted (Rothman & Cosden, 1995).

Craig, Craig, Withers, Hatton & Limb (2002) write that "it is clear that stigma has a major impact on people with disabilities and that service-providers [such as teachers] ... can play a role in maintaining stigma either by collusion or denial" (p. 63). Carpenter and Morgan (2003) have suggested that "There are inbuilt opportunities within curriculum that allow schools to give positive support to the emotional well-being of young people with special educational needs." (p.203) and further that "these particularly rest in [the areas of] personal, social and health education and citizenship..." (p. 203). Eisenman and Tascione (2002) discussed the role of instructors in mediating a discussion on disability issues and social stigma in finding that "the mediating influence of positive adult voices and concerns about social stigma were evident in students responses, which prompted us to question teachers' and families' responsibilities for engaging young people in dialogue about special education and disability" (p. 35).

The stigma of individuals with disabilities as being perceived as less intelligent (Scherer, 2004), without academic prowess, and incapable of having success in life (Hiebert, Wong, & Hunter, 1983) perhaps lead non-special education service personnel and administration to restrict access to technology support materials and infrastructure. This negative perception could be seen to act to widen the digital divide of technology access for individuals with disabilities in schools. This of course, as stated, is simply a possibility, as further investigation within participants' specific schools would need to be performed regarding perceptions of disability.

Implications for Professional Practice

In terms of removing barriers associated with the technology infrastructure in schools, and thus closing the divide related to access, teacher involvement seems to be of key importance. Research has indicated that by having teachers involved in the processes of planning, distribution, procurement, and funding related to technology in schools they obtain a sense of empowerment, control, and stake in their schools' functioning (White, 1992). By having teachers involved in the distribution of resources within schools, perhaps the issue of equity of distribution may become perceived as one of fairness and parity. By decentralizing the planning process from a centralized board office to individual schools, more space may be made for technology inclusion in plans related to school improvement, special education, curriculum, and professional development (Kleiman, 2006).

To change misconceptions associated with special education, schools must be willing to plan for inclusion. Baker and Donnelly (2001) observed that school policy and practices endorsing the principles of inclusion that emphasise equality, acceptance and valued participation may ameliorate school culture in this manner. A culture of inclusion may also be established through curricular means to sensitize staff and students, to both the unique needs of individuals with disabilities (Carpenter & Morgan, 2003), and the similarities they share with their peers (Ellis & Abreu-Ellis, 2006).

CONCLUSION

It appears that special education teachers interviewed in this study perceived the digital divide as omnipresent in school culture. It was manifest in staff and administrative attitudes and actions that served to stigmatize disability and actively hinder access to technology, thus providing little space for successful assistive technology integration that was computer dependent. School culture could possibly be ameliorated by teacher engagement in decision-making and planning for the equitable distribution and access to technology and by school administration and staff fostering a culture of inclusion within schools to quash the stigma.

REFERENCES

Baker, K., & Donnelly, M. (2001). The social experiences of children with disability and the influence of environment: A framework for intervention. *Disability & Society, 16*(1), 71–85.

Bronack, S. (2006). Learning unplugged: The internet divide in American schools. *Electronic Magazine of Multicultural Education.* Retrieved March 23, 2007, from http://www.eastern.edu/publications/emme/2006Spring/bronack.pdf

Bryant, D. P., & Bryant, B. R. (2003). *Assistive technology for people with disabilities.* Toronto: Pearson Education, Inc.

Carpenter, B., & Morgan, H. (2003). Count us in: The role of schools and colleges in meeting the mental health needs of young people with learning disabilities. *British Journal of Special Education, 30*(4), 202–206.

Cleary, P. F., Pierce, G., & Trauth, E. M. (2006). Closing the digital divide: Understanding racial, ethnic, social class, gender and geographic disparities in Internet use among school age children in the United States. *Universal Access in the Information Society, 4*(4), 354–373.

Cooper, J., & Weaver, K. D. (2003). *Gender and computers: Understanding the digital divide.* Mahwah, NJ: Lawrence Erlbaum Associates.

Craig, J., Craig, F., Withers, P., Hatton C., & Limb, K. (2002). Identity conflict in people with intellectual disabilities: What role do service-providers play in mediating stigma? *Journal of Applied Research in Intellectual Disabilities, 15*, 61–72.

Creswell, J. W. (2005). *Educational research: Planning, documenting, and evaluating quantitative and qualitative research.* Toronto: Pearson.

Eisenman, L. T., & Tascione L. (2002). How come nobody told me? Fostering self-realization through a high school English curriculum. *Learning Disabilities Research & Practices*, *17*(1), 35–46.

Ellis, J. B., & Abreu-Ellis, C. (2006). Documenting life narratives as digital video: Anchoring instruction to student documentaries to reduce stigma on campus. *International Journal of Technology, Knowledge, and Society*, *2*(5), 75–82.

Erlandson, D. A., Harris, E. L., Skipper, B. L., & Allen, S. D. (1993). *Doing naturalistic inquiry: A guide to methods*. London: Sage Publications.

Fairlie, R. W. (2004). Race and the digital divide. *Contributions to Economic Analysis & Policy*, *3*(1). Retrieved March 26, 2007, from http://www.bepress.com/bejeap/contributions/vol3/iss1/art15

Green, S., Davis, C., Karshmer, E., Marsh, P., & Straight B. (2005). Living stigma: The impact of labelling, stereotyping, separation, status loss, and discrimination in the lives of individuals with disabilities and their families. *Social Inquiry*, *75*(2), 197–215.

Hasselbring, T. S., & Glaser, C. H. (2000). Use of computer technology to help students with special needs. *Children and Computer Technology*, *10*(2), 102–122.

Hendrix, E. (2005). Permanent injustice: Rawls' theory of justice and the digital divide. *Educational Technology & Society*, *8*(1), 63–68.

Hiebert, B., Wong, B., & Hunter, M. (1982). Affective influences on learning disabled adolescents. *Learning Disability Quarterly*, *5*(4), 334–343.

Kleiman, G. M. (2006). Myths and realities about technology in K-12 Schools. *Harvard Education Letter*. Retrieved March 9, 2007, from http://www.edletter.org/dc/kleiman.htm

Lexis. (2005). Individuals with Disabilities Education Act of 1997, 20 U.S.C. § 1400 *et seq*.

Lancy, D. F. (1992). *Qualitative research in education: An introduction to the major traditions*. New York: Longman.

Lincoln, Y. S., & Guba, E. G. (1985). *Naturalistic inquiry*. Beverly Hills, CA: Sage Publications.

Means, B. (1998). *Models and prospects for bringing technology-supported education reform to scale*. Presented as part of an interactive symposium, Educational Technology for School Reform: Ways to Win (and Ways to Lose) at the annual meeting of the American Educational Research Association, San Diego, CA.

Merriam-Webster, Incorporated. (n.d.) *Accommodation*. Retrieved March 18, 2007, from http://www.m-w.com/cgi-bin/dictionary?va=accommodation

Morrow, S., & Smith, M. (1995). Constructions of survival and coping by women who have survived childhood sexual abuse. *Journal of Counseling Psychology*, *42*, 24–33.

Patton, M. Q. (1990). *Qualitative evaluation and research methods*. Thousand Oaks, CA: Sage.

Rothman, H. R., & Cosden, M. (1995). The relationship between self-perception of a learning disability and achievement, self-concept and social support. *Learning Disability Quarterly*, *18*(3), 203–212.

Sandelowski, M. (1995). Sample size in qualitative research. *Research in Nursing & Health*, *18*(2), 179–183.

Scherer, M. J. (2004). *Connecting to learn: Educational and assistive technology for people with disabilities*. Washington: American Psychological Association.

Smith, T. E. C., Polloway, E. A., Patton, J. R., & Dowdy, C. A. (1998). *Teaching students with special needs in inclusive settings*. Toronto: Allyn & Bacon.

Warschauer, M., Knobel, M., & Stone, L. (2004). Technology and equity in schooling: Deconstructing the digital divide. *Educational Policy*, *18*(4), 562–588.

White, P. A. (1992). Teacher empowerment under "Ideal" school-site autonomy. *Educational Evaluation and Policy Analysis*, *14*(1), 69–82.

Williams, D., Coles, L., Wilson, K., Richardson, A., & Tuson, J. (2000). Teachers and ICT: Current use and future needs. *British Journal of Educational Technology*, *31*(4), 307–320.

Jason Brent Ellis
Dwight Schar College of Education
Ashland University

MICHAEL O'SULLIVAN

INFORMATION AND COMMUNICATIONS TECHNOLOGY TEACHING AND SOCIAL JUSTICE

INTRODUCTION

Harnessing the potential of Information and Communications Technology (ICT) in teaching social justice from a global perspective is a formidable but, I argue, necessary task. For more than a century, the widespread implementation of so-called "progressive education" has been resisted by educational authorities and conservative teachers. In spite of the many obstacles, determined educational reformers have introduced progressive curriculum and child-centred pedagogies at the classroom level. These educators have advocated a commitment to social change that addresses social injustice at home and abroad. Beginning with John Dewey's (1916/1966; 1938/1997) "social problem-solving," progressive education has come to include, *inter alia:* conscientization (Freire, 1970); the greening of education (e.g., Greig, Pike, & Selby, 1987); worldmindedness and interconnectedness (Selby, n.d.); and most recently, the global citizenship approach recently espoused by many writers (e.g., I. Davies & Issitt, 2005; Evans, 2006; Hébert & Wilkinson, 2002). And, yet, the practitioners of socially relevant, social justice-based education, continue to remain, as Schweisfurth (2006) has characterized it, "at the periphery of the concerns of the [teaching] profession as a whole" (p. 49).

The headwinds confronting today's progressive global citizenship educators can be explained by an attitude inherent within, and beyond, a profession that deems issues, like widespread poverty, the HIV/AIDS pandemic, and global warming, to be inappropriate subjects for examination in the educational curriculum. In fact, attempts to do so have been hindered by educators who, while often paying lip-service to the significance of these issues, have suggested that teaching from a global perspective draws attention to issues considered unsuitable, and potentially controversial, for most students (L. Davies, 2006; Schweisfurth, 2006). Society's youngest citizens, however, are aware of these issues and acknowledge the injustice of many aspects of the current global arrangement. They are anxious to learn how they can engage with these global challenges. Schools, reformers argue, have a responsibility to harness this student concern so that young people and, indeed, teachers can develop values, skills, and knowledge in order to address these issues meaningfully (Pike & Selby, 1988; Selby, n.d.; Tye, 1999).

This tug-of-war between global citizenship educators and their detractors will not end now that ICT is so ubiquitous within the classroom. The Internet offers a compelling opportunity to teach social justice from a global perspective. Although

J. A. Kentel and A. Short (eds.), Totems and Taboos: Risk and Relevance in Research on Teachers and Teaching, 241–254.

most teachers tread well-worn and approved paths, others have recognized the potential of global connectedness through ICT and have implemented models of curricular integration within their classrooms, thus making their programs more globally relevant. The latter have taught educational researchers a great deal. Indeed, it is useful to examine the classroom practice of these teachers: In the case-study presented in this article, teachers at a specific elementary school have "dually reshaped the practice of global education pedagogy in compelling and authentic ways…[by recasting] the learning of democratic citizenship and civic participation" (M. O'Sullivan, 2005, p. 1).

This paper examines the efforts of teachers at one small-town Ontario elementary school to implement a computer-mediated learning approach that both reflects the learning needs of the present "Nintendo generation" of students and expands the possibilities of introducing important global experiences into the classroom.

It is interesting to observe how recently educators debated whether "novelty-bound" electronic-mediated learning would or could survive in the educational milieu. In 1999, for example, Balaisis considered the impact ICT *might* play in the efforts of teachers to improve appropriate learning environments for our youth. Today, there is no doubt that, whatever concerns we may have or had about ICT (e.g., the so-called "digital divide" [Attewell, 2001] or "digital screening" [Anderson, 2005]), our world has become web-mediated by communication technologies. Not only does its inevitability manifest itself in a persistent connectedness within our daily routines, but its synergistic effect confirms one fact: all teachers in the northwest European and North American society (and increasingly, and at an incredible rate, elsewhere as well) must embrace ICT or they will become irrelevant to students who have come "most naturally to and from this *connected* world" (Papert, cited in Shields & Berkman, 2000, p. 4).

This paper assumes that ICT is an essential educational tool for both cognitive and pedagogical reasons. Moreover, it can facilitate teachers' ability to understand their students' learning styles. ICT-connectedness has the ability to "generate new cultural meanings and understandings of the world" (Inda & Rosaldo, cited in Monahan, 2002, p. 4), essential to a humanist and globally conscious philosophy of education. As this pedagogical approach relies on an understanding of human experience and of its critical intelligence, it may also inspire social reform at the grassroots and, importantly, at the elementary school–level. Edmund O'Sullivan (1999) advocated such a transformative approach to teaching and learning, by suggesting that "holistic education [is wedded] to a planetary consciousness while maintaining [a] critical perspective" (p. 64).

More than ever, education needs to empower and not to dictate. In this way, ICT must be used to advance socially progressive, globally responsible, and research-based learning theories in schools. Being responsible and visionary, especially in relation to the welfare of our planet, can help to redress growing socioeconomic disparities and to address the human need for meaning, purpose, and belonging.

Brian O'Sullivan (1999) noted that global education, originally conceived as having an unambiguously transformative intent had itself been transformed from its original progressive role into one that prepares students to compete within the global marketplace. In order to realize its potential, ICT can help exceed basic or functional skills (e.g., how to input data, how to do a simple Google search) and achieve a higher order of thought. The parallel with the "old literacies" is clear. Learners are hardly empowered if their skills do not extend beyond the basics of functional reading, writing, and numeracy; they became truly literate only when they can "read the world" (Freire & Macedo, 1987). It is possible that ICT can change students' perceptions of themselves within the world and enable them to research, access, and manoeuvre in the context of multiple information sources. Current and future generations will be able to grapple with complex global and social issues only with these skills.

In spite of its potential, ICT is far from universally used in the classroom, and its potential remains largely unfulfilled (Cox et al., 2003). The case study presented herein illustrates how ICT has fulfilled some of this potential in helping realize the goals of a globally oriented curriculum and in demonstrating the profound effect on student learning. Ironically, it reveals an old truth that educational administrators frequently forget: Teachers will only embrace "lasting pedagogical changes ... when [they] are successfully persuaded by direct or vicarious experience that a new technique is worthwhile" (Harris, 2005, p. 37).

Hardly surprisingly, ICT will be considered worthwhile if teachers can recognize its ability to achieve learning outcomes, especially at the higher levels. I would suggest that, if it is to have an impact on student learning, ICT needs to be taught and integrated across the curriculum. Both traditional and new literacies require rudimentary and advanced skills in order to realize progressive and transformatory ends. It is important to realize that, as Rassool (1989) argues, critical and emerging literacies are far from being mutually exclusive. Computers and multimedia technology, rather than eradicating reading, have led to

> the omnipresence of textuality, and, relatedly, reading and interpreting texts in our daily lives [and that] in order to operate effectively within these textual environments, requires a more sophisticated range of knowledges, literacy and communication skills than the linear and functional skills traditionally associated with basic literacy. (p. xi)

TEACHING THE "NINTENDO GENERATION": REACHING STUDENTS WHO WORK AND THINK DIFFERENTLY THAN DO THEIR TEACHERS

Perhaps the most compelling argument for advancing the use of ICT in the classroom is the fact that students today have been thoroughly inculcated by electronic media. They have acquired skills that cannot be ignored by educators. Schroeder (2004) cites research that applied the Myer-Briggs Personality Type Indicator to 4,000 new students. The results indicated that students who prefer the realm of concepts, ideas, and abstractions (e.g., the realm inhabited most comfortably by their teachers) were in the minority (40%), while their peers who prefer so-called *sensing learning patterns* (e.g., a preference for the concrete, practical, and immediate) were now in the majority (60%, Schroeder, p. 3). This dichotomy of learning styles among students and between a majority of students and their teachers causes an imbalance that needs to be addressed by teachers. "The implications for pedagogy demand greater active modes of teaching and learning …that actively engages [students'] senses [such as] carefully monitored experiential learning, peer critiques, team projects, service learning, field experiences, developing simulations, and utilizing the case method approach" (Schroeder, p. 9).

Schroeder's (2004) deductive case-method approach corresponds to the thought processes of computer-savvy kids, in moving from practice to theory, from utility to conceptualization: a reversal of the traditional pedagogical technique. One could also say that this approach is also more relevant because "students [can] apply theoretical perspectives to real-life-situations" (Schroeder, p. 9).

Mark Prensky (1998) is another astute observer of the impact of technology on learning styles. Complementing the research of Schroeder (2004), Prensky's examination of youth learning styles has been transformed into commercially successful electronic educational and training materials widely accessible in U. S. schools. Although specifically addressing learning styles in the workplace, "Reaching Younger Workers Who Think Differently" is applicable to the classroom. Stating that "every parent, educator and manager knows that 'Nintendo children–those born after 1970 and raised on video and computer games, Walkmans, the internet, etc.–are different" (p. 1), Prensky considers how cognitive styles have changed as the result of frequent computer use. These include:

- The need for speed;
- The electronic ability to "multi-task" or engage in so-called "parallel-processing" (e.g., the connected experience of chatting, posting, and surfing for information simultaneously);
- The ability to random-access or engage in "clicking around";
- Graphic primacy or the heightened role of image;
- The blending of play and work with fantasy and reality; and
- The Pay-off for patience–undoubtedly the most difficult for teachers to comprehend in their apparently attention-deficit challenged students (pp. 2-6).

The new cognitive style puts ICT centre-stage for anyone who "feels [owning a computer] is almost like a birthright [and where] being connected is a necessity" (p. 6).

The research is compelling. If, as Schroeder (2004) states, either 60% of the students studied in research exhibit learning styles associated with the "Nintendo generation" (p. 3) or the other 40% are barely computer-literate, then educators face a difficult challenge. This challenge extends beyond adjusting teaching techniques; it requires adopting new teaching strategies. In so doing, we cannot abandon the classroom situation entirely; indeed, it should not be a matter of "ICT all the time." Far from abandoning "old literacies," we must harness students' love of technology, their "parallel-processing" learning styles, and their wish for independence in the acquisition of knowledge. As such, they can meet, exceed, and enrich curricular learning expectations while simultaneously instilling the values, skills, and knowledge associated with critically thinking, globally aware citizens.

Fortunately, we have some emerging models in meeting this challenge, including the experience of the teachers of W. H. Knight Elementary School (pseudonym), near Toronto. This is the subject of our case study.

W. H. KNIGHT ELEMENTARY SCHOOL'S GLOBAL EDUCATION PROGRAM: SOME BACKGROUND

W. H. Knight Elementary School is a midsized, small-town school located about 100 km from downtown Toronto. What makes this school unique is its school-wide and fully integrated global education program. The program developed in 2001 when the self-described "computer-challenged" grade 1 teacher, J.C., assumed responsibility as the school's ICT site manager.

THE BEGINNING OF THE TECHNOLOGICAL REVOLUTION AT W. H. KNIGHT: THE GRADE 1 COMMUNITY STUDY

One of J. C.'s first steps as site manager was to implement Industry Canada's (now defunct) School Net Grassroots Program as part of his goal to support the School's ICT interests. The program provided the framework and financial support for J. C. and the other grade 1 teachers to produce a community study unit about their town in the fall of 2001, as part of the provincial curriculum. As grade 1 pupils studied different aspects of their town through field trips and guest speakers, their grade 8 reading-buddies posted the younger students' findings on the webpage they were assigned to construct. Guided by J. C., the older students also managed to create a project webpage for the participating teachers so that both the school body and parents could view the findings. Consisting primarily of photographs of activities in key community buildings and of the guest speakers who had come to the school, the website also posted student artwork.

Importantly, this effort opened J.C.'s and his colleagues' eyes to ICT's potential as a teaching and learning tool at the primary school level–and beyond. From here, curricular activities were soon to link the local with the wider world, starting with a computer-mediated joint environmental project with a school in New Brunswick, a visit by Dutch students to W. H. Knight, and an ongoing relationship with young people in Sierra Leone.

Thus, it was the grade 1 classes' community study that marked the beginning of what W. H. Knight Teacher-Librarian, C. C., described as the school's "technological revolution" and prepared the way for the global program that followed. (Notes prepared by C. C. for the author). Elaborating on this assessment, J. C. wrote:

> The process for me began, oddly enough, not by examining global issues but by examining the local community … from a grade 1 perspective through a collaborative web-based project in conjunction with grade 8 students. Through the success of this Grassroots Program, I became interested in how technology can help us as a school to communicate and to collaborate with each other within the school and beyond. (Notes prepared by J. C. for the author)

In questioning J. C. about his wholehearted involvement with global education, I expected him to emphasize experiences like his four years teaching in a First Nations school or something similarly "consciousness raising." While he acknowledged that he had learned a great deal about Aboriginal culture, his newly found fascination with ICT was responsible for leading him to "the global side."

Meanwhile, the Grassroots Program granted the school additional funding on the basis of the impressive quality of the grade 1 study and the student body's successful integration of ICT. The school's principal, A. T., used this money to provide teachers with release-time associated with ICT improvement.

In the summer of 2003, J. C. attended the annual conference of i-EARN (International Education and Resource Network) Canada in Japan. Established in 1988, the organization defines itself as

> The world's largest non-profit global network that enables teachers and young people to use the Internet and other ICT technologies to collaborate on projects that both enhance learning and make a difference in the world. (International Education and Resource Network, 2007)

The development of W. H. Knight's global education program, with a heavy emphasis on ICT, can be traced to J. C.'s return from Japan. In addition to several program ideas, he had made two contacts:

- Gary, a secondary school teacher from the Netherlands who, after a successful visit by his students to New Brunswick the previous year, hoped to replicate his experience elsewhere in Canada and was looking to partner with a school in another region of the country; and
- Andrew, the founder of The Freetown Centre for the Rehabilitation of Child Soldiers and War Affected Youth in Sierra Leone.

Before going to Japan, J. C. had been in e-mail contact with the Freetown Centre's Director, Andrew Greene. Even after meeting with him in Japan, J. C. could not imagine the extent to which subsequent collaboration with Andrew and the Centre would have on W. H. Knight's global program. The relationship "sort of evolved on its own," J. C. explained. We shall return to this relationship shortly.

The possibility of a Dutch exchange was explored a few months later in Calgary. Attending a Network of Innovative Schools (NIS) ceremony to accept an innovation award that had been granted to W. H. Knight, J. C. and the school principal, A.T., spent time with Gary, the ICT teacher from the Valley Middle School (pseudonym) in New Brunswick. Gary's school had been partnered with the Dutch school the year before. Hearing more about the experience, J. C. and A. T. were encouraged to accept a visit by the Dutch students.

DEEPENING THE INTEGRATION OF ICT THROUGH THE GRASSROOTS PROGRAM

During the 2003-04 academic year, W. H. Knight became involved in six projects undertaken within the framework of the Grassroots Program. Three of these initiatives were ambitious school-wide projects, and all of them brought ICT into the classroom in such a way that provincial curricular expectations were not only met but exceeded.

The Grassroots Program units included: a science and technology project extending from kindergarten to grade 8; an art project studying world art along with student artwork, originally posted on the school's website; and the Twin School Project. The latter effort involved a study of environmental issues by grade 7 and 8 students at W. H. Knight and their counterparts from the Valley Middle School. The two schools posted results of their environmental studies electronically, resulting in

> both students and teachers [beginning] to develop ICT proficiencies, starting from their own comfort levels, learning new concepts and skills as they were required by the projects. Teachers, like the students, were learning new skills based on the needs of the projects as opposed to learning in a more traditional, top-down fashion. (Notes prepared by J. C. for the author)

TEACHER ENTHUSIASM FOR THE STUDENTS' ICT PROGRESS

It is hard to know who was more excited about ICT, Grade 2 teacher M. B. or her students. She would have liked to have spent more time learning the required skills: "Oh, I wish I were 15 years younger!" She was frustrated by the fact that her grade 2s' computer skills would be utilized in someone else's grade 3 class. Likening it to missing your child's first word or first steps, M. B. explained how grade 2 students developed skills with the program PowerPoint©:

> They've done PowerPoint© with me about Flat Stanley. I could see them increasingly being able to do that on their own. [With] Power Point©, we took pictures [and] we decided what we were going to do. I put the pictures on the screen, and they did the writing. I can see this particular bunch of kids eventually being able to do that all on their own.... [This is] great for kids who can't write a lot but [who] can show the visuals. I think we are really lucky. (Interview, June 7, 2005)

Special Education teacher, S. L., articulated how computer literacy empowered her students:

> On the computers [these] kids shine. Some of them do the computer work better than some of the other kids and better than some of the teachers and that is where they become...leader[s]. I don't mind that at all. Being a teacher [means] you have to give up some of that control. It amazes me how quickly they catch on too. I remember teaching [the program] Inspiration, which is fairly easy....I thought that I'd have to break it down, step by step, but I didn't have to. I guess they had such extensive previous experience with applications from other programs that they were able to transfer it to this one. (Interview, June 14, 2005)

S. L. further noted how proud the students felt about be ing able to write their "Messages of Hope" to commemorate victims of the December 2004 Tsunami. She observed their frequent visits to the site, proudly rereading what they and their peers had written.

Grade 1 teacher C. B. was also proud of her own new-found computer skills and pleased how they made her teaching more interesting. Never having previously had an interest in or use for such technology, she found her teaching offered a new energy through media like the Smart Board©; as used to compose e-mail messages from her class to children in Japan (Interview, June 7, 2005). Grade 2 teacher M. B. quickly recognized how ICT can contribute to realizing the objectives of a broader initiative, the global education program. This, in turn, constituted "a spark that some of us really needed to continue to make our teaching more interesting, providing us with an opportunity to help the kids do some problem solving and critical thinking" (Interview, June 7, 2005).

At the time of the community study, S. C. was teaching grade 1 and was collaborating closely with J. C. She wrote about her journey from being "computer illiterate" to becoming a proficient computer user:

> When J. C. approached the grade 1 teachers with his plan to create a social studies website on community members and places, I was panic-stricken. As a complete computer illiterate, I was unsure about what he wanted to do and how to go about the whole project. It turned out that we just did the same great social studies unit we always did, but we took more pictures and did some write-up activities with the students. You have to do shared writing activities anyway; [but] once J. C. showed me how to hook up the computer to the television (three or four times until I got it right), it was easy to add the words as a class, and [to] add the pictures. We started slowly, adding colour to the text, discussing where the picture should go, that sort of thing. We were covering quite a few curriculum expectations at the same time. (Notes prepared by S. C. for the author)

Summarizing its significance, J. C. acknowledged that the impact of the Grassroots Program extended well beyond ICT:

> It soon became evident that when students and teachers were working on these projects, not only were they covering a wide variety of curriculum expectations, but they were also learning valuable technological skills far above and beyond what the curriculum required. In addition, students were more engaged in what they were doing and character traits, such as respect, tolerance, empathy, cooperation, caring, etc., were being naturally developed in powerful ways. It was the success of these projects and the fact that they were visible to the whole school and beyond that fostered the ever expanding growth of global projects in our school. (Notes prepared by J. C. for the author)

THE SIERRA LEONE CHILD SOLDIER PROJECT

The Sierra Leone project involved youth who were affected by war and their recovery through the intensive use of ICT. For W. H. Knight, this meant that older students used modern technology to gather information, to communicate with their African counterparts, and to develop an understanding of global issues.

Global awareness certainly does not have to, indeed, cannot, rely on international travel to achieve its objectives. For the vast majority of elementary and secondary students, such a modality is out of the question. Global education based on ICT must be taught in the classroom. In developed countries, most schools offer relatively easy access to ICT, while in the developing world, there is minimal but slowly growing access. The example of the Freetown Centre for the Rehabilitation of Child Soldiers and War-Affected Youth in Sierra Leone shows that, with determined leadership such as that provided by Andrew Greene, even the poorest of the poor can "become connected."

Although hosting the delegation of Dutch students was undeniably enriching for both groups, the relationship that developed between W. C .Knight students with the former child soldiers of the Sierra Leone Centre through ICT-mediated contact was particularly significant (O'Sullivan & Vetter, 2007).

Only in his mid-20s, the Sierra Leonese journalist, Andrew Greene, had been deeply moved by the profound physical and psychological devastation that had been caused by his country's civil war. Motivated by his empathy for armies of soldiers as young as 7 or 8 years old, he established with the support of i-EARN a centre to help rehabilitate these children and their traumatized victims. The Centre provides daily after-school programs including counselling and involvement in organized sports and music therapy (the latter leading to the recording of an internationally marketed CD). It also provides Internet access to facilitate communication with young people around the world. It has been acknowledged how sharing their stories has helped these former child soldiers' slow progress toward recovery. With virtually no ICT equipment at the beginning, however, Andrew and the young people had to rely on expensive and heavily used Internet cafes located far from the Centre.

From the beginning, the Centre organized community outreach activities including the Saturday night youth debates on a range of issues from the "Positive Music Project" and "Rap 4 Rights" to health campaigns about the HIV/AIDs pandemic and drug abuse in the country (Sierra Leone Centre, 2007). Most notably, these efforts have garnered support through a network of loyal supporters worldwide, through the Internet.

Although he had been in e-mail contact with Andrew before meeting him at the 2003 i-EARN conference in Japan, it was that personal, face-to-face contact that inspired J. C. to propose a partnership between W. H. Knight and the Sierra Leone Centre. I-EARN contacts along with the support from other international agencies allowed Andrew to raise the funds necessary to facilitate the installation of Internet access at the Centre. Among the donations, one of particular importance has been a video camera purchased by W. H. Knight students from money they received as a NIS award. With it, the Centre's young people have been able to post stories electronically, such as the video documentary entitled "My Last Hope", which explored the impact of war, HIV/AIDS, and unemployment on the local youth of Sierra Leone.

The UN Human Development Index of 2006 notably ranked Sierra Leone as the second worst country on the planet in which to live. The implications for the life chances of the country's youth are undeniable, especially for those so traumatized by a vicious and prolonged civil war. In spite of living in a country that is "still trying to meet the literacy and technical skills demands of the first industrial revolution" (Razzool, 1999, p. 14), the Centre's children have been able to propel their communicative skills two centuries forward, thanks to the guidance of a visionary leader and the strong desire to share their lived experience with the outside world.

In establishing a close collaboration with the Sierra Leone Centre, the W. H. Knight students gained a rich insight into a microcosm of African society. They were exposed to issues ranging from the horrors of civil war and child soldiering to the spirit of resilience that inspired these children to struggle for peace, dignity, and a drug-free environment, in spite of victimization, trauma, and crushing poverty. W. H. Knight students saw these African kids successfully shed their victim status to become protagonists in confronting some of their country's many problems. Allowing Canadian children to make these connections is central to viewing problems and teaching from a global perspective.

In this Canadian–Sierra Leone relationship, we are compelled to ask what these young people have learned about addressing global issues with global solutions. Certainly, the creation of international connections and feelings of long-distance friendship and solidarity constitute a good start. The Sierra Leonese and Canadian children have all learned and will continue to learn much from each other about their shared realities and their interconnectedness.

This partnership has resulted in a mutual benefit to both the Centre's ex child soldiers and the students of W. H. Knight. Far from being charity, the relationship has been truly reciprocal. The Canadian school's staff and students benefited considerably from the relationship. Through their e-mail communication, DVDs, and recent music CD, the Sierra Leonese young people have demonstrated clearly the ability of all individuals to affect change in their own lives and in those of other circumstances.

Similarly, W. H. Knight students have been able to provide both moral and material support to their partners in Sierra Leone. Moral support, according to Andrew in recent conversation with the author, has relied on an exchange of e-mails between students in Canada and those in Sierra Leone, where experiences, stories, and aspirations have been mutually shared. On a more material level, the "Children Connecting Children for Peace" project allowed staff and students in Ontario to support "the establishment of Community Access Centres–15 or more computers connected to the Internet–so that the students in Sierra Leone can begin to bridge the digital divide" (W. H. Knight School website). According to Andrew, the Centre allows war-affected children in Sierra Leone "to communicate and [to] collaborate with other students all over the world in an effort to promote peace on our planet, as well as participate in a myriad of other projects and activities that the Centre will provide for them" (Interview, March 9, 2005).

During the 2004-05 school year, Andrew lived in Montreal on a Jeanne Sauvé Scholarship awarded in recognition of his work. During this time in Canada, he visited W. H. Knight twice. These visits had a powerful impact both on the staff and on students of all ages. Indeed, kindergarten teacher S. C. described the impact Andrew had on her young students when he spoke to them about being a "child of peace" and making the world a fair place in which to live (Interview, June 14, 2005)

Similarly, grade 2 teacher M. B. wrote at length about the impact of Andrew's visit. Not only was it personally "one of the most rewarding experiences of my teaching career," but,

> Andrew…spoke to [the grade 2 students] about the child soldier situation in a way they could…understand. The children had time to digest the information and to ask questions….We had informed the parents of the content of the presentation just in case the students were upset at home. All of the students handled the information in a manner that was far more mature than I could have ever imagined. They asked Andrew insightful and meaningful questions. They did not focus on the child soldier issue; rather they were concerned about the welfare of the orphans. The students brought the situation to a level they could understand–one of immediate needs: parents, home, family…. As a result, with some guidance, we decided to support the students in Sierra Leone in a small way. The students decided to raise money for…a video camera and Internet access (for the Centre in Freetown). I hope that we continue to support their Internet access for as long as I remain at the school. We arranged a used book sale. The response was overwhelming. We raised over $300.00. (Notes prepared for the author)

M. B. described the reaction of her grade 2 students to the stories about child soldiers who were the age of her students. At first very upset and asking how a child could do to other children what these child-soldiers had done, they came ultimately to consider what they themselves might have done. What might they have been forced to do? M. B. explains:

> They talked about that. They didn't understand why the children did what they did, but [when] we said they needed to put themselves in [those children's] shoes and [when] Andrew talked to them…they [understood] that one [often doesn't] have a choice. (Interview, June 7, 2005)

Noddings (2002) addresses this in the framework of "situational ethics," in which the development of a child's moral character acknowledges contextual limitations. What would *you* have done in the *particular circumstances in which these children found themselves*? Such profound moral issues engage these children. It is not an abstract dilemma but involves real-world choices. In this regard, M. B.'s own understanding was expressed when she said: "So, they are just developing their understanding of a different part of themselves and using their thinking skills and their inference skills in order to form their own opinions" (Interview, June 7, 2005).

It is not difficult to exaggerate the importance to both W. H. Knight staff and students and to the war-affected youth of Sierra Leone that this ongoing connection has had. The Ontario students have learned about the destructive impact of civil war on children and their families, the importance of peace on children's lives, the possibility of improving one's circumstances (even minimally), a considerable knowledge about one corner of Africa, and the abiding satisfaction of extending solidarity. This kind of situation can empower educators not only through contributing to the development of a globally aware youth but through meeting, and then exceeding, the professional responsibilities of delivering the provincial curriculum.

CONCLUSION

Rassool (1999) argued a decade ago that computers and multimedia technology would not eradicate the "old" literacies (reading, writing, numeracy) but would require the addition of "multi-faceted new skills and competencies" (Skutnabb-Kangas, 1999, p. xi). She argued that:

> Computers and multimedia technology, rather than eradicating reading, have led to "the omnipresence of textuality, and, relatedly, reading and interpreting texts in our daily lives" and that "in order to operate effectively within these textual environments, requires a more sophisticated range of knowledges, literacy and communications skills than the linear and functional skills traditionally associated with basic literacy. (p. xi)

At W. H. Knight, the traditional literacies continue to flourish (according to teacher anecdotes and EQAO test results) along with the new literacies as reflected in enhanced teacher and student ICT competencies. It is an environment where students not only apply their ICT skills–some acquired at home, many acquired at school–to curricular learning, but they do so enthusiastically. Impressively, this pedagogical extension is capable of supporting a potentially transformative global education program.

A. T., the principal at the School, had a clear understanding of the centrality of ICT to the school's program from the very beginning. She wrote:

> Students and teachers no longer have to leave the building to interact with another school or community, down the street or across the world. In today's world, a teacher raising their students' awareness of what other people in other communities do day-to-day and what they value is vital both to prepare for the world of work and also for "the work of life." Helping a student understand diversity and develop tolerance in their local community as well as their national and global communities will develop well-rounded citizens ...a fundamental goal of our educational system. A classroom teacher is the key to making a difference. (Notes prepared for the author)

Freire suggested that "the act of learning to read and write has to start from the very comprehensive understanding of the act of *reading the world*, something which human beings do before reading the words" (cited in Berthoff, 1987, p. xiii).

Is it possible that W. H. Knight School students have *read the world* even before the youngest of them has been able to "read the words?" Many of the teachers at the school would argue that deep and meaningful transformations have taken place in their students. The ultimate test, of course, will be to ask these students 5, 10, or 15 years after they leave the school about how or when their values, skills, and knowledge were established and about whether they still remain globally aware. Unfortunately, frequently these students attend high schools that do not support global awareness or innovation ICT programs. Recent W. H. Knight graduates have returned to the school complaining about how bored they are in their new schools.

Until global education, enriched by the potential of the existing and evolving ICT, becomes the established approach in all schools, the results, however impressive at one site, will remain an isolated case. As educators, we must adopt similarly successful models and generalize W. H. Knight's experience to other schools. Faculties of Education along with Board and Ministry officials have a particular responsibility in this regard.

A unique feature of the W. H. Knight experience lies in the history of their global education initiative. The efforts of a single grade 1 teacher were able to persuade other teachers to supplement a long-standing community study unit with an ICT component. Knowing very little about ICT, J. C. enlisted his students' grade 8 reading-buddies to help build a website. Inspired by the potential of ICT, he attended the i-EARN conference in Japan and made several key contacts. As a result of the quality of the work, additional resources flowed into the school and, supported by a principal who quickly had become an indispensable ally, the program took the form previously described.

The school's "technological (and global) revolution" can both be seen to correspond to the previously noted progressive learning theories applicable to the 'Nintendo generation' as well as to correct the disconnectedness many young people (and teachers) feel when confronted with global problems. Just how ICT can facilitate this connectedness requires further investigation–but the early evidence is promising.

REFERENCES

Anderson, N. (2005). "Mindstorms" and "mindtools" aren't happening: Digital streaming of students via socio-economic disadvantage. *E-learning, 2*(2), 144–152.

Attewell, P. (2001). The first and second digital divides. *Sociology of Education, 74*, 252–259.

Balaisis, J. (1999). *The potential for experiential learning in the transformation of young adults*. Unpublished doctoral thesis. Toronto, ON: Ontario Institute for Studies in Education, University of Toronto.

Berthoff, A. E. (1987). Foreward. In P. Freire & D. Macedo (Eds.), *Literacy: Reading the word & the world* (pp. xi–xiii). South Hadley, MA: Bergin & Garvey.

Bigelow, B., & Peterson, B. (Eds.). (2002). *Rethinking globalization: Teaching for justice in an unjust world*. Milwaukee, WI: Rethinking Schools.

Cox, M., Webb, M., Abbott, C., Blakeley, B., Beauchamp, T., & Rhodes, V. (2003). *ICT and pedagogy: A review of the research literature*. Produced by Becta for the Department for Education and Skills (DfES). London, England: British Educational Communications and Technology Agency. Retrieved March 3, 2007, from http://partners.becta.org.uk/page_documents/research/impact_ict_schools.pdf

Davies, I., & Issitt, J. (2005). Reflections on citizenship education in Australia, Canada and England. *Comparative Education, 41*(4), 389–410.

Davies, L. (2006). Global citizenship: Abstraction or framework for action? *Educational Review, 58*(1), 5–25.

Dewey, J. (1966). *Democracy and education.* New York: The Free Press. (Original work published 1916).
Dewey, J. (1997). *Experience and education.* New York: Touchstone. (Original work published 1938).
Evans, M. (2006). Characterizations of citizenship education pedagogy in Canada and England: Implications for teacher education. *Citizenship Teaching and Learning, 2*(1), 40–54.
Freire, P. (1970). *The pedagogy of the oppressed.* New York: Continuum.
Freire, P., & Macedo, D. (1987). *Literacy: Reading the word and the world.* South Hadley, MA: Bergin & Garvey.
Greig, S., Pike, G., & Selby, D. (1987). *Greenprints for changing schools.* York, UK: WWF & Kogan Page.
Harris, J. (2005). Is it worth it? Deciding if technology is worth the time, effort and money. *i.e. magazine.* Retrieved March 11, 2007, from http://downloads.smarttech.com/media/education/pdf/ieAutumn.pdf
Hébert, Y. M., & Wilkinson, L. (2002). *The citizenship debates: Conceptual, policy, experiential, and educational issues. Citizenship in transformation in Canada.* Toronto, ON: University of Toronto Press.
International Education and Resource Network. (2007). *Annual conference of i-EARN.* Retrieved March 3, 2007, from http://www.iearn.org
Monahan, T. (2002). *Globalization, technological change, and public education.* New York: Routledge.
Noddings, N. (2002). *Educating moral people: A caring alternative to character education.* New York: Teachers College Press.
O'Sullivan, B. (1999). Global change and educational reform in Ontario and Canada. *Canadian Journal of Education, 24*(3), 311–325.
O'Sullivan, E. (1999). *Transformative learning: Educational vision for the 21st century.* Toronto, ON: University of Toronto Press.
O'Sullivan, M. (2005). *Every teacher a global teacher, every student a global learner: The global education program at W. H. Knight Elementary School.* Unpublished paper presented to the Faculty and Graduate Student Colloquium on Global Education, September 23, Faculty of Education, York University, Toronto, ON.
O'Sullivan, M., & Vetter, D. (2007). Teacher-initiated, student-centered global education in a K to 8 school. *Journal of Teaching and Learning, 4*(2), 13–28.
Pike, G., & Selby, D. (1988). *Global teacher, global learner.* London: Hodder & Stoughton.
Pike, G., & Selby, D. (1995). *Reconnecting: From national to global curriculum.* Surrey, UK: World Wildlife Fund for Nature, UK.
Prenksy, M. (1998, January). Reaching younger workers who think differently. *Across the Board.* Retrieved March 3, 2007, from http://www.twitchspeed.com/site/article.html
Rassool, N. (1999). *Literacy for sustainable development in the age of information.* Clevedon, UK: Multilingual Matters.
Schroeder, C. C. (2004). *New students – new learning styles.* Retrieved February 14, 2007, from http://www.virtualschool.edu/mon/Academia/KierseyLearingStyles.html
Schweisfurth, M. (2006). Education for global change: Teacher agency and curricular structure in Ontario schools. *Educational Review, 58*(1), 41–50.
Selby, D. (n.d.). *Global education as transformative education.* Retrieved August 15, 2006, from http://www.citizens4change.org/global/intro/global_education_introduce. htm
Shields, M. K., & Berkman, R. E. (2000). Children and computer technology: Analysis and recommendations. *The Future of Children, 10*(2), 4–30.
Sierra Leone Centre. (2007). *Community outreach activities.* Retrieved March 3, 2007, from http://www.iearnsierraleone.org
Skutnabb-Kangas, T. (1999). Foreword. In R. Rassool, *Literacy for sustainable development in the age of information* (pp. vii–xvi). Clevedon, UK: Multilingual Matters.
Tye, K. A. (1999). *Global education: A worldwide movement.* Orange, CA: Interdependence Press.

Michael O'Sullivan
Faculty of Education
Brock University

EPILOGUE

Funabulism, the risky walk, cannot be embarked on without first calling upon the riggers, the ones who lay out the path to be tread. Without this sort of engineering, the base of support does not exist; the walk has no direction, no possibility to challenge, no opportunity for risk. The totem (risky and relevant research) similarly acts as the emblem of what is possible when taboos are challenged and faced with bravado. The challenge for the scholar is to attend to the contest while maintaining the inner balance integral to forward movement. The path, like the tightrope, will shift with each motion making it essential for challengers to balance from the core.

Of late, fearsome stunts such as rolling down Niagara Falls in a wheel-barrel have been banned and are no longer practiced; they are taboo. The authors in this collection of works have challenged the constraints that could result in research that is unthinkable, prohibited, and forbidden. Hence, as we forge ahead in research on teachers and teaching we do so with recognition of the researchers and participants who dare to lay out the path and disrupt the totems and taboos that have stalled educational growth.

CONTRIBUTORS

Christine Arnold is a Concurrent Education Student in the 4th year of education studies at Brock University. She is currently looking forward to starting her Masters of Education in the field of Teaching and Learning Studies.

Idit Avni is an inspector of ICT in Education at the Israeli Ministry of Education. She earned an MA in Development of Educational Systems from the University of Haifa and in Educational Leadership from Humberside University of England. Her interests are ICT in Education, teacher professional development and narrative research.

Iman Awadyeh, is a director of testing in Arabic at the Israeli National Authority for Measurement and Evaluation in Education. Her Masters thesis studied the professional growth of teacher leaders. She is currently engaged in developing diagnostic tests for Arabic language acquisition.

Aysen Bakioglu, is a professor in the Department of Educational Science at Marmara University in Istanbul, Turkey. Her research interests focus on the effectiveness and professional development of principals, career phases, self evaluation at the university, school based professional development, international standards and quality indicators and accreditation of universities. She is the country representative of The International Study Association on Teacher Thinking.

Aviva Ben-Hefer, M.Ed., has taught in experimental and open schools, and gifted students. Currently offers guidance/instruction in writing programs to school directors and teacher teams, and teacher continuing education programs in Israel and developing countries (sponsored by the Israel Foreign Ministry and UNICEF).

Maryann Brown is a Senior Research Fellow in the School of Education at the University of Ballarat, Australia. She is currently employed in a non-government co-education (Kindergarten to Year 12) school as a Curriculum Coordinator. Her research interests are in the areas of professional learning, educational change and teachers' narratives.

Jude Butcher is the Director of Australian Catholic University's Institute for Advancing Community Engagement. He has been member of Boards of Catholic Education for more than 10 years and is also Chair of the Board of the Edmund Rice Centre for Justice and Community Education. He was Head of School of Education at Australian Catholic University for New South Wales for many years. He has been leader of the Partners in Learning Project between the University and Wollongong Catholic Education Office since 2000 and sees Religious Education as central to the life and work of Catholic schools.

Anne Chodakowski is a doctoral student in the Faculty of Education at Simon Fraser University. Her teaching background is in secondary English and drama. Her main areas of interest are imaginative teacher education and somatic understanding.

Dina David holds a Masters' degree in Womens' Studies from Bar-Ilan University. She is a teacher and a poet, facilitates womens' reading circles, and has a consulting business focused on women's personal and professional development.

Ms. Leisa Desmoulins is a PhD candidate within the Graduate Studies and Research Department of the Faculty of Education at Lakehead University in Thunder Bay, Canada. This paper, E/raced: Aboriginal youth and public schooling, is part of her dissertation research which follows other community-based research and teaching work using an anti-racism frame to focus on relationships amongst racialized peoples in cities and within institutions.

Kieran Egan is a professor of Education at Simon Fraser University. He is the author of a number of books, including The Educated Mind (University of Chicago Press) and most recently The Future of Education: Re-imagining the school from the ground up (New Haven: Yale University Press.)

Graham English is a lecturer in the School of Religious Education at Australian Catholic University. Previously he was in the Religious Education Department of the Catholic Education Office, Archdiocese of Sydney. Graham is an author and cartoonist who has brought both a substantive and creative richness to the Religious Literacy Project with Wollongong Catholic Education Office.

Freema Elbaz-Luwisch is an associate professor in the Faculty of Education, University of Haifa; her main interests are in narrative inquiry, teachers' lives, and teacher education for multiculturalism. Her book, *Teachers' Voices: Storytelling and Possibility*, was published by Information Age in 2005.

Jason Brent Ellis is an assistant professor of instructional and assistive technologies at Ashland University. His research focuses on technology use by students with disabilities in higher education and ways of leveling the digital divide through policy and pedagogical interventions.

Ozge Hacifozlioglu, is an assistant professor at the University of Bahcesehir, Computer Instructional Technologies Teacher Development Department, Istanbul. Her research area is educational administration. She completed her PhD in Educational Administration with the thesis entitled as "Quality Indicators in European Higher Education" institutions. She is the co author of articles published in the national and international arena.

Kristin Johnston has been involved in Religious Education for some time as well as the piloting of the role of the Religious Education Coordinator in schools in the 1970s. She has been involved in both the Religious Education Department and the Professional Studies Department at Australian Catholic University reflecting her long interest in integrating Religious Education into the total education process. Her doctoral studies included a focus on the evaluation of the role of Religious Education coordinators in the implementation of Religious Education curricula. Kristin was involved from the early stages of the Religious Literacy Project.

Jana Kalin, PhD in pedagogy, is an assistant professor for the didactics at the Department of Pedagogy and Andragogy at the Faculty of Arts of the University of Ljubljana, Slovenia. Her research interests include the questions about instruction, pre-service and in-service teacher education, teachers' professional development, evaluation of educational process.

Jeanne Adèle Kentel is currently employed in the Carnegie Faculty of Sport and Education at Leeds Metropolitan University. Prior to this post she was an assistant professor of Health and Physical Education at Brock University and taught in elementary, secondary, and teacher education programs in Alberta and British Columbia, Canada. She completed her Doctor of Philosophy in Curriculum Studies at the University of Alberta.

Susana Klein, born in Uruguay, worked till 2005 at the Israeli Ministry of Education as a teacher and senior mentor. A doctoral candidate at the University of Haifa, she teaches in a principals' program and an MA practicum in qualitative research.

Michael Kompf is Professor of Education at Brock University, Canada. Interests include developmental issues for adult learners and teachers; personal construct psychology; global policies and practices in higher education; and philosophies of inquiry. An ISATT member since 1985, Michael is serving his fourth term as Chair and is a member of several professional associations.

Manfred Lang is senior researcher at the IPN (Institute for science education) in Kiel, Germany. He is involved in European projects about discursive planning of teacher education. A central idea is change of teachers' work as collabaration across boundaries. He is a contributor to the recently published book " Professional Development and School Improvement. Science Teachers' Voices in School-based Reform" (Studienverlag, Innsbruck, 2006) co-authored with John Olson and edited by Manfred Lang and others.

Per F. Laursen is a professor of Educational Professionalization at the Department of Curriculum Research at the Danish School of Education, University of Aarhus. His research interests focus on teacher education, professional development and classroom management.

Marcos Tarciso Masetto is a professor of Didactics at Universidade de São Paulo and a member of the faculty of the Postgraduate Program in Education of the Pontifical Catholic University of São Paulo, Brazil .His chief research interest concerns the preparation of educators for teaching in higher education environments.

Maria da Graça Nicoletti Mizukami is a Professor of the Federal University of Sao Carlos. She is currently lecturing, supervising and researching learning and professional development of teachers at the Mackenzie Presbyterian University in Sao Paulo, Brazil.

Dr. Shannon Moore is an Assistant professor Brock University and holds a PhD in Counseling Psychology. Her scholarship emphasizes community-based implementation of UN human rights and justice instruments. This focus bridges critical theory, social justice and mental health. As a clinical counsellor, she has practiced in Canada and the UK.

Hanna Morag, M.Ed in Educational Leadership from Humberside University of England, is manager of a computer center in the Haifa Ministry of Education. Her interests are in guiding and supporting teachers in developing language skills of students in a digital environment.

Dr Sue Morón-García is a teacher and pedagogic researcher with over twenty years' experience (school, adult and higher education). She is currently Senior Lecturer Higher Education Research & Development, the Centre for the Study of Higher Education, Coventry University, UK.

Hiam Nassraldeen, a Druze woman born in Daliat El Carmel, earned her M.A. in education, University of Haifa. An English teacher, pedagogical supervisor at Gordon College, and research assistant (Faculty of Education, University of Haifa), her main interests are in gender and multiculturalism.

Säde-Pirkko Nissilä, PhD, MA, a Principal Lecturer in The School of Higher and Vocational Teacher Education, in Oulu University of Applied Science. She has worked as an English and Latin lecturer in the senior secondary school and a foreign language didactics lecturer in the University of Oulu before the present job. Her areas of interest are professional identity and growth, human dynamics, intercultural communication, reflection, mentoring and innovative higher education.

Patricia O'Gorman is Head of Religious Education and part of the Leadership Team of the Catholic Education Office in the Diocese of Wollongong. She is responsible for Religious Education K-12 and coordinates faith formation courses across the Diocese. She is a member of the Partners in Learning Project with Australian Catholic University and was a core writer of the Diocesan Religious Education Curriculum K-6.

John Olson is professor emeritus at Queens University, Ontario, Canada. He is interested in the way teachers respond to change and what their accounts can tell us about the change process itself and about what they value in their work. He is a contributor to the recently published book " Professional Development and School Improvement. Science Teachers' Voices in School-based Reform." (Studienverlag, Innsbruck, 2006) edited by co-author Manfred Lang.

Michael W. O'Sullivan is an Associate Professor in comparative education at Brock University, Saint Catharines, Ontario, Canada. His research interests include the impact of globalization on education and issues relating to global education and global citizenship education in elementary and secondary schools.

Francine Peterman is a professor and urban teacher educator for the Department of Curriculum and Foundations at Cleveland State University. Peterman writes about urban teaching and teacher preparation, standards for urban teacher education, inquiry-based teaching and learning, and the invention of cultures and practices that support renewal that is socially just.

Mark Raue is Head of the Religious Education & Learning Services Team and part of the Leadership Team of the Catholic Education Office in the Diocese of Wollongong. Prior to working in the Catholic Education Office he was a secondary teacher in the Archdiocese of Sydney for many years. He holds overall responsibility for Religious Education, Faith Formation, general curriculum and learning services in the Wollongong Diocese.

Beth Riolo is an Education Officer in the Religious Education & Learning Services Team of the Catholic Education Office in the Diocese of Wollongong and is the Wollongong coordinator of the Religious Literacy Project an initiative of the Partners in Learning Project with Australian Catholic University. Previously she was a primary teacher, and was a core writer of the Diocesan Religious Education Curriculum K-6 (a joint collaboration between the Archdiocese of Sydney and Dioceses of Armidale and Lismore).

Frances Rust is Senior Vice President for Academic Affairs and Dean of Faculty at the Erikson Institute. Between 1991 and 2007, Rust was professor of education in the Steinhardt School of New York University. Her research and teaching focus on teacher education and teacher research.

Shukri Sanber is a senior lecturer at the Australian Catholic University. His academic interest is educational assessment, teacher research and program evaluation. He has made major contribution towards the successful implementation of the Assessment of Religious Literacy project in partnership with the Wollongong Catholic Education Office.

Tova Shaul, born in Israel, received her Masters degree in education from the University of Haifa in 2001. She has worked for the Ministry of Education since 1990. During this period she has taught literature and has been a mentor to teachers.

Fany Shimoni is a doctoral candidate at the University of Haifa, and works as a senior teacher in preschool education at Gordon Teachers College. Her interests are in training and mentoring of kindergarten student-teachers and teachers during internship.

Andrew Short is an instructor at Brock University within the Graduate and Undergraduate department in the Faculty of Education, and an adjunct instructor in the department of Applied Linguistics. His research interests include Higher Education theory and practice, the roles of university teachers, Second Language Acquisition, and Teaching of English as a Second Language (TESL) programs in Higher Education contexts. Andrew is a member of the ISATT executive and the editor of the ISATT newsletter.

Chava Simon earned a PhD from the University of Haifa; she is a senior teacher in special education at Sha'anan Teachers College. Her interests and publications are in narrative research, parenting young adults, and an alternate construction of fatherhood and its significance in teacher education.

Tony Steel is a member of staff of the Institute for Advancing Community Engagement and lecturer in Theology at Australian Catholic University. Prior to this Tony was Leader of the Spirituality Team at the Catholic Education Office, Archdiocese of Sydney. He has had extensive experience in teaching and administrative roles in Catholic secondary schools.

Barbara Šteh, PhD in psychology, is an assistant professor of educational psychology at the Department of Pedagogy and Andragogy at the Faculty of Arts of the University of Ljubljana. Her research interests are conceptions of learning, knowledge and teaching, the quality of teaching/learning, teacher autonomy and professional development.

Mark G. Storz is Associate Professor of Education at John Carroll University in Cleveland and the Associate Dean for Graduate Studies in the College of Arts and Sciences. Storz writes about urban education, educational equity, and young adolescents.

Keith Trigwell is Professor and Director of the Institute for Teaching and Learning at the University of Sydney, Australia. He was previously a faculty member at the University of Oxford, has a PhD in chemistry, university teaching experience in chemistry and education, and over 100 publications.

Printed in the United Kingdom
by Lightning Source UK Ltd.
135208UK00001B/82-207/P

9 789087 905651